Praying—

with the Saints—

to God Our Mother

Praying—
with the Saints—
to God Our Mother

Daniel F. Stramara Jr.

CASCADE *Books* • Eugene, Oregon

PRAYING—WITH THE SAINTS—TO GOD OUR MOTHER

Copyright © 2012 Daniel F. Stramara Jr. All rights reserved. Except for brief quotations in critical publications or reviews, no part of this book may be reproduced in any manner without prior written permission from the publisher. Write: Permissions, Wipf and Stock Publishers, 199 W. 8th Ave., Suite 3, Eugene, OR 97401.

Cascade Books
An Imprint of Wipf and Stock Publishers
199 W. 8th Ave., Suite 3
Eugene, OR 97401

www.wipfandstock.com

ISBN 13: 978-1-61097-491-2

Cataloging-in-Publication data:

Stramara, Daniel F., Jr.

    Praying—with the saints—to God our mother / Daniel F. Stramara Jr.

    xii + 448 p. ; 23 cm. Includes bibliographical references.

    isbn 13: 978-1-61097-491-2

    1. Saints—Prayers and devotions—English. 2. God—Motherhood. I. Title.

BV245 S79 2012

Manufactured in the U.S.A.

*Dedicated to the women in my life
who have enabled me to see the feminine face of God,
especially my wonderful wife, Clare,
who has been loving, patient, and supportive;
to our beautiful daughter, Julianna,
who inspires the delight and joy of love;
to my loving mother, Audrey, who formed me and embodies grace;
to my sister, Andrea, who exhibits creativity and playfulness;
to my maternal grandmother, Violet, who nurtured me;
to my paternal grandmother, Verna, who saw me as precious;
and to my maternal great grandmother, Mary (Gram),
who displayed gentleness and care.*

*Every scribe who becomes a disciple of the Kingdom of Heaven
is like a steward of the house who draws out from the storeroom
things both new and old.*
—Matthew 13:52

Contents

List of Illustrations / x

Acknowledgments / xi

Introduction / 1

Scriptural Readings and Doxologies / 13

Select Psalms in Greek as Used by the Apostles / 15

Christian Scriptures That Use Feminine Imagery / 75

Suggested Alternative Doxologies / 115

Thematic Readings for Non-Feast Days / 117

God Is beyond Human Description / 119

The Divine Nature Possesses Feminine Qualities / 126

God Almighty / 162

God the Second Person: Wisdom / 176

God the Third Person: The Holy Spirit / 181

God Almighty Eternally Gives Birth to the Second Person / 202

Relationships in the Trinity Can Be Expressed in Feminine Terms / 229

The One, Holy, Catholic, and Apostolic Faith / 235

Wisdom Delighted in the Children of the Earth and Became Incarnate / 242

Christ Is Our Mother / 251

God Provides Us with Life-Giving Milk / 262

God as Maternal Bird or Animal / 276

Christ as the Woman Searching for the Lost Coin / 293

Sacramental Life in Christ: Mystery of the Church / 297

The Mystery of Baptism / 299

The Mystery of Chrismation/Confirmation / 304

Contents

    The Mystery of Eucharist / 306
    The Mystery of Matrimony / 314
    The Mystery of Religious Profession (Male) / 315
    The Mystery of Religious Profession (Female) / 317
    The Mystery of Holy Orders / 318
    The Mystery of Anointing of the Sick / 320
    The Mystery of Last Rites / 321
    The Grieving Process / 322
    The Mystery of the Final Resurrection / 324

Liturgical Calendar: Fixed Feast Days / 325

    January 1—Solemnity of Mary, Mother of God / 327
    January 6—Solemnity of the Epiphany / 328
    January 25—Feast of Paul's Conversion / 329
    February 2—Feast of the Presentation of the Lord / 331
    February 22—Feast of the Chair of St. Peter / 332
    March 19—Solemnity of St. Joseph, Husband of Mary / 333
    March 25—Solemnity of the Annunciation / 335
    June 25—Solemnity of the Birth of John the Baptist / 337
    June 29—Solemnity of Sts. Peter and Paul / 338
    June 30—Synaxis of the Twelve Apostles / 339
    July 22—Feast of Mary Magdalene / 341
    August 6—Solemnity of the Transfiguration / 342
    August 15—Solemnity of the Assumption of Mary / 343
    August 29—Feast of the Beheading of John the Baptist / 345
    September 8—Feast of the Birth of Mary, Mother of God / 346
    September 14—Feast of the Exaltation of the Cross / 347
    September 29—Feast of the Archangels / 348
    November 1—Solemnity of All Saints / 349
    November 2—Feast of All Souls / 351
    November 21—Feast of the Presentation of Mary in the Temple / 352
    December 8—Solemnity of the Immaculate Conception of Mary (West): Feast of the Conception of St. Anna of Mary (East) / 353
    December 25—Solemnity of the Birth of Christ / 355
    Christmas Week / 356
    December 27—Feast of John the Apostle and Evangelist / 363

Contents

Liturgical Calendar: Moveable Feast Days / 365

Baptism of the Lord / 367
Christian Unity Sunday—Second Sunday of Ordinary Time (West) / 368
Ash Wednesday (West)—First Day of the Great Fast (East) / 369
Sunday of Orthodoxy—First Sunday of Lent (East) / 371
Lenten Daily Readings / 372
Palm Sunday / 387
Holy Thursday / 388
Good Friday / Great and Holy Friday / 389
Great and Holy Saturday / 392
Easter / Great and Holy Pascha / 393
Feast of Divine Mercy—Second Sunday after Easter (West) / 394
Solemnity of the Ascension of our Lord / 395
Fathers of the First Ecumenical Council—
    Sunday before Pentecost (East) / 398
Solemnity of Pentecost / 399
Feast of the Holy Spirit—Monday after Pentecost (East) / 400
Solemnity of the Holy Trinity—First Sunday after Pentecost (West) / 402
Solemnity of Corpus Christi—Thursday after Holy Trinity (West) / 403
Solemnity of the Sacred Heart of Jesus—
    Friday after Second Sunday after Pentecost (West) / 404
Fathers of the Fourth Ecumenical Council—
    Fourth Sunday after Pentecost (East) / 406
Fathers of the First Six Ecumenical Councils—
    Seventh Sunday after Pentecost (East) / 407
Solemnity of Christ the King—Last Sunday in Ordinary Time (West) / 409
Advent Daily Readings / Nativity Fast (East) / 410
Devotion to the Sacred Heart of Jesus (West) / 417
Afterword / 420

Appendix A: Chronological List of Authors and Church Writings / 421

Appendix B: Alphabetical List of Authors and Their Critical Sources / 425

Appendix C: Liturgical Hours / 441
  Compline—Night Prayers / 441
  Morning Prayer—Abbreviated Format / 443
  Evening Prayer—Abbreviated Format / 444

Bibliography / 445

Illustrations

1   Holy Spirit / 1

2   Holy Trinity / 117

3   God the Generatrix / 325

4   Pelican with Her Young / 365

Illustrations by Daniel F. Stramara Jr.

Acknowledgments

I would like first of all to thank my wife, Clare, and daughter, Julianna, for all of their patience and loving support as I spent months upon months working on this book. You have my deepest gratitude.

Likewise, the work of previous translators was a boon to me when wrestling with passages. I am indebted to your hard work. And thanks to all of my teachers throughout the years who taught me ancient and modern languages. These have become invaluable tools in my regular research, but especially with regard to this book.

Also the help of librarians must not be overlooked. Without the aid of Verna Rutz and Ellie Kohler, our former and current librarian in charge of interlibrary loans at Rockhurst University's Greenlease Library, as well as the help of Ron Crown at Saint Louis University's Pius XII Memorial Library, accessing some of the critical texts would have been impossible. Librarians are an invaluable asset to researchers; thanks to all!

The encouragement as well as critical eye of my colleague Bill Stancil, who read the manuscript, is very much appreciated. And thanks to Rockhurst University for granting me a semester sabbatical to work on this project, and to the Thomas More Center for a subsequent summer grant. Likewise a big thank you to Chris Spinks and Nathan Rhoads and the team at Cascade Books for making this book a reality.

Finally, without the help of the Holy Spirit directing me to texts, helping me translate them and then weave this Office of Readings together, I never could have done it. A deep heartfelt thank you!

June 12, 2011
The Solemnity of Pentecost and of the Holy Trinity
(concurrence of East & West)

Introduction

Let the word of Christ dwell in you abundantly,
as you teach and admonish one another in all wisdom,
singing psalms, hymns, and spiritual songs,
with gratitude in your hearts to God.

—Colossians 3:16

About the Topic

God is a wondrous life-giving mystery to be experienced personally. The rich bounty of God's love overwhelms us and defies scrutiny. No matter how much we try to comprehend God, totally understand God, we can't; we can only partially know God. The Scriptures, as well as Christians throughout the centuries, have warned against putting God in a box, making images of God and turning them into idols. No one image can capture the infinite graciousness of God's total presence; no one metaphor can exhaust the immeasurable liberality of God's complete loving presence (known as "immanence"). That is why the Scriptures abound with various analogies and metaphors, struggling to paint a comprehensive picture of God's loving relationship with us. Genesis tells us that God created us in the image of God, male and female God created us. Appropriately, Moses and the prophets after him were not afraid to compare God's love for us to that of a mother for her child, or to utilize other feminine analogies and metaphors. The Scriptures, as well as Christian tradition, emphasize that God is neither male nor female, that the infinite Divine Nature cannot be circumscribed by such categories pertaining to finite nature. God's very Being transcends these attributes and surpasses their richness while at the same time encompasses them.

Masculine metaphors of God afford us deep and beautiful insights into God's inexhaustible love for humanity. The majority of us are quite familiar with these. Unfortunately, the Christian populace is not as aware of the feminine imagery employed by the Scriptures as well as Christians throughout history, providing yet another window into the vastness and enduring strength of God's relationship with us. God is neither male nor female, but possesses qualities we deem as masculine and feminine, while at the same time surpassing such life-giving qualities. Regrettably, for us humans, we usually come into consciousness about something only when we really concentrate on it, and thus end up possibly excluding other vital realities. This book runs that risk. I have purposely focused on feminine analogies and metaphors of God and not masculine ones. However, as will be evident, the two are not exclusive. Many writers, both biblical and Christian, felt quite at ease moving back and forth between masculine and feminine imagery.

About the Purpose

The purpose of this book is to enable one to experience and to appreciate in a prayerful and meditative manner various feminine aspects of God. While this book is primarily a book of prayer, it can also be used by the serious scholar as an anthology of scriptural and Christian texts depicting God in feminine imagery; Appendix B lists the critical sources used in the translations.

It is my express hope that *Praying—with the Saints—to God Our Mother* can enrich your personal life and encounter with God, as well as bear fruit in Christendom as a whole: secular and religious, lay and academic, as well as within the various Christian churches and traditions.

The purpose of this book is to promote a healthy spirituality that embraces both the masculine and the feminine qualities of God. However, by its very nature, *Praying—with the Saints—to God Our Mother* emphasizes the feminine aspects of God, but not to the exclusion of the masculine. While honoring the masculine, it celebrates the feminine. Furthermore, femininity is far broader and richer than just motherhood. In this book are images of God as a woman who is sister, friend, teacher, guide, architect, baker, and so forth. Likewise God is depicted in female animal form: she-bear, leopardess, lioness, hen, mother bird, as well as other living creatures.

About the Format

Because I wish this book of prayer to be ecumenical I have chosen to use the format of prayer and meditation that predates all divisions within the one, holy, catholic, and apostolic faith. The structure is that of "monastic" prayer, commonly known as the Liturgy of the Hours. I in no way intend this book to replace the Liturgy of the Hours as used within the Roman Catholic Church or Orthodox Office of Readings; rather, it is to serve as a complement. Early Christian men and women assembled together to pray the Psalms, meditate on the Scriptures, and draw inspiration and encouragement from other writings and songs composed by recognized spiritual authorities.[1] This was regularly done in the morning and evening of every day. For biblical witnesses to the regular practice of Christian prayer see Luke 11:1–13 & 18:1–8; Ephesians 5:18–20 & 6:18; Colossians 4:2; and 1 Thessalonians 1:2 & 5:16–20. Quite often prayer was done at home (Acts 2:46; 10:9; 12:5, 12). Those men and women who withdrew into the desert in imitation of Jesus, escaping the distractions of the world in order to focus upon

---

1. For a good survey of the history of Christian prayer see Taft, *Liturgy of the Hours* as well as Uspensky, *Evening Worship*.

Introduction

God, eventually gave concrete form to this method of prayer and reflection. The morning was devoted to pondering how the Law, Prophets, and Writings prepared the way for the New Covenant revealed in Jesus Christ. Thus the scriptural texts chosen for the morning office in this book are usually taken from these books. The evening prayer celebrates the riches bestowed on us by God Almighty through the Word of God in the Holy Spirit. Consequently, the biblical texts are regularly drawn from the New Testament. In each office of prayer, three or more psalms were recited, usually chanted from side to side. A canticle was also sung. This structure is followed throughout the book. For those who have used the Liturgy of the Hours or other books for the Divine Office, you will only have to flip to the front of the book to find the indicated psalm and scriptural reading. The song, known as the "canticle," is up to you. Everything else is printed in sequence except for the standard format for Morning Prayer and Evening Prayer, which is provided at the very end of the book. You will also have a choice of a doxology to use (see below).

About the Content

The vast majority of modern English-speaking Christians read translations of the Psalms based upon the original Hebrew. However, for over fifteen hundred years this was not the case. Early Greek-speaking Christians used the Greek translation of the Hebrew Bible, known as the Septuagint (abbreviated as LXX). In fact, nearly 97 percent of all the quotations in the New Testament from the Law, Prophets, and Writings were taken from the LXX, not from the original Hebrew. To this present day, the Septuagint version of the Bible is the official text used by Christians who call themselves Orthodox. In the West, the Scriptures were quickly translated into Latin; this version was naturally based upon the Greek. This Old Latin version of the Psalms was popular and survived in various renditions. Consequently, it is the Greek version of the Psalms which has been prayed by Christians, both East and West, for nearly nineteen hundred years, except for those Christians from the sixteenth century onward known as Protestants who used translations based on the Hebrew Bible. The purpose of the book is to recapture the experience of previous generations of Christians who recognized the feminine aspects of God. Most of them prayed and meditated upon the Greek version of the Psalms, and thus I have purposely chosen to make my own translation of them from the Septuagint. *The Psalms will thus follow that numbering.* Besides, this will provide you with variety in your prayer life.

The Scriptures play a vital role in the life of every Christian. The books of the Bible are authoritative and consequently authoritative translations were made. The Jews refer to their own Hebrew Bible as the Tanak, standing for Torah (Law), Neviim (Prophets), and Ketuvim (Writings). I will refer to the Hebrew Bible as the Tanak (abbreviated TNK) and all translations based upon this version will be noted as such. As already mentioned, the authoritative Greek version of the Bible is called the Septuagint, meaning "seventy," abbreviated using the Roman numeral (LXX). The same applies to the Latin Vulgate (abbreviated VULG), the authoritative Bible in the Western Catholic

PRAYING—WITH THE SAINTS—TO GOD OUR MOTHER

Church. There is one other ancient authoritative version of the Bible that I have used, the Syriac, known as the Peshitta (PESH). The Peshitta is an Aramaic/Syriac translation of the Tanak and the Greek New Testament. It is authoritative among Syriac-speaking Christianity and churches that developed out of Antioch. Where I have made my own translation from the New Testament Greek and I wish you to use my version, the passage is followed by NT. If no abbreviation follows a scriptural reference it means you are to use whichever translation you prefer.

Christians consider certain books to be canonical, or authoritatively binding, thus forming the Bible. I, myself, am a Catholic Christian. Some quotations will be from books not found in the Protestant Bible. However, I am not attempting to impose my own beliefs and persuasions upon you, the prayerful reader. What I am trying to do is present the experience of all Christians in their encounter with God before the Protestant Reformation. Catholics have more books in their Bible than do Protestants; Orthodox Christians have even more. Thus I have chosen to use the largest canon of the Bible, that belonging to Orthodox Christianity. For the Protestant reader, these extra books are known as the Apocrypha, and are considered merely inspirational. For the Catholic reader, the extra books you will encounter are known as "extra-canonical." For Catholic and Orthodox Christians, equal authority resides in the Scriptures and the Apostolic Tradition. For Catholics, the extra-canonical books, nevertheless, form part of the Church's Tradition.

Case in point: one scriptural reading is taken from 4 Esdras, a book not considered canonical by any church but for centuries (even still) included in the Latin Vulgate after the New Testament. This book was quoted by numerous early church authorities such as Clement of Alexandria, Cyprian, Tertullian, Commodianus, Ambrose, Athanasius, and Gregory of Nyssa (known by Catholic and Orthodox Christians as Fathers of the Church).[2] Several extracts from 4 Esdras were incorporated into the Roman Catholic Liturgy.[3] In fact, a verse from this book persuaded Columbus and his royal sponsors that there was land to be discovered west of the Atlantic. Fourth Esdras has impacted Western civilization in numerous ways.[4]

I have also chosen to use one text found in 1 Enoch. Perhaps this extra-canonical book is more familiar to Christians. The New Testament epistle known as Jude contains a direct quote from it and mentions Enoch by name. This book forms part of the canonical Scriptures of Ethiopian Orthodox Christians. First Enoch was also used at Qumran and is found in the Dead Sea Scrolls. Besides Jude 14–15 being a quotation from 1 Enoch 1:6, verses 6 and 16 of Jude are also influenced by it. Understandably, many early Church Fathers considered 1 Enoch inspired and meditated upon it, for example, Justin Martyr, Irenaeus, Origen, Clement of Alexandria, and Tertullian.[5] First Enoch, as well as other biblical books not found in the Tanak but used by Christians

---

2. See Myers, *I and II Esdras*, 131–34.
3. See Stuhlmueller, "Apocrypha," 1:552.
4. See Metzger, "Fourth Book of Ezra," 1:523.
5. See Isaac, "I Enoch," 1:8.

throughout the world and throughout the centuries (i.e., Apocrypha), are employed as sources for passages in both Morning and Evening Prayer.

A regular part of the Liturgy of the Hours is a time for meditation upon a passage written by some spiritual authority. The question of authority can be a sticky issue. I have chosen to quote in the Liturgy of the Hours only passages taken from the Fathers of the Church and saints recognized by the Catholic Church. A word of explanation is in order. In 1 Corinthians 11:1 the Apostle Paul exhorts, "Take me for your model, as I take Christ." Elsewhere Paul states, "Take as your models everybody who is already doing this and study them as you used to study us" (Phil 3:17). Christians are to emulate other Christians who have more fully conformed their lives to Christ than we have (see also 1 Thess 1:6–7; 2 Thess 3:7–9; Heb 6:12 and 13:7). Eventually, the issue arose of deciding who ought to be held up publicly as a model of Christian virtue and teaching. The Roman Catholic Church, of all the catholic apostolic churches, over time devised a method and system for deciding who is worthy of such a widespread status. Every Christian is called to be a saint, but in certain people the splendor of Christ and the power of the Holy Spirit more brightly shine. I have chosen to use writings from those Christians who have been sanctioned by the Catholic Church. There are three ascending levels of Catholic sainthood: Venerable (Ven.), Blessed (Bl.), and Saint (St.). The names of the men and women quoted herein will be preceded by their recognized Catholic title and position.

However, a few saints will also be quoted who are not formally recognized as such by the Roman Catholic Church. Originally there was one, holy, catholic, and apostolic church. This body of Christians became divided in the fifth century into two major camps: the "new" Oriental Orthodox Churches and the original Catholic Orthodox Churches. Eventually there was another split, a schism between East and West in the eleventh century, resulting in the Roman Catholic Church and the Eastern Orthodox Churches. Over the centuries, various non-Roman Christians sought communion with the Church of Rome; these have formed what are known as the Eastern Catholic Churches. The Roman Church is only one of more than eighteen Catholic Churches in communion with the bishop of Rome, who is known as the pope. Because all the Catholic Churches in communion with the bishop of Rome recognize the various Orthodox Churches as fully apostolic and preserving the catholic faith, men and women who are regarded as saints in these particular churches will also be quoted. One such illustrious (Greek) Orthodox saint is Gregory Palamas. His spiritual authority and learning in Orthodoxy is comparable to that of St. Thomas Aquinas in the West.

Vatican II has this to say regarding the teachings of the Orthodox Church: "In the study of revealed truth, East and West have used different methods and approaches in understanding and confessing divine things. It is hardly surprising, then, if one tradition has come nearer to a full appreciation of some aspects of a mystery of revelation than the other, or has expressed them better."[6]

---

6. Vatican II, "Decree on Ecumenism," §17, p. 466.

Because of the length of this book, quotes from non-canonized Christians—whether they are Catholic or Orthodox, as well as Protestant—will be found in a forthcoming book. Many would expect to find excerpts from Dame Julian of Norwich in this volume; however, she has never been canonized by the Catholic or Orthodox Churches and thus her texts are not included in this book. Reformers such as Luther, Calvin, and Zinzendorff, not to mention other Protestant renowns, also used feminine metaphors when speaking about God. As should be evident by now, and as will become strikingly clear later, Christians throughout every century and belonging to every church affiliation have celebrated the feminine aspects of God. Meditational passages in this book have been drawn from eight non-canonized but officially recognized Fathers of the Church, thirteen authoritative church documents (five of which are from Ecumenical Councils), and seventy-five Catholic and Orthodox saints speaking almost every language, and spanning every century. In Appendix A you will find a complete chronological list of these Fathers, documents, and Catholic/Orthodox saints.

One further point needs to be made. Saints are noted for conforming their lives to Christ under the inspiration of the Holy Spirit to the glory of God Almighty. The Catholic Church also accords various extra titles to certain saints for their teaching authority. Listed according to importance, we have Apostolic Fathers (those who lived and taught from AD 70–125), Post-Apostolic Fathers (AD 125–175), Fathers of the Church (AD 175–787), and Doctors of the Church, who are outstanding teachers acclaimed as authorities. Some Fathers of the Church are also Doctors, thus possessing the highest honor. But one need not live before 787 to be a Doctor of the Church, nor must one be a man; there are three female Doctors of the Church: Sts. Catherine of Siena, Teresa of Avila, and Thérèse of Lisieux. In the Catholic Church there are thirty-three Doctors.[7] Every single one of them utilized feminine imagery to express a facet of God's infinite love.

Finally, there is the peculiar case regarding St. Gregory of Nyssa, who was highly influential during the Second Ecumenical Council, known as Constantinople I. For some reason, he is not yet acclaimed by the Roman Catholic Church as a Doctor of the Church, even though he is a weighty and brilliant authority whom the Seventh Ecumenical Council hailed as the "Father of the Fathers." Two Eastern Catholic Churches in communion with Rome acknowledge Gregory of Nyssa as a "Doctor of the Church": the Syro-Malabar Catholic Church and the Chaldean Catholic Church. Because the Seventh Ecumenical Council, recognized by Rome, as well as two Eastern Catholic Churches, accord Gregory of Nyssa the title of Doctor of the Church, I have likewise, thus raising the number by my reckoning to thirty-four Doctors.

I have used authors sanctioned by the Catholic Churches as well as Orthodox to demonstrate that speaking about God in feminine terms is not contrary to the Catholic Church's Tradition. In fact, it is part and parcel of the Apostolic Tradition as demon-

---

7. According to reports coming out of Rome, Pope Benedict XVI will declare Hildegard of Bingen a Doctor of the Church in October 2012. When this happens, she will be the fourth female Doctor of the Church.

strated by several authors included herein. Authors will be followed by the date of their death so that one can appreciate the persistency and continuity of this tradition.

About the Translations

One of the most difficult jobs is to translate accurately from one language into another. All translations are my own and are based on the most critical text available, unless noted otherwise. While I am concerned with the authenticity of the text in question and the historical meaning the author most probably had in mind, I am more intent upon presenting the possible historical perception that the Christian community had when pondering these texts. This is especially true for the Psalms, which were prayed in a christological context. I have striven to be faithful to the actual wording and to maintain any vagueness that might have permitted an alternate understanding of the text. For example, the Hebrew version of Isaiah 46:3 is polyvalent, that is to say, open to various interpretations. It reads:

> Listen to me, O House of Jacob,
> and all the remnant of the House of Israel,
> whom I have borne since your conception,
> whom I have carried since you were born.

The Hebrew does not make it explicit if God "carried" Israel internally or externally. Because the passage is open to a feminine interpretation—God carrying us within God's own womb—I have used this passage. It could legitimately be heard in this fashion. Such a contention is verified by the Vulgate. When Jerome translated this text he explicitly brought out the feminine possibility in his Latin translation:

> Listen to me, O house of Jacob,
> and all the remnant of the house of Israel,
> you who are carried by my uterus [*meo utero*],
> you who are borne by my womb [*mea vulva*].

I have always attempted to be faithful to the original wording. However, sometimes I felt some modifications to be necessary for flow in the English language.

1) The Psalms were originally written as poetry to be sung. Accordingly, I have tried to maintain some semblance of meter, rhyme when appropriate, plays on words and the like. To do this, at times it was necessary to add an adjective or adverb so that the beat could be facilitated in public recitation. In all cases, what I perceive to be the meaning of the text was never violated. Reputable translations were always consulted. Some admirably captured the beauty of a turn of phrase, or the full force of a verb. I am indebted to their insights and sometimes a wording has been borrowed, not out of plagiarism, but out of praise for the translator. In the final analysis there are only so many ways in which a sentence can validly be translated. Biblical translators can appreciate my predicament.

2) Unlike English, nouns in most languages have a grammatical gender: masculine, feminine, or neuter. Verbs likewise take corresponding feminine and masculine

endings. Some nouns are grammatically masculine but can refer to either sex of an animal, or some are feminine. Case in point: Isaiah 31:5 refers to birds that are hovering. The noun is grammatically feminine in the singular but becomes masculine in form when plural. In the following verse the verb is in the feminine plural. The verb means "to hover" (especially above a nest); thus I chose to bring out the validly possible feminine metaphor:

> Like mother birds hovering over their young
> Yahweh Sabaoth will shield Jerusalem;
> to protect and save,
> to spare and deliver.

But in order to do this, I needed to add the word "mother" to convey the underlying feminine grammatical, as well as metaphorical, text. God being compared to a mother bird is common in the Scriptures.

Also because certain nouns are feminine, this permitted the original authors to create images revolving around women. For example, the word for "wisdom" in Hebrew (as well as in Greek and Latin) is feminine. When Wisdom is personified it is presented as a woman. Many of us are familiar with such passages, especially from Proverbs.

In Hebrew, the word for "spirit" is also feminine. I have not utilized every text in which "spirit" is grammatically followed by a feminine adjective or verb with a feminine ending. However, I have chosen to garner some texts so that the reader can experience how many Aramaic- and Syriac-speaking Christians considered the Holy Spirit to be feminine, inasmuch as they considered God masculine. (Jesus spoke Aramaic.) Recall that God, in and of God's self, is actually neither male nor female. This grammatical feminine gender of the Spirit allowed Christians to depict the Spirit as mother.

3) Sometimes the richness of a particular word needed to be brought out by more than one word in English. One such word is the Hebrew *rachemim*, usually translated as "compassion" or "mercy." Its root is the noun *rechem*, which unequivocally means "womb." Thus, in certain passages wherein I believed the context warranted it, I translated *rachemim* as "maternal compassion." In fact, Hebrew has five other words for compassion, pity, or mercy. The underlying womb motif in *rachemim* should not be overlooked. In the famous scene where Solomon must decide to which of two women a certain baby belongs, he purposely proposes to have the child divided in half. He discerns which woman is the true mother by the one who has pity or compassion (*rachemim*), in other words, the one whose womb is moved for her baby's welfare. This is lost upon the English reader. In the following text, once again from Isaiah, the feminine imagery is explicit; thus this passage has been used by many. But the richness of the maternal nature of God is missed when *rachemim* has been translated merely as "pity" or "mercy."

> For Yahweh comforts his people
> and displays maternal compassion on his afflicted ones.
> Zion was saying, "Yahweh has abandoned me;

the Lord has forgotten me."
Can a mother forget the baby at her breast,
feel no maternal compassion for the child of her womb?
Even should she forget,
I will never forget you. (Isa 49:13–15)

4) Perhaps nothing is more challenging than the very terms used to refer to God. The Hebrew for "God" is *elohim*. This noun is actually a plural form, literally "gods," and at times it is used to refer to the gods of the heathens. However, whenever it refers to the One God of Israel the verb is almost always in the singular, except, for example, in Genesis 1:26—"God said, 'Let us make man in our own image...'" While the grammatical form of *elohim* is masculine plural, it is theologically understood as singular and thus grammatically followed by the verb in the masculine singular. However, the grammatical singular of *elohim* is *eloah*, which is feminine. In one sense, *elohim* is the perfect word for God because it displays and contains within itself the plurality of the masculine and the feminine. It is plural and yet singular, masculine yet feminine. The term *eloah* appears several times in the Scriptures and is always followed by the verb in the masculine singular. Scholars believe that rectification of *elohim* and *eloah* to be followed by a masculine singular was a conscious act on the part of the copyists who transmitted the written text. However, there is one instance in which the Hebrew text has kept *eloah* followed by a feminine direct object. It is Job 40:2, "Will the one who contends with Shaddai correct? Let the one who accuses Eloah answer her." Because in the ears of any Semitic speaker *eloah* is clearly a feminine noun, possessing the feminine ending, I have chosen not to translate it as "God" but keep it in its original Hebrew/English spelling. I am intending it to carry a feminine aura. Such an intention can be argued when it is realized that the author of Job regularly used *eloah* in parallel with *shaddai*, another puzzling term.

Shaddai as a name for God is most ancient. English Bibles, following the Septuagint translation, render it as "Almighty." Scholars still debate its actual meaning; thus I have not resolutely concluded that *shaddai* has the feminine meaning I attach to it, but in this book of prayer I am underscoring that valid possibility. Early on, scholars believed that *el shaddai* meant "God of the Mountain." However, Albright in 1935 pointed out that the Hebrew word *shad* means "breast," and that in the mind of the ancients, a mountain rising up from a plain resembles a breast mounted above the abdomen.[8] Having known this, and read other scholarly references arguing that on linguistic grounds *el shaddai* possibly means "God the Breasted One," I did my own contextual analysis of the divine name. I was struck at how many times *el shaddai* is used in a context referring to the blessing of fertility (see Genesis 17:1–22; 28:1–5; 35:8–12; 43:14; 49:25 as well as Ruth 1:1–22 where this blessing was lacking). Of particular interest is the explicit avowal that *el shaddai* bestows "blessings of breast and womb" (Gen 49:25). Naturally, God the Breasted One would grant such graces of fertility. I mention this because my own independent research was confirmed when I read a scholarly article

---

8. See Albright, "Names Shaddai and Abram."

by Cross.⁹ He too believes, because of linguistic and textual analysis, that *shaddai* can validly be interpreted to mean "breasted one," and was understood as such by the early Hebrews. Of further interest is the contention by Walker that *shaddai* comes from the Akkadian word *shagzu* and was an epithet for the god Marduk meaning God the Womb-Wise, or God the Midwife.¹⁰ Whatever the case may be, understanding *shaddai* as a feminine name for God is neither unreasonable nor without scholarly support. This feminine nuance is further strengthened when it is paralleled with *eloah*. This cannot be mere coincidence. Consequently, I have rendered the Hebrew for *shaddai* in English and at times followed it by "God the Breasted One."

Finally, a word should be said about the psalms I have chosen. I have purposely utilized psalms that address God as "you," or ones in which God speaks in the first person. Because I am pondering the feminine side of God, I felt it inappropriate to use psalms that constantly refer to God as "he." I, personally, have nothing against referring to God as "he," but thought that this would be distracting in this context. Nevertheless, some readers might be disconcerted that on occasion "he, him, and his" are found. I must be faithful to the original text. Furthermore, the ancient authors, whether biblical or Christian, felt quite at ease employing both analogies at the same time. I have respected their experiences and practices. Other normal rules of non-gender biased translation have been followed, such as avoiding unnecessary "he who has" and related phrases, replacing it with "anyone" or "whoever." I refer the reader to such gender-inclusive translations of the Scriptures as the New Jerusalem Bible, the Revised New American Bible, and the New Revised Standard Version. Inevitably, I will not please everyone, but I have chosen to be grammatically accurate and faithful to the original wording and meaning of the texts, without being slavishly so. Any errors or oversights are my own.

About the Doxology

In the early church there were a variety of doxologies; eventually "Glory be to the Father and to the Son and to the Holy Spirit . . ." became standard. St. Basil the Great († 379), a very important Doctor of the Church, argued that there were various ancient doxologies and that these were legitimate.¹¹ Because a doxology must be used in the Liturgy of the Hours, I needed to address the issue of coming up with an alternate to the canonical doxology that brings out the masculine side of the relationality within the Holy Trinity. Proposed doxologies such as "Creator, Redeemer, and Sanctifier" are unacceptable from a Catholic/Orthodox point of view because 1) they do not safeguard the relationship among the divine Persons within the Trinity, 2) each of the Persons is Creator, Redeemer, and Sanctifier, and 3) such a doxology only emphasizes God's relationship with us and not God's eternal nature as the Divine Community of Love.

9. See Cross, "Yahweh and the God of the Patriarchs."
10. See Walker, "New Interpretation."
11. See Basil of Caesarea, *De spiritu sancto* 1.3 & 29.71 (PG 32:72B–C & 200B–201A).

Introduction

However, it is important to note that Fathers and Doctors of the Church gave voice to their praise of God in terms beyond the traditional "Glory be." St. Theophilus of Antioch was the first to use the term "Trinity" around AD 180. The text is *Ad Autolycus* 2.15, in which he has "God, His Word and His Wisdom." The relationality is preserved but in English the possessive pronoun is masculine; see also *Clementine Homilies* 16.12 where Spirit is also feminine Wisdom. St. Gregory of Nazianzus († 389), a Doctor of the Church who was acclaimed as "the Theologian" by the Orthodox Church, praises God as "Mind and Word and Spirit, one in relationship and divinity."[12] Such a doxology is appealing to me because it is gender neutral. However, the metaphors are intellectual and abstract. Furthermore, for a book of prayer such as this, the feminine side of God should be celebrated in the doxology. In fact, St. Aphrahat († ca. 345), another Father of the Church, wrote: "Glory and honor to the Father and to his Son and to his Spirit, she who is living and holy; let the mouths of everyone render praise, above and below, for ever and ever, Amen."[13] Such a conception in the Syrian Church is refreshing. Nevertheless, as shall be seen, the Doctor of the Church St. Ephrem the Syrian († 379) depicted all three divine Persons as feminine. Moreover, according to the Ecumenical Councils, all three Persons are equal; whatever is ascribed to one is equally ascribed to the other, except for their terms expressing origin of relationship. If a doxology is to be truly theologically balanced, all three Persons must be equal, i.e., all three masculine, or all three feminine, or all three neuter.

Thus after the section of the Psalms and Scriptures you will find a list of possible doxologies you can employ, many based off of early church writings and some created by myself. In no way is this list to infer that I consider the traditional doxology as incorrect or theologically problematic; the issue is, however, pastoral. It will be up to the reader or praying community to decide which form will be used. If *Praying—with the Saints—to God Our Mother* is used publicly, I suggest that the first line of the doxology be recited only by the one leading the prayer; the refrain "as it was in the beginning . . ." can be a communal response, thus avoiding confusion concerning which wording is being adopted. Of course, one is free to alternate the various doxologies between the morning and evening office or after each psalm.

May this book of prayer and meditation deepen your relationship with the God of our ancestors, and may She abundantly bless you as you prayerfully ponder another rich and life-giving facet of the Holy Trinity.

Stand firm, then, brothers and sisters,
and maintain the traditions that we taught you,
whether by word of mouth or by letter.

—2 Thessalonians 2:15

---

12. See Gregory of Nazianzus, *Oratio* 12.1 (PG 35:844B).
13. See Aphrahat, *Demonstrationes* 23.61 (PS 2:128).

PRAYING—WITH THE SAINTS—TO GOD OUR MOTHER

You must remain faithful to what you have learned and firmly believe;
knowing full well who your teachers were,
and how, ever since you were a child,
you have known the Holy Scriptures—
from these you can learn the wisdom
that leads to salvation through faith in Christ Jesus.
All Scripture is inspired by God
and useful for instruction and refuting error,
for guiding people's lives
and teaching them to be upright.
This is how someone who is dedicated to God
becomes fully equipped and ready for every good work.

—2 Timothy 3:14–17

Scriptural Readings and Doxologies

Select Psalms in Greek as Used by the Apostles

Psalm 1

1. Blessed the fellow who has not walked in the counsel of the wicked;
nor loitered along the path of sinners;
nor sat in the seat of the pestilent.
2. But whose delight is in the law of the Lord;
meditating on the law day and night.

3. Such a person will be like a tree planted by babbling brooks,
a tree which will yield its fruit in due season,
and its leaves shall not wither and fall.
Whatever that one does shall prosper.
4. Not so the wicked, not so;
rather they are like the chaff which the wind scatters
from the face of the earth.

5. Therefore the wicked shall not stand up in judgment,
nor sinners in the counsel of the righteous.
6. For the Lord knows the way of the righteous;
but the way of the wicked shall perish.

Psalm 2

1. Why did the nations rage? And peoples imagine vain things?
2. The kings of the earth rose up and the rulers assembled together,
against the Lord and against his Anointed; saying:

3. Let us break their bonds asunder and throw off from us their yoke.

4. The one who dwells in the heavens shall laugh them to scorn;
the Lord will treat them with derision.
5. Then will he address them in his wrath,
and cause them distress in his fury.

6. But as for me, I was made king by him on Zion, his holy mountain,
7. announcing the Lord's decree—
the Lord said to me:
"You are my Son, today I have begotten you.
8. Ask me, and I will bequeath you the nations as your inheritance,
and the ends of the earth for your possession.
9. You shall rule them with a rod of iron;

you shall dash them in pieces as a potter's jar."

10. Now therefore, O kings understand:
be instructed all you who judge
the earth.
11. Serve the Lord with fear,
and rejoice in him with trembling.

12. Hold fast to instruction lest the Lord be angry,
and you should fall away from the right path.
Whenever his indignation is suddenly kindled,
happy are all those who have trusted in him.

Psalm 3

1. O Lord, why have those who afflict me multiplied?
Many rise up against me.
2. Regarding my life, many say,
"There is no deliverance for this one in God."

3. But you O Lord are my protector;
my glory and the lifter of my head.
4. I cried aloud to the Lord,
and from the holy mountain he heard me.

5. I laid down to rest and slept;
then I awoke because the Lord protects me.
6. I will not fear myriads of people;
encircling round about to beset me.

7. Arise O Lord; save me my God!
You have smitten all who were my enemies without cause.
You have broken the teeth of sinners.

8. Deliverance belongs to the Lord!
Let your blessing be upon your people.

Psalm 4

1. When I called out,
my righteous God heard me.
In the midst of distress you have given me space;
be gracious to me and hear my prayer.
2. O you children of earth, how long will your hearts be weighed down?
Why do you love vanity, and seek after falsehood?

3. Know that the Lord has worked marvels for his holy one;
the Lord will hear me when I cry out to him.
4. Be provoked to anger, but sin not.
What you say in your hearts,
feel compunction for upon your beds.

5. Offer a sacrifice of righteousness,
and trust in the Lord.
6. Many say, "Who will show us good things?"
The light of your countenance, O Lord,
has been revealed to us.

7. You have put gladness into my heart;
they have been filled with an abundance of grain, wine, and oil.
8. Now I will lie down in peace and truly sleep,
for only you, O Lord, have caused me to dwell securely.

Psalm 5

1. Hearken to my words, O Lord;
attend to my cry.
2. Listen to the sound of my plea, my Sovereign and my God!
For to you, O Lord, I will pray.

3. In the morning you shall hear my voice;
in the morning I will wait for you and raise my eyes.
4. For you are not a God who desires iniquity;
therefore the wicked shall not dwell with you.

5. Nor shall the transgressors remain in your presence;
You, O Lord, hate all who do evil.
6. You will destroy all who lie;
the Lord abhors the bloody and deceitful fellow.

7. As for me, because of your abundant mercy I will enter your house;
I will worship before your holy temple, in reverence of you.
8. Lead me, O Lord, in your righteousness because of my enemies;
make my path straight before you.

9. For there is no truth in their mouth;
their heart is vain; their throat an open grave;
with their tongues they have spoken deceit.
10. Judge them, O God! Let them fall by their own devices;
according to the multitude of their crimes cast them out;
because they have provoked you, O Lord.

11. But let all who trust in you, rejoice.
They shall exult forever and you will dwell among them.
All who love your name shall glory in you.
12. For you, O Lord, will bless the righteous;
You have bestowed us with an armor of favor.

Psalm 6

1. O Lord, rebuke me not in your wrath, nor reprove me in your anger.
2. Pity me, O Lord, for I am weak.
Heal me, O Lord, for I am troubled to my bones.

3. My soul is vexed exceedingly;
but O Lord, for how much longer?
4. Return, O Lord, deliver my soul;
save me for your mercy's sake.

5. For in death no one mentions you;
in Hades who will give you thanks?
6. I am weary with my groaning.
Every night I bedew my bed
and drench my couch with my tears.

7. My sight is troubled because of my wrath;
I am worn down in the midst of my enemies.
8. Depart from me, all you workers of iniquity,
for the Lord has heard the sound of my weeping.

9. The Lord has heard my supplication;
the Lord has accepted my prayer.
10. Let all my enemies be put to shame and greatly troubled.
Let them be turned back and quickly put to shame.

Psalm 7

1. O Lord, my God, in you have I placed my trust.
Save me from all my persecutors and deliver me,

2. lest at any moment my enemy seize me like a lion,
while there is no one to ransom me,
none to save me.

3. O Lord, my God, if I have done this—
if there be iniquity on my hands;
4. if I have requited with evil those who did me wrong;
then let me fall empty-handed at my enemies' hands.

5. Let the enemy pursue my soul and take it;
let him trample my life to the ground,
and cause my honor to lay in the dust.

6. Arise, O Lord, in your indignation.
Be exalted to the boundaries of my enemies.
Awake, O Lord my God, according to the judgment you decreed.
7. And when the assembly of the peoples encompasses you,
ascend on high above them.

8. The Lord will judge the peoples.
Judge me O Lord according to my righteousness;
and according to my innocence be for me.
9. Let the wickedness of sinners be brought to an end.
You will indeed direct the righteous,
O God who searches the hearts and innermost being. . . .

14. Behold my enemy has travailed with injustice;
has conceived trouble and given birth to iniquity.
15. He has dug a pit and covered it; into the trench which he dug,
he will fall.
16. His mischief will return upon his own head;
on his forehead his injustice will fall.
17. Because of the Lord's righteousness I will give thanks;
I will sing praises to the name of the Lord Most High.

Psalm 8

1. O Lord, our Lord, how wonderful is your name in all the earth;
for your magnificence is exalted above the heavens!
2. Out of the mouths of babes and sucklings you have perfected praise,
on account of your enemies, so as to destroy the enemy and avenger.

3. When I survey the heavens, the work of your fingers,
the moon and the stars which you have established,
4. what is a human being that you should be mindful of him?
or a mere mortal that you should visit him?

5. You made him a little lower than the angels,
with glory and honor you crowned him,
6. and set him over the work of your hands.
You have put all things under his feet:

7. all flocks and herds,
even beasts of the field,
8. birds of the air and fishes of the sea,
all creatures traversing the salty paths.

9. O Lord, our Lord, how wonderful is your name in all the earth!

Psalm 9

1. I will praise you, O Lord, with my whole heart,
I will recount all your marvelous deeds.
2. I will be glad and rejoice in you;
to your name I will sing, O Most High.

3. When my enemies are turned back,
they shall grow faint and perish in your presence,
4. for you have upheld my cause
and my right.
You sat upon the throne,
O Righteous Judge.

5. You have rebuked the nations,
and the ungodly have perished.
You have blotted out their name forever,
even for ages and ages. . . .

7. But the Lord endures forever,
and prepares his throne for judgment;
8. This one will judge the world in righteousness,
and will pass judgment with rectitude.

9. The Lord has been a refuge for the distressed,
a propitious helper in time of affliction.
10. Let those who know your name place their hope in you,
for you, O Lord, have not failed those who fervently seek you.

Psalm 11

1. Save me, O Lord, for the godly one has failed,
for truths are scarce among the children of the earth.
2. They spoke empty words, one to another, neighbor to neighbor,
their lips are deceitful; they have spoken with a duplicitous heart.

3. May the Lord destroy all lying lips,
and the tongue which wags with wonderful words!
4. those who boast: "We will magnify our own tongue,
our lips are our own, who is the Lord to us?"

5. "Because of the oppression of the poor,
because of the groans of the needy,
now will I arise," declares the Lord.
"I will set them in safety and speak about it boldly."

6. The utterances of the Lord are pure—
as silver refined in the fire,
tested in the fiery furnace,
purified seven times over.

7. You, O Lord, will keep us and preserve us,
from this generation and forever more.
8. The wicked walk round and round in circles,
in your greatness you have observed carefully the children of the earth.

Psalm 12

1. How long, O Lord will you forget me, forever?
How long will you turn your face away from me?
2. How long shall I ponder counsels in my mind and sorrows in my heart?
How long shall my enemy be left to exalt over me?

3. Look down and listen to me, O Lord my God.
Enlighten my eyes lest I sleep in death;
4. lest my enemy gloat: "I prevailed against him."
Those who afflict me will rejoice if I be moved.

5. But I have placed my trust in your mercy;
my heart will rejoice in your salvation.
6. I will sing to the Lord my great benefactor;
I will sing psalms to the name of the Lord Most High.

Psalm 13

1. The fool has said in his heart, "There is no God."
They are corrupt and abominable in their designs.
There is none who does good; no, not even one.
2. The Lord looked down from heaven upon the children of the earth,
to see if there were any
who understood or sought after God.

3. They have all gone astray, altogether become vile.
There is none who does good; no, not even one.
Their throat is an open grave;
with their tongues they have spoken deceit.

The viper's poison drools from their lips;
their mouths are full of cursing and bitterness;
their feet are swift to shed blood;
destruction and misery fill their paths.

The path to peace they have not known;
there is no fear of God before their eyes.

4. Will all the workers of iniquity remain ignorant?
They devour my people like bread;
they have not called upon the Lord.
5. They were seized with terror,
where there was no cause for fear,
for God dwells among a righteous generation.

6. You are ashamed of the counsel of the poor,
because the Lord is their hope.
7. Who from Zion will bring Israel's salvation?
When the Lord brings back his captive people,
let Jacob rejoice and Israel be glad.

Psalm 14

1. O Lord, who shall dwell in your sanctuary?
And who shall encamp on your holy mountain?

2. Whoever walks blamelessly,
and practices righteousness,
speaking truth from the heart.
3. Who has not deceived with the tongue,
nor done evil to neighbor,
nor given them reproach.

4. In whose sight an evil-doer is discounted,
while honoring all who fear the Lord.
Who makes an oath to a neighbor
and does not renege.
5. Who has not lent money at interest,
nor taken bribes against the innocent.

Whoever acts likes this,
shall never be shaken.

Psalm 15

1. Preserve me, O Lord,
for I have placed my hope in you.
2. I said to the Lord, "You are my Lord;
for you have no need of my goods."

3. Because of the holy places which are in his land,
he has marvelously displayed all his designs in them.
4. Their infirmities were multiplied,
to these holy places they hastened.
I will no longer assemble meetings for blood-vengeance,
neither will I remember their names upon my lips.

5. The Lord is the portion of my heritage and my cup;
You are the one who restores me my rightful inheritance.
6. The boundaries have fallen to me in the best of places,
for this inheritance of mine is the best for me.

7. I will bless the Lord who has granted me understanding,
even during the night my instincts have instructed me.
8. I saw the Lord continually before me,
at my right hand that I should not be shaken.

9. Therefore my heart rejoiced and my tongue exulted;
furthermore my flesh shall dwell in the hope
10. that you will not leave my soul in Hades,
nor allow your holy one to see corruption.

11. You have made known to me the paths of life.
You will fill me with joy with your presence;
at your right hand there are delights forever.

Psalm 16

1. Give heed, O Lord, to my justification;
and attend to my supplication.
Give ear to my prayer,
not made with deceitful lips.
2. Let my judgment come forth from your presence;
let my eyes behold your equity.

3. You have proved my heart;
you have visited me by night.
You have tested me as by fire,
and found in me no wrong.
4. May my mouth not speak the deeds of these fellows.
I, because of the words of your lips,
guarded myself against hardened ways.

5. Direct my footsteps in your paths,
so that my steps may not stumble.
6. I cried out, because you, O God, had heard me.
Incline your ears to me and give heed to my words.

7. Display your mercy in wondrous fashion,
O, you, who with your right hand,
save from their adversaries,

those who place their hope in you.
8. Guard me as the apple of your eye.
In the shadow of your wings you will shelter me
9. from the presence of the wicked who afflict me.

My enemies have encompassed my soul.
10. They have sealed themselves up with their fat.
With their mouths they have spoken proudly.
11. They have cast me out and now encircle me,
with their eyes cast down, inclined to the ground.

12. They laid wait for me like a lion eager for prey,
like a lion's whelp lurking in hidden places.
13. Arise, O Lord, thwart them and cause them to stumble.
Deliver my soul from the ungodly.
Wrest your sword from your enemies' hands.

14. O Lord, destroy them from the earth;
scatter them in their lifetime.
Though their belly was filled from your storehouse,
they satiated themselves with swine and left the remains for their children.

15. But as for me, I shall appear before you in righteousness;
and I shall be satisfied when your glory appears.

Psalm 17

1. I will love you, O Lord, my strength.
2. The Lord is my support, my refuge, and my deliverer.
My God is my helper in whom I will trust:
my protector, the horn of my salvation and my defender. . . .

25. With the holy you will be holy;
and with the innocent you will be innocent.
26. With the favored you will show favor,
and with the cunning you will be cunning.

27. For you will save the lowly,
and humble the eyes of the proud.
28. For you, O Lord, will light my lamp;
my God will shed light on my darkness.

29. Because of you I shall be delivered from a roving band;
and because of my God I shall leap over a wall.
30. As for my God, his way is faultless;
the oracles of the Lord are tried in fire;
my God, a Protector of all who have hope.
31. For who is God besides the Lord?
And who is God except our God?

Psalm 18

1. The heavens declare the glory of God;
the firmament proclaims his handiwork.
2. Day unto day utters a word,
night unto night announces knowledge.

3. There are no speeches nor are there words
in which their voices are not heard.
4. To every land their voice has gone forth,

and their message, to the ends
of the world.

In the sun he has placed his tabernacle.
5. He is like a bridegroom coming forth
from his chamber.
He will rejoice as a giant about to run
his course.

6. His going forth is from the one end
of heaven,
and his circuitous route to the other end
thereof;
no one shall be hidden from his
radiant heat.

7. The law of the Lord is perfect,
converting souls.
The testimony of the Lord is faithful,
making infants wise.

8. The statutes of the Lord are right,
rejoicing the heart.
The command of the Lord is bright,
enlightening the eyes.

9. The fear of the Lord is pure,
enduring forever.
The judgments of the Lord are true,
justified as being so;

10. more to be desired than gold,
or many precious stones,
sweeter than honey,
or the honeycomb.

11. These indeed your servant keeps,
in keeping them there is great reward.

12. Who will understand transgressions?
Purge me from my hidden sins,
13. and from those of others, spare your
servant.

If they do not gain dominion over me,
then will I be blameless,
and clean from great sin.

14. Thus the words of my mouth,
and the meditations of my heart,
will be continually pleasing
in your sight,
O Lord, my helper and my redeemer.

Psalm 21

1. O God, my God, attend to me; why
have you forsaken me?
Far be my salvation from the account of
my transgressions!
2. O my God, shall I cry to you by day
and you not listen?
cry to you by night and it all be in vain?

3. You indeed dwell in a holy sanctuary,
you the praise of Israel.

4. Our ancestors placed their hope
in you,
they hoped and you delivered them.
5. They cried out to you and were saved;
in you they trusted and were not put
to shame.

6. But I am a worm, not even
a human being;
a reproach to all, the contempt
of people.
7. All who have seen me laughed me
to scorn;
they spoke openly and shook
their heads:

8. "He hoped in the Lord, let him
deliver him,
let him save him, since he delights
in him."

9. For you are the one who drew me out of the womb;
my hope from my mother's breast.
10. I was cast on you since
my very birth;
from my mother's womb you have been my God.

11. Don't keep aloof from me, for trouble is near,
for there is no helper, [save you].

12. Many bulls have encompassed me—
fat bulls beset me round about.
13. Against me they have opened wide their mouth,
like a ravenous lion, a roaring lion.

14. I am poured out like water
and all my bones are distended;
my heart sinks within me like melted wax.
15. My strength is dried up like a potsherd,
and my tongue is glued to my palate;
you have brought me down to the dust of death.

16. For many dogs have encircled me;
the assembly of the wicked has encompassed me;
they have pierced my hands
and my feet.
17. They have numbered all my bones,
have stared at me, observing me.
18. They distributed my garments among themselves,
and have cast lots for my raiment.

19. Therefore, O Lord, delay
not my help.
Draw near to my assistance.
20. Deliver my soul from the sword;
my only-begotten from the power of the dog.
21. Rescue me from the mouth of the lion;
and this lowliness of mine from the unicorns' horns.

22. I will declare your name to my brethren;
in the midst of the congregation I will sing praise to you.
23. Let those who fear the Lord praise him!
All you offspring of Jacob glorify the Lord!
Let all the seed of Israel fear him!

Psalm 22

1. The Lord tends to me as a shepherd, thus I shall want nothing;
2. in a verdant pasture, has caused me to dwell;
near restful waters, has refreshed me.

3. The Lord has restored my soul,
guided me on the paths of righteousness,
for the sake of the Lord's name.

4. For even if I walk in the midst of the shadow of death,
I will fear no evils, for you are with me;
your rod and your staff, these have comforted me.

5. You have prepared a table before me,
in the presence of those who afflict me.
You have anointed my head with fine oil,
and your cup of choice wine is the very best.

6. Surely your mercy shall follow me all the days of my life;
and my dwelling shall be in the Lord's house to the length of days.

Psalm 24

1. To you, O Lord, I have lifted up my soul.
2. O my God, in you have I placed my trust;
let me not be ashamed,
nor let my enemies deride me.

3. For none who wait on you shall be put to shame;
let them be ashamed who vainly transgress.
4. Show me your ways, O Lord,
and teach me your paths.

5. Lead me in your truth, and teach me;
for you O God, are my Savior—
for you have I waited all the day long.

6. Remember your compassion, O Lord, and your tender mercy,
for they are from everlasting.
7. Remember not the sins and follies of my youth,
but according to your mercy remember me,
for your goodness' sake, O Lord. . . .

16. Look down upon me and have mercy,
for I am an only child and poor.
17. The afflictions of my heart have been multiplied;
deliver me from all my distresses.

18. Behold my humiliation and my trouble,
and forgive me all my sins.

19. Behold my enemies for they have increased;
they have hated me with an unjust hatred.

20. O preserve my soul and deliver me;
let me not be put to shame,
for I have placed my hope in you.
21. The innocent and upright clung to me,
because I waited for you, O Lord.
22. God redeem Israel from all affliction!

Psalm 25

1. Judge me, O Lord, for I have conducted myself in innocence;
trusting in the Lord I shall not be shaken.
2. Examine me, O Lord, and prove me:
purify my innermost being and my heart.

3. For your mercy is ever before my eyes,
and I have taken delight in your truth.
4. I have not sat with the council of the vain,
and will not enter the company of transgressors.

5. I have hated the assembly of the wicked,
and will not take my seat among the godless.
6. I will wash my hands in innocence,
and will walk round your altar, O Lord,

7. that I may hear the sound of praise,
and declare all your wonderful deeds.
8. O Lord, I have loved the beauty of your house,

and the abode of the tabernacle
of your glory.

9. Destroy not my life with the ungodly,
nor my life with blood-thirsty fellows
10. in whose hands are iniquities,
and whose right hand is filled with
bribes.

11. Whereas I have conducted myself
in innocence;
redeem me and be merciful to me.
12. My footsteps have been in rectitude;
in the assemblies I will bless you,
O Lord.

Psalm 26

1. The Lord is my Light and my Savior;
whom shall I fear?
The Lord is the Defender of my life;
of whom shall I be afraid?

2. When evil-doers drew near
to devour my flesh;
my persecutors and my enemies,
they fainted and fell.
3. Though an army be arrayed
against me,
my heart will not succumb to fear.
Though a war should be waged
against me,
in this I place my hope:

4. One thing I asked of the Lord,
this will I eagerly seek:
that I may dwell in the house
of the Lord
all the days of my life;
that I may behold the beauty of the Lord
and survey God's temple. . . .
7. Hear, O Lord, my wail which
I uttered;

have mercy on me and hearken to me.
8. To you my heart said, "I have sought
your face."
Your face, O Lord, will I continue
to seek.

9. Turn not your face away from me,
withdraw not in anger from your
servant.
Be my helper, forsake me not.
O God, my Savior, overlook me not.

10. For my father and mother have
forsaken me,
but the Lord has taken me in.
11. Instruct me, O Lord, in your way,
and guide me in the right path, mindful
of my enemies.

12. Deliver me not to the will of those
who afflict me;
for unjust witnesses have risen up
against me,
and injustice has lied to her very self.

13. I believe I shall see
the goodness of the Lord
in the land of the living.
14. Wait on the Lord and be of
good courage!
Let your heart be strengthened and wait
on the Lord!

Psalm 27

1. To you, O Lord, I have cried:
My God, do not pass me by in silence.
If you should pass me by in silence,
I shall be like those who go down
to the Pit.

2. Hearken to the sound of my
supplication,

when I pray to you,
when I lift up my hands to your holy
temple.

3. Do not draw my life away
with sinners,
nor destroy me with the workers
of iniquity,
with those who speak of peace with
their neighbors,
yet conceive mischief in their hearts.

4. Requite them according
to their deeds,
according to the wickedness
of their designs.
Give to them according to the works
of their hands;
render their full recompense to them.

5. Because they ignored the works
of the Lord
and the operations of his hand,
you will pull them down,
and never rebuild them. . . .

9. Save your people,
and bless your inheritance.
Shepherd them,
and lift them up forever.

Psalm 29

1. I will extol you, O Lord, for you upheld me,
and did not allow my enemies to rejoice over me.
2. O Lord my God, to you I cried,
and you healed me.
3. O Lord, you have raised my soul
from Hades,
and delivered me from among those
who descend to the Pit. . . .

8. To you, O Lord, I will I cry;
and to my God will I make supplication.
9. What profit is there in my blood,
by my going down to destruction?

Can dust give you praise,
or shall it declare your truth?
10. The Lord heard and had compassion
upon me;
the Lord has become my helper.
11. You transformed my mourning
into joy;
you ripped my sackcloth from off of me
and girded me with gladness,

12. that my glory may sing praise to you
and I may no longer be pierced
with sorrow.
O Lord my God,
I will give thanks to you forever.

Psalm 30

1. In you, O Lord, I have trusted; let me never be put to shame.
because of your righteousness rescue me
and deliver me.
2. Incline your ear to me; hasten to
deliver me!
Be for me a protecting God and a house
of refuge to save me.

3. For you are my strength
and my refuge;
therefore for your name's sake you will
guide me and sustain me.
4. You will lead me out of the snare they
have hidden for me;
because you, O Lord, are my protector.

5. Into your hands I commit my spirit;
you have redeemed me O Lord,
God of Truth.

6. You have hated those who waste their time with vanities;
but as for me, I have placed my hope in the Lord.

7. I will exult with joy and be glad in your mercy,
because you have looked upon my humiliation,
and have saved my soul from many distresses.
8. You have not hemmed me in within my enemies' grasp;
instead you have established my footsteps in a broad expanse.

9. Pity me, O Lord, for I am afflicted,
with indignation my eye was troubled,
my soul and even my bosom.

10. For my life has been spent with grief,
and my years consumed with groaning;
my strength has been weakened through poverty,
and all my bones have experienced trouble.

11. Among all my enemies I have become a reproach;
and especially so to all my neighbors,
even an object of terror to my friends.
They who saw me out and about fled from me.

12. I have been forgotten as someone dead,
no longer remembered;
I have become like a shattered vessel.
13. For I have heard the slander of many who dwelt round me,
when they assembled together, arrayed against me,
they plotted how to take my life.

14. But as for me, I hoped in you, O Lord;
I said, You are my God.
15. In your hands are my lots;
deliver me from the hands of my enemies,
and from those who are persecuting me.

16. Let your face shine on your servant;
save me in your mercy.
17. O Lord, let me not be put to shame,
because I have called upon you.
Let the ungodly be covered in shame,
weighed down to the depths of Hades.

18. Let those deceitful lips become mute
which speak injustice against the righteous
with pride and contempt.

19. How abundant is the multitude of your kindness, O Lord,
which you have secretly stored up for those who fear you!
You have drawn them out for those who hope in you,
in the presence of the children of the earth.

20. In the secret of your presence,
you will hide them from mortal vexation;
you will shelter them in the tabernacle,
from the contradiction of tongues.

21. Blessed be the Lord,
for magnificently displaying such mercy in a fortified city.

22. But I said in my ecstasy,
I am cast out from your presence;
therefore, you, O Lord, did hearken
to the sound of my supplication
when I cried out to you.

23. O love the Lord, all you saints,
because the Lord seeks after truth
and requites those who act with
insolence.

24. Be of good courage,
let your hearts be strengthened,
all you who place your trust in the Lord.

Psalm 31

1. Blessed are they whose transgressions
are forgiven,
and whose sins are covered over.
2. Blessed the fellow to whom the Lord
will impute no sin,
and in whose mouth there is no guile to
be found.

3. Because I kept silent,
my bones grew old,
from my crying all day long.
4. Because day and night your hand
weighed heavy upon me,
I was reduced to misery by
a piercing thorn.

5. I acknowledged my sin,
and did not hide my iniquity.
I said, "Against myself I will confess my
iniquity to the Lord."
Thus you forgave the wickedness
of my heart.

6. Because of this, every pious person
shall pray to you in due season,
even a deluge of many waters would not
approach him.
7. You are my refuge from the affliction
which encircles me,
my joy, to redeem me from those who
encompass me.

8. I will instruct you and guide you in
the way you should go;
I will steadfastly fix my eyes upon you.
9. Be not like horse and mule,
which have no understanding,
whose mouths you must restrain with
bridle and bit,
when they do not respond to you.

10. Many are the scourges of the sinner,
but mercy will encompass the one who
trusts in the Lord.
11. Be glad in the Lord and exult you
righteous,
and glory all you who are upright
of heart.

Psalm 34

1. Judge them, O Lord, those who
wrong me.
Fight against those who are at war
with me.
2. Grab shield and buckler,
and rise to my defense.

3. Wield a sword and fend off
my pursuers;
say to my soul, I am your deliverance.
4. Let those who seek my life be
ashamed and confounded;
let those who devise evils against me be
thwarted and put to shame.

5. Let them be like dust before the wind,
with an angel of the Lord
afflicting them.
6. Let their path be dark and slippery,
with an angel of the Lord pursuing
them.

7. For without cause they have hid their
destructive snare for me,

and without basis they have reproached
my soul.
8. Let a snare which they see
not catch them,
and the trap which they have
hidden snap;
and by that very snare let them
fall victim.

9. But my soul shall exult in the Lord,
and take delight in his salvation.
10. All my bones shall declare,
O Lord, who is like you!
Delivering the poor from the hand
which is stronger,
the poor and needy from their
despoilers.

11. Unjust witnesses arose,
and charged me with things I knew not.
12. They paid me back evil for good,
even bereavement to my soul.

13. But I, when they troubled me,
clothed myself in sackcloth,
and humbled my soul with fasting,
and my prayer shall be directed
to my bosom.
14. I behaved kindly towards them,
as to one of our neighbors or to
a brother.
I humbled myself as one mourning,
as one sad of countenance.

15. But they rejoiced over me gathering
together,
scourges were brought against me, and I
didn't know it.
They were scattered, but they felt no
compunction.
16. They tested and tortured me,
they sneered at me most
contemptuously,
they gnashed their teeth at me.

17. O Lord, when will you look down
upon me?
Deliver my soul from their malice,
my only-begotten from the lions.
18. I will give you thanks in the great
assembly,
amid vast throngs I will praise you.

19. Let not those who are my enemies
for no reason,
rejoice over me;
those who hate me without cause,
who wink at each other.
20. For indeed in my presence they
spoke peaceably,
but with rage they were weaving plots.

21. Then their mouths opened wide
against me,
blurting, "Aha! Aha! Our own eyes have
seen it!"
22. You, O Lord have seen!
Do not remain silent!
O Lord, do not draw away from me!

23. Rise up, O Lord, and attend
to my trial,
O my God and my Lord, for the sake of
my cause.
24. Judge me, O Lord,
according to your righteousness,
O Lord my God;
and let them not rejoice on my account.
25. Let them not say in their hearts,
Aha! Aha! It is to our mind!
Nor let them say,
We have swallowed him alive!
26. Let them be confounded and
ashamed together,
who rejoice over my calamities;
let them be clothed with shame and
confusion,
who make great claims against me.

27. Let those who desire my justification,
exult with joy and be filled
with gladness.
Let those who desire the peace
of your servant,
continually repeat, "The Lord be
magnified!"
28. Thus shall my tongue speak of your righteousness,
and of your praise all the day long.

Psalm 35

5. O Lord, your mercy dwells
in the heavens,
and your truth is as high as the clouds.
6. Your righteousness is as solid as the mountains of God,
and your judgments are as great as the deep abyss.

7. As you, O Lord, have greatly multiplied your mercy;
let the children of the earth trust in the shelter of your wings.
8. They shall be fully satiated with the fatness of your house,
and you shall cause them to drink the full stream of your delights.

9. For with you is the wellspring of life,
and in your light we shall see light.
10. Extend your mercy to those who know you,
and your righteousness to those who are upright of heart.

11. Let not the foot of pride come against me,
nor the hand of sinners shake me.
12. There, all the evil doers have fallen!
They are cast out and will not be able to stand.

Psalm 37

1. O Lord, rebuke me not in your wrath;
nor chastise me in your anger.
2. For your darts are fixed deeply
within me,
and your hand is pressed heavily
upon me.

3. There is no health in my flesh because of your anger;
there is no peace for my bones because of my sins.
4. For my transgressions have soared over my head;
they have pressed heavily upon me like a weighty burden.

5. My wounds become infected
and malignant,
on account of my foolishness.
6. I have been in misery,
totally bent over—
all the day long I have been
in mourning.

7. For my soul was filled with illusions;
and there is no healthy soundness
in my flesh.
8. I have been afflicted and exceedingly depressed;
I have roared because of the groaning of my heart.

9. But all my desire is laid before you,
and my groaning is not hidden
from you.

10. My heart panted, my strength
failed me,
and the light of my eyes has left me.

11. My friends and neighbors stayed
away from me,
they drew near but stopped;

even my nearest relatives stood aloof.
12. And those who sought my life
pressed against me;
those who sought my ruin
spoke vanities,
they devised deceits all the day long.

13. But I, as someone deaf, heard not;
and as someone dumb, opened not
my mouth.
14. In fact, I became like a person who
doesn't hear,
and in whose mouth no reproofs
are found.

15. For in you, O Lord, I placed
my trust;
you O Lord, my God will hearken.
16. For I said, Perhaps my enemies will
rejoice over me,
Indeed, when my feet slipped, they
boasted and gloated.

17. For I am prepared for plagues,
my terrible situation continually
before me.
18. For I will declare my lawlessness,
and express sorrow for my sin.

19. But my enemies live and are stronger
than I!
And those who hate me unjustly are
multiplied!
20. Those who reward evil for good
slandered me,
all because I follow righteousness.

21. Do not utterly forsake me, O Lord,
my God;
do not stand far away from me.
22. Draw near to my aid,
O Lord of my salvation.

Psalm 38

1. I said, I will watch my ways,
so I won't sin with my tongue.
I set a guard over my mouth,
while the sinner stood in my presence.

2. I was dumb and humbled myself,
and kept silent from profitable speech,
yet my grief was renewed.

3. My heart grew hot within me,
a fire would be set ablaze by
my musings,
thus I spoke with my tongue:

4. O Lord make known to me my end,
and the number of my days, what it is,
that I might know what I lack.

5. Behold you have made my days old,
yet my existence is as nothing
before you.
The universe is nothing but vanity,
and every living person.

6. Surely Man walks about in an illusion,
still he is disquieted in vain.
He stores up treasures,
yet knows not for whom he shall
gather them.

7. And now, what is my expectation?
Is it not the Lord?
In you is my sustaining hope.

8. Deliver me from all my
transgressions.
You have made me a reproach
to the foolish.
9. I was dumb and opened
not my mouth,
because you are the One who made me.

10. Remove your scourges from me,
I have fainted because of the strength of your hand.
11. With rebukes you have corrected Man for iniquity;
and caused his life to vanish like a spider's web,
nevertheless, everyone is disquieted in vain.

12. Give ear to my prayer, O Lord,
hearken to my supplication.
Attend to my tears, be not silent,
for I am a sojourner in the land,
and a stranger as all my ancestors were.

13. O spare me,
that I may be refreshed,
before I depart,
and be no more.

Psalm 39

5. O Lord my God, you have multiplied your marvelous deeds,
and in your thoughts none shall be likened to you.
I declared aloud and spoke of them,
they defied all numbering.
6. Sacrifice and offering you desired not,
but a body you prepared for me;
whole-burnt offerings and sacrifices for sin,
these, you required not.

7. Then I said, Behold I come,
in the volume of the book it is written regarding me:
8. I desired to do your will, O my God,
your law resides in the midst of my heart.

9. I have preached righteousness in a great congregation,
Behold I will not refrain my lips from speaking,
You, O Lord, can bear witness.

10. I have not hidden your righteousness in my heart,
your truth and your salvation I have proclaimed.
I hid not your mercy and truth from the great assembly.

11. But you, O Lord, remove not your compassion from me,
your mercy and your truth have helped me constantly.
12. For innumerable evils have encompassed me,
my transgressions have taken hold of me
—thus I could not see clearly;
they are more numerous than the hairs of my head,
therefore my heart failed me.

13. Be pleased, O Lord, to deliver me.
O Lord, draw near to my assistance.
14. Let those who seek my life
to destroy it,
be utterly confounded and ashamed.
Let those who wish evil upon me,
be turned back and put to shame.

15. Let those who say to me, Aha! Aha!
quickly receive shame as their reward.
16. Let all who seek you, O Lord,
exult and rejoice in you;
let those who love your salvation continually say,
"May the Lord be magnified!"

17. As for me, I am poor and needy;
the Lord will take care of me.
You are my helper and defender;
O my God, do not delay.

Psalm 41

1. As the deer earnestly pants for springs of water,
so pants my soul for you, O God.
2. My soul has thirsted
for the living God.
When shall I come and appear
before God?
3. My tears were my food day and night,
when they continually said to me,
Where is your God?

4. I remembered these things,
and poured out my soul within me;
for I will go to the place of your marvelous tabernacle,
even to the house of God,
with shouts of exultation and thanksgiving,
and the sound of those who celebrate the festival.

5. Why then are you sad, O my soul?
And why do you trouble me?
Hope in God, for I will give him thanks,
God, the healthy glow of my countenance.

6. O my God, my soul has been troubled within me;
therefore I will remember you
from the land of Jordan and Hermon,
straddling the little mountain.

7. Deep calls unto deep,
in the roar of your raging waters;
all your billows and waves passed over me.
8. By day the Lord will execute mercy,
and make it manifest by night.
Let a prayer to the God of my life accompany me.

9. I will say to God, You are my helper,
so why have you forsaken me?
Why do I go about downcast
while my enemy oppresses me?

10. While my bones were crushed,
those who afflicted me reproached me
incessantly saying every day:
Where is your God?

11. Why are you sad, O my soul?
And why do you trouble me?
Hope in God, for I will give him thanks,
the health of my countenance
and my God.

Psalm 42

1. Judge me, O God, and plead my cause
against an ungodly nation:
deliver me from the unjust
and deceitful fellow.
2. For you, O God, are my strength; then why have you cast me off?
Why do I go about sad of countenance
while the enemy oppresses me?

3. O send forth your light
and your truth;
these have guided me and brought me
to your holy mountain,
even directed me to your holy tabernacle.

4. Thus I will go to the altar of God,
to the God who gladdens my youthfulness.
I will give thanks to you on the harp,
O God, my God.

5. Why are you sad, O my soul?
And why do you trouble me?
Hope in God, for I will give him thanks,

the health of my countenance
and my God.

Psalm 44

1. My heart has uttered a good word,
I declare my works to the king.
My tongue is the quill of a speedy writer.

2. You are fairer than mere mortals;
grace is poured out upon your lips,
therefore God has blessed you forever.

3. Gird your sword upon your thigh,
O Mighty One!
To your comeliness and beauty
give splendor!
4. Bend your bow, and prosper
and reign,
for the sake of truth, meekness
and justice!
Your right hand shall guide you
wondrously!

5. Your arrows are sharpened,
O Mighty One.
Nations shall fall under your sway;
even those in the heart of the king's
enemies.

6. Your throne, O God, is forever
and ever,
the scepter of your kingdom is a scepter
of rectitude.
7. You have loved righteousness and
hated iniquity,
therefore God, your God,
has anointed you
with the oil of gladness above
your fellows.

8. There is myrrh, stacte, and cassia
wafting from your robes,
from the ivory palaces which have gladdened you.
9. Kings' daughters assemble in honor
of you;
the queen stood at your right hand,
clothed in vestments of gold and fine
embroidery.

10. Listen, O daughter, and take note:
Incline your ear, forget your people and
your father's house,
11. because the king has desired your
beauty,
because he is your Lord.

12. The daughters of Tyre shall bow
down to him bearing gifts,
the richest people of the land shall sup-
plicate your favor.
13. All this glory is for the daughter of
the king within;
she is enwrapped in golden fringed
finery and embroidery.

14. The virgins in her train shall be
brought to the king.
Those who are related to her will be
introduced to you.
15. They shall be brought forth with
gladness and rejoicing.
They shall be ushered into the temple of
the king.

16. In place of your ancestors, children
are born to you;
you shall make them princes over
all the land.
17. They shall cause your name to be
remembered,
from generation to generation.
Therefore the nations shall give you
thanks for ever,
even for ages and ages to come.

PRAYING—WITH THE SAINTS—TO GOD OUR MOTHER

Psalm 46

1. Clap your hands all your nations;
Shout to God with voices of exultation.
2. For the Lord Most High is awesome,
great king over all the earth.

3. He has subdued peoples under us,
the nations under our feet.
4. He has chosen us as his inheritance,
the beauty of Jacob which he loved.

5. God has ascended with shouts of acclamation,
the Lord to the sound of trumpet blasts!
6. Sing praises to our God, sing praises!
Sing praises to our King, sing praises!

7. For God is king over all the earth;
sing praises with heartfelt understanding.
8. God reigns over the nations;
God sits upon his holy throne.

Psalm 49

7. Hear, my people and I will speak to you, Israel,
and I will bear witness to you: I am God your God.
8. I will not reprove you for your sacrifices,
your burnt-offering which are always before me.
9. Nor will I take any bullocks from your house,
nor he-goats from your flocks.

10. For all the wild beasts of the thicket are mine,
the cattle on the mountainsides and oxen.
11. I lay claim to all the birds of the air,
and the ripe fruits of the field belong to me.

12. If I were hungry, I would not inform you,
for the world is mine and all its fullness.

13. Do I eat the flesh of bulls,
or drink the blood of goats?
14. Sacrifice to God a sacrifice of praise,
and pay your vows to the Most High.
15. Call upon me in the day of affliction,
and I will deliver you and you will praise me.

16. But to the sinner God has said,
"Why do you declare my ordinances,
or take up my covenant in your mouth?
17. As for you,
you have hated instruction,
and cast my words behind you.

18. If you saw a thief, you kept pace with him;
and cast in your lot with adulterers.
19. Your mouth has abounded in wickedness,
and your tongue has fashioned deceit.
20. You sat down and spoke against your relative,
even against your mother's offspring you caused scandal.

21. You did these things
and I kept quiet.
You wickedly supposed that I was like yourself.
But now I will reprove you and set the matter before you."
22. Now consider this, you who forget God,
lest you be rent to pieces,
and there be no deliverer.

Psalm 50

1. Have mercy upon me, O God,
according to your great mercy;
and according to the multitude of your compassions,
blot out my transgression.

2. Wash me thoroughly from my iniquity,
and cleanse me from my sin.
3. For I am conscious of my iniquity,
and my sin is continually before me.

4. Against you alone have I sinned,
and done what is evil in your sight,
thus you may be justified
in your decrees,
and may be vindicated when
you are judged.

5. For behold, I was molded
in iniquities,
and in sins did my mother conceive me.
6. For behold, you love truth,
you have manifested to me
the secret and hidden things of your wisdom.

7. Sprinkle me with hyssop and I shall be purified;
wash me, and I shall become whiter than snow.
8. Cause me to hear gladness and joy
and these weary bones shall rejoice.

9. Turn your face away from my sins,
and blot out all my iniquities.
10. Create a clean heart in me, O God,
and renew a right spirit in my
inner depths.
11. Cast me not away from your presence,
and take not your Holy Spirit from me.

12. Restore to me the joy of your salvation;
establish me with your directing Spirit.
13. Then will I teach transgressors
your ways,
and the ungodly shall return to you.
14. Deliver me from blood-guilt O God,
the God of my salvation,
and my tongue shall joyfully proclaim
your righteousness.

15. O Lord, open my lips,
and my mouth shall declare your praise.
16. For if you desired sacrifice, I would
have rendered it.
In whole-burnt offerings you take no pleasure.
17. Sacrifice for God is a contrite spirit.
A broken and humbled heart you will
not spurn, O God.

18. Deal favorably, O Lord, with Zion
according to your good pleasure;
Let the walls of Jerusalem be built up.
19. Then shall you be pleased with a
sacrifice of righteousness,
an offering and whole-burnt sacrifices,
then shall they offer up calves upon
your altar.

Psalm 53

1. Save me, O God, by your name,
and judge me by your might.
2. O God, hear my prayer;
give ear to the words of my mouth.

3. For strangers have risen up
against me,
and the mighty have sought my life;
they have not set God before their eyes.

4. For behold, God comes to my aid.
The Lord is the protector of my life.
5. The Lord will repay my enemies with evil.
Utterly destroy them in your truth!

6. Willingly I will offer you sacrifices,
I will give thanks to your name O Lord,
for it is good.
7. For you have rescued me from all afflictions,
and my eye has witnessed
my enemies' fate.

Psalm 54

1. Give ear, O God, to my prayer,
and do not disregard my supplication.
2. Attend to me and hearken to me,
I was grieved in my meditation and troubled;

3. because of an enemy's voice and oppression of a sinner;
because they brought iniquity against me, seething with rage.
4. My heart was troubled within me,
and the dread of death fell upon me.
5. Fear and trembling gripped me,
and darkness enshrouded me.
6. And I said, "O that I had wings like those of a dove,
that I might fly away and find rest."

7. Behold! I have fled far and away,
and sought refuge in the wilderness.
8. I waited on the one who would deliver me
from distress of spirit and wild tempest.

9. Overwhelm, O Lord, and divide their tongues,
for I have seen iniquity and contradiction in the city.

10. Day and night transgression keeps its rounds upon the walls;
iniquity, sorrow and unrighteousness are in its midst,
11. and usury and fraud have not departed from its streets.

12. For if an enemy had reproached me,
I would have endured it,
and if one who hated me had spoken boastfully against me,
I would have hid myself from him.

13. But you, O like-minded soul, my guide, my intimate friend!
14. Who in companionship did sweeten my meals!
In the house of God, we used to walk in unanimity!

15. Let death come upon them,
and let them go down alive into Hades;
because there was wickedness in their dwellings,
even in the midst of them.

16. I cried out to God,
and the Lord hearkened to me.
Evening, morning and noon I shall declare and proclaim,
and the Lord shall hearken to my voice.

Psalm 56

1. Have mercy upon me, O God, be merciful to me,
for my soul has trusted in you;
and in the shadow of your wings
I will hope,
until this iniquity passes away.
2. I will cry to God the Most High,
to the God who has been kind to me . . .

5. Be exalted above the heavens, O God,
and let your glory be over
all the earth . . .
7. My heart, O God is ready,
my heart is ready:
I will sing, indeed, I will sing Psalms.
8. Awake my glory;
awake psaltery and harp:
I will awake early.

9. I will give thanks to you among the peoples, O Lord,
I will sing to you in the midst
of the nations.
10. For your mercy has been magnified
even to the heavens,
and your truth exalted even to the clouds.
11. Be exalted above the heavens,
O God,
and let your glory be over all the earth!

Psalm 60

1. Hearken, O God, to my supplication,
attend to my prayer.
2. From the ends of the earth I have cried to you,
when my heart was despondent, you lifted me up on a rock.

3. You guided me because you were my hope,
a tower of strength in the face
of the enemy.
4. I shall dwell in your tabernacle forever,
I shall take shelter in the cover
of your wings.

5. For you, O God, have heard
my prayers;
you have granted an inheritance to
those who fear your name.

6. You will add days upon days to the king's reign,
and extend his years to generation after generation.

7. He will continue forever in the presence of God.
Who will seek out his mercy and truth?
8. Thus I will sing to your name forever and ever,
that I may, day after day, fulfill my vows.

Psalm 62

1. O God, my God, I cry to you early in the morning;
my soul has thirsted for you,
how often has my flesh longed for you,
in a barren and trackless desert.

2. Thus have I appeared before you in the sanctuary,
to contemplate your power
and your glory.
3. Because your mercy is better than life,
my lips shall render you praise.

4. Thus I will bless you
throughout my life,
and in your name I will lift
up my hands.
5. Let my soul be filled as with marrow and fatness,
that my joyful lips may
praise your name.

6. Inasmuch as I remembered you upon my bed,
in the early hours I have meditated
upon you.
7. For you have been my helper,
and in the shelter of your wings
I will rejoice.

8. My soul has clung closely to you;
your right hand has supported me.
9. But as for those who sought my life in vain,
they shall descend into the depths of the earth.

10. They shall be delivered up to the edge of the sword,
they shall become morsels for the jackals.
11. But the king shall rejoice in God,
everyone who swears by him shall be praised,
for the mouth of those who speak lies has been stopped up.

Psalm 64

1. Praise is befitting for you, O God, in Zion;
and to you shall a vow be paid.
2. Hearken to my prayer,
to you all flesh shall come.

3. The words of transgressors have overpowered us,
but you can pardon our sins.
4. Blessed is the one whom you have chosen and adopted,
he will dwell in your courts.
We shall be satisfied with the good things of your house;
your temple is holy, wondrous in righteousness.

5. Listen to us, O God, our savior,
the hope of all the ends of the earth,
and of those who travel in the distant seas.
6. You establish the mountains by your might,
girt round about by your power.

7. You stir up the depths of the sea,
causing the crashing sound of its waves.

8. The nations shall be in tumult;
those who inhabit the far reaches terrified at your signs.
You will cause the exiting of morning and evening to bring joy.

9. You have visited the earth and watered it;
you have abundantly enriched it.
The river of God is bursting with water,
You have provided its supply for such is your provision.
10. Saturate her furrows,
and augment her productivity.
By these showers on it,
it will be gladdened,
the crops will spring up.

11. Bless the crown of the year with your goodness,
and let the fields be filled with fertility.
12. Let the mountains of the wilderness become fertile;
and the hills be girt round about with joy.
13. The rams of the flock have put on thick coats,
and the valleys abound in rich grain;
they shall cry aloud and sing hymns of praise.

Psalm 66

1. May God be merciful to us and bless us,
and cause his face to shine upon us.
2. May all know your way upon the earth,
among the nations your saving help.

3. Let the peoples, O God,
give you thanks,
let all the peoples render you thanks.
4. Let the nations rejoice and exult,
for you shall judge peoples in equity,
and will guide the nations
upon the earth.

5. Let the peoples, O God,
give you thanks,
let all the peoples render you thanks.
6. The earth has yielded her fruit,
may God, our God, bless us!
7. May God truly bless us,
and may all the ends of the earth
revere God.

Psalm 68

1. Save me, O God,
for the waters have inundated me.
2. I am stuck in deep mire,
and there is no underlying support.
I am come into the depths of the sea,
and a tempest has overwhelmed me.

3. I am weary with crying;
my throat is hoarse;
and my eyes failed
while I waited on my God.

4. Those who hate me without cause
are more numerous than the hairs on
my head.
My enemies who unjustly persecute me
have become strong;
I have made restitution for what I did
not steal.

5. O God, you are aware of my
foolishness,
and my mistakes are not hidden
from you.

6. Let not those who wait on you,
O Lord of Hosts,
be put to shame on account of me.
Let not those who seek you,
experience confusion on my account,
O God of Israel.

7. For I have suffered reproach
for your sake,
confusion has covered my face.
8. I have become an alien to my
relatives,
and a stranger to my mother's children.
9. For zeal for your house has
consumed me,
and the reproaches of those who reproached you,
these have fallen upon me.

10. I have bowed down my life
with fasting,
but this has become a source of reproach to me.
11. I put sackcloth on for my garment,
thus I became a proverb to them.
12. Those who sit in the gate spoke
against me;
those who drink wine composed a song
about me.
13. But I will offer my prayer to you,
O Lord;
it is a propitious time, O God, in the
multitude of your mercy;
hear me in the truth of your saving help.
14. Save me from the mire,
so that I may not be stuck;
let me be delivered from those
who hate me,
and rescued from the watery depths.

15. Let not a deluge of water engulf me;
let not the watery abyss swallow me;
nor the cistern shut its mouth on me.

16. Hear me, O Lord, for your loving mercy is tender,
according to your abundant compassion look down on me.
17. Turn not your face away from your servant,
for I am sorely afflicted;
hasten to hear me.

18. Draw near to my soul and redeem it;
deliver me, in spite of my enemies.
19. For you know my reproach, my shame and my confusion;
all those who afflict me stand poised before me.

20. My soul anticipated reproach and misery,
I waited for a condoler,
but there was none,
for someone to comfort me,
but found none.

21. They gave me gall for my food,
and for my thirst, gave me vinegar to drink.
22. Let their table become a snare before them,
a source of recompense and a stumbling-block. . . .

29. I am needy and grief-stricken,
but the saving grace of your face has upheld me.
30. I will praise the name of my God with a song;
I will magnify God with praise.

31. This will be more pleasing to God,
than a young calf having horns and hooves.
32. Let the poor see and rejoice;
diligently seek God and you shall live.

Psalm 69

1. O God, come to my assistance;
O Lord, make haste to help me.
2. Let those who seek my life be ashamed and confounded;
let those who wish me ill, be thwarted and put to shame.

3. Let those who say to me, Aha! Aha!
be turned back and suddenly covered with shame.
4. Let all who seek you rejoice and be glad in you;
Let those who love your saving help,
continually say, God be magnified!

5. But I am poor and needy;
O God help me.
You are my helper and deliverer;
O Lord do not delay.

Psalm 70

1. I have placed my hope in you, O Lord,
let me never be put to shame.
2. In your righteousness, deliver me and rescue me;
incline your ear to me and save me.

3. Be for me a protecting God
and a stronghold to save me,
for you are my fortress and refuge.

4. Deliver me, O God, from the grasp of the sinner,
from the hand of the transgressor and unjust person.
5. For you are my support, O Lord;
you are my hope, O Lord,
from my youth.

6. I have depended on you
from the womb;
from my birth you have been
my protector.
I continually sing hymns
concerning you.
7. To many I became a wonder,
as it were,
but you have been my strong helper.
8. Let my mouth be filled with praise,
that I may sing of your glory and majesty all day.

9. Do not cast me off in the time of my
old age;
do not forsake me when
my strength fails.
10. For my enemies have spoken
against me,
and my assassins have taken
counsel together,

11. saying, "God has forsaken him,
pursue and take him, for he has no
deliverer."
12. O God, do not be far removed
from me;
O my God, draw near to my assistance.

13. Let those who plot against my life
be ashamed and utterly fail;
let those who seek my ill
be clothed with shame and dishonor.

14. But as for me,
I will continually hope,
and I will praise you more and more.
15. My mouth shall declare your
righteousness,
your saving help all the day long;
for I know no other practices.

16. I will go forth in the might of the
Lord,

O Lord I will boast of your
righteousness alone.
17. You have taught me, O God, from
my youth,
even still I declare your wonders.

18. Even until I am old
and advanced in years,
forsake me not, O God,
until I shall have declared your might
to all the generation that is yet to come,
even your power and righteousness.

19. O God, the great works you
have wrought
are as high as the heavens!
O God, who can be compared with you?

20. O what trials many and sore have
you shown me!
Yet you relented and restored my life,
and brought me back from the depths of
the earth.
21. You have multiplied your
saving mercy,
and returned and comforted me,
and brought me back from the depths of
the earth.

22. Therefore I will praise you with a
musical instrument,
even I, regarding your truth, O God.
I will sing and play to you on the harp,
O Holy One of Israel.

23. My lips shall rejoice
when I sing to you,
and my soul, which you have redeemed.
24. Moreover, even my tongue
shall meditate on your righteousness,
all the day long,
while those who seek my harm,
shall be ashamed and confounded.

PRAYING—WITH THE SAINTS—TO GOD OUR MOTHER

Psalm 71

1. O God, give your judgment
to the king,
and your righteousness to the king's son;
2. that he may judge your people with
righteousness,
and your poor with judgment.

3. Let the mountains and hills
raise peace and prosperity for
your people.
4. He shall judge the poor of your
people with righteousness,
and save the children of the needy
and lay low the false accuser.

5. He shall endure as long as the sun,
and stand before the moon forever.
6. He shall come down as heavy showers
upon a fleece
and as raindrops falling upon the earth.

7. In his days righteousness shall
spring up
and abundance of peace until the moon
be no more.
8. And he shall reign from sea to sea,
from the great river to the ends
of the earth.

9. Ethiopians shall bow down
before him,
and his enemies shall lick the dust.
10. The kings of Tarshish and the islands
shall bring presents
The kings of Arabia and Saba
shall offer gifts.

11. And all kings shall worship him;
all the nations will serve him.
12. For he has delivered the poor from
the oppressor;
and the needy who had no helper.

Psalm 72

1. How good is God to Israel,
to the upright of heart!
2. But as for me, my feet almost
stumbled,
my steps had nearly slipped.

3. For I was jealous of transgressors,
seeing how sinners prosper.
4. For there is no sign of reluctance in
their death;
they are steadfast in their affliction.

5. They experience not the trials
of others,
nor are they afflicted like others.
6. Therefore haughtiness
has possessed them;
they have clothed themselves with injustice and impiety.

7. Their injustice springs forth
in fat supply;
they have fulfilled the intention
of their heart.
8. They have taken counsel
and spoke wickedly;
they uttered injustice to high heaven.

9. They have set their mouth
against heaven;
and their tongue has wagged
over all the earth.
10. Therefore my people shall return
to this,
and fullness of days shall be found
with them.
11. Indeed they said,
"How does God know?
Is there any knowledge
in the Most High?"

12. Behold, these are the sinners,
the ones who always prosper,
possessing great wealth.

13. Then I said, "I have in vain kept my heart just,
and washed my hands in innocence.
14. All the day long I have been plagued,
and my reproof was every morning."

15. If said, I will make an open declaration;
I would have been treacherous to your children's generation.
16. Yet I undertook to understand this,
but alas, it is too difficult for me.
17. When I go to the sanctuary of God,
then I may understand the final outcome.

18. It is because of their crafty dealings,
that you have dealt thus with them.
You have cast them down,
when they thought they were exalted.

19. How they have become desolate!
They have vanished in a flash!
They have perished
because of their lawlessness.

20. Like the dream of someone rising from sleep,
you, O Lord, in your city will spurn their phantom.
21. Therefore, my heart has been filled with joy,
and my stomach—tied in knots—has been relieved.

22. Yet I was despicable and knew it not;
I had become like a brute beast
before you.
23. Nevertheless, I am always with you,
because you held me by my right hand.

24. You have guided me by your counsel,
and taken me to yourself in glory.
25. For what is there in heaven for me besides you?
And what have I desired on earth other than you?

26. Have my heart and my flesh failed?
God is the life of my heart.
God is my portion forever.

27. For behold, those who remove themselves from you,
shall utterly perish.
You have destroyed everyone
who leaves you
to play the whore.

28. Thus it is good for me
to cleave to God,
to place my trust in the Lord,
that I may proclaim all your praises,
in the gates of the daughter of Zion.

Psalm 76

13. O God, your path is in holiness.
What god is as great as our God?
14. You are the God who works wonders,
you have made known among the peoples your power.
15. You redeemed with your arm your people,
the children of Jacob and Joseph.

16. The waters saw you, O God,
the waters saw you and trembled,
and the abyss was deeply troubled.
17. Great was the roaring of waters,
the clouds uttered a sound,
for your bolts were passing through them.

18. The sound of your thunder rumbled round,
and your lightening illumined the world;
the earth trembled and quaked.
19. Your way was through the sea,
and your paths through many waters,
but your footsteps could not be known.

20. You guided your people as sheep,
by the hand of Moses and Aaron.

Psalm 79

1. Attend, O Shepherd of Israel,
who leads Joseph like a flock.
You who sit upon the cherubim,
manifest yourself.

2. Before Ephraim, Benjamin and Manasseh,
stir up your power
and come to our salvation.
3. Turn us around, O God,
let your face shine,
and we shall be saved.

4. O Lord, the God of hosts,
how long will you be angry
with the prayer of your servant?
5. How long will you feed us
with the bread of tears,
and cause us to drink tears by measure?

6. You have made us a laughing stock to our neighbors;
and our enemies have mocked us round about.
7. Turn us around, O God,
let your face shine,
and we shall be saved.

8. You have transplanted a vine out of Egypt;
your have uprooted the heathen and planted it.
9. You prepared a way before it,
and caused it to take root,
and the land was filled.

10. Its leafy shade covered the mountain,
and its tendrils, the cedars of God.
11. It sent forth its branches to the sea,
and its spreading boughs to the river.

12. Then why have you broken down its hedge,
that all who pass by the roadside may pluck it?
13. The boar from the forest has laid it waste;
and the wild beast has devoured it.

14. O God of Hosts, return
we beseech you;
look down from heaven and see and visit this vine.
15. Restore that which your right hand has planted,
and look on the Son of Man whom you strengthened for yourself.

16. It is burnt up and uprooted,
at the rebuke of your countenance they will perish.
17. Let your hand be upon your right hand man,
on the Son of Man whom you made strong for yourself.

18. Thus will we not depart from you;
you shall give us life,
and we will call upon your name.
19. O Lord, God of hosts,
turn us around.
Let your face shine
and we shall be saved.

Psalm 80

1. Exult with joy in God our helper!
Shout aloud to the God of Jacob!
2. Take up a psalm and produce
the timbrel,
the sweet sounding psaltery with a harp.

3. Blare the trumpet at the new moon,
in the glorious day of our feast.
4. For it is an ordinance for Israel,
and a statute written by the God
of Jacob,

5. who established it as a testimony
in Joseph,
when he came forth from the land
of Egypt;
he heard a language which he understood not.
6. He removed his back from burdens;
his hands slaved away
at making baskets.

7. In affliction you called upon me,
and I delivered you.
I heard you in the secret place
of the tempest;
I tested you in the water
of contradiction.

8. Hear, my people, and I will testify
to you,
O Israel, if you will hearken to me.
9. There shall be no new god
among you,
nor shall you worship a strange god.

10. For I am the Lord your God,
who brought you out of the land
of Egypt.
Open wide your mouth and I will fill it.

11. But my people did
not heed my voice,
and Israel did not hearken to me.
12. So I let them go after
the habits of their own hearts;
they will pursue their own customs.

13. If my people had hearkened to me,
if Israel had walked in my ways,
14. I would have quickly routed
their enemies,
and laid my hand upon those who
afflicted them.

Psalm 81

1. God stands in the assembly of gods,
and in their midst will judge gods.
2. How long will you judge unjustly,
and favor the person of sinners?

3. Do justice to the orphan and poor,
render justice to the oppressed
and needy.
4. Rescue the needy,
and deliver the poor
from the sinner's hand.

5. They know not, neither do
they understand;
they walk about in darkness.
All the foundations of the earth
shall be shaken.

6. I have said, "You are gods,
all of you, children of the Most High."
7. But you shall die as mortals,
and fall as one of the rulers.

8. Arise O God,
judge the earth;
for you shall inherit all nations.

Praying—with the Saints—to God Our Mother

Psalm 83

1. How lovely are your dwellings,
O Lord of hosts!
2. My soul longs and faints for the
courts of the Lord;
my heart and my flesh have exulted in
the living God.

3. Yea, the sparrow has found itself
a home;
and the turtle-dove a nest for herself,
where she may lay her young,
even your altars, O Lord of hosts,
my King and my God.

4. Blessed are those who dwell
in your house;
they shall praise you for ever and ever.
5. Blessed the fellow whose help is from
you, O Lord,
who has planned in his heart to go up to
6. the valley of weeping, to the appointed place,
for there the Lawgiver will bestow
blessings.

7. They shall go from strength
to strength;
the God of gods will be seen in Zion.
8. O Lord, God of hosts, hear my prayer;
give ear O God of Jacob.

9. Behold, O God our Defender,
and look upon the face
of your anointed.
10. For one day in your courts
is better than a thousand [elsewhere];
I would rather be dejected in the house
of God,
than dwell in the tents of sinners.

11. For the Lord loves mercy and truth;
God will grant grace and glory.
The Lord will not withhold good things
from those who walk in innocence.
12. O Lord of hosts,
blessed the fellow who trusts in you!

Psalm 84

1. O Lord you have favored your land;
you have turned back the captivity
of Jacob.
2. You have forgiven your people their
transgressions;
you have covered over all their sins.

3. You have caused all your wrath
to abate;
you have turned away from
your fierce anger.
4. Turn us around, O God
of our salvation,
and turn your anger away from us.

5. Will you be angry with us forever?
Or will you extend your wrath
from generation to generation?
6. O God you will relent and give us life,
and your people will rejoice in you.
7. Show us your mercy, O Lord,
and grant us your salvation. . . .

10. Mercy and truth have met
each other;
righteousness and peace have kissed
one another.
11. Truth has sprung up from out
of the earth,
and righteousness has peered down
from heaven.
12. For the Lord will grant goodness,
and our land shall yield her fruitfulness.
13. Righteousness will precede the Lord,
and shall establish his steps along
the way.

Psalm 85

1. Incline your ear, O Lord,
and hearken to me,
for I am indeed poor and needy.
2. Preserve my life, for I am holy;
save your servant, O God,
who hopes in you.

3. Have mercy on me, O Lord,
for to you will I cry all the day long.
4. Gladden the soul of your servant,
for to you, O Lord,
I have lifted up my soul.

5. For you, O Lord, are kind and gentle,
and bountiful in mercy to all who call
upon you.
6. Give ear, O Lord, to my prayer;
attend to the sound of my supplication.

7. In the day of my woe
I cried out to you,
because you have heard me.
8. For there is none like you among the
gods, O Lord,
and there are no works compared
to yours.

9. All the nations which you have made
shall come,
and worship before you, O Lord,
and they shall glorify your name.
10. For you are great and work wonders;
you are the only God, the Great One.

11. Guide me, O Lord, in your path,
that I may walk in your truth.
Let my heart rejoice,
that I might revere your name.

12. I will give thanks to you, O Lord,
my God,
with all my heart,
and I will glorify your name forever.
13. For your mercy towards me is great;
you have delivered my life from the
deepest hell.
14. O God, transgressors have risen up
against me,
an assembly of violent people has
sought my life,
and they have not set you
before their eyes.

15. But you, O Lord God, are compassionate and merciful,
longsuffering, abounding in mercy
and truth.
16. Look down upon me and have
mercy on me,
give your strength to your servant,
and save the offspring of your
handmaid.

17. Vouchsafe for me a token for good,
and let those who hate me see it
and be ashamed,
for you, O Lord, have helped me
and comforted me.

Psalm 88

1. O Lord, I will sing of your
mercies forever;
I will proclaim your truth with my
mouth to all generations.
2. For you have said: "Mercy shall be
built up forever.
Your truth shall be established
in the heavens.

3. I have made a covenant
with my chosen;
I swore a pledge to my servant, David.
4. I shall establish your seed forever,

and build up your throne to all
generations."

5. The heavens declare your wonders,
O Lord,
and your truth in the assembly of the
holy ones.
6. For who in the heavens shall be compared to the Lord?
And who shall be likened to the Lord
among the sons of God?

7. God is glorified in the council of the
holy ones,
great and fearful to all who
are around him.
8. O Lord, God of hosts,
who is like you?
You are mighty, O Lord, and your truth
encompasses you.

9. You rule over the raging of the sea,
and calm the tumult of its waves.
10. You have humbled the proud like
someone slain;
with your mighty arm you have scattered your foes.

11. Yours are the heavens, and yours
is the earth.
You have founded the world
and its fullness.
12. You have created the north
and the west;
Tabor and Hermon will rejoice
in your name.

13. Yours is the mighty arm;
let your hand be strengthened, your
right hand exalted.
14. Justice and judgment are the foundation of your throne;

mercy and truth shall process before
your presence.

15. Blessed the people who know the
sound of joy!
They shall walk, O Lord, in the light of
your presence.
16. In your name they shall rejoice all
the day long,
and in your righteousness they shall be
exalted.

17. For you are the boast
of their strength,
and in your good pleasure our horn
shall be exalted.
18. For from the Lord is support,
even from the Holy One of Israel,
our King.

19. Then you spoke in a dream to your
children, saying:
"I have set help on one who is mighty,
I have exalted a chosen one from out of
my people.
20. I have found David to be my servant,
I have anointed him with holy oil.

21. For my hand shall support him,
and my arm shall strengthen him.
22. The enemy shall have no advantage
over him,
and the son of lawlessness shall not hurt
him again.

23. I will hew down his enemies
before him,
and I will put to flight those
who hate him.
24. And my truth and my mercy shall
surround him,
and in my name his horn
shall be exalted.

25. I will place his left hand in the sea,
and his right hand in the river.
26. He shall call upon me, saying:
'You are my father, my God,
and the support of my salvation.'

27. And I will set him as a first-born,
high above all the kings of the earth.
28. I will keep my mercy
with him forever,
and my covenant with him
shall be firm."

Psalm 89

1. O Lord, you have been our refuge,
from one generation to the next.
2. Before the mountains existed,
or the earth and the world were formed,
even from age to age, you are.

3. Do not turn humanity back to its lowly state,
when you said, "Return you children of earth."
4. For a thousand years in your sight,
are as the yesterday which is past,
and as a watch in the night.

5. Years shall be vanity to them;
let the morning pass away like grass.
6. In the morning let it flower
and pass away,
in the evening let it droop, become withered and dried.

7. For we have perished in your anger,
and in your wrath we have been sorely troubled.
8. You have set our transgressions before your eyes,
our age is seen in the light of your face.

9. For all our days have perished,
indeed in your anger we have perished;
our years have spun on like a spider.
10. The days of our years number
seventy years,
perhaps by reason of strength,
they last eighty,
but the greater part of them is labor and trouble,
for weakness overtakes us
and we are chastised.

11. Who knows the spite of your wrath?
And who knows how to number days
because of your dread rage?
12. Thus make known your right hand,
and those who are instructed by wisdom
in the heart.

13. Return, O Lord, how long?
Be pacified with your servants.
14. We have been satiated in the morning by your mercy,
and we greatly exalted and rejoiced.

15. Let us rejoice all our days,
in return for the days you humbled us,
the years wherein we experienced evil.
16. Look upon your servant and upon your handiwork,
and give guidance to their offspring.

17. May the brightness of the Lord our God shine upon us,
and may you prosper for us the work of our hands.

Psalm 90

1. The one who dwells in the help of the Most High
shall find shelter in the shadow of the God of Heaven.

2. That one shall say to the Lord, "You are my helper and my refuge;
O my God, I will place my hope in him."
3. For he shall deliver you from the snare of the hunters
and from every troubling matter.
4. He shall overshadow
with his shoulders,
and you shall trust beneath his wings.
His truth shall encompass you
like a shield.

5. You shall not fear any terror
of the night,
nor any arrow flying by day,
6. nor any evil that prowls
in the darkness
nor calamity and evil spirit at noon-day.

7. A thousand shall fall at your side,
ten thousand at your right,
but not one shall come near you.
8. With your own eyes you shall behold
and see the reward of sinners.

9. For you, O Lord, are my hope.
You, my soul, have made the Most High
your refuge.
10. No evil shall befall you,
no scourge shall approach
your dwelling.

11. For he shall give his angels charge
over you,
to guard you in all your ways.
12. They shall bear you up
upon their hands,
lest you dash your foot against a stone.

13. You shall tread upon the asp
and the basilisk,
and you shall trample the lion
and the dragon.

14. Because he has placed his hope in me, I will deliver him;
I will protect him, because he has known my name.
15. That one shall call upon me and I will hearken;
I am present in the midst of affliction,
and I will deliver him and glorify him.

16. I will satisfy him with
abundance of days,
and make known to him my salvation.

Psalm 91

1. It is good to give thanks to the Lord,
and to sing praises to your name,
O Most High,
2. to proclaim your mercy
in the morning,
and your truth every night,

3. with a ten-string psaltery,
with a song on the harp.
4. For you, O Lord, have made me glad
with your works,
and in the operations of your hands I
will rejoice.

5. How great are your works, O Lord!
Your thoughts are exceedingly deep!
6. A foolish fellow cannot know;
nor can a senseless person
understand this.

7. When the sinners sprang up
like grass,
all the workers of iniquity came to light,
that they should be utterly
destroyed forever.
8. But you are the Most High forever,
O Lord.

9. For behold your enemies shall perish,
and all the workers of iniquity
shall be scattered.
10. But my horn shall be exalted as that of a unicorn,
and my old age rejuvenated
with fresh oil.

11. My eye has espied around
in the midst of my enemies,
and among the wicked who
rise against me,
my ear shall hear.

12. The righteous shall flourish like a palm tree,
and be multiplied like a cedar
in Lebanon.
13. Those who are planted in the house of the Lord,
shall flourish in the courts of our God.

14. Then they shall be multiplied in a ripe old age,
and they shall be prosperous that they may proclaim:
15. that the Lord, my God, is upright,
and that there is no unrighteous in God.

Psalm 100

1. I will sing to you, O Lord,
of mercy and judgment,
2. I will sing a psalm and conduct myself wisely
in a blameless way.
When will you come to me?
I walked in the integrity of my heart,
in the midst of my house.

3. I have not set before my eyes any unlawful thing,
those who commit transgressions
I have detested.

4. A perverse heart has not
cleaved to me.
When the wicked withdrew from me,
I no longer acknowledged him.

5. The one who privately slanders
his neighbor,
such a person I have expelled.
6. With one of haughty eye and insatiable heart,
I would not share a meal.

7. My eyes shall look upon the faithful of the earth,
that they may dwell with me.
Whoever walked in a blameless way,
the same ministered to me.

8. The arrogant did not dwell
in the midst of my house,
Whoever spoke unjustly was not rewarded in my eyes.
9. Early on I destroyed all the sinners of the land,
to root out from the city of the Lord
all evildoers.

Psalm 101

1. O Lord, hearken to my prayer,
and let my cry reach you.
2. Do not turn your face away from me.
On the day when I am afflicted,
incline your ear to me.
On the day when I shall call upon you,
speedily give heed to me.

3. For my days have dissipated
like smoke,
and my bones are parched like kindling.
4. I am cut down like blades of grass,
and my heart is withered,
because I have forgotten to eat my food.

5. Because of the sound of my groaning,
my bones have stuck to my flesh.

6. I have become like a pelican
in the wilderness,
like a night-owl in an abandoned house.
7. I have spent sleepless nights,
I have become like a solitary bird on a roof.

8. All day long my enemies have reproached me,
and those who formerly praised me
have sworn against me.
9. For I have eaten ashes
as if it were bread,
and my drink has been mingled
with weeping,
10. because of your anger
and your wrath,
for you have lifted me up only
to dash me down.

11. My days have declined like a shadow,
and I am withered up like dry grass.
12. But you, O Lord, endure forever,
and your memorial lasts for all generations. . . .

25. In the beginning, you, O Lord,
laid the foundations of the earth;
and the heavens are your handiwork.
26. They shall perish,
but you shall perdure.
They shall grow old like a garment,
and as a cloak you shall fold them up,
and they shall be changed.

27. But you remain the same,
and your years do not falter.
28. Let the children of your servants
pitch their tents,
and let their seed prosper forever.

Psalm 102

1. Bless the Lord, O my soul;
and all that is within me, bless his holy name.
2. Bless the Lord, O my soul;
and forget not all his praises;

3. who forgives all your transgressions,
and heals all your infirmities;
4. who redeems your life from corruption,
and crowns you with mercy and compassion;
5. who satisfies your desire
with good things
so that your youthfulness may be renewed like that of an eagle.

6. The Lord executes mercy
and judgment
for all who are wronged.
7. He made known his ways to Moses,
his will to the children of Israel.

8. The Lord is compassionate
and merciful,
longsuffering, abounding in mercy.
9. He will not always be angry;
nor will he be wrathful forever.

10. He has not dealt with us according
to our sins,
nor repaid us according to
our iniquities.
11. For as high is the heaven
above the earth,
the Lord has correspondingly increased
mercy for those who revere him.

12. As far as the east is from the west,
accordingly he has removed our transgressions from us.

13. As a father displays compassion
towards his children,
the Lord takes pity on those
who revere him;
14. for he knows our make-up,
and remembers that we are dust.

15. A human being's days are like grass;
like a blossom of the field
so shall she bloom.
16. For the dry wind blows over it, and
it shall cease to exist,
and one shall no longer recognize
her place.

17. Yet the mercy of the Lord is from
generation to generation
for those who revere him;
and his righteousness endures to the
children's children;
18. so that they keep his covenant,
and remember to observe his
commandments.

19. The Lord has established his throne
in heaven,
and his kingdom rules over all.
20. Bless the Lord all you his angels,
mighty in strength to perform
his bidding,
to heed the voice of his commands.

21. Bless the Lord all you his hosts,
you ministers of his that perform
his will.
22. Bless the Lord, all you his works,
in every place of his dominion.
Bless the Lord, O my soul!

Psalm 103

1. Bless the Lord, O my soul!
O Lord, my God, you are very great!
You have clothed yourself with praise
and honor;
2. you who robe yourself with light as
with a garment,
stretching out heaven
like a leather tunic;

3. who vaults his chambers with waters
who makes the clouds his chariots,
who walks on the wings of the wind;
4. who makes his angels spirits,
and his ministers flaming fire;

5. who establishes the earth
on its firm foundation,
it shall not be displaced from age to age.
6. The abyss, like a garment,
is his vestment,
the waters shall stand upon the hills.

7. At your rebuke the waters
shall depart;
at the voice of your thunder they shall
be alarmed.
8. They go up to the mountains,
and reach down to the plains,
to the place you have founded for them.

9. You have set a boundary which they
shall not pass,
neither shall they turn back again to
cover the earth.
10. You are the one who causes springs
to burst forth in the valleys,
the waters shall flow between the
mountains.

11. They shall give drink to all the wild
beasts of the field,
the wild asses shall quench their thirst.
12. The birds of heaven shall build their
nests beside them,

from between the rocks they shall raise
their voices.

13. You are the One who waters the
mountains from celestial chambers,
the earth shall be satisfied with the fruit
of your labors.
14. You are the One who causes grass to
grow for the cattle,
and the green plants for the service
of humans,
to bring forth bread from the earth;

15. as well as wine to gladden the
people's hearts,
to make their face glisten with oil,
and bread to strengthen the heart.
16. The trees of the plains shall be laden
with fruit,
even the cedars of Lebanon which you
have planted.

17. There the sparrows shall build
their nests;
the heron's house takes precedent
among them.
18. The high mountains are for the deer;
the rocky crag is refuge for the rabbit.

19. He made the moon for
marking times;
the sun knows its time to set.
20. You established darkness,
and it was night,
when all the wild animals of the forest
prowl about.

21. The young lions roar for their prey,
and seek their food from God.
22. The sun rises and they are
gathered together;
and they shall lie down in their
dens to rest.

23. People shall go out to work,
to labor until evening.
24. How great are your works, O Lord!
You made everything by wisdom;
the earth is full of your creativity.

25. There is this great and expansive sea;
innumerable are the creeping
creatures there,
small animals as well as large.
26. There the ships ply their passage;
and the dragon you formed to play
therein.

27. All things wait upon you,
to give them their food in due season.
28. When you give it to them, they shall
gather it;
when you open your hand,
all will be filled with your bounteous
goodness.

29. But when you turn away your face,
they shall be troubled.
When you take away their breath,
they shall perish and return
to their dust.

30. You shall send forth your Spirit,
and they shall be created;
and you shall renew the face
of the earth.

31. Let the glory of the Lord be forever;
the Lord shall take pleasure
in his works.
32. He gazes upon the earth and makes
it tremble;
He touches the mountains,
and they smoke.

33. I will sing to the Lord all my life;
I will sing praise to my God as long as I
exist.

34. May my conversation be
pleasing to him,
and so I shall be glad in the Lord.

Psalm 107

1. My heart is ready, O God,
my heart is ready,
I will chant and sing psalms in my glory.
2. Awake psaltery and harp,
I will wake up early in the morning.

3. I will publicly give thanks to you,
O Lord,
I will sing praises to you among
the nations.
4. For your mercy is great above
the heavens,
and your truth soars above the clouds.

5. Be exalted above the heavens, O God,
and let your glory shine upon
all the earth.
6. So that your beloved ones
may be delivered,
save with your right hand
and hearken to me.

Psalm 109

1. The Lord said to my Lord:
Sit on my right,
until I make your enemies
your footstool.
2. The Lord will send out from Zion
a rod of power;
take up your rule in the midst
of your enemies.

3. With you is dominion in the day
of your power,
in the splendors of your holy ones.
From the womb before
the morning star,
I have begotten you.

4. The Lord swore an oath,
and will not take it back:
You are a priest forever,
according to the order of Melchizedek.

5. The Lord at your right hand
has dashed in pieces
kings in the day of his wrath.

6. He shall judge among the nations,
multiply the corpses,
crush the heads of many on the earth.

7. He shall drink from the brook
by the wayside,
therefore, he will lift up his head.

Psalm 112

1. Praise the Lord, you servants;
praise the name of the Lord!
2. Let the name of the Lord be blessed,
henceforth and forever more.

3. From the rising of the sun
to its setting,
let the name of the Lord be praised.
4. The Lord is exalted above
all the nations,
above the heavens his glory.

5. Who is like the Lord our God,
who dwells on high,
6. overseeing the things below,
in heaven and on earth,

7. who lifts up the poor from the earth,
and raises the needy from the dunghill,
8. to seat him with royalty,
even with the rulers of his people,
9. who settles the barren woman
in a home,
making her a joyful mother of children?

Praying—with the Saints—to God Our Mother

Psalm 113A

1. At the departure of Israel from Egypt,
of the house of Jacob from
a barbarous people,
2. Judah became his holy claim,
and Israel his dominion.

3. The sea had sight and took flight,
the Jordan turned back on its course.
4. The mountains skipped like rams,
the hills like yearling lambs.

5. What did you see O sea,
that you took flight?
6. And you, O Jordan,
that you turned back in fright?
7. You mountains that you skipped
like rams?
And you hills like yearling lambs?

8. At the presence of the Lord,
the earth trembled,
at the presence of the God of Jacob,
9. who turned the rock into pools
of water,
and the flinty rock into watery
fountains.

Psalm 113B

9. Not to us, O Lord, not to us,
but to your name give the glory,
because of your mercy and truth;

10. lest the nations should say:
Where is their God?
11. But our God dwells in heaven,
and on earth;
doing whatsoever he wills.

12. The idols of the nations,
are silver and gold,
the work of human hands.

13. They have a mouth
but cannot speak;
they have eyes, but cannot see.

14. They have ears, but cannot hear;
they have nostrils, but cannot smell.
15. They have hands, but cannot touch;
they have feet, but cannot walk,
nor can they make a sound through
their throat.

16. Let those who make them,
become like them,
and all who have trusted in them.

17. The house of Israel trusted in the
Lord,
their helper and their protector.
18. The house of Aaron trusted
in the Lord,
their helper and their protector.
19. Those who fear the Lord have
trusted in the Lord,
their helper and their protector.

Psalm 117

8. It is better to trust in the Lord,
than to trust in human might.
9. It is better to hope in the Lord,
than to place hope in rulers.

10. All the nations encompassed me,
in the Lord's name I warded them off.
11. They completely encircled me,
but in the Lord's name I fended
them off.

12. They encompassed me like bees
about a honeycomb,
and violently blazed like fire
among thorns,
but in the Lord's name I drove them off.

13. Hard-pressed, I was on the verge of falling,
but the Lord supported me.

14. The Lord is my strength and my song,
and has become my salvation.
15. A sound of rejoicing and deliverance,
in the tents of the just!
The right hand of the Lord exercised power!

16. The right hand of the Lord has exalted me,
The right hand of the Lord has wrought mightily!
17. I shall not die,
but I shall live,
and recount the deeds of the Lord!
18. The Lord chastised me with correction,
but has not delivered me over to death.

19. Open to me the gates of righteousness;
I pass through them and give thanks to the Lord.
20. This is the gate of the Lord;
the righteous enter through it.

21. I will give thanks to you,
for you have heard me,
and become my salvation.

22. The stone which the builders rejected,
the very one,
now has become the chief cornerstone.
23. Through the Lord this has happened,
and it is marvelous in our eyes.

24. This is the day which the Lord has made,
let us rejoice and be glad in it.
25. O Lord, save, I beseech you,
O Lord, grant prosperity indeed!
26. Blessed is the one who comes in the name of the Lord.
We have blessed all of you from the house of the Lord.

Psalm 118

9. How can a youth make his way prosperous?
By keeping your words.
10. With all my heart I have diligently sought you;
do not let me fall away from your commandments.
11. I have hidden your oracles in my heart;
so that I would not sin against you.
12. Blessed are you, O Lord,
teach me your decrees.
13. With my lips I have declared,
all the judgments of your mouth.
14. I have taken delight in the path of your testimonies;
as much as in all riches.
15. I will mull over your commandments,
and consider your ways.
16. I will meditate on your decrees;
I will not forget your words.

17. Grant recompense to your servant,
that I may live and keep your words.
18. Pull the veil from my eyes,
that I may perceive the wondrous things of your law.
19. I myself am a stranger in the land,
do not hide your commandments from me.

20. My soul has longed vehemently,
for your judgments at all times.
21. You have rebuked the haughty,
cursed are they who turn away from
your commands.
22. Remove from me reproach
and contempt,
for I have sought diligently
after your testimonies.
23. For rulers sat and spoke out
against me,
but your servant was mulling over
your decrees.
24. For your testimonies are
my meditation,
and your decrees are my counselors.

25. My life has clung to the ground;
keep me alive according to your word.
26. I declared my ways and you hearkened to me;
teach me your decrees.
27. Instruct me in the way
of your statutes,
and I will mull over your
wondrous deeds.
28. My soul has slumbered
with heaviness;
strengthen me with your words.
29. Remove me from the path
of injustice;
and have mercy on me through
your law.
30. I have chosen the way of truth,
and have not forgotten your judgments.
31. I have clung to your testimonies,
O Lord;
do not put me to shame.
32. I have run the way of your
commandments,
whenever you enlarged my heart.

33. Train me, O Lord, in the way
of your statutes,
and I will diligently seek after them
at every occasion.
34. Instruct me that I may search out
your law,
and keep it with all my heart.
35. Guide me in the path of your
commandments,
for I have taken delight in them.
36. Incline my heart to your testimonies;
and not to covetousness.
37. Turn my eyes away from
beholding vanity;
give me life in your way.
38. Confirm your oracle to your servant,
that I may revere you.
39. Take away my reproach
which I dreaded;
for your judgments are pleasant.
40. Behold, I have desired your
commandments;
grant me life by your righteousness.

41. Let your mercy come upon me,
O Lord,
your salvation according to your word.
42. And so I shall answer those who
reproach me,
because I trusted in your words.
43. Do not take the word of truth utterly
out of my mouth;
because I have placed my hope in your
judgments.
44. I shall continually keep your law,
even forever and ever.
45. I have roamed about
in an open space,
because I diligently sought
your commandments.
46. I spoke of your testimonies
before kings,
and was not overcome with shame.

47. I meditated on your commandments,
which I loved exceedingly.
48. I have lifted my hands to your precepts which I loved,
and mulled over your decrees.

49. Remember your words
to your servant,
for which you have caused me to hope.
50. This has comforted me in my humiliation,
for your oracle has kept me alive.
51. The haughty have greatly transgressed,
but I have not swerved away
from your law.
52. I remembered your judgments of old, O Lord,
and thus was comforted.
53. Despondency gripped me on account of sinners—
those who totally forsake your law.
54. My songs were your decrees,
in the place of my pilgrimage.
55. I remembered your name in the night, O Lord,
and have faithfully kept your law.
56. This was my state of affairs,
for I diligently sought your precepts.

57. You are my portion, O Lord,
I said I would keep your law.
58. I entreated your presence
with my whole heart,
have mercy on me according
to your oracle.
59. I pondered over your ways
in my mind,
and I turned my footsteps
to your testimonies.
60. I prepared myself and was not disheartened,
to put your commandments
into practice.
61. The snares of sinners entrapped me;
but I did not forget your law.
62. I rose at midnight
to give you thanks,
for the judgments of your righteousness.
63. I am a companion of all
who revere you,
and of those who keep your commandments.
64. The earth is full of your mercy, O Lord;
teach me your decrees.

65. You have dealt kindly with your servant, O Lord,
according to your word.
66. Teach me kindness, instruction and knowledge,
because I have believed in your commandments.
67. Before I was humbled, I habitually transgressed,
for this reason I have steadfastly kept your word.
68. You, O Lord, are gracious,
thus in your graciousness teach me your precepts.
69. The injustice of the proud was puffed up against me,
but I will search out your commandments with all my heart.
70. Their heart has been curdled like milk,
thus I meditated on your law.
71. It is good that you humbled me,
that I may learn your decrees.
72. The law of your mouth
is good for me,
better than thousands of gold
and silver pieces.

73. Your hands have made me
and fashioned me;
instruct me that I may learn
your commandments.
74. Those who revere you will see me
and rejoice,
because I have placed my hope
in your words.
75. I know, O Lord, that your judgments
are righteous,
and that you have humbled me
by your truth.
76. Let your mercy, I pray,
be for my comfort,
according to your promise
to your servant.
77. Let your tender mercies reach me
that I may live;
for your law is my meditation.
78. Let the proud be ashamed, for they
sinned against me unjustly;
but I will mull over your
commandments.
79. Let those who revere you turn to me,
as well as those who know
your testimonies.
80. Let my heart be blameless
in your decrees,
that I may not be put to shame.

81. My soul faints for your salvation;
I have hoped in your words.
82. My eyes failed waiting
to see your promise,
saying: "When will you comfort me?"
83. For I am like a wineskin covered
with hoarfrost,
yet I have not forgotten your decrees.
84. How many are the days
of your servant?
When will you deal out judgment
on my persecutors?
85. Transgressors told me idle tales,
but your law, O Lord, told me otherwise.
86. All your commandments are truth.
They persecuted me unjustly; help me!
87. They almost finished me off
in the earth;
but I did not forsake your
commandments.
88. According to your mercy
give me life,
and I will keep the testimonies
of your mouth.

89. You are forever, O Lord,
your word remains in heaven.
90. Your truth endures for all
generations;
you have founded the earth and it
remains.
91. By your arrangement, day shall
continue,
for all things are subjected to you.
92. Were it not that your law is my
meditation,
I would have perished in my affliction.
93. Let me never forget your decrees,
for through them you have
given me life.
94. I indeed am yours, save me,
for I have diligently sought out
your decrees.
95. Sinners lay in wait for me
to destroy me;
yet I understood your testimonies.
96. I have seen a limit to all perfection,
yet your commandment is very broad.

97. O how I loved your law, O Lord!
It is my meditation all day long.
98. You have made me wiser in your
precept than my enemies;
because it is mine forever.
99. I have more understanding than all
my teachers,

because your testimonies are my meditation.
100. I understood more than the elders,
for I diligently sought out your commandments.
101. From every evil path
I curbed my feet,
that I might keep your words.
102. I have not turned aside
from your judgments,
because you yourself indoctrinated me.
103. How sweet are your oracles
to my palate,
more so than honey in my mouth!
104. From your precepts
I gained understanding;
therefore I despise every path
of injustice.

105. Your law is a lamp to my feet,
and a light for my footsteps.
106. I have sworn
and determined to keep
the judgments of your righteousness.
107. I have been greatly afflicted, O Lord,
give me life according to your word.
108. Please accept, O Lord,
my spontaneous words,
and teach me your judgments.
109. My life is continually in my hands,
but I have not forgotten your law.
110. Sinners set a trap for me,
but I wandered not away
from your precepts.
111. I have inherited
your testimonies forever,
because they are the joy of my heart.
112. Incline my heart
to perform your decrees,
forever is my reward.

113. I have detested transgressors,
but loved your law.

114. You are my helper
and my protector;
I have placed my hope in your words.
115. Depart from me, you evildoers,
for I will diligently seek the commandments of my God.
116. Uphold me according to your promise, and enliven me,
and let me not be ashamed
of my expectation.
117. Come to my assistance
and I shall be saved,
thus I will continually meditate
on your decrees.
118. You have brought to naught all who depart from your precepts;
because their inward thought is wicked.
119. I reckoned all the sinners of the earth as transgressors,
therefore I have loved your testimonies.
120. Penetrate my flesh with reverence for you,
for I am afraid of your judgments.

121. I have exercised judgment
and justice,
do not deliver me up to my oppressors.
122. Be surety for your servant for good;
let not the haughty falsely accuse me.
123. My eyes have failed looking for your salvation,
and for the promise
of your righteousness.
124. Deal with your servant according
to your mercy,
and teach me your decrees.
125. I am your servant, instruct me;
then I shall know your testimonies.
126. It is time for the Lord to act;
they have totally broken your law.
127. Therefore I have loved your commandments,
more than finest gold
or sparkling topaz.

128. Thus I direct myself according to all your statutes,
I detested every wicked way.

129. Your testimonies are wonderful, therefore my soul diligently
sought them.
130. The manifestation of your words,
will enlighten and instruct children.
131. I opened my mouth
and drew breath,
because I earnestly longed
for your commandments.
132. Look down upon me and have mercy on me,
the same way you do to those who love your name.
133. Order my steps according
to your promise,
and let no iniquity have dominion
over me.
134. Deliver me from people's false accusations,
and I will keep your commandments.
135. Let your face shine
upon your servant,
and teach me your decrees.
136. My eyes flowed
with streams of water,
because I did not keep your law.

137. You, O Lord, are righteous,
and your judgments are upright.
138. You have charged as your testimonies,
righteousness and perfect truth.
139. Zeal for your house has totally consumed me,
because my enemies have forgotten your words.
140. Your promise has been thoroughly tested in fire,
thus your servant has loved it.

141. Although I am young and accounted for nothing,
I have not forgotten your decrees.
142. Your righteousness is an everlasting righteousness,
and your law is truth itself.
143. Afflictions and distress found me,
but your commandments were my meditation.
144. Your testimonies are an everlasting righteousness;
grant me understanding and I shall live.

145. I cried out with all my heart,
"Hear me, O Lord";
I will diligently search your decrees.
146. I cried out to you, "Save me";
and I will keep your testimonies.
147. I arose before the crack of dawn
and cried out,
on your words I have placed my hope.
148. My eyes were wide awake before the dawn,
that I might meditate on your oracles.
149. Hear my voice, O Lord, according to your mercy,
according to your judgment
grant me life.
150. Those who persecuted me unjustly have drawn near,
since they were far removed
from your law.
151. You are near, O Lord,
and all your ways are truth.
152. From of old I have known
your testimonies,
because you have established
them forever.

153. Behold my affliction
and rescue me,
for I have not forgotten your law.
154. Plead my cause and deliver me,
on account of your word grant me life.

155. Salvation is far from sinners,
for they haven't diligently
sought your decrees.
156. Many are your tender mercies,
O Lord,
according to your judgment
grant me life.
157. Many are they who persecute me
and oppress me,
but I have not wavered
from your testimonies.
158. I saw people acting foolishly
and was grieved,
because they have not kept our oracles.
159. Behold, I have loved your commandments, O Lord,
in your mercy grant me life.
160. The beginning of your words
is truth,
and all of your righteous judgments
last forever.

161. Rulers persecuted me
for no reason at all,
but my heart was awestruck
by your words.
162. I will truly exult because
of your promises,
as one who finds much spoil.
163. I hate and abhor injustice;
I have loved your law.
164. Seven times a day
I have praised you,
because of your righteous judgments.
165. Much peace have those who love
your law,
and for them there is no
stumbling block.
166. I have waited for your saving help,
O Lord,
and have loved your commandments.
167. My soul has kept your testimonies,
and has exceedingly loved them.

168. I have kept your commandments
and your testimonies,
because all your ways are before me,
O Lord.

169. Let my supplication come before
you, O Lord,
according to your promise, grant me
understanding.
170. Let my petition enter before you,
O Lord,
according to your promise, deliver me.
171. Let my lips utter a hymn,
when you have taught me your decrees.
172. Let my tongue resound
with your promises,
because all of your commandments
are righteous.
173. Let your hand be quick to save me,
for I have chosen your commandments.
174. I have longed for your saving help,
O Lord,
and your law is my meditation.
175. My soul shall live and praise you,
and your judgments shall help me.
176. I have gone astray like a lost sheep,
seek your servant, for I haven't forgotten
your commandments.

Psalm 120

1. I lifted my eyes to the mountains,
from whence shall come my help.
2. My help is from the Lord,
the maker of heaven and earth.

3. May your foot not slip,
nor your keeper slumber.
4. Behold, the Keeper of Israel,
shall neither slumber nor sleep.

5. The Lord shall preserve you;
the Lord at your right hand shall be
your shelter.

6. The sun shall not scorch you by day,
nor shall the moon harm you by night.

7. The Lord shall guard you
from all evil;
the Lord shall preserve your life.
8. The Lord shall keep watch over your
coming and going,
from now and forever more.

Psalm 121

1. I was glad when they said to me:
"Let us go into the house of the Lord."
2. We have planted our feet
in your courts, O Jerusalem.

3. Jerusalem has been built as a city,
whose compactness is complete.
4. For there the tribes go up,
the tribes of the Lord as a witness
for Israel,
to give thanks to the name of the Lord.

5. For there are set the thrones
for judgment,
thrones for the house of David.
6. Pray, I beseech you, for the peace
of Jerusalem,
and prosperity for those who love you.

7. Let peace, I pray, be within
your stronghold,
and let prosperity dwell in your palaces.
8. For the sake of my relatives
and neighbors,
I have invoked peace upon you.
9. For the sake of the house of the Lord
our God,
I have purposely sought your welfare.

Psalm 122

1. I have raised my eyes to you,
who dwells in the heavens.
2. Behold, as the eyes of servants
are fixed on the hands of their masters,
and as the eyes of a maidservant,
are fixed on the hands of her mistress,
even so our eyes are fixed on the Lord
our God,
until God display compassion
towards us.

3. Have mercy upon us, O Lord,
have mercy upon us,
for we are exceedingly filled with
contempt.
4. Indeed, our life has been
exceedingly filled;
let reproach come upon the prosperous,
and contempt fall upon the haughty.

Psalm 123

1. If the Lord had not been in our midst,
let Israel say;
2. if the Lord had not been in our midst,
when people rose up against us,

3. then would they have swallowed
us up alive,
when their anger blazed out against us,
4. then the waters would have
drowned us,
and our life would have gone under the
torrent.
5. Indeed our soul would have sunk,
beneath the overwhelming waters.

6. Blessed be the Lord,
who has not given us as prey
to their teeth!

7. Our life has escaped like a bird
from the fowler's snare,
the snare was shattered,
and we have escaped.

8. Our help is in the name of the Lord,
who made heaven and earth.

Psalm 124

1. Those who trust in the Lord shall be as Mount Zion,
whoever dwells in Jerusalem shall never be shaken.
2. The mountains encompass her,
and the Lord encompasses his people,
from now and forever more.

3. For the Lord will not permit,
the rod of sinners,
over the lot of the righteous,
lest the righteous stretch forth
their hands to iniquity.

4. Do good, O Lord,
to those who are good and upright
in heart.
5. But those who swerve into
crooked paths,
the Lord will drive away with the workers of iniquity.
Peace be upon Israel!

Psalm 125

1. When the Lord returned the captives of Zion,
we were like those who are comforted.
2. Then our mouth was filled with joy,
and our tongue with exultation;
then would they say among the nations:
"The Lord has done great things
for them."

3. The Lord has done great things for us,
and we have become overjoyed.
4. Bring back, O Lord, our captives,
like streams in the south.

5. Those who sow in tears,
shall reap rejoicing.
6. They trudged along weeping,
sowing their seed,
but they shall come skipping for joy,
carrying their sheaves.

Psalm 126

1. Unless the Lord build the house,
the builders have labored in vain.
Unless the Lord keep watch
over the city,
in vain has the guard kept watch.

2. It is vain for you to rise early.
Rise up after you are rested,
you who eat the bread of grief,
when sleep is granted to his beloved.

3. Behold the inheritance of the Lord,
children, the reward of the fruit
of the womb.
4. As arrows in the hand
of a mighty warrior,
so are the children of those
who were expelled.

5. Blessed whoever shall satisfy
his desire with them!
They shall not be put to shame,
when they speak to their enemies
in the gateways.

Psalm 127

1. Blessed are all who revere the Lord,
who walk in his ways.

2. You shall eat the fruit of your labors,
blessed are you, and it shall be well
with you.

3. Your wife shall be as a fruitful vine
attached to the sides of your house.
Your children shall be
as young olive plants,
encircling your table.

4. Behold, thus shall the man be blessed,
who reveres the Lord.
5. May the Lord bless you out of Zion,
and may you see the prosperity
of Jerusalem,
all the days of your life.

6. And may you see
your children's children.
Peace upon Israel.

Psalm 129

1. Out of the depths,
have I cried to you, O Lord.
2. O Lord, hearken to my voice,
let your ears be attentive
to the sound of my supplication.

3. If you, O Lord,
should mark iniquities,
O Lord, who shall be left standing?
4. For there is propitiation with you.
5. For the sake of your name I have
waited O Lord;
my soul has waited for your word.

6. My soul has placed its hope
in the Lord,
from the morning watch until night.
7. Let Israel hope in the Lord,
for with the Lord there is mercy,
and bountiful redemption.

8. And he himself will redeem Israel
from all its iniquities.

Psalm 130

1. O Lord, my heart is not haughty,
neither are my eyes lofty.
Neither have I trafficked
in great matters,
or in things too marvelous for me.

2. If I had not been humble,
but exalted my soul
like a weaned child
from its mother's breast,
how you would have repaid my soul!

3. Let Israel hope in the Lord,
henceforth and forever more.

Psalm 131

1. O Lord, remember David,
and all his meekness,
2. how he swore to the Lord,
made a vow to the God of Jacob:

3. "I will not enter my own house,
nor lay down to rest on my bed,
4. nor give sleep to my eyes,
and slumber to my eyelids,
nor rest to my temples,
5. until I find a place for the Lord,
a dwelling for the God of Jacob."

6. Behold we heard of it in Ephrata,
we found it in the fields of the woods.
7. Let us enter into his tabernacles;
let us worship at the place
where his feet stood.

8. Arise, O Lord, and come
into your rest,
you and the ark of your holiness.

9. Your priests shall clothe themselves
with righteousness,
and your holy ones shall exult with joy.
10. For the sake of your servant David,
turn not your face away from your
anointed.

11. The Lord has sworn
in truth to David,
and will not annul it:
"From the fruit of your loins,
I will set one on your throne;
12. If your children keep my covenant,
and these my testimonies which I shall
teach them,
their children also shall sit
upon your throne.

13. For the Lord has elected Zion,
has chosen her as a dwelling for himself.
14. This is my resting place forever,
here will I dwell, for I have chosen her.
15. I will abundantly bless her provision;
I will satisfy her poor with bread.

16. I shall clothe her priests
with salvation,
and her saints shall exceedingly exult.
17. There will I cause to spring up a
horn for David;
I have prepared a lamp for my anointed.
18. I will clothe his enemies with shame,
but upon himself my holiness
shall flourish."

Psalm 132

1. Behold indeed! What is so good
or so pleasant,
as for brothers and sisters
to dwell together?
2. It is like precious ointment
upon the head,
running down upon the beard,
even the beard of Aaron,
running down to the fringe of his robe.

3. It is like the dew of Hermon,
which comes down on the mountains
of Zion,
for there the Lord invoked the blessing,
life for evermore.

Psalm 133

1. Now, I pray you,
bless the Lord,
all you servants of the Lord,
who stand in the house of the Lord,
in the courts of the house of our God.

2. Lift up your hands by night
in the holy places,
and bless the Lord.
3. May the Lord bless you out of Zion,
the maker of heaven and earth.

Psalm 136

1. By the rivers of Babylon,
there we sat and wept,
remembering Zion.
2. Upon the willows
in the midst of it,
we hung up our harps.

3. For there our captors asked us
the words of a song,
and those who carried us away,
asked for a hymn:
"Sing us one of the songs of Zion."

4. How could we sing the Lord's song,
in a foreign land?
5. If I should forget you,
O Jerusalem,
let my right hand be forgotten!
6. May my tongue cleave to my throat,
if I should not remember you,

if I do not prefer Jerusalem,
as the chief subject of my joy.

Psalm 137

1. I will give thanks to you, O Lord,
with my whole heart,
and I shall sing psalms to you in the presence of the angels,
because you have listened to all the words of my mouth.

2. I will worship
before your holy temple,
and I will give thanks to your name,
on account of your mercy
and your truth,
for you have magnified your holy name
above all else.

3. On whatever day I invoke you,
speedily answer me,
thus you shall abundantly supply me
with your power in my soul.

4. Let all the kings of the earth,
render you thanks, O Lord,
for they have heard
all the words of your mouth.

5. And let them sing
in the ways of the Lord,
for great is the glory of the Lord.

6. For the Lord is on high,
yet looks after the lowly,
and knows lofty matters from afar.

7. Though I should walk,
in the midst of affliction,
you will grant me life.

Against the wrath of my enemies,
you have stretched forth your hand,
indeed, your right hand has saved me.

8. O Lord, you will repay them,
on my behalf.
O Lord, your mercy endures forever;
do not overlook the work of your hands.

Psalm 138

1. O Lord, you proved me,
and you have known me.
2. You know my sitting down
and my rising up.
You understand my thoughts from afar.

3. You have kept track of my footsteps
and laying down,
indeed, you have foreseen all my ways.
4. For there is no unrighteous word,
to be found upon my tongue.

5. Behold, O Lord, you know all things:
the last as well as the first;
you have fashioned me,
and placed your hand upon me.

6. This knowledge of yours is too marvelous for me,
I cannot even come close to it.
7. Where could I go from you Spirit?
And where can I flee from your presence?

8. If I should ascend to heaven,
you are there;
if I should descend to the grave,
you are present.
9. If I wing my way to the rising sun
in the east,
or dwell in the farthest reaches
of the western sea,

10. even there your hand
would guide me,
and your right hand would hold me.

11. When I said: "Surely darkness will
trample me under foot,"
then to my astonishment,
night became luminous.
12. For darkness cannot grow dark
apart from you,
and night can be made
as brilliant as day;
the darkness of the one, as the light of
the other.

13. For you, O Lord,
created my inner parts,
have supported me
from my mother's womb.
14. I will give thanks to you,
for you are dreadfully wondrous;
wondrous are your works,
as my soul well knows.

Psalm 140

1. O Lord, I cried out to you,
hearken to me;
attend to the sound of my supplication,
whenever I call out to you.

2. Let my prayer come before you
as incense,
the raising of my hands
like an evening sacrifice.
3. Set a watch, O Lord, over my mouth,
and a bolted door over my lips.

4. Do not let my heart turn aside
to evil deeds,
to form excuses for sins with those who
work iniquity,
nor let me keep company with their
chosen bands.

5. Let the righteous correct me with
mercy and reprove me,
but do not let the oil of the sinner
anoint my head,
for this is still my prayer in the midst of
their pleasures.

Psalm 141

1. With my voice I cried out to the Lord;
with my voice raised, I pleaded
to the Lord.
2. I will pour out before him
my supplication;
I will openly declare my affliction.

3. When my spirit was fainting
within me,
and you knew my footsteps,
in the very path upon which I traveled,
they hid a trap for me.

4. I looked to the right and took stock,
there was no one there who knew me.
A means of escape was cut off from me,
and there was no one who sought my
well-being.

5. I cried out to you, O Lord, and said:
"You are my hope, my lot in the land of
the living."
6. Attend to my supplication,
for I am brought very low.
Deliver me from my persecutors,
for they are stronger than I.

7. Bring my life out of this prison,
that I might give thanks to your name,
O Lord.
The righteous shall wait for me,
until I receive recompense.

Psalm 142

1. O Lord, hearken to my petition;
give ear to my supplication
in your truth;
answer me in your righteousness.

2. Enter not into judgment
with your servant,
for in your sight no living person
can be justified.
3. For the enemy has eagerly
pursued my soul,
has driven my life to the ground,
has caused me to be holed up
in dark holes,
like those who have been long dead.

4. Therefore my spirit was grieved
within me;
my heart was deeply troubled
within me.
5. I remembered the days of old,
and meditated on all your works;
I mused on the works of your hands.

6. I stretched out my hands to you;
my soul thirsts for you
like parched land.

7. Speedily hear me, O Lord;
my spirit has fainted.
Do not turn your face away from me,
or I shall become like those who sink in the pit.

8. Cause me to hear your mercy
in the morning,
because I have placed my hope in you.
Make known to me, O Lord,
the path on which I should walk,
for I have lifted up my soul to you.

9. Deliver me from my enemies, O Lord,
because I have fled to you for refuge.
10. Teach me to put your will into practice,
because you are my God.
Let your good Spirit guide me into the upright land.

11. For the sake of your name, O Lord,
grant me life;
in your righteousness,
you shall bring my life out of tribulation.
12. And in your mercy,
you will utterly destroy my enemies,
and wipe out all who afflict my soul,
because I indeed am your servant.

Psalm 144

1. I shall exalt you, my God, my King,
and I shall bless your name forever,
even to the ages of ages.
2. Every day I shall bless you
and praise your name forever,
even to the ages of ages.

3. Great is the Lord and exceedingly praiseworthy,
his greatness knows no bounds.
4. Generation upon generation shall praise your deeds,
and they shall declare your power.

5. They shall speak of the glorious magnificence of your holiness,
and they shall describe at length your marvelous deeds.
6. They shall discourse about the power of your awesome works,
and they shall describe at length your great majesty.

7. They shall overflow with memories
of your abundant goodness,
and shall greatly rejoice
in your righteousness.
8. The Lord is compassionate
and merciful,
longsuffering and abounding in mercy.

9. The Lord is good to those
who wait patiently,
and his compassionate mercies are upon
all his works.
10. O Lord, let all your works
praise you,
and all your holy ones bless you!

Psalm 145

1. Praise the Lord, O my soul.
2. I shall praise the Lord while I live;
I shall sing to my God as long as I exist.

3. Do not trust in rulers,
or in any human offspring,
in whom there is no salvation.
4. Their breath shall be exhaled,
and they shall return to their earth;
on that day all their thoughts
shall perish.

5. Blessed is the one whose help
is the God of Jacob;
whose hope is in the Lord his God,
6. who made heaven and earth,
the seas and everything in them;
who keeps truth forever;
7. who executes justice for the wronged;
who provides food for the hungry.
The Lord liberates those held
in bondage.
The Lord grants wisdom to the blind.

8. The Lord restores the broken-hearted.
The Lord loves the righteous.
9. The Lord protects the resident alien,
and shall adopt the orphan
and the widow,
but destroy the way of sinners.
The Lord shall reign forever;
your God, O Zion, for all generations.

Christian Scriptures That Use Feminine Imagery

TNK = Hebrew, LXX = Greek, VULG = Latin, PESH = Syriac, NT = Greek New Testament

Hebrew Texts

Genesis 1:1–2 TNK

In the beginning, when God created the heavens and earth, the earth was a formless void, and darkness covered the face of the deep, but the Spirit of God, she hovered, brooding over the face of the waters.

Genesis 1:26–27 TNK

God said, "Let us make Man in our own image, in the likeness of ourselves, and let them be masters of the fish of the sea, the birds of the air, the cattle, all the wild animals and all the creatures that crawl upon the earth." And so God created Man in his image; in the image of God he created him, male and female he created them.

Genesis 17:1–8 TNK

When Abram was ninety-nine years old, God appeared to Abram and said, "I am El Shaddai—God, the Breasted One. Walk in my presence and be blameless. I will establish my covenant between myself and you and exceedingly increase your numbers." Then Abram fell on his face; and God spoke to him as follows: "For my part, my covenant with you is this: you will become the father of many nations. Thus you will no longer be called Abram, but your name shall be Abraham for I have made you the father of many nations. I will make you abundantly fertile; thus I will make you into nations, and kings will issue from you. And I will maintain my covenant between myself and you, and your descendants after you, from generation to generation, as an everlasting covenant, to be your God and the God of your progeny after you. And I will give to you and your descendants after you the land in which you are now sojourneying, the entire territory of Canaan, as a perpetual possession; and I will be their God."

Genesis 17:1–4, 9–14 TNK

When Abram was ninety-nine years old, God appeared to Abram and said, "I am El Shaddai—God, the Breasted One.

Walk in my presence and be blameless. I will establish my covenant between me and you and exceedingly increase your numbers." Then Abram fell on his face; and God spoke to him as follows: "For my part, my covenant with you is this: you will become the father of many nations. . . ." God further said to Abraham, "You for your part must keep my covenant, and your descendants after you, from generation to generation. This is my covenant that you must keep between myself and you and your descendants after you: every male among you must be circumcised. You must circumcise the flesh of your foreskin, and this will serve as the sign of the covenant between myself and you. As soon as your males are eight days old, every one of them, generation after generation, they must be circumcised, including slaves born within the household as well as those bought from a foreigner not of your progeny. Whether born within the household or purchased, they must all be circumcised. Thus my covenant shall be in your flesh as a perpetual pact. But the uncircumcised male, whose foreskin has not been cut off, that person must be cut off from his people; he has broken my covenant."

Genesis 17:1–4, 15–21 TNK

When Abram was ninety-nine years old, God appeared to Abram and said, "I am El Shaddai—God, the Breasted One. Walk in my presence and be blameless. I will establish my covenant between me and you and exceedingly increase your numbers." Then Abram fell on his face; and God spoke to him as follows: "For my part, my covenant with you is this: you will become the father of many nations. . . ." And God concluded saying to Abraham, "As for your wife Sarai, you must no longer call her Sarai; her name shall be Sarah. I shall bless her, thus indeed I will give you a son by her. I shall bless her so that she shall be a mother of nations; kings of peoples will issue from her." Now Abraham bowed to the ground and laughed, thinking to himself, "Can a child be born to a hundred year old man? Or can Sarah, a ninety year old woman, give birth?" So Abraham said to God, "May Ishmael live in your presence!" But God replied, "Nevertheless, your wife Sarah shall bear you a son and you will name him Isaac. I shall maintain my covenant with him, as an everlasting covenant, even for his descendants after him. As to Ishmael, I heard your request. I hereby bless him so that he will be fruitful and greatly increase in numbers. He will be the father of twelve princes, and I shall make him into a great nation. But I will establish my covenant with Isaac, whom Sarah will bear to you by this time next year."

Genesis 28:1–5 TNK

Then Isaac summoned Jacob, blessed him and commanded him saying, "You must not marry any of the Canaanite women. Arise, go to Paddan-Aram, the house of Bethuel your mother's father, and there choose for yourself a wife from the daughters of Laban, your mother's brother. May El Shaddai—God the Breasted One, bless you, make you fruitful, and cause you to multiply so that you become a company of peoples. May God bestow on you the blessing of Abraham, to you and your descendants after you, so that you may take possession of the land where you sojourn, which God granted to Abraham." Then Isaac sent Jacob on his way, and Jacob traveled to Paddan-Aram, to Laban son of Bethuel the Aramaean, and brother of Rebecca, mother of Jacob and Esau.

Genesis 35:9–13 TNK

God appeared to Jacob again as he returned from Paddan-Aram, and blessed him. God said to him, "Your name is Jacob; but you will no longer be called Jacob, but your name shall be Israel." (That is why he called himself Israel.) God said to him, "I am El Shaddai—God, the Breasted One. Be fruitful and multiply. A nation, indeed a throng of nations, will come from you, even kings will spring from your loins. The land which I gave to Abraham and Isaac I now give to you; and this country I will give to your descendants after you." Then God departed from him.

Genesis 43:1–14 TNK

Now the famine in the land only grew more severe. So when they had finished eating the grain which they had brought back from Egypt their father said to them, "Go back and buy us some food." "But," Judah replied, "the man solemnly warned us, 'You will not be permitted in my presence unless your brother is with you.' If you are willing to send our brother along with us, then we will go down and purchase supplies for you. But if you won't send him, we won't go, for the man told us, 'You will not be permitted in my presence unless your brother is with you.'" Then Israel demanded, "Why did you bring this misery upon me by telling the man you had another brother?"

They replied, "He kept interrogating us, asking about ourselves and our family, demanding, 'Is your father still alive? Do you have another brother?' So we answered him point for point. How were we supposed to know that he would say, 'Bring your brother down here?'" Judah then spoke to Israel his father, "Send the boy with me and we will depart at once, so that we all may survive and not die, we, you, and our children. I myself will stand as surety for him. You can hold me personally responsible for him. If I do not bring him back and set him before your eyes, I will bear the blame before you all my life. As it is, if we hadn't wasted so much time we would have been there and back by now, twice over!"

So their father Israel said to them, "If it has to be that way, then do this: Put some of the best produce of the land in your sacks and take them down to the man as a gift—a little balsam, some honey, gum, myrrh, pistachio nuts, and almonds. And make sure you take double the amount of money with you, for you must return the sum that was put back in the mouth of your sacks; it might have been an accident. Take your brother and be off. Go back to the man. May El Shaddai—God, the Breasted One, grant you maternal compassion in the presence of the man so that he will permit your other brother and Benjamin to return with you. As for me, if I must be bereaved of my children, then bereaved I must be."

Genesis 48:1–4 TNK

Some time later, Joseph was informed, "Your father's health is failing." So he took with him his two sons: Manasseh and Ephraim. When Jacob was told, "Look, your son Joseph has come to you," he mustered his strength and sat up in bed. Jacob recounted to Joseph, "El Shaddai—God, the Breasted One, appeared to me at Luz in Canaan and blessed me, saying, 'I shall make you fertile and increase your numbers so that I can make you into a company of peoples. And I will give this very land to your descendants after you to be a perpetual possession.'"

Genesis 49:9 TNK versicle

Judah is a lion's whelp;
You stand over your prey, my son.
Like a lion he crouches, laying in wait,
even like a lioness, who dare rouse him?

Genesis 49:25–26 TNK

The God of your father helps you,
El Shaddai, God, the Breasted One,
blesses you:
with blessings of heaven above,
blessings of the abyss lying below,
blessings of breasts and womb,
blessings of grain and flowering bloom,
blessings of the ancient mountains,
with bounties of the everlasting hills.

Exodus 6:3 TNK versicle

To Abraham, Isaac, and Jacob I appeared as El Shaddai—God, the Breasted One.

Exodus 33:18–23 TNK

Moses said, "Please show me your glory." Then Yahweh replied, "I shall cause all my beauty to pass before you, and in your presence I shall pronounce my name 'Yahweh.' I will be gracious to whom I will be gracious, and I will have maternal compassion on whom I will have maternal compassion. But my face you cannot see, for no one sees me and survives." So Yahweh continued, "Here is a place near me. You must stand on the rock and when my glory passes by, I shall put you in a cleft of the rock and place my hand over you until I pass by. Then I shall remove my hand so that you might see my back, but the front of me is not to be seen."

Numbers 11:4–12 TNK

Now the rabble in the midst of the people had strong cravings for other food and so the Israelites began to wail again, bewailing, "If only we could eat meat! Think of the fish we used to eat in Egypt for free, the cucumbers, the melons, the leeks, the onions, and the garlic! But now we are famished and we never see anything except this manna!"

Now the manna was tiny like coriander seed and looked like resin. The people went around gathering it and ground it up in handmills or crushed it in the mortar. They cooked it in a pot and fashioned it into cakes. It tasted like pancakes made with oil. When the dew descended on the camp at night, the manna fell with it.

Now Moses heard the people bemoaning, each family at the entrance of their tent. Yahweh's anger greatly blazed against them and Moses was grieved and asked Yahweh, "Why have you brought this trouble on your servant? What have I done to displease you, that you foist the burden of all these people on me? Was it I who conceived all these people? Was it I who gave them birth? For you tell me, 'Carry them in your bosom as a nurse carries a suckling infant, to the land which I promised your ancestors.'"

Numbers 24:2–9 TNK

When Balaam lifted his eyes and surveyed Israel, encamped by tribes, then the Spirit of God, she came upon him so that he uttered his oracle:
The oracle of Balaam son of Beor,
the oracle of one whose eyesight
is perfect,
the oracle of one who hears the words
of God,
who beholds a vision from Shaddai,
fallen in ecstasy with unveiled eye:

How beautiful are your tents, O Jacob,
how fair your encampments, O Israel;
like valleys that spread out,
like gardens beside a river,
like aloes planted by Yahweh,
like cedars beside running waters!
Water will flow from his buckets;
and his seed will have waters abundant.
His king will be greater than Agag,
and his kingdom will be greatly exalted.

God has brought him out of Egypt;
he possesses the wild ox's might.
He shall devour the corpses
of his enemies,
shattering their bones to pieces,
piercing them with his arrows.

He crouches like a lion,
laying in wait like a lioness;
who dare rouse him?
Blessed are those who bless you,
cursed those who curse you!

Numbers 24:2–3, 15–17 TNK

When Balaam lifted his eyes and surveyed Israel, encamped by tribes, then the Spirit of God, she came upon him so that he uttered his oracle:
The oracle of Balaam son of Beor,
the oracle of one whose eyesight is
perfect,
the oracle of one who hears the words
of God,
who has knowledge
from the Most High,
who beholds a vision from Shaddai,
fallen in ecstasy with unveiled eye:

I see him, but not now;
I behold him, but not near:
a star will come out of Jacob,
a scepter will rise out of Israel;
it shall smite the brow of Moab,
the forehead of all Sheth's children.

Deuteronomy 30:1–5 TNK

Moses said, "When all these things come to pass for you, the blessing as well as the curse which I set before you, and when you take them to heart, wherever among the nations Yahweh your God has dispersed you, and when you return to Yahweh your God and obey his voice with all your heart and with all your soul according to everything that I am commanding you today, you and all your children, then Yahweh your God will bring back your captives and have maternal compassion upon you and gather you back from all the nations in which Yahweh your God had scattered you. Even if you have been banished to the far distant horizons, even from there Yahweh your God will gather you and reclaim you, and bring you back to the land which your ancestors possessed, so that you might take possession of it and be made more prosperous and numerous than even your ancestors were."

Deuteronomy 32:9–11 TNK

Yahweh's portion is his people,
Jacob his allotted inheritance.
He found him in a desert land,
in a barren and howling wasteland.
He shielded, reared and guarded him,
as the apple of his eye,
just like an eagle incites her nestlings,
hovering over her young,
that spreads her wings to catch them,
and carries them on her pinions.

Deuteronomy 32:12–14 TNK

The Lord alone is Israel's guide,
there is no alien god with him.
God gives the heights of the earth for him to ride,
nourishes him on the produce
of the slopes,
nurses him with honey from the crag,
and oil out of the flinty rock.

God supplies curds from the cattle, milk from the flock,
With fine meat from the pastures,
Herds of Bashan and goats,
With the finest grains of wheat to eat,
and blood of the grape to drink as wine.

Deuteronomy 32:15–18 TNK

Jeshurun grew fat and kicked.
(You became fat, gross and gorged.)
He abandoned the God who made him, and disowned the Rock, his Savior.
They roused his jealousy
with strange gods,
with abominable idols they provoked his wrath.
They sacrificed to demons
which are not God,
to gods they had never known,
gods only recently appeared,
ones which your ancestors
never revered.
You neglected the Rock who bore you;
you forgot the God
who gave birth to you.

Nehemiah 9:13–17 TNK

You descended on Mount Sinai and spoke to them from the heavens. You imparted to them just ordinances, reliable rules, good statutes, and commandments. Your Holy Sabbath you revealed to them; you established commandments, statutes, and laws for them through your servant Moses. You gave them bread from heaven to satisfy their hunger and brought forth water from the rock to slake their thirst. You told them to enter and take possession of the land which you had sworn with outstretched hand to give them. But they and our ancestors grew arrogant and stiff-necked, obeying not your commands. They refused to listen and failed to remember the miracles that you performed within their midst. They became obstinate and in their rebellion made up their minds to return to their former bondage. But you, O Eloah, are ever forgiving, gracious, full of maternal compassion, slow to anger, and abounding in steadfast love. Therefore, you did not abandon them.

Christian Scriptures That Use Feminine Imagery

Nehemiah 9:18–21 TNK

Even when they cast for themselves a molten image of a calf and said, "This is your God who brought you up out of Egypt!" and committed atrocious blasphemies, you, in your exceeding maternal compassion, did not abandon them in the wilderness: the pillar of cloud did not desert them, but guided them on their path by day, nor did the pillar of fire by night cease to light the way ahead of them by which they were to travel. Your benevolent Spirit you bestowed upon them, that she might instruct them. Furthermore, you did not withhold your manna from their mouths and you gave them water for their thirst. For forty years you cared for them in the desert, they lacked nothing, their clothing did not wear out, and their feet did not become swollen.

Nehemiah 9:26–31 TNK

[Your children] grew disobedient and rebelled against you, in fact, they cast your law behind their backs, slaughtered your prophets who had admonished them in order to turn them back to you, and they committed atrocious blasphemies. Therefore you delivered them into the hands of their enemies who oppressed them. But in the midst of their oppression they cried out to you, and you, you heard them from the heavens and because of your magnificent maternal compassion you granted them deliverers who rescued them from their enemies' grasp. But as soon as they experienced a respite, they again returned to doing evil in your sight, so you abandoned them into the clutches of their enemies who in turn crushed them. And when they cried out to you again, you heard from the heavens and because of your maternal compassion delivered them time after time. You warned them so they would come back to your Law, but they became arrogant and would not obey your commandments. They sinned against your ordinances in whose observance is found life. They turned a stubborn back, stiffened their necks, and refused to listen. Nevertheless, you were patient with them for many years, admonishing them by your Spirit through your prophets. Yet they paid no attention, so you handed them over to the people of the country. But because of your magnificent maternal compassion you did not destroy them completely or abandon them, for you are a gracious and compassionate God.

Job 28:12–19 TNK

But whence can Wisdom be found?
And where is the abode of
Understanding?
No human being knows the path to her,
and she cannot be found on earth where they live.
The abyss says, "She is not in me";
and the sea notes, "She dwells not with me."
She cannot be purchased with solid gold,
nor can her price be weighed
in sterling silver,
nor can she be valued with the fine gold
of Ophir,
precious agate or sapphire.
Neither gold nor crystal compares
with her,
nor can she be exchanged for a dress
of golden filigree,
not to mention coral and jasper;
the price of Wisdom

is beyond rosy pearls.
The topaz of Cush
cannot compare with her,
nor can she be valued against the purest
refined gold.

Job 28:20-27 TNK

Where does Wisdom come from?
Where is the dwelling of
Understanding?
She is hidden from the eyes of every living creature,
even concealed from the birds
of heaven.
Destruction and Death declare,
"Our ears have only heard rumors
about her."
God alone understands her path
and knows where her dwelling place is.
For he surveys the ends of the earth,
and observes everything beneath
the heavens.
When he established the weight
of the wind,
and gauged the measure of the waters,
when he imposed rules on the rain,
and mapped a trek for thunderstorms,
then he beheld Wisdom
and assessed her,
looked her through and through,
and appraised her.

Job 32:6-9 TNK

Elihu, son of Barachel the Buzite, responded and said:
"I am still young and you are aged,
thus I was timid and hesitant
to impart to you my knowledge.
I thought, Days of experience
should speak
and many years should teach wisdom.
But the Spirit, she who dwells
in humanity,
even the Breath of Shaddai, she grants
understanding.
Many days do not guarantee wisdom,
nor do the aged necessarily understand
correctly."

Job 33:1-6 TNK

But now, Job, listen to my speech;
pay attention to all my words.
Behold, I open my mouth;
my words are on the tip of my tongue.
I utter words from an upright heart,
and my lips sincerely profess knowledge.
The Spirit of God, she has made me;
the Breath of Shaddai—
the Breasted One,
she gives me life.
Answer me, if you can;
prepare yourself and refute me.
Behold, I am just like you before God;
I, too, was molded from a piece of clay.

Job 38:1-11 TNK

Then Yahweh answered Job from out of
the tempest.
"Who is this that obscures divine counsel with ignorant mutterings?
Brace yourself and muster
up your strength.
Now I will pose the questions
and you will answer me.
Where were you when I set
the earth's foundations?
Pray, tell me, since you possess
such understanding!
Who determined its dimensions? Surely,
you know.
Or who stretched the measuring line
across it?
Into what were its pillars sunk?
Or who laid its cornerstone,

while the morning stars sang
in harmony,
and all the angelic hosts shouted for joy?
And who pent the sea up behind
locked doors,
when it bolted forth from my womb?
when I wrapped it in a raiment of billowy clouds,
and made enveloping darkness its swaddling bands;
when I fixed its limits,
and set bar and door in place,
saying, 'This far you may come
and no further;
here your haughty waves must halt!'"

Job 38:1–3, 22–29 & 40:2 TNK

Then Yahweh answered Job from out of the tempest.
"Who is this that obscures divine counsel with ignorant mutterings?
Brace yourself and muster
up your strength;
Now I will pose the questions and you will answer me....
Have you taken a tour of the storehouses of snow?
Or have you inspected the treasury of hailstones
which I reserve for seasons of distress,
for days of battle and war?
What is the way from whence the lightning is dispatched,
or the place from whence the east wind blows over the earth?
Who forges a channel for
the torrents of rain,
or plots a path for the thunderstorms,
to water the land where no one lives,
a barren desert with no one in it,
to slake the thirst of a desolate land,
and make a wasteland
sprout forth grass?
Does the rain have a father?
Or who begets the drops of dew?
From whose womb comes the ice?
And who gives birth to the hoarfrost of heaven?...
Will the one who contends with Shaddai correct [her]?
Let the one who accuses Eloah
answer her."

Job 5:17 TNK versicle

Blessed is the person
whom Eloah corrects!
Therefore do not despise the discipline of Shaddai.

Job 6:14 TNK versicle

Whoever withholds faithful love
from a friend,
forsakes the fear of Shaddai.

Job 8:3 TNK versicle

Does God pervert judgment,
or Shaddai distort justice?

Job 8:5 TNK versicle

Look to God
and plead with Shaddai.

Job 11:7 TNK versicle

Can you fathom the depths of Eloah,
or probe the far reaches of Shaddai?

Job 13:3 TNK versicle

I wish to speak with Shaddai;
I desire to argue my case with God.

PRAYING—WITH THE SAINTS—TO GOD OUR MOTHER

Job 22:26 TNK versicle

Surely you shall delight in Shaddai,
and lift up your face to Eloah.

Job 27:10 TNK versicle

Will the godless take delight in Shaddai,
calling on Eloah at all times?

Job 27:11 TNK versicle

I will teach you about the power of God;
I will not conceal the secrets of Shaddai.

Job 31:2 TNK versicle

What is my lot from Eloah above,
my heritage from Shaddai on high?

Job 37:22–23 TNK versicle

Eloah is clothed in awesome majesty;
Shaddai is far beyond our reach—
pre-eminent in power and justice,
abounding in righteousness.

Psalm 22:9–11 TNK

It was you who drew me out from the womb like a midwife,
and confided me to my mother's breasts.
On you I was cast from my birth,
from my mother's pregnancy you have been my God.
Do not be far from me,
for trouble is close at hand,
and there is no one to aid me.

Psalm 27:10 TNK versicle

Though my father and my mother abandon me,
yet Yahweh will take me in.

Psalm 40:9–13 TNK

I proclaim your righteousness
in the great assembly;
See, I do not seal my lips,
as you well know, Yahweh.

Your righteousness I did not hide
within my heart;
your faithfulness and salvation
I announce.
I don't conceal your steadfast love
and truth
from the great assembly.

You, O Yahweh, do not withhold
your maternal compassion from me;
may your steadfast love and truth
always protect me.

For troubles surround me,
they are beyond number;
my sins have overtaken me,
and I cannot see.

They are more numerous
than the hairs of my head,
and my heart fails me.

May it please you, O Yahweh,
to rescue me!
Yahweh come quickly to help me!

Psalm 51:1–5 TNK

Have mercy on me O God,
according to your steadfast love;
according to the greatness of your maternal compassion,
blot out my transgressions.

Wash me thoroughly of my iniquity,
and from my sin, totally cleanse me.

For I know my transgressions,
and my sin is constantly before me.

Against you, you alone, have I sinned,
and what is evil in your sight
I have done,
that you may display your saving justice
when you sentence,
and your vindication may be made
known when you judge.

Indeed, in guilt I was born,
and in sin my mother conceived me.
Surely you desire truth in the bowels,
thus you teach me wisdom in my inmost being.

Psalm 68:8–15 TNK

O God, when you went forth at the head
of your people,
when you marched through
the barren desert,
the earth trembled, the heavens hurled
down rain
at the presence of God, the One of Sinai,
at the presence of God,
the God of Israel.

An abundance of rain you showered
down, O God;
you refreshed the land, your weary
inheritance.
Your people settled in it;
you provided from your bounty for the
needy, O God.

The Lord announced the word;
women bear glad tidings
of a great army:
"Chiefs and their armies are fleeing;
they flee,
while the women are at home dividing
the booty.
While you rested among the keep
of sheep,
the wings of the Dove with silver
were sheathed,
and her feathers were covered
with a golden sheen;
thus while Shaddai scattered
the chieftains,
she caused it to snow on
the Dark Mountain."

Psalm 69:16 TNK versicle

Answer me, O Yahweh, for your steadfast love is bounteous,
in your abundant maternal compassion,
turn to me.

Psalm 79:8–12 TNK

Do not hold against us the guilt of previous generations,
may your maternal compassion quickly
come to greet us,
for we are utterly languishing.

Help us, O God our Savior,
because of the glory of your name.
Deliver us and wipe away our sins,
for the sake of your name.

Why should the nations say,
"Where is their God?"
Let it be seen among the nations,
even before our very eyes,
vengeance for the shedding of your
servants' blood.
May the groans of the captive come
before you,
by the might of your arm, preserve
those condemned to death.

Pay back our neighbors sevenfold into their bosom,
the reproach that they have leveled against you, O Lord.

Psalm 91:1 TNK versicle

Whoever dwells in the shelter of the Most High,
shall rest in the shadow of Shaddai.

Psalm 103:8 TNK

Maternally compassionate and gracious is Yahweh,
slow to anger and abounding in steadfast love.

Psalm 131:1–3 TNK

Yahweh, my heart is not haughty,
I do not fix my eyes on things too high.
I am not concerned with great affairs,
or wonders beyond my grasp.
I have calmed and quieted my soul,
like a child being weaned from its mother's breast,
like a babe being weaned so is my soul within me.
Let Israel place its hope in Yahweh,
now and forever more.

Psalm 143:7–12 TNK

Quickly answer me, O Yahweh,
for my spirit faints.
Hide not your face from me,
lest I become like those who descend into the pit.

At dawn let me hear of your steadfast love,
for I place my trust in you.
Show me the path that I should take,
for I lift up my soul to you.
Rescue me from my enemies,
O Yahweh,
in you I take refuge.

Teach me to do your will,
for you are my God;
your benevolent Spirit,
may she lead me on level ground.
For your name's sake, O Yahweh,
preserve my life;
in your righteousness,
deliver me from distress.
In your steadfast love,
silence my enemies,
and destroy all my foes,
for I am your servant.

Psalm 145:1–10 TNK

I will exalt you, O my God,
the Sovereign,
I will praise your name forever and ever.
Day after day I will bless you,
I will extol your name forever and ever.
Great is Yahweh and most worthy to be praised,
his greatness is unfathomable.

Generation after generation will laud your deeds,
will proclaim your mighty works.
They will speak of the glorious splendor of your majesty,
and I will ponder
your wonderful works.

They will declare the power of your dreadful deeds,
and I shall recount
your awesome greatness.
They will celebrate the fame of your great generosity,
and joyfully sing of your righteousness.

Yahweh is gracious and maternally compassionate,
slow to anger, rich in steadfast love.
Yahweh is generous to all,
displaying maternal compassion
to all creatures.
All your creatures shall thank you,
O Yahweh,
and your faithful ones will bless you.

Proverbs 1:8 TNK versicle

Listen, my child,
to your father's instruction,
and do not forsake
your mother's teaching.

Proverbs 7:4 TNK versicle

Say to Wisdom, "You are my sister."

Proverbs 1:20–33 TNK

Wisdom calls aloud in the street,
she raises her voice
in the public squares;
in the intersections she cries out,
she delivers her speeches
in the city gateways.
"You simple people, how much longer
will you love your base ways?
How much longer will mockers make
merry in mockery
and fools despise knowledge?
Pay heed to my warning.
I will pour out my spirit upon you;
I will make my thoughts known to you.
Because I called and you rejected me,
stretched out my hand and no one paid
any attention,
since you ignored all of my advice
and rejected all my warnings;
I in turn will chuckle at your calamity,
I will mock when misfortune overwhelms you,
when catastrophe overtakes
you like a storm,
when disaster sweeps down upon you
like a whirlwind,
when distress and anguish befall you.
Then they will call upon me, but I will
not answer;
they will diligently search for me but
not find me.
Because they despised knowledge
and chose not the fear of the Lord,
since they did not accept my counsel,
and have spurned all my rebukes,
they will eat the fruit of their ways,
and gorge themselves
on their scheming.
For the base are killed by their
waywardness,
and fools are destroyed by their
complacency;
but whoever listens to me
will live in security,
experience tranquility,
and fear no malady."

Proverbs 3:13–19 TNK

Blessed the person
who discovers Wisdom,
the person who gains Understanding,
for she is more profitable than silver,
and yields a better revenue than gold.
She is more precious than rosy pearls,
and nothing you desire can compare
with her.
Long life lies in her right hand;
in her left—riches and honor.
Her ways are totally pleasant,
and all her paths are peace.
She is a tree of life to those
who embrace her;
those who cling to her will be blessed.
By Wisdom Yahweh fixed
the earth's foundations,

by Understanding, set the heavens
in place.

Proverbs 4:4–9 TNK

Let your heart lay hold of my words;
keep my commands and you will live.
Obtain Wisdom; obtain Understanding.
Do not disregard her or deviate from
my words.
Do not desert her
and she will protect you.
Love her and she will watch over you.
The beginning of wisdom is:
obtain Wisdom;
at the cost of all you have,
obtain Understanding.
Esteem her, and she will exalt you.
She will honor you if you embrace her.
She will place a garland of grace upon
your head,
a crown of splendor she will bestow
upon you.

Proverbs 8:1–11 TNK

Does not Wisdom call out?
Does not Understanding
raise her voice?
On the city walls above the crossroads
she takes her stand;
beside the gates leading into the city,
in the entryways she cries aloud:
"To you, O people, I call,
my voice beckons to the children
of the earth.
You simpletons, gain cunning;
fools, gain common sense.
Listen, for I have something
important to say,
when I open my lips,
what is right pours forth.
My mouth declares the truth,
for wickedness is abhorrent to my lips.
All the words from my mouth are just,
not one of them is crooked or perverse.
To the discerning, they are all straight,
to those attaining knowledge,
they are right.
Acquire my instruction instead of silver,
knowledge of me rather than finest gold.
For Wisdom is more precious
than rosy pearls,
and nothing you most desire can compare with her."

Proverbs 8:12–21 TNK

I, Wisdom, dwell with discretion,
and I obtain judicious knowledge.
To revere Yahweh is to hate evil;
I hate pride and arrogance,
wicked behavior and perverse speech.
Counsel and sound judgment are mine;
understanding and power belong to me.
By me royalty reigns
and rulers regulate justly;
by me princes govern
as do all nobles.
I love those who love me;
and those who seek me find me.
With me are riches and honor,
enduring wealth and prosperity.
My fruit is better than gold,
even the finest,
and my yield surpasses
the choicest silver.
I walk in the way of righteousness,
along the paths of justice,
to bestow wealth on those who love me,
to make their treasuries replete.

Proverbs 8:22–31 TNK

Wisdom declares:
The Lord begot me, the first-born
of his way,
before his deeds of old.

From eternity I was poured forth,
from the beginning, before the foundation of the earth.
When the watery abyss did not exist I was given birth,
when there were no springs abounding with water.
Before the mountains were settled,
before the hills, I came to birth;
before he made the earth and the fields,
even the first particles of the world.
I was there when he fixed the heavens firmly in place,
when he scored a circumference on the face of the abyss,
when he made firm
the cloudy skies above,
when he strengthened the fountains of the deep,
when he assigned the sea its boundary
so that the waters would not overstep his command,
when he marked out the foundations of the earth,
then I was at his side as an artisan
delighting him day after day,
ever dancing in his presence,
playfully dancing everywhere
in his world,
and delighting in the children
of the earth.

Proverbs 8:32–36 TNK

Wisdom delivers her discourse:
Now then my children, listen to me,
blessed are those who keep my ways.
Give heed to my instruction and become wise,
do not reject it.
Blessed is whoever listens for me,
watching daily at my doorstep,
waiting day by day at my gateway.

For whoever encounters me finds life,
obtaining favor from Yahweh;
but whoever misses me meets
self-injury,
all who despise me court death.

Proverbs 9:1–6, 11 TNK

Wisdom has constructed
her own house,
she has chiseled her seven columns,
she has slaughtered her livestock,
mixed her spiced wine,
and prepared her table.
She has dispatched her maids
and announced from the city heights:
"Whoever is simple? Come this way!"
To those lacking judgment,
she proclaims:
"Come, feast on my food,
and imbibe the spiced wine
which I mixed!
Leave your simple ways
at the doorway and live,
and enter the path to understanding.
For by me your days will be multiplied,
and years will be added to your life."

Isaiah 11:1–3 TNK

A shoot will sprout from
the stump of Jesse,
from his burgeoning roots
a bud shall blossom.
The Spirit of Yahweh, she shall rest
upon him:
a Spirit of Wisdom
and of Understanding,
a Spirit of Counsel and of Power,
a Spirit of Knowledge and of the Fear
of Yahweh,
so that he will delight
in revering Yahweh,
and not judge by what he sees

with his eyes,
nor decide by what he hears
with his ears.

Isaiah 30:18 TNK versicle

Yet Yahweh longs to be gracious to you,
the Exalted One to show maternal compassion to you.

Isaiah 31:4-5 TNK

Indeed, this is what Yahweh says to me,
"Just as the full grown or young lion
growls over his prey,
when a band of shepherds is summoned
against him,
and is not frightened by their shouting
or daunted by their clamor,
so too Yahweh Sabaoth descends
to do battle
on Mount Zion and on her ridges.
Like mother birds hovering
over their young
Yahweh Sabaoth will shield Jerusalem;
to protect and save,
to spare and deliver."

Isaiah 42:10-16 TNK

Sing to Yahweh a new song!
Let his praises resound from the ends
of the earth,
by those who sail the seas,
and all creatures within them,
by the coastlands and their inhabitants.
Let the desert and its towns
raise their voices,
the settlements where Kedar lives.
Let the people of Sela sing for joy,
let them shout from
the mountain peaks.
Let them give glory to Yahweh
and let them proclaim his praises
in the islands.
Yahweh marches forth like a hero,
like a warrior rouses passion.
He shouts, sounding the war cry,
he displays his might against his foes.
"For a long time I have kept silent,
have been quiet, holding myself
in check.
But now like a woman in childbirth,
I groan, I gasp, I pant all at once.
I will lay waste to mountains and hills,
will wither all their vegetation;
I will transform torrents
into dry territory,
and bring drought to pools of water.

But I will lead those who are blind by
a way they knew not,
along unfamiliar paths
I will guide them.
I will transform the darkness
into light before them,
and turn rough places into level ground.
These are the things I shall do,
I shall not abandon them."

Isaiah 45:9-12 TNK

Woe to anyone who contends
with his Maker;
a potsherd among potsherds
of the earth!
Does the clay say to its potter,
"What are you making?"
or "Your work lacks handles."
Woe to anyone who asks a father,
"What are you begetting?"
or a mother, "What are you
giving birth to?"
Thus says Yahweh,
the Holy One of Israel and his Maker:
Will you question me
about my children,

or give me orders about the works
of my hands?
It was I who made the earth
and created humanity upon it.
My own hands stretched out
the heavens
and I marshaled all of their starry array.

Isaiah 46:1-5 TNK

Bel bows down, Nebo stoops,
their idols are borne by beasts
and cattle;
the loads you are carrying are a burden
to a weary beast.
They stoop and bow down together,
powerless to save those who bear them;
they themselves go into captivity.
Listen to me, O House of Jacob,
and all the remnant of the House
of Israel,
whom I have borne since your
conception,
whom I have carried
since you were born.
Even to your old age I am the same,
even when your hairs are gray I will
bear you.
It is I who made you and I will bear you;
I will carry you and I will save you.
To whom will you compare me,
or count as my equal?
To whom will you liken me,
that we may be equated?

Isaiah 49:13-16 TNK

Thus says Yahweh:
Shout for joy, O heavens;
and rejoice, O earth!
Burst forth in song, O mountains!
For Yahweh comforts his people
and displays maternal compassion on
his afflicted ones.
Zion was saying, "Yahweh has abandoned me;
the Lord has forgotten me."
Can a mother forget the baby
at her breast,
feel no maternal compassion for the
child of her womb?
Even should she forget,
I will never forget you.
See, I have engraved you on the palms
of my hands.

Isaiah 51:1-3 TNK

Listen to me, you who pursue
righteousness,
who seek after Yahweh.
Look to the Rock from
which you were hewn,
and to the Pit from which
you were quarried.
Consider Abraham your father
and Sarah who gave you birth.
When he was just one I called him,
I blessed him and made him numerous.
Yahweh will surely comfort Zion,
have maternal compassion
on all her ruins;
will make her deserts like Eden,
and her wastelands like the garden
of Yahweh.
Joy and gladness shall be found in her,
thanksgiving and the sound of singing.

Isaiah 53:1-7 TNK

Who would dare believe
what we have heard?
To whom has the arm of Yahweh
been extended?
He sprouted like a tender sapling
before him,
like a shoot breaking
through arid ground.

He possessed no striking features
that would cause us to look at him;
no attractive appearance
that we should fix our eyes upon him.
He was shunned and rejected by others,
a man of sorrows accustomed
to suffering,
a man to make people
look the other way.
He was despised; we didn't even give
him a second thought.

Yet ours were the sufferings he bore,
ours the sorrows he shouldered.
But we reckoned him as someone
under a curse,
struck down by God, brought low.
Yet he was pierced for our faults,
crushed for our sins.
On his back lies the punishment that
makes us whole,
and through his wounds
we have been healed.

All of us had gone astray like sheep,
each going his or her own way.
Yet Yahweh weighed him down
with the sins of us all.
Though treated harshly, he bore it,
never opening his mouth.
Like a lamb led to the butcher-house,
like a ewe that is dumb
before her shearers,
never opening its mouth.

Isaiah 54:7–13 TNK

I did for a brief moment abandon you,
but with magnificent maternal compassion I shall bring you back.
In a flood of fury I hid my face
for but a moment,
but in everlasting and steadfast love
I shall shower you
with maternal affection,
declares Yahweh your Redeemer.
This is to me like the days of Noah
when I swore that Noah's waters
would never flood the world again.
So now I have sworn never to be angry
with you,
never to rebuke you again.
Though the mountains be moved
and the hills be shaken,
yet my unfailing love for you shall not
be moved,
nor my covenant of peace ever shaken,
declares Yahweh who displays maternal
compassion.
O afflicted one, battered by storms and
uncomforted,
behold, I shall set your stones in solid
cement
and lay your foundations
with sapphires;
I will build your battlements
with rubies,
your gateways bejeweled with beryl,
and all your walls with precious gems.
All your children will be taught
by Yahweh
and great will be your children's
well-being.

Isaiah 63:7–9 TNK

I will recount the acts of Yahweh's steadfast love,
the praiseworthy deeds of Yahweh,
because of all that Yahweh
has done for us,
for the great generosity shown the
House of Israel
according to his maternal compassion
and abundant acts of steadfast love.
He said, "Surely they are my people,

children who will not prove false";
so he became their Savior
in all their distress.
It was neither messenger nor angel,
but his presence that saved them.
Out of love and maternal compassion,
he himself redeemed them,
lifted them up and carried them
all the days of old.

Isaiah 63:14–15 TNK

The Spirit of Yahweh,
she led them to rest.
Thus you guided your people
and gained for yourself a glorious name.
Look down from heaven, look down
from your holy and glorious abode.
Where is your fervent care, your wondrous might,
the trembling of your womb and maternal compassion?

Isaiah 66:9–13 TNK

Shall I bring a mother to the point of giving birth,
and yet not let her child be delivered?
declares Yahweh.
Or shall I, who cause conception,
then close her womb? asks your God.
Rejoice with Jerusalem,
and be glad for her,
all you who love her!
Exultantly rejoice with her,
all you who mourned for her!
O that you may be suckled and satisfied
from her consoling breasts,
that you may drink deeply with delight
from her overflowing
and swollen breasts.
For this is what Yahweh proclaims:
Behold, I will extend prosperity to her
like a river,
and like an overflowing stream, the
wealth of nations.
You will nurse and be carried
on her hip,
and fondled in her lap.
As a mother comforts her child,
so shall I comfort you;
you will be comforted in Jerusalem.

Jeremiah 31:18–20 TNK

Without a doubt
I have heard Ephraim groaning:
"You disciplined me,
and I learned a lesson,
like an untamed calf.
If you allow me, I will come back,
for you are Yahweh my God.
After I had strayed I repented,
and once I understood I beat my breast.
I am deeply ashamed and blush,
because I bear the disgrace
of my youth."
"Is not Ephraim a dear son to me,
the child in whom I delight?
As often as I speak against him,
I still remember him lovingly.
Therefore my womb yearns for him
and I must have great maternal compassion upon him,"
declares Yahweh.

Ezekiel 3:14 TNK versicle

Then the Spirit lifted me up and she carried me away.

Ezekiel 3:24 TNK versicle

Then the Spirit entered me and she raised me to my feet.

PRAYING—WITH THE SAINTS—TO GOD OUR MOTHER

Ezekiel 8:1–4 TNK

In the sixth year, in the sixth month, on the fifth day, I was sitting at home and the elders of Judah were seated around me, when suddenly the Power of the Lord Yahweh, she fell upon me. I looked, and there was a figure with the appearance of a human being. From what seemed to be the waist downward there was fire, and from the waist upwards there was a brilliance resembling glittering amber. Something that looked like a hand reached out and grabbed me by the hair of my head. And the Spirit, she lifted me up between earth and heaven and she took me to Jerusalem in visions from God to the entrance of the inner north gate, where the idol provoking jealousy was positioned. And there before me was the glory of the God of Israel, like that which I had seen on the plain in a vision.

Hosea 11:1–4 TNK

When Israel was a child I loved him,
out of Egypt I called my son.
The more I called out to them,
the further they went away from me;
they sacrificed to the Baals
and burned incense to idols.
Yet it was I who taught Ephraim
how to walk,
taking them by the arms,
but they did not realize
that I was the one caring for their well-being,
that I was drawing them
with human cords,
with leading-strings of love,
that, towards them, I was like a parent
lifting an infant to one's cheeks,
and that I stooped down to feed him.

Hosea 13:4–8 TNK

But I am Yahweh your God
who brought you out of Egypt;
you shall acknowledge no God but me,
there is no Savior except me.
It was I who cared for you in the desert,
in the land of sweltering heat.
I pastured them and they were satisfied;
but once satisfied, their hearts became bloated with pride,
therefore they forgot me.
So now I shall pounce upon them
like a lion,
like a leopard I will lurk by the roadside,
like a mother bear robbed of her cubs I will attack them,
and rip out their hearts
from their breasts,
like a lioness I will devour them
on the spot,
as a ferocious beast tears apart her prey.

Hosea 14:4 TNK versicle

In you the orphan finds maternal compassion.

Micah 7:18–20 TNK

Who is a god like you,
who removes guilt
and pardons transgression;
who does not stay angry forever,
but rather delights in displaying steadfast love?
Once more have maternal compassion upon us,
tread our faults underfoot,
and cast all our sins
into the depths of the sea.
Grant Jacob your faithfulness,
and Abraham your steadfast love,
as you swore to our ancestors
from days of old.

Septuagint Texts

Deuteronomy 1:29–31 LXX

I said to you, "Do not be terrified; do not be afraid of them. The Lord your God who goes before you, the same, shall fight against them according to all which was done for you in the land of Egypt, and in that wilderness which you saw on your journey to the mountain of the Amorites. You saw how the Lord your God tenderly carried you as a nursling—as any human being would nurse its child—such the Lord did throughout the whole journey which you have traveled, until you arrived at this place."

Judith 16:13–15 LXX rectified with presumed original Hebrew

I will sing to my God a new song:
O Lord, you are great and glorious,
wondrous in strength and invincible.
Let all creatures serve you,
for you spoke and they came into being;
you sent forth your Spirit
and she created them;
there is none that can resist your voice.
Should mountains be toppled
from their foundation
to mingle with crashing waves,
should rocks melt
like wax before your face,
to those who revere you
you would still show maternal
compassion.

Song of Songs 1:1–4 LXX

The Song of Songs which is Solomon's.
Let him kiss me with the kisses
of his mouth,
for your breasts are better than wine;
and the fragrance of your ointments
is better than all spices.
Your name is an ointment poured forth,
thus the young maidens love you.
They have drawn you;
we will run after you
for the fragrance of your ointments.
The king has brought me
into his chamber,
Let us be abundantly joyful
and glad in you.
We will love your breasts
more than wine;
Uprightness loves you.

Wisdom 1:4–7 LXX

For into a wickedly crafty soul Wisdom
will never enter,
nor will she dwell in a body
dominated by sin;
for the Holy Spirit of instruction
flees deceit,
and will remove herself from thoughts
void of understanding,
and will be ashamed when unrighteousness enters.
For Wisdom is a loving
spirit of humanity
and she will not acquit
a blasphemer's words,
for God is witness to his inmost feelings,
a true observer of the heart
and hearer of the tongue.
For the Spirit of the Lord has completely
filled the world,
and that which holds everything together knows every utterance.

Wisdom 6:12–20 LXX

Wisdom is brilliant and unfading;
indeed, she is readily seen by those who
love her,
she is easily found

by those who seek her.
She anticipates those who desire her
by making herself known first.
Whoever rises early to find her,
will encounter no difficulty,
but will discover her sitting
at the entrance.
To transfix one's desires on her
is perfect comprehension,
and whoever keeps watch for her will
quickly be without cares.
For she herself goes about in search
of those who are worthy of her,
graciously appearing to them
on their journeys;
and she encounters them
in their every thought.
The beginning of Wisdom is a truly
sincere desire for instruction,
and concentration on instruction
is love of her,
and love of her is the keeping
of her laws,
and paying heed to her laws is assurance
of incorruptibility,
and incorruptibility renders
one near to God;
so the desire for Wisdom leads
to sovereignty.

Wisdom 6:22 LXX versicle

What Wisdom is and how she came to be, I will tell you, and will not hide any mysteries from you, but will trace her steps from the beginning of her origin, thus establishing knowledge of her in full light.

Wisdom 7:7–14 LXX

Therefore I prayed and understanding was granted to me;
I entreated and the Spirit of Wisdom
came to me.
I preferred her over scepters
and thrones,
and considered wealth as nothing in
comparison with her.
Neither did I liken her
to any priceless gem,
for all the gold in the world
is as a few grains of sand
compared with her,
and silver shall be reckoned
as mere clay before her.
I loved her more than health
and a shapely physique,
and I chose to have her
rather than light,
since her radiance never wanes.
All good things came to me
along with her,
and riches beyond counting
are in her hands.
I delighted in all these things,
because Wisdom presides over them,
though I did not realize that she
is their mother.
Diligently I learned, and liberally
will I share;
I will not hide her riches.
For she is an inexhaustible treasury
for humanity;
those who acquire her gain friendship
with God,
commended for the gifts that come
from instruction.

Wisdom 7:21–22 LXX versicle

Now I comprehend everything: both
hidden and observable,
for Wisdom, the designer of everything,
she has instructed me.

Wisdom 7:21–26 LXX

I learned what is both secret
and manifest,
for Wisdom, the artistic designer
of the universe,
has instructed me.
For in her resides a spirit:
intelligent, holy, unique,
manifold, subtle, mobile,
clear, unsullied, lucid,
invulnerable, benevolent, keen,
irresistible, beneficent, loving humanity,
steadfast, dependable, carefree,
all-powerful, overseeing everything, and
permeating all spirits:
intelligent, pure and very subtle.
For Wisdom moves more speedily than
any motion;
she pervades and penetrates everything
thanks to her purity.
Indeed, she is the breath
of the power of God,
pure emanation of the glory
of the Almighty,
thus nothing defiled can find its way
into her.
For she is the reflection
of the Eternal Light,
the spotless mirror of God's
dynamic activity,
and the image of God's goodness.

Wisdom 7:27—8:1 LXX

Although Wisdom is one,
she can do everything,
remaining unchanged in herself, she
renews all creation.
Passing into holy souls generation
after generation,
she renders them friends of God
and prophets.
For God loves nothing so much as the
one who dwells with Wisdom.
For she is more majestic than the sun,
and more resplendent
than all the starry expanse.
Compared with light, she is found to be
far superior,
for light is replaced by night,
but against Wisdom evil cannot prevail.
She robustly reaches from one extent of
the universe to the other,
and she administers all things well.

Wisdom 8:2–8 LXX

I loved Wisdom and diligently sought
after her from my youth;
I desired to make her my bride
and became deeply enamored
of her beauty.
She glorifies her wholesome generation
by sharing in God's life,
indeed, the Lord of all creation
loves her.
For she is an initiate in the knowledge
of God,
and one who chooses
to accomplish his works.
If wealth be a desirable possession
in this life,
then what is richer than Wisdom who
produces everything?
And if it be the intellect that is at work,
who, more than she, is the designer of
all being?
And if anyone loves righteousness,
her labors are virtues,
for she teaches self-control
and prudence,
righteousness and fortitude;
nothing in life is more profitable
for human beings.
And if anyone longs

for much experience,
she knows past things
and divines future events;
she understands circumlocutions
and resolves enigmas;
she displays foreknowledge of signs
and wonders,
and of the fulfillment of epochs
and times.

Wisdom 8:9–13 LXX

Therefore I determined to take Wisdom
as my life's partner,
knowing that she would be a counselor
in good times,
and a comfort in the midst of cares
and sorrows.
Because of her, admiration shall be
accorded me by the multitudes,
and honor in the presence of the elders,
even though I am young.
I shall be found keen in judgment,
and in the sight of the mighty
I shall be admired.
When I am silent they will wait for me,
and when I utter a word they
will hang on it;
and when I discourse at length
they will put their hands over their lips.
Moreover, by means of Wisdom I shall
attain immortality,
and bequeath an everlasting memorial
to my successors.

Wisdom 8:16–21 LXX

Arriving in my house, I shall take my
repose with Wisdom,
for companionship with her
is void of bitterness,
when sharing life with her there
is no pain,
but only gladness and joy.
When I considered these things
within myself,
and thought about them in my heart,
that immortality is kin to Wisdom,
and blessed delight shares
her friendship,
and in the labor of her hands are
inexhaustible riches,
and in the experience of her company
lies understanding,
and renown in fellowship
with her discourses,
I went about seeking how to receive her
into myself.
As a child, by nature I was physically
well-endowed,
I also received a good soul as my lot;
or rather, being good, I entered an
undefiled body.
But I realized that I could not possess
Wisdom
unless God grant her to me—
that in itself was an insight to know
whose gift she is—
and so I petitioned the Lord.

Wisdom 9:1–4, 9–11 LXX

O God of our ancestors and Lord
of mercy,
who made the universe by your Word,
and by Wisdom have fashioned
human beings
to have dominion over the creatures you
have made,
to govern the world in holiness
and righteousness,
and to execute judgment in integrity
of soul,
grant me Wisdom,
consort of your throne,
and do not reject me from among
your children. . . .

With you is Wisdom, she who knows your works,
she who was present when you made the world,
who understands what is pleasing in your sight,
and what is right according to your commandments.
Send her forth from the holy heavens,
and dispatch her from your throne of glory,
that she may accompany me and labor with me,
causing me to learn what is well pleasing to you.
Because she knows and understands everything,
she will guide me wisely in my actions,
and safeguard me in her glory.

Wisdom 9:17—10:6 LXX

Who could be cognizant
of your counsel,
unless you granted Wisdom,
sent your Holy Spirit from on high?
Thus the paths of those on earth have been rectified,
and humans have been taught what pleases you,
and have been saved by Wisdom.
It was she who safeguarded the first-formed father of the world,
when he had been created alone;
she delivered him from his fall
and bestowed on him power
to master all things.
But when a wicked one in his anger departed from her,
he was undone by his own fratricidal fury.
And when the earth was flooded because of him,
it was Wisdom again who saved it,
steering the righteous
on worthless wood.
It likewise was she,
while the nations were concurring in wickedness
and thus confounded,
who found the upright soul and preserved him blameless before God,
and fortified him against his own intestinal fortitude for his son.
She it was who, while the ungodly were completely perishing,
rescued a righteous soul who
fled from the fire
which fell on the Five Cities.

Wisdom 10:9–12 LXX

Wisdom delivered from ordeals those who served her.
When the righteous man fled from his brother's wrath,
she guided him on straight paths;
she showed him the kingdom of God,
and imparted knowledge of holy things;
she prospered him in his labors,
and increased the results of his efforts.
When his oppressors were gripped by covetousness,
she stood by his side
and made him wealthy.
She protected him from enemies,
and kept him safe from those who laid in wait for him.
In his arduous struggle
she granted him victory
that he might learn that piety is stronger than anything.

Wisdom 10:9, 13–14 LXX

Wisdom delivered from ordeals those
who served her.
She did not forsake the righteous man
when he was sold,
but rescued him from the sting of sin.
She descended with him into the pit,
and did not depart while
he was in chains,
and thus she brought him
the scepter of a kingdom
and authority over his masters.
As for those who accused him,
she showed them to be liars,
and bestowed upon him
everlasting glory.

Wisdom 10:15—11:1 LXX

It was Wisdom who delivered a holy
people and blameless stock
from the nation that oppressed them.
She entered the soul of
a servant of the Lord,
and withstood dread potentates with
portents and signs.
She rendered to the holy ones a reward
for their labors,
guided them on their
wondrous journey;
she became a shelter to them by day,
and a starry light by night.
She brought them through the Red Sea,
and led them through deep waters.
But their enemies, instead, she drowned,
and cast them up from the depths
of the abyss.
Therefore the righteous plundered
the ungodly,
and sang hymns to your holy name,
O Lord,
and with one accord praised your
champion hand.
For Wisdom opened the mouths
of the dumb,
and caused the tongues of babes to
speak clearly.
She prospered their works by the hand
of a holy prophet.

Sirach 14:20–27 LXX

Blessed the one who meditates
on Wisdom
and reflects on Understanding;
who ponders her ways in the heart
and studies her secrets;
who tracks her like a scout
and lies in wait by her route;
who peers in through her windows
and eavesdrops at her portals;
who encamps near her house
and drives a tent peg in her walls;
who pitches a tent beside her
and dwells in an excellent lodging;
who sets one's children under her shade
and lodges beneath her branches;
who is sheltered by her from the heat
and in her glory finds a home.

Sirach 15:1–8 LXX

Whoever fears the Lord
will act accordingly,
and whoever grasps the Law
will obtain Wisdom.
She shall go to meet him like a mother,
and welcome him like a virgin bride.
She shall give him the bread of understanding to eat,
and the water of wisdom to drink.
He will lean upon her and will not falter,
he will rely upon her
and not be put to shame.
She shall exalt him above his neighbors,
and in the midst of the assembly she will
open his mouth.

He will discover happiness and a crown of gladness,
he will inherit an everlasting name.
Fools shall not attain her,
and sinners shall not see her.
She stands aloof from the proud,
and liars never think of her.

Sirach 24:1–9 LXX

Wisdom recounts her own praises,
in the midst of her people she glories in herself.
In the assembly of the Most High she opens her mouth,
in the presence of his hosts she extols her fame:
I proceeded from the mouth of the Most High,
and covered the earth like a misty cloud.
I had my abode in the highest heavens,
and my throne was set in a pillar of cloud.
I alone encompassed the circuit of heaven,
and marched through the bottom of the abyss.
Over the waves of the sea and the whole earth,
and over every people and nation I have held sway.
Among all of these I sought a resting place,
and in whose inheritance I might encamp.
Then the Creator of everything issued me a command,
and the One who created me assigned a resting place for my tent,
saying, "Pitch your tent in Jacob, and make Israel your inheritance."
From eternity, in the beginning, he created me,
and for all eternity I shall never cease.

Sirach 24:1, 10–22 LXX

Wisdom recounts her own praises,
in the midst of her people she glories in herself. . . .
In the holy tabernacle I ministered before the Most High,
and thus in Zion my dwelling was established.
In the beloved city he granted me rest,
yea, in Jerusalem my authority reigned.
I struck root in a privileged people,
in the Lord's portion and heritage.
I grew tall like a cedar in Lebanon,
like a cypress on Mount Hermon,
like a palm tree in Engedi,
like a rose bush in Jericho,
like a fair olive tree in the field,
and like a plane tree I grew lofty.
Like cinnamon and aromatic acanthus, I yielded a perfume,
like choicest myrrh a beautiful fragrance,
like galbanum, onycha, and labdanum,
like the fume of frankincense in the tabernacle.
I have spread out my branches like a terebinth,
and my many branches are glorious and graceful.
I am like a beautifully budding vine,
and my blossoms bear fruit, splendid and rich.

Sirach 24:1–3, 18–22 LXX

Wisdom recounts her own praises,
in the midst of her people she glories in herself.
In the assembly of the Most High she opens her mouth,
in the presence of his hosts she extols her fame:
I proceeded from the mouth of the Most High,

and covered the earth like a misty cloud.
. . .
I am the mother of pure love
and reverence,
of knowledge and of holy hope;
I am bestowed upon all of my children,
from all eternity on those
appointed to me.
Come to me, you who yearn for me,
and take your fill of my fruits,
for my remembrance
is sweeter than honey,
my inheritance better
than the honeycomb.
All who feast on me will hunger
for more;
all who imbibe me will thirst for more.
Whoever obeys me will never
be put to shame,
and whoever is in my service
will never falter.

Baruch 4:4–8, 30 LXX

O Israel, happy are we:
what pleases God
has been revealed to us.
Take courage, my people,
Memorial of Israel!
You were sold to the nations,
but not for destruction.
You angered God;
and thus were handed over
to your enemies.
You provoked your Creator,
by sacrificing to demons,
and not to God.
You had forgotten the Eternal God
who suckled you,
and you grieved Jerusalem
who nursed you. . . .
Be of good heart, O Jerusalem,
for the One who gave you that name
will comfort you.

Hosea 2:19–20, 23 LXX

I will betroth you to myself forever;
yes, I will betroth you to myself
in righteousness and justice,
and in mercy and tender compassion.
I will betroth you to myself
in faithfulness,
and you shall know the Lord. . . .
I will love that which was not loved,
and will say to that which
was not my people,
"You are my people!"
and they shall reply,
"You are the Lord, my God!"

Hosea 13:5–8 LXX

I tended you like a shepherd
in the wilderness,
in an uninhabited region.
according to their pastures,
they were abundantly filled.
But their hearts became puffed up,
therefore they forgot me.
Thus I shall be to them as a panther,
and as a leopardess.
I will meet them on the road to Assyria,
as a mother bear robbed of her cubs,
and I will break open the encasing of
their heart,
and like a lioness
I shall devour them there.
The wild beast of the field shall rip them
to shreds.

Greek New Testament

Matthew 11:16–19 NT

To what shall I compare this generation?
It is like children sitting in the market-
places, screaming out to others:

"We played the pipes for you, yet you wouldn't dance;
we sang a dirge, but you wouldn't mourn." For John came neither eating nor drinking, and they say, "He's possessed." The Son of Man came, eating and drinking, yet they say, "Look, a glutton and a drunkard, a buddy of tax collectors and sinners." But Wisdom is proved right by her deeds.

Matthew 13:33-35 NT

He told them another parable, "The kingdom of heaven is like the yeast a woman took, kneading it in three large measures of flour until the whole batch was leavened." All these things Jesus spoke to the crowd in parables, indeed, he said nothing to them except in parables. Thus was fulfilled what was spoken through the prophet:
I will open my mouth in parables,
I will utter what has been hidden from the foundation of the world.

Matthew 23:37-39 NT

O Jerusalem, Mother Jerusalem, you who kill the prophets and stone those who are sent to you! How often I wanted to gather your children as a mother bird gathers her young under her wings, yet you were not willing. Look, your house will be left to you alone, for I assure you, you will not see me any more until you say: "Blessed is the one who comes in the name of the Lord!"

Second translation:
Jerusalem, O Jerusalem, she who puts the prophets to death and stones those who are sent to her! How often I longed to huddle your children around me, as a mother bird huddles her nestlings under her wings, yet you would have none of it. Look, your dwelling will be deserted, for I tell you, you will not see me again until you say: "Blessed is the one who comes in the name of the Lord!"

Luke 7:31-35 NT

To what can I compare the people of this generation? What are they like? They are like children sitting about in the market place shouting to one another:
"We piped you a tune but you didn't dance;
we wailed but you didn't weep."
For John the Baptist came not eating bread and not drinking wine, and you remark, "He's possessed." The Son of Man came eating and drinking, and you say, "Look, a glutton and a drunkard, a buddy of tax collectors and sinners." Yet Wisdom is justified by all her children.

Luke 11:47-51 NT

Woe to you, because you build the tombs of the prophets whom your ancestors killed. Consequently you are witnesses and in total agreement with the deeds of your ancestors; they did the butchering, you do the building. Accordingly the Wisdom of God declared, "I will send them prophets and apostles, some they shall slaughter and others persecute." She said this so that this generation will be held accountable for all the blood of the prophets that has been shed since the foundation of the world, from the blood of Abel to the blood of Zechariah, who perished between the altar and the sanctuary. Indeed, I assure you, this generation will be held responsible.

Luke 13:34-35 NT

Jerusalem, O Jerusalem, she who kills the prophets and stones those who have been sent to her! How often I wanted to gather your children together as a mother bird gathers her own brood under her wings, but you didn't want that. Look, your house is left to you desolate. I tell you, by no means will you see me again until the time comes when you say, "Blessed is the one who comes in the name of the Lord."

Luke 15:8-10 NT

What woman, having ten silver coins, if she were to lose one, would not light a lamp and sweep the house, searching painstakingly until she found it? And having found it would she not call her friends and neighbors together, saying, "Rejoice with me, I have found the money I lost." In the same way, I tell you, there is rejoicing among the angels of God over one repentant sinner.

John 1:9-14 NT

The Word was the true Light
which enlightens all peoples;
it was penetrating into the world.
He was present within the world
which had come into being
through him,
yet the world did not perceive him.
He came to his own creations,
yet his own people did not receive him.
But to those who did accept him
he bestowed upon them the power
to become children of God,
to all who believe in the name of him
who were given birth to
not out of human generation
or urge of human nature,
or human will,
but born by God.
And so the Word was made flesh
so that he might dwell within our midst.

John 1:15-18 NT

John bore witness to him and
proclaimed,
This is the one of whom I said:
The one who comes after me
has surpassed me,
because he existed before me.
From his fullness all of us have received,
one blessing after another,
for the Law was delivered
through Moses,
while grace and truth have come
through Jesus Christ.
No one has ever seen God;
it is the only-begotten God,
being in the bowels of the Father,
who has revealed God.

John 3:1-6 NT

Now there was a Pharisee named Nicodemus, a leader of the Jews, who came to Jesus by night and said, "Rabbi, we know that you are a teacher come from God, for no one can perform the signs you do, unless God were with him." Jesus answered: "In all honesty, I tell you, unless someone be born from above, it is impossible to see the kingdom of God." Nicodemus replied, "How can anyone who is already old be born? Surely it isn't possible to enter into one's mother's womb a second time and be born again?" Jesus answered, "I tell you the truth, unless someone be born of water and Spirit, it is impossible to enter into the kingdom of God. What is born of the flesh is flesh, but what is born of the Spirit is spirit.

Christian Scriptures That Use Feminine Imagery

You should not be surprised that I told you that you must be born from above."

John 16:17–21 NT

Some of his disciples said to one another, "What does he mean when he tells us, 'In a little while you will no longer see me, and then a short while later you will see me again,' and, 'I am going to the Father?'" They kept talking back and forth, "What does he mean by 'a little while?' We don't know what he's talking about." Jesus knew that they wanted to interrogate him, so he said, "You are trying to find out from one another what I meant when I said, 'In a little while you will no longer see me, and then a short while later you will see me again.'
I tell you the truth,
you will weep and wail,
while the world will celebrate;
you will be grief-stricken,
but your grief will be turned into joy.
When a woman gives birth,
she experiences pain,
because her hour has come,
but when she has given birth to the baby,
she no longer remembers the suffering because of her joy that a child has been born into the world."

[In the ancient world, when a woman was pregnant, she was secluded and removed from sight, only to return after having given birth.]

1 Corinthians 3:1–2 NT

But I, brothers and sisters, was not able to address you as spiritual people, but as still worldly, mere infants in Christ. I provided you with milk and not solid food, for you were not yet capable of digesting it.

Hebrews 1:1–9 NT

At various times in the past and through various different ways, God spoke to our ancestors through the prophets; but in our own time, the last days, God has spoken to us in his Son, the Son whom he appointed to inherit everything and through whom he created the ages. He is the reflection of God's glory and the perfect copy of God's very being, sustaining the universe by his powerful word. When he had made purification for sins, he took his seat at the right hand of the Divine Majesty on high; thus he is now as far above the angels as the title which he has inherited is superior to their own name. God has never said to any of the angels, *You are my Son, today I have given birth to you*; or, *I will be a father to him, and he a son to me*. Again, when he brings the First-born into the world, he says, *Let all the angels of God worship him*. And concerning the angels he says, *He makes his angels spirits and his ministers flames of fire*; but to his Son he declares, *O God, your throne shall endure forever and ever, and your royal scepter is the scepter of virtue. You love righteousness and detest wickedness. Therefore, O God, your God has anointed you with the oil of gladness, above all your rivals.*

James 1:13–18 NT

When being tempted, no one should say, "God is tempting me." For God cannot be tempted by evil allurements, and does not tempt any one; but everyone is tempted by being attracted and enticed by that person's own desires. Once the desire has conceived, it gives birth to sin, and when sin is fully grown, it gives birth to death. Don't be deceived, my beloved brothers and sisters. Every good endowment and every perfect gift comes from above, descending from the Father of lights, with whom there is no alteration or shadow due to change. He purposely gave birth to us by the word of truth, so that we might be a sort of first-fruits of all creation.

1 Peter 1:3-5 NT

Blessed be the God and Father of our Lord Jesus Christ, who in plenteous mercy has given birth to us again into a living hope through the resurrection of Jesus Christ from the dead, and into an inheritance which is incorruptible, undefiled and never waning. It has been reserved in the heavens for you who are being safeguarded by God's power through faith until the manifestation of the salvation which is ready to be revealed at the end of time.

1 Peter 1:25—2:3 NT

The word of the Lord remains forever, and this is the word which was preached to you. Therefore, rid yourselves of all malice and all deceit, hypocrisy, envy, and every form of slander. Like newborn babes, crave pure spiritual milk, so that thanks to it, you may grow up into salvation, since you have tasted that the Lord is good.

OLD PESHITTA

Matthew 23:37-39 PESH

O Jerusalem, Jerusalem, murderess of the prophets and stoner of those who are sent to her! How often I wanted to gather your children as a hen gathers her chicks under her wings, and yet you were not willing. Behold, your house will be left desolate! For I assure you, you will not see me any more until you say: "Blessed is the one who comes in the name of the Lord!"

Luke 1:26-35 PESH

Now in the sixth month the angel Gabriel was sent from God to Galilee, to a city called Nazareth, to a virgin who was acquired by dowry for a man named Joseph of the house of David; the virgin's name was Mary. And the angel went in and said to her, "Peace be with you, O full of grace; our Lord is with you, O blessed among women." When she saw him, she was disturbed by his message and wondered what kind of greeting this could be. But the angel said to her, "Fear not, Mary, for you have found favor with God. For behold, you will conceive and give birth to a son, and you will name him Jesus. He will be great, and he will be called the Son of the Most High. The Lord God will grant him the throne of his father David. And he will rule over the house of Jacob forever, and there will be no limit to his kingdom." Then Mary asked the angel, "How can this be, for no man has known me?" The angel answered saying to her, "The Holy Spirit, she will come upon you, and the Power of the Most High, will overshadow you; thus the one who will be born of you is holy, and he will be called the Son of God."

Luke 4:1-2 PESH

Now Jesus, filled with the Holy Spirit, returned from the Jordan, and the Spirit, she carried him away into the desert for forty days, so that he might be tempted by the adversary. And he did not eat anything for all those days. But when they were over, at last he grew hungry.

Luke 12:8-12 PESH

I say to you, "Whoever will acknowledge me before mortals, the Son of Man will acknowledge before the angels of God. But whoever denies me before mortals, I will deny before the angels of God. And whoever utters a word against the Son of Man will be forgiven; but whoever blasphemes against the Holy Spirit will not be forgiven. When they drag you to the synagogues before the leaders and authorities, do not worry about how you will respond or what you will say; for the Holy Spirit, she will teach you at that very moment what you ought to say."

John 1:15-18 PESH

John bore witness concerning him and cried out saying, "This is the one about whom I said, 'He is coming after me, and yet he is ahead of me, for he was before me.'" Indeed, of his fullness we have all received, grace following upon grace. For the Law was given by Moses, but truth and grace came into being through Jesus Christ. No one has ever seen God; but the first-born of God, who is in the womb of his Father, has declared him.

John 7:37-39 PESH

Now on the greatest day, which is the last day of the Feast, Jesus stood up and exclaimed, saying, "If anyone is thirsty, let him come to me and drink. Whoever believes in me, just as the Scriptures have said, 'Rivers of living water will flow from within him.'" He said this regarding the Spirit, whom they who believe in him were to receive; for the Spirit, she was not yet given, since Jesus had not yet been glorified.

John 14:12-17 PESH

Amen, amen, I say to you, "Whoever believes in me will do the works which I do, and even greater than these will he do because I am going to my Father. And whatever you ask for in my name I will do it for you so that the Father may be glorified through his Son. If you ask me in my own name, I will do it. If you love me, keep my commandments. Likewise I shall ask of my Father, and he will give you another Comforter to be with you forever, even the Spirit of Truth, whom the world cannot receive because it has not seen her and does not know her. But you know her because she abides with you and is in you."

John 14:19-26 PESH

"The world will not see me, but you will see me. Because I live, you also shall live. In that day you will know that I am with my Father, and you are with me, and I am with you. Whoever possesses my commandments and obeys them is the one who loves me; and whoever loves me will be loved by my Father, and I will love him and reveal myself to him." Judah (not of Iscariot) said to him, "My Lord, why will you reveal yourself to us and not to the world?" Jesus answered, saying to him, "Whoever loves me keeps my word, and my Father will love him, and we will come and make our abode within him. But whoever does not love me does not keep my word; and this word which you hear is not my own but the Father's who sent me. I have spoken these things to you while I am with you. But the Comforter, the Holy Spirit whom my Father will send in my name, she will teach you everything and she will remind you of everything I have told you."

John 15:16–26 PESH

"You did not choose me, but I chose you. And I have appointed you that you, too, might go forth and produce fruit and that your fruit might endure, so that whatever you ask of my Father in my name, he will grant it to you. I command these things to you in order that you may love one another. If the world hates you, know full well that it hated me before you. If you were of the world, the world would love its own; but you are not of the world for I have chosen you out of the world. This is why the world despises you. Remember the word which I told you, that no servant is greater than his master. If they have persecuted me, they will persecute you likewise; if they kept my word, they will keep yours also. But they will do all of these things to you on account of my name because they do not know the one who has sent me. If I had not come and spoken to them, they would be without sin; but now they have no excuse for their sins. Whoever hates me likewise hates my Father. If I had not done deeds before their eyes, such as no one has even done, they would be without sin; but now they have seen and hated me and also my Father, so that the word which is written in their Law might be fulfilled, *'They hated me for no reason.'* But when the Comforter comes, whom I shall send to you from my Father, the Spirit of Truth who proceeds from my Father, she will testify on my behalf.

John 16:12–16 PESH

I have many other things to tell you, but you cannot grasp them now. But when the Spirit of Truth has come, she will guide you into the whole truth, for she will not speak from herself, but what she hears she will speak; and she will make known to you things which are to come in the future. She will glorify me because she will take of my own and reveal it to you. Everything that my Father has is mine; this is the reason why I told you that she will take of my own and reveal it to you.

1 Thessalonians 4:1–8 PESH

From henceforth my brothers and sisters, we beseech you and earnestly beg of you in our Lord Jesus that as you have been taught by us how you are to live so that you may please God, and already are doing, you will do more so. For you know what commandments we have given you in our Lord Jesus. For this is the will of God, namely your sanctification, that you should refrain from all fornication, that each one of you should know how to keep his possessions in sanctification and honor; and not through lustful passion, as the rest of the people do who do not know God; and that no one should take advantage of or exploit his brother in this regard, because our Lord is the avenger of such matters, as we also have forewarned you about and testified to. For God has not called you to uncleanness but to holiness. Therefore, whoever commits an injustice does not wrong a human being but God who has granted you his Spirit, she who is holy.

ETHIOPIC TEXTS

1 Enoch 5:7–9

For the elect there shall be light and joy and peace, and they shall inherit the earth. But for you, the godless, there shall be a curse. Then shall Wisdom be granted to the elect, and all of them shall live and sin no more, either through witlessness or pride, for those who possess Wisdom shall be humble. In an intelligent person she is illumination, and to the prudent she is understanding; and they shall not return to sin again. Thus they shall not be condemned all the days of their lives, nor die because of divine fury or wrath. But they shall complete the number of the days of their lives, and their lives shall grow increasingly in peace, and the years of their joy shall be multiplied forever in gladness and eternal peace all the days of their lives.

1 Enoch 42:1–2

Wisdom found no place
where she might dwell,
so a dwelling place was found
for her in the heavens.
Wisdom went forth in order to dwell
among the children of Adam,
but she found no dwelling place,
thus she permanently took her seat in
the midst of the angels.

VULGATE TEXTS

Deuteronomy 32:9–11 VULG

The Lord's portion is his people,
Jacob the lot of his inheritance.
He found him in a deserted land,
in a place of horror, of vast wilderness.
He led him around and taught him,
took care of him like the apple of his eye.
As the eagle provoking her nestlings to fly,
hovering over them,
she spread her wings and took him up,
carrying him on his shoulder.

Psalm 109:1–7 VULG

1. The Lord said to my Lord,
"Sit at my right hand
until I make your enemies
your footstool."

2. The Lord will send forth the scepter
of your power out of Sion
to rule in the midst of your enemies.

3. With you is the principality
in the day of your might
in the splendor of the saints.
From the womb before the daystar,
I gave birth to you.

4. The Lord has sworn a solemn oath
and will not renege:
"You are a priest forever
according to the Order of
Melchisedech."

5. The Lord at your right hand
has shattered kings on the day
of his wrath.

6. He will pass judgment among
the nations
filling up the gaping holes.
He will crush heads
in the populous lands.

7. He will drink from the torrent
by the wayside,
therefore he will raise up his head.

PRAYING—WITH THE SAINTS—TO GOD OUR MOTHER

Proverbs 1:20, 22 VULG versicle

Wisdom preaches abroad,
in the open gates of the city,
she proffers her word, saying:
"O children, how long will you love
childishness?"

Proverbs 8:22–25 VULG

Wisdom recounts:
"The Lord possessed me in the beginning of his ways,
before he made anything else
from the beginning.
I was established from eternity,
from antiquity before the earth
was made.
The depths did not yet exist,
and I was already conceived,
neither had the fountains
of water erupted.
The mountains with their heavy mass
were not yet constituted,
before the hills came into being,
I was given birth to.

Song of Songs 1:1–3 VULG

Let him kiss me with the kisses
of his mouth!
Your breasts are far better than wine.
Your breathed name is better than
the fragrance of diffused ointments.
This is why the young maidens love you.
Draw me! We will run after you.
The king has brought me
into his chambers,
We will rejoice and be glad in you.
The memory of your breasts is better
than wine.
How right it is to love you!

Sirach 4:1–11 VULG

My child, don't defraud
the poor of alms;
and don't turn your eyes
away from the poor.
Do not heap grief on the hungry;
and do not exasperate the downtrodden.
Do not afflict someone in distress;
and do not defer giving
to those in anguish.
Do not belittle the request
of the afflicted;
and do not turn your face
away from the beggar.
Avert not your eyes from the destitute
due to disgust,
and give no petitioner grounds to curse
you in return.
For the prayer of someone who curses
you in bitterness,
shall be heard, for his Creator will hear.
Make yourself a friend of the community
of the poor;
humble your attitude before your elders;
and bow your head in respect
before the great.
Incline your ear to the poor;
and pay your debts;
answer peacefully with words full
of mildness.
Deliver those who suffer injustice, out of
the hands of the powerful;
and do not be fainthearted
in your spirit.
In judging be merciful to the orphan
like a father,
and as a husband
to their widowed mother.
Thus you shall be like an obedient child
to the Most High,
and he will have more tender mercy
towards you than a mother.

Sirach 4:12–21 VULG

Wisdom inspires life into her children,
protects those who seek after her,
and leads them in the path of justice.
Whoever loves her, loves life,
and those who watch for her shall embrace her sweetness.
Those who hold her fast
shall inherit life;
and wherever she enters, God will give a blessing.
Those who serve her shall be servants to the Holy One,
and God loves those who love her.
Whoever listens to her
shall judge nations;
and whoever fixes his gaze upon her
shall remain secure.
Whoever trusts her, shall inherit her,
and his progeny shall be confirmed.
She walks with him in the midst
of temptation,
at first she chooses him.
She will bring upon him, fear, dread, and trials;
and she tries him in the crucible
of her discipline
until she tests him with her precepts
and trusts his soul.
Then she shall strengthen him,
and make his paths straight,
giving him joy.
And she shall disclose her
secrets to him,
enriching him with treasures of knowledge and understanding of justice.

Sirach 24:1–11 VULG

Wisdom shall laud her own self
and in God she shall be honored,
in the midst of her people
she shall glory,
in the congregations of the Most High
shall open her mouth,
in the sight of his power shall glory,
in the midst of the people be exalted,
in the holy assembly be admired,
in the multitude of the elect be praised,
and among the blessed she shall be blessed, saying:
I came forth from the mouth of the Most High,
the firstborn before all creatures.
I was made in heaven so that an inexhaustible light might rise
and as a mist I covered all the earth.
I dwelt in the heights
and my throne is in a column of cloud.
I alone have encompassed
the circuit of heaven
and into the depths
of the abyss penetrated,
and in the waves of the sea walked,
and in all the earth stood,
and in every people and in every nation
I have held primacy.
By my power I trod through every high and low heart,
and in all of these I sought rest;
I shall abide in God's inheritance.

Sirach 24:4, 12–21 VULG

In the multitude of the elect Wisdom
will be praised,
and among the blessed she shall be blessed, saying:
Then the Creator or all commanded and spoke to me,
and the One who created me found rest
in my tabernacle
and said to me:
"Dwell in Jacob,
and in Israel claim inheritance;
Strike root in my elect."

From the beginning, before the ages,
I was created,
and to the world to come, I shall not
cease to be;
and in the holy dwelling place I ministered in his presence.
And thus I was established in Zion
and in the sanctified city
I similarly rested;
in Jerusalem was power set.
I struck root in an honorable people
and in the portion of my God,
his inheritance,
and in the full assembly of the saints is
my abode.
Like a cedar in Lebanon was I exalted,
and like a cypress on Mount Zion.
Like a palm tree in Cades was I exalted,
and like a rosebush in Jericho.
Like a splendid olive tree in the fields
and a planetree by waters on the plane
path, I was exalted.
Like cinnamon and aromatic balm,
I produced fragrance;
like choice myrrh I wafted
a sweet aroma,
like storax, galbanum, onycha,
and aloes,
and like uncrushed frankincense
I perfumed my dwelling;
and my fragrance is as pure balsam.

Sirach 24:4, 22–31 VULG

In the multitude of the elect Wisdom
will be praised,
and among the blessed she shall be
blessed, saying:
"Like a terebinth I have stretched out
my branches,
and my branches are dignity and grace.
Like a vine I have yielded fruit and a
sweet fragrance,
and my flowers are the fruit of honor
and respectability.
I am the mother of fair love
and of reverence,
of knowledge and of holy hope.
In me is all grace of the way
and of truth,
in me all hope of life and of virtue.
Turn to me all who love me
and be filled with my generativity.
For my spirit is sweeter than honey,
and my inheritance better than honey
and the honeycomb.
My memory endures to unending
generations.
They who eat me, shall hunger still;
and they who drink me,
still thirst they will.
Whoever hears me shall
not be confounded,
and they who operate through me
will not sin.
Whoever elucidates me will have
eternal life."

Sirach 24:39 VULG versicle

Wisdom's thoughts are more unbounded than the sea,
and her counsels more deep than the
great ocean.

Sirach 24:40–47 VULG

I, Wisdom, have poured forth rivers.
I am like a watercourse out of a river
from immense waters;
I, like a channel of a river,
and like an aqueduct,
flowed out of paradise.
I said, "I will water my garden of plants
and abundantly irrigate the fruits of my
meadow."

Lo and behold, my watercourse overflowed,
and my river came close to being a sea.
For I cause doctrine to shine forth like the morning light,
and I will announce it
to the distant shores.
I will penetrate to the deepest parts of the earth,
gaze upon all who are sleeping,
and illuminate all who hope in God.
I will continue to pour forth doctrine as prophecy
and bequeath it to those
who seek wisdom,
and not cease to instruct their progeny,
even until the holy Age arrives.
Therefore see that I have not labored for myself alone,
but for all who diligently seek the truth.

Wisdom 6:23–24 VULG

Love the light of Wisdom,
all you who preside over peoples.
Now what Wisdom is,
and what was her origin,
I will declare.
I will not hide from you the mysteries of God,
but will investigate her from the beginning of her birth,
and bring to light knowledge of her.
I will not pass over the truth.

Isaiah 1:2 VULG

Hear O heavens, and give ear O earth,
for the Lord has spoken,
I have suckled children
and reared them,
but they have spurned me.

Isaiah 46:3–5 VULG

Listen to me, O house of Jacob,
and all the remnant of the house of Israel,
you who are carried by my uterus,
you who are borne by my womb:
Even to your old age I remain the same,
and to your gray hairs I will carry you.
I made you and I will bear you;
I will carry and I will save.
To whom have you likened me and equated me,
compared me and made me similar?

Isaiah 66:9–13 VULG

Shall I who cause others to give birth,
myself not give birth, says the Lord?
Shall I who grant generation to others,
myself be barren, demands the Lord your God?
Rejoice with Jerusalem,
and be glad with her,
all you who love her.
Rejoice for joy with her,
all you who mourn for her;
that you may suck and be filled
with the breast of her abundant consolation;
that you may extract milk
and flow with delights
from the abundance of her glory.
For thus says the Lord,
I will bring upon her,
as it were, a river of peace,
like an overflowing torrent—
the glory of the nations,
which you shall suck;
you shall be carried at the breasts,
and upon the knees
they shall caress you.
As one whom a mother caresses,
so shall I comfort you,

and you shall be comforted
in Jerusalem.

Hosea 1:10 & 2:1, 14 VULG

And the number of the children of Israel
shall be as the sands of the sea,
that is without measure,
and they shall not be numbered.
And it shall come to pass in the place
where it will be said to them:
"You are not my people";
it will be proclaimed:
"You are children of the Living God!"

Say to your brothers,
"You are my People,"
and to your sisters, "You have obtained
loving kindness." . . .
Therefore, behold,
I will suckle her with milk,
and I will lead her into a solitary place,
and I will speak to her heart.

Matthew 23:37–39 VULG

"Jerusalem, Jerusalem, you who kill the prophets and stone those who are sent to you! How often I wanted to gather your children together just as a hen gathers her little chickens under her wings, but you refused. Behold your house will be left to you desolate. Therefore I tell you, you will not see me again until you say: 'Blessed is the one who comes in the name of the Lord.'"

4 Esdras 1:22–30 VULG

Thus says the Lord Almighty, "When you were in the desert, at the bitter stream, and blaspheming my name, I did not rain down fire upon you for your blasphemies; instead I cast a beam into the water and made the stream sweet. What am I to do with you, O Jacob? You would not obey me, O Judah. I shall turn to other nations and give them my name so that they will keep my statutes. Because you have forsaken me, I myself shall forsake you; when you beg me for mercy, I will show you no mercy. When you call upon me, I will not listen to you; for you have defiled your hands with blood, and your feet are swift to commit murder. It is not as though you have forsaken me, rather you have forsaken yourselves," declares the Lord.

Thus says the Lord Almighty, "Have I not entreated you as a father does his sons, as a mother pleads with her daughters, and as a nursemaid with her children, that you should be my people and I should be your God, that you should be my children and I should be your father? I gathered you as a hen gathers her brood under her wings. But now, what am I to do with you?"

Suggested Alternative Doxologies

Gender Neutral

1. Glory be to the Trinity: to God Almighty, to the Divine Word and to Wisdom—the Spirit, as it was in the beginning is now and ever shall be world without end. Amen. (Based on Theophilus of Antioch, *Ad Autolycum* 2:15 combined with 1.7)

2. Glory be to the Holy Trinity: Mind and Word and Spirit, one in relationship and divinity; as it was in the beginning is now and ever shall be world without end. Amen. (Based on Gregory of Nazianzus, *Oratio* 12.1)

3. Glory be to the Triune God, from whom, through whom, and in whom all things exist; as it was in the beginning is now and ever shall be world without end. Amen. (Based on Augustine, *De doctrina christiana* 1.5; PL 34:21B)

4. Glory be to God Almighty with the Only-Begotten and with the Holy and Life-Giving Spirit, now and always and for all eternity. Amen. (Based on Cyril of Jerusalem, *Catechetica* 7.16)

5. Glory be to the Begetter, to the Only-Begotten, and to God's Holy Spirit; as it was in the beginning is now and ever shall be world without end. Amen.

6. Glory be to God Almighty, to the Only-Begotten and to God's Holy Spirit; as it was in the beginning is now and ever shall be world without end. Amen.

7. Glory be to you, O God Almighty and to your Only-Begotten and to your Holy Spirit, as it was in the beginning is now and ever shall be world without end. Amen.

8. Glory be to the Progenitor and to the Offspring and to the Emission, as it was in the beginning is now and ever shall be world without end. Amen.

9. Glory be to the Progenitor and to the Offspring and to the Effluence, as it was in the beginning is now and ever shall be world without end. Amen.

10. Glory be to the Unbegotten and to the Only-Begotten and to the Emitted, as it was in the beginning is now and ever shall be world without end. Amen.

PRAYING—WITH THE SAINTS—TO GOD OUR MOTHER

11. Glory be to the Holy Trinity: the Anointer, the Anointed, and the Anointing, as it was in the beginning is now and ever shall be world without end. Amen. (Based on Gregory of Nyssa, *In inscriptiones Psalmorum* 2.11)

12. Glory to you O Unoriginate, and to you O Only-Begotten; glory to you, O Holy Spirit, proceeding from the former and resting on the latter; as it was in the beginning is now and ever shall be world without end. Amen. (Based on a monastic doxology from Mt. Athos)

13. Glory to the Trinity, Three Persons in Unity, as it was in the beginning, is now and always for all eternity. Amen.

14. Glory to the Trinity, Three Persons in Unity, as it was from all eternity, is now into infinity. Amen.

15. Glory to God in the Holy Trinity,
    Word and Spirit in sublime unity,
    One in Godhead and full divinity,
    Three in Persons of equal majesty.

16. Glory to our God almighty and supreme,
    and praise to the Word, Wisdom's eternal sweet theme;
    glory to the Spirit, love's eternal warm beam,
    to the Three in One, whom equally we esteem.

FEMININE FORMULAE

17. Glory be to the Mother and to the Offspring and to the Breath of Life, as it was in the beginning is now and ever shall be world without end. Amen.

18. Glory be to the Generative Womb and to the Offspring and to the Heartbeat, as it was in the beginning is now and ever shall be world without end. Amen.

19. Glory be to God the Mother and Daughter Wisdom and the Spirit of Truth, as it was in the beginning is now and ever shall be world without end. Amen.

20. Glory be to El Shaddai, Hokmah, and Ruach, one in relationship and divinity; as it was in the beginning is now and ever shall be world without end. Amen.

The above doxology was created from biblical feminine names: *hokmah* is Hebrew for "wisdom" (here applied to the Second Person) and *ruach* is Hebrew for "spirit." However, such a doxology will be experientially void of meaning until one has prayed over the Scriptures and personally appropriated them.

Thematic Readings for Non-Feast Days

as when speaking about God one uses the terms, sleep, wrath, indifference, hands, and even feet, and the like.

But we both know and confess that God is without beginning and without end, eternal and everlasting, uncreated, unchangeable, inalterable, simple, uncompounded, incorporeal, invisible, impalpable, uncircumscribed, infinite, incomprehensible, indefinable, unfathomable, good, just, maker of all created reality, all-powerful, all-ruling, all-seeing, the provider, the sovereign, and the judge of all. We likewise know and confess that God is one, that is to say, one essence that is known and has being in three Persons . . . one in all things except in the being unbegotten, the being begotten, and the procession.

Day 2

Morning Prayer

Antiphon: Who could ever know the mind of God?

Psalm 41:1–11 ✠ Psalm 56:1–11 ✠ Psalm 102:1–22

Scripture: Isaiah 55:6–9

Reading: St. Cyril of Jerusalem, bishop, Father and Doctor of the Church † 386

Catechetical Lectures 6.6–7

The One who was brought forth without change from all eternity knows the One who begot, and the One who begot knows the One who is brought forth. Since then angels are ignorant [regarding the nature of the Divine begetting]—for, as we have previously said, the Only-Begotten reveals things with and through the Holy Spirit to each angel according to its capacity, let no human being be ashamed to admit ignorance.

Right now I am speaking out loud, and all people do so on occasion, but exactly how we speak, we cannot properly say. How then can I describe in detail the One who gives the power of speech? I have a soul, yet I am incapable of talking about its characteristics. How then shall I be able to discourse about the Giver of souls?

For spiritual devotion it suffices us simply to know that we have a God, a God who is One, a God who Is, who is eternal, ever the self-same, without a progenitor, with none mightier, no successor to expel the sovereign, who is honored by many titles, is all-powerful, and in substance uniform. For although God is called Good, Righteous, Almighty, Sabaoth, this does not mean that there is any variation or difference in God, but rather, that being One and the Same, God is the source of countless operations flowing from the Godhead. God does not exceed in measure in one thing and experience deficiency in another, but rather is in all things God's own self. God is not abounding in loving-kindness and therefore diminished in wisdom, but possesses wisdom to the same degree as loving-kindness.

Evening Prayer

Antiphon: You have never seen God's form.

Psalm 1:1–6 ✠ Psalm 35:5–12 ✠ Psalm 56:1–11

Scripture: John 1:15–18 NT

Reading: St. Cyril of Jerusalem, bishop, Father and Doctor of the Church † 386

Catechetical Lectures 6.7–8

God is holy and almighty, surpassing all things in goodness, majesty, and wisdom, concerning whom we can declare neither form nor shape. For *you have never heard his voice or seen his form*, says the Sacred Scripture. Therefore Moses says to the Israelites, *Be strictly on your guard concerning your very souls, for you saw no form*. For if it is totally impossible to imagine God's likeness, how will thought even approach God's substance?

Many have been the imaginations of many people, yet all have failed. Some have speculated God to be fire; others like a winged person, because of a beautiful text, badly perverted, *You shall hide me under the shadow of your wings*. They have neglected that our Lord Jesus Christ, the Only-Begotten, spoke in a similar manner concerning himself to Jerusalem, *How often would I have gathered your children together, as a hen gathers her young under her wings, but you would not*. For while God's protective power is compared to shielding wings, failing to understand, they sank to the level of human affairs, and conceived of God's unsearchable Being in terms of human experience.

Day 3

Morning Prayer

Antiphon: You cannot find an exact equivalent when translating from one language to another.

Psalm 54:1–16 ✠ Psalm 16:1–15 ✠ Psalm 60:1–8

Scripture: Sirach Prologue 1–26

Reading: St. Jerome, priest, Father and Doctor of the Church † 420

Letter to Pope Damasus 18B

The Septuagint version reads: "And one [*unum*] of the seraphim was sent to me"; Aquila's and Theodotion's versions have: "And one [*unum*] of the seraphim flew to me"; Symmachus has: "And one [*unus*] of the seraphim flew to me." Every day a seraph is sent to us, daily the lips of those who groan and utter: *Woe is me because I have felt remorse*, are cleansed, and when they have been freed from their sins, they prepare themselves for God's service.

Now regarding the use of "flew" by the other interpreters instead of "was sent," understand this as referring to the swift coming of the divine message to us who are deigned worthy of association with God. There is a difference in gender in the translations as well. The Septuagint, Aquila, and Theodotion render seraphim in the neuter gender, while Symmachus has it in the masculine. It is unthinkable that sex exists among God's angelic spirits, since even the Holy Spirit according to the grammatical rules of the Hebrew language is expressed in the feminine gender: *ruach*; in Greek by the neuter: *to pneuma*; and in Latin in the masculine: *spiritus*.

Thus we must understand that when there is a discussion regarding the above and when something is rendered in the masculine or the feminine, it is does not so much signify sex as indicate a linguistic idiom; on the one hand God himself, the Invisible and Incorruptible, is propounded in almost all languages in the masculine grammatical gender, whereas sex does not pertain to God.

Evening Prayer

Antiphon: In the Divine Nature there is no sexual gender.

Psalm 6:1–10 ✠ Psalm 62:1–11 ✠ Psalm 35:5–12

Scripture: Galatians 3:23–28

Reading: St. Jerome, priest, Father and Doctor of the Church † 420

Commentary on Isaiah XI 40.9–11

According to the Hebrew language Spirit is feminine in gender, and in our own Latin language Spirit is masculine in gender, and the Greek word is neuter. Therefore, in the Divine Nature there is no sexual gender.

Letter to Pope Damasus 18B

Thus we must understand that when there is a discussion regarding the above and when something is rendered in the masculine or the feminine, it is does not so much signify sex as indicate a linguistic idiom; on the one hand God himself, the Invisible and Incorruptible, is propounded in almost all languages in the masculine grammatical gender, whereas sex does not pertain to God.

Day 4

Morning Prayer

Antiphon: May one illumination come upon us from the One God, one in diversity and diverse in unity, which is a paradox. (Gregory of Nazianzus *Theological Orations* 28.1)

Psalm 64:1–13 ✠ Psalm 2:1–12 ✠ Psalm 118:9–16

Scripture: Genesis 1:26–27 TNK

Reading: St. Gregory Nazianzus, Patriarch, Father and Doctor of the Church † 389

Theological Orations 29.2

The three predominant opinions concerning God are Anarchy, Polyarchy, and Monarchy. The first two are the sport of the children of the Greeks; let them play with their ideas! Now Anarchy is something lacking order, and Polyarchy is factious and thus leads to anarchy and disorder. Demonstrably, both of these lead to the same thing: disorder, and this in turn to dissolution, for disorder is the first sign of dissolution. But Monarchy is what we esteem, a monarchy, however, that is not limited to one Person. For it is possible that Unity, if at variance with itself, attains a state of plurality, but one which is constituted by an equality of nature and concordance of will, as well as identity of movement and convergence of its constituents to unity—something which is inconceivable for created nature—so that while numerically distinct there is no division of essence. Therefore, Unity, from all eternity, having arrived by motion to Duality, culminated itself in Trinity. This is what we mean by Father and Son and Holy Spirit, namely first, the Progenitor and Emitter, without passion, of course, and without any time or in any corporeal manner, as well as second, the Offspring, and third, the Emission. For I do not know how to express this in terms completely devoid of visual things. . . . Let us confine ourselves, therefore, within our human limitations, and speak of the Unbegotten and the Begotten and That which Proceeds from the Father.

Evening Prayer

Antiphon: Thanks be to God for God's inexpressible gift: God's very self!

Psalm 91:1–15 ✠ Psalm 46:1–8 ✠ Psalm 9:1–10

Scripture: Revelation 21:1–7

Reading: St. Gregory of Nyssa, bishop, Father and Doctor of the Church † ca. 395

Against Eunomius 2:144–46, 148–49

While we avoid all manner of concurrence with any absurd notion in our thoughts about God, we utilize a great variety of designations for him, adapting our terminology to various concepts. Because no single title has been discovered to encompass the Divine Nature directly applicable to the subject itself, we therefore employ many titles, each person according to various interests attaining some particular idea about God, attempting to designate the Divinity, as we hunt among the pluriform variety of terms, for the one to shed some light on our understanding regarding the One we seek. When we ask ourselves and inquire about what the Divinity is, we propound various responses. . . .

PRAYING—WITH THE SAINTS—TO GOD OUR MOTHER

I claim, therefore, that people have the right to such word-building, adapting the appellations to their subject as each person deems fit, and that what our controversialist sets forth as some dreaded, frightening, bogy-monster is not in fact monstrous. Likewise, I claim that we are justified in permitting the use of neologisms in respect to everything that can be named, and in the case of God as well. Now God is not an expression, nor does God's being consist in speech or sound. Rather, God is, according to himself, whatever by faith God is believed to be, while what is named by those who speak about God is not what God actually is, for the nature of the One who Is, is inexpressible. Yet God receives his titles from what are believed to be God's actions regarding our life.

Day 5

Morning Prayer

Antiphon: Your womb, O God, is beyond comprehension!

Psalm 72:1–28 ✠ Psalm 8:1–10 ✠ Psalm 138:1–14

Scripture: Job 28:20–27 TNK

Reading: St. Ephrem, deacon, Father and Doctor of the Church † 373

Hymns on Virginity 52.6–7

> You have humbled the pride of those who boldly dispute.
> You have silenced the voice of assailing researchers.
> You have confounded the faction of attacking scrutinizers.
> They hoped to investigate your Light,
> but your immensity could not be grasped so as to be investigated.
> Your manifestation could not be dissected so as to be comprehended.
> Your outflowing could not be quelled so as to measure your Source.
> You have hidden yourself in your Parent.
> If his Womb can be investigated, then its Offspring can be comprehended as well.
> Your being brought forth confounds us and is beyond comprehension,
> and your seeking out overtakes us and is unsearchable.
> Your Light fills us but is unable to be held.
> Who has searched out our Sun?
> Your extent cannot be seized that we could know it.
> Your manifestation is beyond grasp that we could measure it.
> If the Supreme Being were comprehensible, the bringing forth could be investigated.
> If the Parent had been interpreted,
> then it would be easy for his Offspring to be explained.

God Is beyond Human Description

Day 1

Morning Prayer

Antiphon: From the greatness and beauty of creation, we may, by analogy, contemplate their original Author. (Wisdom 13:5)

Psalm 5:1–12 ✠ Psalm 8:1–9 ✠ Psalm 148:1–14

Scripture: Wisdom 13:1–5

Reading: St. John of Damascus, priest, Father and Doctor of the Church † 749

The Orthodox Faith 1.11
    Since in Divine Scripture we find many things said symbolically concerning God as if God possessed a body, it is necessary to realize that because we are human beings clothed in this thick mantle of flesh, we are incapable of thinking or speaking about the divine, sublime, and immaterial operations of the Godhead without making use of images, types, and symbols that correspond to our own nature. That being the case, everything that is said about God as if God were corporeal is said symbolically and contains a loftier meaning, for the Deity is simple and formless. . . . Thus, to state matters simply, all the things which are said about God as if God existed in a body, these statements contain some hidden meaning, and through things relating to our nature, instruct us about matters which transcend our nature.

Evening Prayer

Antiphon: We are incapable of thinking or speaking about the divine, sublime, and immaterial operations of the Godhead unless we make use of images, types, and symbols that correspond to our own nature. (John of Damascus *Orthodox Faith* 1:11)

Psalm 133:1–3 ✠ Psalm 18:1–14 ✠ Psalm 8:1–9

Scripture: 1 Timothy 6:11–16

Reading: St. John of Damascus, priest, Father and Doctor of the Church † 749

The Orthodox Faith 1.2
    What can be known is one matter, and what can be expressed another; just as it is one thing to speak, and yet quite another to know. Moreover, many of the things pertaining to God which are faintly perceived cannot be appropriately described, so that we are required to express in human conceptions things which transcend us, such

Evening Prayer

Antiphon: The Spirit reaches the inner depths of God.

Psalm 15:1–11 ✠ Psalm 50:1–19 ✠ Psalm 138:1–14

Scripture: 1 Corinthians 1:18–25; 2:6–10

Reading: St. Ephrem, deacon, Father and Doctor of the Church † 373

Hymns on the Nativity 13.7–9

> If anyone seeks your Hidden Nature
> behold it dwells in heaven in the immense Womb of Divinity!
> And if anyone seeks your visible body,
> behold it rests and peers out from the minuscule womb of Mary!
> The intellect becomes lost among your many attributes O Rich One!
> Chamber upon inner chamber are in your Divinity,
> contemptible spectacles in your humanity.
> Who will fathom you, O Immense Ocean, who reduced yourself?
> We sought to see you as God, but lo, you are a human being.
> We sought to see you as a man, but lo, the ensign of your divinity is resplendent.
> Who can bear your contrariety O True One?

Day 6

Morning Prayer

Antiphon: Now we see as in a mirror.

Psalm 91:1–15 ✠ Psalm 118:17–24 ✠ Psalm 118:25–32

Scripture: Hosea 1:10; 2:1, 14 VULG

Reading: St. Francis de Sales, bishop, Doctor of the Church † 1622

Treatise Concerning the Love of God 3.11

> For just as the mirror doesn't contain the thing itself that one sees in it but only the representation and species of it (which representation, fixed by the mirror, produces another in the eye of the beholder), in the same manner, the word of faith doesn't contain the things it announces but only represents them. And this representation of divine matters, which is in the word of faith, thereby produces yet another, that our understanding, aided by God's grace, accepts and receives as a representation of holy truth. Thus, our will delights in it and embraces it as an honorable, profitable, lovable, and excellent truth. In this way, the truths signified in the Word of God are by it represented to our understanding as things reflected in the mirror and through the mirror, represented to the eye, so that, as the great Apostle declared, to believe is to *see as in a mirror*.

But in heaven, Theotimus, O my God, what blessings! The Divinity will unite herself to our understanding, without the mediation of any species or representation whatsoever, but she will apply herself and join herself to our comprehension, making herself so present to it, that this intimate presence will take the place of any representation or species. O Good God! What sweetness for human understanding, to be forever united with its sovereign object, receiving not its representation but its very presence, not the image or species, but the very essence of divine Truth and Majesty! There we shall be like most happy children of the Divinity, having the honor to be nourished with her divine substance itself, imbibed by our soul, through the mouth of our understanding. And what surpasses all sweetness is, that just as mothers are not content to nourish their little babies with their milk, which is their own substance, but they even put the nipple of their breast into its mouth, so that these infants might receive their mother's substance not in a spoon or some other instrument, but even in and by their own substance—thus the maternal substance serves not only as conduit but also as nourishment to be received by the dearly beloved nursling. So too God, our Father, is not content to make us receive his very substance in our understanding, that is to say, cause us to see his Divinity, but by a profundity of his sweetness he will himself apply his substance to our spirit, so that we no longer will understand it by means of species or representation but in and through itself, so that his paternal and eternal substance serves as species as well as the object of our understanding. Then shall be fulfilled in a most excellent manner these divine promises: *I will lead her into the wilderness and I will speak to her heart, and give her milk to suck*, and *Rejoice with Jerusalem and be glad with her, that you may suck and be filled with the breast of her consolation, that you may nurse and delight yourself in the overflowing abundance of her glory; you shall be carried at the breasts, and caressed upon the knees.*

The Divine Nature Possesses Feminine Qualities

Day 1

Morning Prayer

Antiphon: Our God is beyond all telling.

Psalm 107:1–6 ✠ Psalm 29:1–12 ✠ Psalm 88:1–28

Scripture: Wisdom 13:1–5

Reading: Minucius Felix, apologist † second century

Octavius 18.7–8

Look at some other examples: bees have but one ruler, flocks have one leader, herds have one head. Regarding heaven, could you possibly believe that the Supreme Power is divided, that the absolute majesty of this truly divine Empire is sundered in twain, when it is evident that God, who is the Parent of all, has neither beginning nor end? God, who brings all manner of life to birth while being self-eternal existed before the world ever was, and was a world unto God's very self. The self-same orders all things by the Word, disposes all by Reason, and by Virtue perfects each and everything that has being.

This God cannot be seen, is too bright for sight, cannot be comprehended, is too pure to be touched, cannot be measured; is too great for our senses, of infinite and immeasurable dimensions being known to God alone. But we possess an understanding that is too constricted to comprehend, and thus we properly measure God when we declare God to be beyond all measurement. In my honest opinion, whoever supposes to know the magnitude of God, diminishes it; and whoever does not wish to diminish it, does not pretend to know it. Neither should you seek a name for God—"God" is the name. We employ titles to distinguish individuals from the masses, such as personal names and designations. But for God who is unique, the term God sums it all up. Were I to say "Father," you would imagine something terrestrial. Were I to say, "King," you would suspect something composed of flesh; if "Lord," you would envision someone mortal. Remove the names piled up and you will clearly perceive God's splendor.

Evening Prayer

Antiphon: God is highly esteemed in God's many facets.

Psalm 18:1–14 ✠ Psalm 117:8–26 ✠ Psalm 118:33–40

Scripture: Titus 3:4–8

Reading: An Apostolic Father of the Church, mid second century

Letter to Diognetus 9.2–6

O how exceedingly great is God's friendship and love for humanity! God neither hated us, nor rejected us, nor remembered our sins, but was long-suffering and patient, and in mercy took our sins upon himself. God gave us his own Son as a ransom for us—the Holy One for the wicked, the Pure One for the evil, the Just One for the unjust, the Incorrupt One for the corrupt, the Immortal for the mortal. For what else but divine righteousness could have covered up our sins? In whom was it possible for us lawless and ungodly people to have been justified if not in the Son of God alone? O sweet exchange! O inscrutable divine operation! O unexpected benefits! That the wickedness of many should be hidden in one righteous person, and the righteousness of One should justify many sinners.

While in former times God convinced us that our human nature is incapable of obtaining life, now God reveals a savior capable of saving those who are incapable. For both of these reasons God wanted us to believe in his loving-kindness and esteem him as Nursing Mother, Father, Teacher, Counselor, Healer, Mind, Light, Honor, Glory, Strength, and Life.

Day 2

Morning Prayer

Antiphon: God declares, I was like a loving parent towards them.

Psalm 118:145–52 ✠ Psalm 26:1–14 ✠ Psalm 118:41–48

Scripture: Hosea 11:1–4 TNK

Reading: Minucius Felix, apologist † second century

Octavius 19.14–15

Plato's language about God is clearer both in content and terminology; his discourse would be truly divine if it were not occasionally tainted by the incorporation of prejudices held by the populace. For Plato, in the Timaeus, God, by reason of this designation, is Parent of the universe, Architect of the soul, Constructor of everything in heaven and on earth; a Being difficult to discover, as Plato instructs us, by reason of its extraordinary and incredible power, and when discovered, impossible to describe in common everyday terms. This approach is pretty much the same as our own; we, likewise, recognize God whom we call Parent of All, but avoid talking about God in popular terms unless questioned.

Evening Prayer

Antiphon: People are without excuse for failing to recognize God, the Parent of all.

Psalm 21:1–11 ✠ Psalm 1:1–6 ✠ Psalm 102:1–22

Scripture: Romans 1:18–23

Reading: Minucius Felix, apologist † second century

Octavius 35.4–5

Those who do not know God are rightly afflicted for their impiety and wickedness; none but the irreligious doubt this. To totally ignore the Parent of all, the Lord of all, is just as criminal as to purposely offend God. Just as ignorance of God is sufficient grounds for punishment, knowledge regarding the same wins pardon.

Thematic Readings for Non-Feast Days

Day 3

Morning Prayer

Antiphon: El Shaddai has made an everlasting covenant with us.

Psalm 129:1–8 ✠ Psalm 118:65–72 ✠ Psalm 68:8–15 TNK

Scripture: Genesis 28:1–5 TNK

Reading: Syrian hymn, mid to late second century

Odes of Solomon 8.8–16

> Hear the Word of Truth,
> and receive the knowledge of the Most High.
> Your flesh may not understand what I am saying to you,
> nor your garment what I am manifesting to you
> Keep my mystery, you who are kept by it;
> keep my faith, you who are kept by it.
> And understand my knowledge, you who know me in truth;
> love my affection, you who love;
> for I shall not turn my face away from my own,
> because I know them.
> Even before they existed,
> I recognized them;
> and set a seal upon their faces.
> I fashioned their members,
> and my own breasts I prepared for them,
> that they might drink my holy milk and live by it.

Evening Prayer

Antiphon: For all alike, God is sustainer and nursing mother and king and judge (Irenaeus, *Proof of Apostolic Teaching* 8).

Psalm 118:49–56 ✠ Psalm 118:73–80 ✠ Psalm 131:1–3 TNK

Scripture: 1 Peter 1:25—2:3 NT

Reading: St. Irenaeus, bishop, Post-Apostolic Father of the Church † 202

Against Heresies 4.38.1

> If someone should object, "What? Could not God have made Man perfect from the beginning?" let that person know that for God, who is always the self-same and unbegotten, all things are possible. But created things, inasmuch as they have subsequently received their beginning of existence, must necessarily be inferior to the one

who created them. For it is impossible for things recently created to be uncreated. Now, precisely because they are not uncreated, they fall short of perfection; for, inasmuch as they are recently created, they are mere infants, and because they are infantile, they are neither accustomed to nor practiced in perfect conduct.

Now, just as a mother is capable of giving mature food to her newborn, but doesn't do so because it is as yet incapable of consuming such a nourishment well beyond its age, thus God likewise could have given from the very beginning, perfection to humanity; but humanity was incapable of receiving it, being still a little infant. And by the way, that is why our Lord, in these last times, having summed up all things within himself, came to us, not as he could have appeared, but as we were capable of seeing him. He easily could have come to us in his inexpressible glory, but in that case we never could have endured the greatness of the glory. Therefore, as to infants, the perfect Food of the Father offered himself to us as milk—this happened when he appeared as a man, so that we, being nourished, as it were, from the breast of his flesh, and having become accustomed by such a flow of milk to ingest and imbibe the Word of God, may be capable to contain within ourselves the Food of Immortality, which is the Spirit of the Father.

Day 4

Morning Prayer

Antiphon: I am the first and I am the last; there is no other God besides me.

Psalm 142:1–12 ✠ Psalm 17:1–31 ✠ Psalm 85:1–17

Scripture: Isaiah 48:12–16

Reading: St. Aphraates, priest, Father of the Church † ca. 350

Demonstrations 17.7

When God resolved to create the world with all of its splendor, God conceived and formed Adam in the womb of his thought. After he had conceived Adam by his reflection, then he conceived the creatures, as it is written: *Before the mountains were conceived or the earth was brought forth in labor.* For humanity is the elder, and according to her conception, she precedes the creatures. But as to what concerns coming to birth, the creatures are the elders, and they precede Adam. Adam was conceived and remained in the reflection of God.

And having thus conceived, God was resolute in thought; he created all the creatures by the word of his mouth. Now when he had finished and embellished the world so that nothing was lacking, then he gave birth to Adam from his reflection and molded man with his own hands. . . . After having conceived Adam and given birth to him, he granted him power over all his creation. This is what the prophet says: *Lord, you have been for us a dwelling place from generation to generation, before the mountains were conceived, before the earth was in its pangs, and before the universe was founded: from everlasting until forever you are the Lord.* It was so that no one dare imagine that there was another god, either in the beginning, or afterwards, that he said: *From everlasting until forever*, just as Isaiah said, *I am the first and I am the last*.

After having given birth to Adam from the womb of his reflection, God formed and breathed into Adam his Spirit; and he endowed him with the knowledge of discernment so that he might discern the good from the evil and know that God created him.

Evening Prayer

Antiphon: Like a child being weaned from its mother's breast, like a babe being weaned so is my soul within me.

Psalm 118:57–64 ✠ Psalm 130:1–3 ✠ Psalm 131:1–3 TNK

Scripture: 1 Corinthians 3:1–2 NT

Reading: St. Hilary of Poitiers, bishop, Father and Doctor of the Church † 367

Homilies on the Psalms 130.5

Then the psalmist continues, *Like a weaned child upon its mother's breast, so will you reward my soul.* We learn that when Isaac was weaned that Abraham held a feast because now that Isaac was weaned he was about to enter boyhood and was passing beyond milk as food. The Apostle feeds with the milk of knowledge all who are immature in the faith and still babes in the things of God. The greatest possible advance, therefore, is to cease needing milk. By a joyful feast Abraham proclaimed that his son had attained stronger food. Likewise, the Apostle denies bread to the carnally minded and those who are little ones in Christ. Thus the prophet prays that because he has not exalted his heart nor walked among things great and wonderful which are beyond him, and because he did not experience humiliation but rather raised his soul to God, that God may reward his soul, lying like a weaned child upon its mother's breast.

Day 5

Morning Prayer

Antiphon: We ought to love God more than our own mother.

Psalm 5:1–12 ✠ Psalm 26:1–14 ✠ Psalm 102:1–22

Scripture: Isaiah 1:1–4

Reading: St. Basil the Great, bishop, Father and Doctor of the Church † 379

The Long Rules 2.2

If the affection of children for their parents is a natural sentiment which is manifested in the instincts of animals and in the predisposition of humans to love their mother from infancy, let us not be less intelligent than children, nor more stupid than wild beasts, by remaining unloving and alienating ourselves from the God who created us. Even if we have not learned from the divine goodness what God's being actually is, nevertheless, we should, by the very fact that we are created, experience an extraordinary love for God and possess a constant remembrance of God as children do for their mother.

Evening Prayer

Antiphon: The One who formed Adam, formed Eve as well; both male and female were fashioned by the Divine Hands (Cyril of Jerusalem, *Catechetical Lectures* 12.26).

Psalm 140:1–5 ✠ Psalm 8:1–9 ✠ Psalm 138:1–14

Scripture: Romans 1:16–20

Reading: St. Cyril of Jerusalem, bishop, Father and Doctor of the Church † 386

Catechetical Lectures 9.2, 15

It is impossible to see the Divine Nature with eyes of the flesh, but from the divine operations it is possible to arrive at some conception of God's power. According to the words of Solomon, *From the greatness and beauty of created things, their Creator is seen, by way of analogy.* . . . Well then enter into your own self and from your own nature consider its Artisan. What fault is there to find in the constitution of your body? Be master of yourself and nothing base will proceed from your members. From the beginning, Adam was naked with Eve in Paradise, but it was not because of his physical nature that he was cast out. The physical nature then is not the cause of sin, but rather those who abuse their physical nature, for the Maker of the physical nature is all-wise.

Who was it that prepared the recesses of the womb for childbearing? Who gave the breath of life to the lifeless thing within it? *Who knit us together with sinews and bones, and clothed us with skin and flesh,* and as soon as the infant is born brings forth fountains of milk from the breasts? . . . You see, O mortal, the Artisan; you behold the Wise Creator.

Day 6

Morning Prayer

Antiphon: God gives birth to creation made in her image.

Psalm 41:1–11 ✠ Psalm 18:1–14 ✠ Psalm use: Job 37:22–23 TNK

Scripture: Job 38:1–3, 22–29; 40:2 TNK

Reading: St. Cyril of Jerusalem, bishop, Father and Doctor of the Church † 386

Catechetical Lectures 9.2, 9

It is impossible to see the Divine Nature with eyes of the flesh, but from the divine operations it is possible to arrive at some conception of God's power. According to the words of Solomon, *From the greatness and beauty of created things, their Creator is seen, by way of analogy....*

Who is the father of the rain? Or who gave birth to the drops of dew? Who condensed the air into clouds, and commanded they carry the water of rain showers, sometimes *bringing golden-hued clouds from the north*, sometimes transforming them all, uniform in appearance, and again changing them into various orbs and other shapes? Who is wise enough to count the clouds? Regarding which in Job it says, *He knows the differences of the clouds, and has bent the heavens down to earth*; and *who counts the clouds by wisdom*, and *the cloud is not torn asunder beneath him.* For although so many measures of water rest upon the clouds, they are not torn asunder, but come down upon the earth in all good order. *Who is the one who brings forth the winds from their storehouses? Who gave birth*, as we mentioned before, *to the drops of dew? Out of whose womb come forth the crystals of ice?*

Evening Prayer

Antiphon: God will never abandon us.

Psalm 133:1–3 ✠ Psalm 26:1–14 ✠ Psalm 131:1–3 TNK

Scripture: Hebrews 13:5–9

Reading: St. Macarius the Great, Desert Father of the Church † 391

Collection of Homilies III 27.3

It isn't true, as some claim who are led astray by misleading teachings, that Man is dead once and for all, and is thus incapable of accomplishing anything good. For an infant, even if it still isn't able to do anything productive, finding itself incapable of standing on its own two feet in order to approach its mother, nevertheless, rolls around, screams, and cries, searching for its mother. And because of this, the mother is deeply moved and delighted; she rejoices that the infant searches for her with anguish and wailing. And if the baby is unable to go to her, simply because of the ardent seeking and desire of the infant, the mother herself will go to embrace it, bound as she is by her love for her baby. She warmly cuddles it and nurses it with much affection. However, when the mother draws near to the baby, it doesn't calm down all at once, but continues to cry until she has embraced it in her arms and bared her breast to suckle it with her own milk, only then do the streams of milk begin to flow and cause the infant to be content. Nevertheless, once the baby is comforted, picked up by the mother and brought to her breast, and once it nurses with delight from the maternal milk, it begins to cry again, because the mother was so slow to come and comfort it, rather having abandoned it much to its distress. For even if one offered the infant a thousand types of food, or gold, silver or other such things, none of these things will provide amusement or comfort or distraction, nothing but its mother's breast. The sight of this causes pleasure, and by drawing nourishment from the breast the baby is content. Beholding the breasts affords joy and delight.

Day 7

Morning Prayer

Antiphon: God is full of maternal compassion.

Psalm 54:1–16 ✠ Psalm 78:8–12 TNK ✠ Psalm 145:1–10 TNK

Scripture: Genesis 43:1–14 TNK

Reading: St. Macarius the Great, Desert Father of the Church † 391

Spiritual Homilies 46.3

An infant has no strength to accomplish anything, and is unable to walk on its own two feet towards its mother, nevertheless it rolls itself over, makes noises, and cries, earnestly seeking for its mother. Meanwhile, the mother is moved with compassion and delights that the little one eagerly seeks after her with pangs and crying even though the infant is powerless to come to her. Yet because of the child's earnestly seeking after her, the mother approaches it herself, completely taken by her love for her infant. She lifts it up, warmly embraces it, and nurses it with deep affection. This is precisely how God, the tenderhearted, acts towards the soul who approaches and pours itself out.

Evening Prayer

Antiphon: In various different ways God has spoken to us.

Psalm 1:1–6 ✠ Psalm 88:1–28 ✠ Psalm 76:13–20

Scripture: Hebrews 1:1–9 NT

Reading: St. Gregory of Nyssa, bishop, Father and Doctor of the Church † ca. 395

Against Eunomius 2.417–19, 420

We determine that the reason why God willingly converses with human beings is God's tender love for humanity. Now because it is impossible for what is naturally circumscribed to rise above its own limitations, let alone grasp the superior nature of the Transcendent, accordingly, God brings his power, so full of tender love for humanity, down to the level of our weakness, even to the extent that we are able to receive it, personally doling out grace and benevolent aid. For just as by a divine dispensation the sun, tempering the intensity of its searing rays by dispersion through the intervening atmosphere, showers down light and heat upon its recipients, being itself unapproachable due to the weakness of our nature; so too, the Divine Power, in a similar manner as in our illustration, even though it infinitely transcends our nature and is inaccessible to immediate participation, like a tenderly responsive mother chiming in with the inarticulate babblings of her babies, the Divine Power doles out to our human nature what it is able to receive. Therefore, in the rich variety of divine manifestations to human beings God adapts to humanity and speaks in a human fashion. . . . God's providential care aids our weakness by becoming acquainted with our own idioms of speech.

Day 8

Morning Prayer

Antiphon: We have wandered away from the Maternal Womb of God.

Psalm 64:1–13 ✠ Psalm 50:1–19 ✠ Psalm 145:1–10 TNK

Scripture: Isaiah 46:3–5 VULG

Reading: St. Gregory of Nyssa, bishop, Father and Doctor of the Church † ca. 395

Inscriptions of the Psalms 2.15

Complaining about those who have fallen away from salvation, he says, *Sinners have become estranged from the maternal source; they have wandered away from the womb.* You would understand this text if you had investigated what the first "maternal source" of human existence is, and what "womb" has been pregnant with humanity. For I believe it is nothing other than God's tender love for humanity and God's goodness, from which we were formed and given birth. For *the One who formed each of their hearts individually*, is the one who said, *Let us make a human being according to our image and likeness.* Furthermore, that one says, *I have given birth to children, and exalted them, and they have rejected me.* And myriads of similar statements can be gathered from the Sacred Scripture, through which one can certainly know what the "womb" is which formed us, and what the "maternal source" is which delivered us into the light through birth.

ಐ 📖 ಞ

Evening Prayer

Antiphon: We can only think about God by way of analogy.

Psalm 6:1–10 ✠ Psalm 102:1–23 ✠ Psalm 118:89–96

Scripture: Acts 17:22–29

PRAYING—WITH THE SAINTS—TO GOD OUR MOTHER

Reading: St. Gregory of Nyssa, bishop, Father and Doctor of the Church † ca. 395

Against Eunomius 2.104, 136, 154

Whatever names we have learned expressive of the knowledge of God, all of these have something in common with and are analogous to the kinds of names which indicate individual human characteristics. . . .

The point in speaking about God is not to conceive some well-sounding and harmoniously beautiful verbage, but to seek out some reverent conception by which what is befitting the thought of God may be safeguarded. . . .

From the greatness and beauty of created things, analogously, Wisdom declares, *the generative Source of the universe may be perceived.* We propound such titles for the Divine Being which transcends all intellect, not to glorify it by the appellations we employ, but to guide ourselves towards the understanding of hidden conceptions by what is said.

Day 9

Morning Prayer

Antiphon: Mother and father mean the same thing because there is neither male nor female in God.

Psalm 72:1–28 ✠ Psalm 8:1–9 ✠ Psalm 88:1–28

Scripture: Song of Songs 3:6–11

Reading: St. Gregory of Nyssa, bishop, Father and Doctor of the Church † ca. 395

Song of Songs 7

Daughters of Zion, see the crown on the king's head which his mother set on him according to the prophet, *You have placed on his head a crown of precious stone.* Now no one can grasp God and carefully and accurately put God into words. For example "mother" is used here in place of "father." Both terms connote the same meaning, because God is neither male nor female (for how can anything transitory like human nature be attributed to God? But when we are one in Christ, the signs of this differentiation are stripped away along with the old man). Therefore, every name is equally capable of indicating God's ineffable nature; neither the concept "feminine" nor "masculine" can utterly defile God's pure nature. Therefore, the father mentioned in the Gospel prepares a wedding for his son, and the prophet declares regarding God, *You have set on his head a crown of precious stone.* Thus the Song says that a crown has been placed upon the bridegroom by his mother. Since the wedding and bride are one, one mother places the crown upon the bridegroom's head. Likewise, it doesn't make much difference whether one calls the Son of God, the Only-Begotten God, or the Son of God's love, for according to Paul each name has the ability to signify a bridal escort which leads the Bridegroom to dwell within us. "Go out then," says the bride to the attendants, "and become daughters of Zion, so that from a high summit (for this is what Zion signifies) you will be able to behold that wonderful sight, the bridegroom bedecked with his crown." Now his crown is the Church encircling his head with living stones, and love is the braiding of his crown, since whether one calls it "mother" or "love," you will not go wrong, for "God is love," as John declares.

Evening Prayer

Antiphon: God is our Mother, the First Cause of our existence.

Psalm 15:1–11 ✠ Psalm 143:7–12 TNK ✠ Psalm 118:81–88

Scripture: Colossians 1:15–20

Reading: St. Gregory of Nyssa, bishop, Father and Doctor of the Church † ca. 395

Song of Songs 6

[The Bride says] I called him by name as much as it was in my power to find the One who lacks a name, but the meaning of a name would not help me secure the One for whom I was searching. For how can the One who is above every name be discovered by the invocation of a name? She declares, "'*I called him, but he did not answer me.*' I knew then that the sheer greatness of his glory and holiness has no limit." Thus the Bride rises again and wanders about in spirit through the spiritual and transcendent realm which she calls a "city" in which there are principalities, dominions, and thrones prescribed to angelic powers. She calls the assembly of the heavenly hosts a "marketplace," and names "boulevards" an innumerable multitude as in among these she might find her Beloved. While the Bride went round about all these places, she inspected the entire angelic army and not having beheld the One whom she sought amid all these long-sought good things, she reasoned with herself, "Can my Beloved then be comprehended?" Next she asks them, *Have you seen the One whom my soul loves?* But their only answer to her question is silence, signifying by their silence that what she seeks is incomprehensible.

After the Bride traversed in spirit throughout that transcendent city without perceiving her Beloved among immaterial and spiritual beings, she abandons everything that she has ever discovered. Thus she realizes that her long-sought-for love is known only in her inability to comprehend his Being, and that every indication becomes an impediment for those who seek after him. Therefore, the Bride notes, "*When I walked by them a little bit*, I passed by every creature and left behind everything that it is intelligible in creation; having abandoned every manner of comprehension, then I found my Beloved by faith. And I will never let him go, now that I found him by faith until he comes into my chamber. The "chamber" indeed is the heart, which becomes an abode of the divine indwelling when it is restored to that state it experienced in the beginning made by "*her who conceived me*." Surely we would be correct in understanding "mother" as the First Cause of our existence.

PRAYING—WITH THE SAINTS—TO GOD OUR MOTHER

Day 10

Morning Prayer

Antiphon: God hears the cries of her children.

Psalm 91:1–15 ✠ Psalm 118:89–96 ✠ Psalm 51:1–5 TNK

Scripture: Hosea 1:10; 2:1, 14 VULG

Reading: St. Gregory of Nyssa, bishop, Father and Doctor of the Church † ca. 395

On the Lord's Prayer 1

    Now everything depends upon the Divine Will and life here below is arranged from above; this is so obvious no one would deny it. And we have learned that other causes affect the success of such prayers. But it is not as if God does not dispense all these things as something good to those who ask; but this occurs so that through these things their superficial faith in God may be made firm. Thus they will eventually learn from their experiences with smaller petitions that God indeed hears their requests, so that they might proceed to the desire for the higher gifts which are more worthy of God. It's the same as we see in our children who for awhile cling to their mother's breast, sucking from it as much as their newborn nature desires. But when the baby has grown up and exhibits the capacity to utter some sort of words, it has second thoughts about the breast, and seeks other things, whether the showy pin or the clothing or some such things that delight infants' eyes. But as the child grows older the mind develops with the body, and the youth leaves behind all childish desires and asks its parents for those things that pertain to adulthood. Likewise, God is not deaf even to the most insignificant human petitions and accustoms the person to look towards God for everything, thereby summoning the person who has received this gracious gift in trifling matters to desire the higher ones.

Evening Prayer

Antiphon: We need to make steady progress in our spiritual growth.

Psalm 18:1–14 ✠ Psalm 76:13–20 ✠ Psalm 118:97–104

Scripture: Philippians 3:8–16

Reading: St. Gregory of Nyssa, bishop, Father and Doctor of the Church † ca. 395

On Infants' Early Deaths

    It appears to me that the present way of life serves as a sort of analogy for the future life which we anticipate, and has an intimate connection with it. Accordingly, the first stage of infants is to be suckled and reared with milk from the breast; then another type of food corresponding to the subject, and intimately adapted to the needs of the child, follows, until at last the youth attains maturity. And so I think, by stages continually adapted to it and in a sort of progression, the soul participates in that truly natural life. According to its capacity and power the soul receives a portion of the blessed state. In fact, we have learned as much from Paul, who had a different type of food for the person who had already grown in virtue compared to that for the infant and the immature, saying, *I gave you milk to drink, and did not nourish you with meat; for you were not yet ready.* ...

For the infant there is a soothing delight in milk, and in its nursing mother's embrace, and in the gentle rocking back and forth that induces and sweetens its slumber. Any happy delight beyond this, the immaturity of its age prevents it from experiencing. In the same manner, those who in their earthly life have nourished their souls on a diet of virtues, and have, as the Apostle said, *exercised the senses of their minds*, will, if they are transported to that incorporeal life, participate in that divine delight, proportionately to the condition and the powers existing within them. They will have more or less of its beneficence according to the capacity that each has attained.

Day 11

Morning Prayer

Antiphon: God our Creator is the foundation and center of the universe.

Psalm 107:1–6 ✠ Psalm 103:1–34 ✠ Psalm 54:1–16

Scripture: Sirach 24:4, 12–21 VULG

Reading: Synesius of Cyrene, bishop, Father of the Church † ca. 414

Hymn 5.59–74, 89–91

> All of creation depends upon your will.
> You are the root of things present and past,
> of all things future and conceivable.
> You are Father and you are Mother.
> You are masculine and you are feminine.
> You are voice and you are silence,
> the True Nature giving birth to nature,
> You the Sovereign, the Eternal of all ages.
> This should readily be proclaimed!
> Glory to You, Foundation of the universe!
> Glory to You, Center of all beings,
> Unity of divine innumerability,
> Original Ruler of every essence!
> You are glorious, utterly glorious!
> To God alone belongs the glory! ...
> O that my soul would take flight!
> That I might dance about the ineffable mysteries,
> blossoming forth from your depths.

PRAYING—WITH THE SAINTS—TO GOD OUR MOTHER

Evening Prayer

Antiphon: The mystery of God's love cannot adequately be put into human words.

Psalm 21:1–11 ✠ Psalm 131:1–3 TNK ✠ Psalm 102:1–22

Scripture: 2 Corinthians 12:1–5

Reading: St. Cheremon, Desert Father of the Church † ca. 400

In Cassian, *Consolations* 13.17

> Pondering the multifaceted bounty of God's gracious design, the blessed Apostle sees himself engulfed in a vastly deep and boundless ocean of God's tender goodness, and exclaims: *Oh the depths of the riches of the wisdom and knowledge of God! How unfathomable are the judgments of God and how unsearchable his ways! For who has known the mind of the Lord?*
>
> O wondrous admiration for Divine Knowledge which threw into a state of awe a man such as the Teacher of the nations! Whoever believes it is possible to measure with human reason the profundity of this unfathomable abyss, attempts to reduce it to emptiness. Indeed, whoever is so certain that one can mentally conceive or perfectly explain the designs through which God works salvation in human beings is definitely resisting the Apostle's statement and with impious audacity declaring that the judgments of God are in fact penetrable and his ways are discoverable. Thus the Lord himself testifies against such as these: *My thoughts are not your thoughts, and my ways are not your ways, for as high are the heavens above the earth, as high are my ways above your ways, and my thoughts surpass your thoughts.*
>
> Therefore the Lord wanted to express, by means of the rapture of human affection, the loving providence which he desires to bestow upon us, with a tenderness which does not grow weary. Not finding any sentiment in all of creation to which he could better match his own, God compared it to the loving devotedness of a mother's heart. He made use of this example, because he could find nothing more tender in all of human nature, and declared: *Can a mother forget her child? Can it be that she might have no compassion for the child of her womb?* Then, even this comparison no longer sufficed, and he transcended it, exclaiming: *Even if she should forget, I will never forget you!*

Day 12

Morning Prayer

Antiphon: Let me confess my sins, confident in your maternal mercy.

Psalm 118:145–52 ✠ Psalm 50:1–19 ✠ Psalm 78:8–12 TNK

Scripture: Jeremiah 17:5–10

Reading: St. Augustine, bishop, Father and Doctor of the Church † 430

Confessions 4.1.1

Let the proud mock, let them laugh who have not yet fallen flat on their faces, felled for their own good by you, O my God. Nevertheless, let me confess my shameful failings, and thereby praise you. Put up with me, I beg you, and let me traverse round about in my present memory the past paths of my erring, and offer you a sacrifice of rejoicing. Without you, what good am I to myself, except a guide to my own downfall? On the contrary, when all goes well with me, what I am but a child nursing on your milk and fed on you, the food that never corrupts.

Evening Prayer

Antiphon: God is our mother because she cherishes and warmly embraces us.

Psalm 118:49–56 ✠ Psalm 130:1–3 ✠ Psalm 26:1–14

Scripture: Romans 4:1–12

Reading: St. Augustine, bishop, Father and Doctor of the Church † 430

Second Discourse on Psalm 26 2.17–18

Be my helper, do not abandon me. For look, I am on my journey, *one thing have I asked you for, to dwell in your house all the days of my life*, to contemplate your delightfulness and be protected as your temple. This one thing have I asked; and I am on my journey to reach it. Perhaps you will say to me, "Be cheerful; put your best foot forward. I have given you free will; you're your own master. Strike out on your path; seek after peace and pursue it. Don't get side tracked; don't get in a rut; don't look back. Persevere on your journey, because whoever perseveres to the end will be saved." But now you with your free will are depending as it were on your own strength to walk. Don't rely on yourself; if God abandons you, from your own path you will depart, fall away, wander, and remain there. Therefore say to God, "You have indeed granted me free will, but without you all my efforts amount to nothing. Be my helper, do not abandon me; do not despise me, O God my Savior. You who fashioned me, help me; you did not create me only to desert me."

For my father and my mother have abandoned me. The psalmist has made himself a little child before God; made God his father, made God his mother. He is father because he created, calls forth, directs, governs. She is mother because she warmly cherishes, nourishes, suckles, encompasses. *My father and my mother have abandoned me, but the Lord has adopted me*, both to govern and to nourish.

PRAYING—WITH THE SAINTS—TO GOD OUR MOTHER

Day 13

Morning Prayer

Antiphon: God rebukes us as a loving parent for our own good.

Psalm 118:9-24 ✠ Psalm 6:1-10 ✠ Psalm 37:1-22

Scripture: Proverbs 1:20-33 TNK

Reading: St. Peter Chrysologus, archbishop, Father and Doctor of the Church † 450

Sermon 45.1-2

Lord, do not rebuke me in your anger, nor reprove me in your rage. Is God inflamed with anger, boiling over with rage? Far from it, brothers and sisters! God is not subjected to passions, nor enkindled to anger, nor agitated by rage. Rather God's anger is the punishment of the reprobate and God's rage is the penalty of sinners. Brothers and sisters, formed from dust and molded from clay, we are trampled underfoot by vices, subjected by our failings, consumed by anxieties, withered in our members, disintegrated by death, and we tremble at putrid tombs. We are found incapable of virtue, yet so capable of vice. Therefore the Prophet, mindful of human frailty and conscious of carnal existence, and because he places no trust in merits, had recourse to the help of God's mercy, so that God's judgment regarding him might consist in loving-kindness rather than severity.

Lord, do not rebuke me in your anger. That is to say: rebuke me, but not in anger; reprove me, but not in rage. Rebuke me as Father, but not as Judge; reprove me not as Lord, but as Parent. Rebuke me, not so as to destroy me, but rather to reprove me. Reprove me, not so as to make an end of me, but rather to reform me.

ೞ 📖 ಆ

Evening Prayer

Antiphon: God is ablaze with love. Come, let us be consumed by love of God.

Psalm 118:57-64 ✠ Psalm 22:9-11 TNK ✠ Psalm 40:9-13 TNK

Scripture: Luke 12:49-53

Reading: St. Peter Chrysologus, archbishop, Father and Doctor of the Church † 450

Sermon 164.5

Christ says, *I have a baptism with which to be baptized, and what ardor I feel until it is completed! I have come to light a fire on earth, and how I wish that it were ablaze!* Christ pursues fire and summons water: what is the connection between such disparate things? Water pursues a flame and a flame thereby increases water: how can things so discordant find one accord? At play here, as we have previously remarked, is a metaphor concerning the Divine Cultivator. In fact, everything germinates because it is full of heat and is nourished by moisture. Accordingly, God, the Parent of the Universe, with a swift interplay of fire and water produces us, and nourishes us, for whom with such intensity, she burns, is red hot, blazes, and pants with passionate affection.

Day 14

Morning Prayer

Antiphon: God is clothed in feminine attire to reveal the Divine Nature.

Psalm 129:1–8 ✠ Psalm 143:7–12 TNK ✠ Psalm 109:1–7

Scripture: Wisdom 13:1–9

Reading: Pseudo-Dionysius, Father of the Church † fifth century

Letter 9.1

Now I thought it important to explain as best as I could . . . the great variety of sacred symbols fashioned by Scripture to reveal God, for if one looks at them from outside the faith they appear to be overflowing with incredible and concocted bizarre tales. For example, concerning the super-essential generation of God, Scripture refers to God's womb forming God within, in a corporeal fashion. It likewise speaks of the Word issuing like a breath of air exhaled from a human heart and the Spirit as breathed out from a mouth. It depicts the divine bosom embracing the Son of God and it presents this to us in a physical manner. . . . God is clothed in feminine garments. . . . Likewise there are those other sacred covenantal signs boldly asserted to portray God, in order that what lays hidden may be exposed and multiplied, what is unique and undivided may be divided up, and multiple types and forms be assigned to what is devoid of shape and form. Scripture does all of this enabling the person to perceive the hidden dignity within these figures and to discover that they are truly mysterious, completely appropriate to God, and abundantly filled with a great theological light.

Evening Prayer

Antiphon: God has great compassion for us and heals us, restoring us to life.

Psalm 138:1–14 ✠ Psalm 6:1–10 ✠ Psalm 29:1–12

Scripture: Mark 5:21–43

Reading: St. Peter Chrysologus, archbishop, Father and Doctor of the Church † 450

Sermon 33.1–2

A certain ruler of the synagogue named Jairus came to Jesus and upon seeing him, he fell at his feet and greatly begged him, saying: My daughter is at death's door, but come, place your hand on her so that she might be well and live. But before my sermon reveals

the mystical meaning of the Gospel, it is befitting at this juncture to discourse a little about the sufferings that parents assume and undergo due to their affection and love for their children. While Jairus' family is standing around, surrounded by sensitive, calm, and supportive neighbors, and the daughter is lying on a soft and comfortable bed, the father throws himself prostrate on the dusty floor, and writhes in distress on the ground. Her body fails her; he pines away in mind and spirit. She experiences unseen sufferings from her languishing state; he, mourning and disheveled, casts himself down in public for all to see. She is dying unto peace; whereas he is living unto anguish.

And certainly we have failed to mention the anxious vows of parents when they try to get pregnant and the succeeding stages of dangers when they bear and raise their offspring. When the children are sick they precipitate distressing labors and constant hardships. But worst of all is the day of the child's death, when the parents' posterity precedes them to the grave! Woe is me! Why are children oblivious to such trials? Why don't they understand? Why don't they break out in a sweat, thereby reciprocating their parents' actions? Nevertheless, the parents' loving devotion remains unfaltering; consequently, whatever parents expend on their children, God the Parent of all will pay back to the parents.

Day 15

Morning Prayer

Antiphon: God takes us up as any loving mother would.

Psalm 142:1–12 ✠ Psalm 130:1–3 ✠ Psalm 26:1–14

Scripture: Numbers 11:4–12 TNK

Reading: Cassiodorus, monk, Father of the Church † ca. 580

Exposition on the Psalms 26:10

Because my father and my mother have abandoned me, the Lord has adopted me. By his "father" he refers to Adam, the first man, and by his "mother," he means Adam's wife, Eve, from whom the human race descends. So these left him with his mortal condition and were not able to nourish him because they had been removed from the light of day. This verse, however, could also be understood as referring to David's parents because he abandoned the house of his father and mother when he was carried away to the position of king by the Hebrew people. The text continues, *the Lord, however, has adopted me,* in place of a real parent. God is father because God establishes and governs, and mother because God nurtures and nurses the weak and little ones with milk.

Thematic Readings for Non-Feast Days

Evening Prayer

Antiphon: We are all children born of God.

Psalm 140:1–5 ✠ Psalm 118:73–80 ✠ Psalm 131:1–3 TNK

Scripture: Romans 11:16–24

Reading: Cassiodorus, monk, Father of the Church † ca. 580

Exposition on the Psalms 130:2

The psalmist says that he has desired the Lord, *As a weaned child upon its mother*. When a little child grows older and is prepared for receiving other foods, it is customary to deny it the milk with which it was regularly nourished by its devoted mother. This is so that the child might graduate to more solid food and its body not become soft by being left in its tender condition. But with what purity of heart and longing and charm does the child seek its mother so that her heart is moved by its crying, and she practically grieves at being thus separated. The prophet compares his religious sentiments with that longing; he shows what great hope, simplicity, and yearning we ought to feel for the Lord. "Weaned" is what is said of those from whom milk has been withdrawn. The comparison is rightly made, for just as infants suck at their mother's breasts, so the infant faithful are nourished by the simplicity of Divine Scripture until they are prepared for solid food. As the Apostle remarks, *I could not speak to you as spiritual people, but as carnal. As children in Christ, I gave you milk to drink, not meat.* The additional phrase, "*upon its mother*," signifies that they are still at the tender age and are lifted towards their mother's breasts.

Day 16

Morning Prayer

Antiphon: Intimacy with God leads us to mystical knowledge.

Psalm 5:1–12 ✠ Psalm 118:105–12 ✠ Psalm 30:1–24

Scripture: Genesis 28:1–5 TNK

Reading: St. Maximos the Confessor, monk, Father of the Church † 662

Letter 8

It's as if I dwell with the children of Esau in Arabia, that is, in the flesh, without being able to attain another life than the present one because of my sensual carnal nature. To dwell here isn't the heritage of the true Israel which is to see God and hasten to emigrate by means of knowledge towards the Lord who mystically is (and is called) the Promised Land containing ineffable bounty where milk and honey flow. For the Lord suckles those who act like his little ones; God fills them with joy until they have grown into adults, nourishing them in stages by the practice of virtue as with milk; and for those who hold him in awe, he fills them with the sweetness of mystical knowledge; and for those who love him he grants them spiritual contemplation like honey.

Evening Prayer

Antiphon: Wisdom delightfully throws herself into creation.

Psalm 133:1–3 ✠ Psalm 89:1–17 ✠ Psalm 103:1–34

Scripture: Proverbs 8:22–31 TNK

Reading: St. Maximos the Confessor, monk, Father of the Church † 662

Ambigua 1.71

"The lofty Word plays in every kind of form, appreciating his world as he wills, here and there" (Dionysius the Areopagite).

The great divine preacher Dionysius the Areopagite asserts, "We must dare to say this as being no less true, that God is the cause of the universe, and in God's wonderful and good desirous love for all things, through the excess of ecstatic loving goodness, is propelled outside of God's self in providential solicitude for all creatures. So enraptured is God by goodness, and loving, and desiring, being moved from his position above all and beyond all, that God descends to be in all according to an ecstatic and transcendent power inseparable from himself." Perhaps, then, as I said, with this in mind, we may find a means of understanding: "The lofty Word plays."

To use examples from our own experience to affirm matters that are above us, it is like parents rousing their children from sluggishness, and indulging them, participate in their childish games. They play with nuts and throw dice with them, or arrange beautifully colored flowers for them, as well as dress up in brightly colored clothes that entice the senses. The parents play hide and seek, astonishing them, as if they have nothing better to do than play in their children's games. But after awhile the parents lead their children on to more advanced things and engage with them in more mature discourse, sharing their own affairs. So perhaps in the above text, [Dionysius] our teacher is saying that God who is above all creation in the meantime leads us through the unfolding story of our nature from the appearance of created things to amazement, as an ascent through contemplating them and subsequent knowledge, quite like how we presently care for our children. God then inspires the contemplation of the more spiritual meaning contained within creation, and ultimately leads us up by means of theology to the most mystical knowledge of himself, as much as this is attainable.

Thematic Readings for Non-Feast Days

Day 17

Morning Prayer

Antiphon: God, who is Grace, is our Mother in all things.

Psalm 41:1–11 ✠ Psalm 118:113–20 ✠ Psalm 30:1–24

Scripture: Proverbs 31:1–9

Reading: St. Bede the Venerable, priest, Father and Doctor of the Church † 735

Allegorical Exposition on the Sayings of Solomon 3.31

The words of King Lemuel, a vision which his mother taught him. Now the name Lemuel means "in whom God dwells." Given what was said above he is called the same name in Latin, in turn meaning: "A vision which a man spoke, with whom God dwells." The mother, in fact, who instructed him in this vision, cannot be more fittingly understood than as Divine Grace, who herself invisibly instructed him within the heart by an understanding of Wisdom so that he himself might show it to those outside.

₰ 📖 ℭ

Evening Prayer

Antiphon: God is father and mother and tutor and whatever else we need.

Psalm 1:1–6 ✠ Psalm 18:1–14 ✠ Psalm 26:1–14

Scripture: Luke 15:8–10 NT

Reading: St. Gregory of Narek, monk and priest † 1003

Prayers 5.1

> You who created me in your glorious image,
> struck as a coin of your Majesty,
> come to the aid of my feebleness.
> You adorned me with reason.
> You made me resplendent by your breath.
> In spirit you enriched me;
> in wisdom you made me flourish;
> in prudence you confirmed me.
> Among living creatures you distinguished me;
> to my being you united an intelligent soul;
> with free will you bedecked me.
> You begot me like a father;
> you nursed me like a mother;
> you raised me like a tutor.

PRAYING—WITH THE SAINTS—TO GOD OUR MOTHER

Day 18

Morning Prayer

Antiphon: There is One God, One Creator, Mother of all creation.

Psalm 54:1–16 ✠ Psalm 103:1–34 ✠ Psalm 85:1–17

Scripture: Song of Songs 1:1–7

Reading: St. Gregory of Narek, monk and priest † 1003

Commentary on the Song of Songs 1:5

Next the text says *like the tents of Kedar*. Kedar signifies "dark"; that is to say, "I was *the tent* of Satan, but because of the mercy of God has shown me I am now fit to be *the tabernacle of Solomon*." The words *the tabernacle of Solomon* refer to the Temple (built by Solomon). In other words, "Now I have become the House of God, like *the tabernacle of Solomon*." Thereby it alludes to the Church of the Gentiles.

Recalling once again her earlier unseemliness, she adds, "*Do not look at me because I am black*." She speaks of the blackness of sin, "having caught me in transgression, *the Sun* (which is God) *looked on me fiercely*." In this manner she indicates the bitterness of the punishments inflicted upon her, and her expulsion from Eden and God's presence. Whose transgression brought all of this about? The Bride remarks, "*The sons of my mother fought with me*." She calls Satan "*my mother's son*," for in fact they are both creatures of the same Creator.

ೞ 📖 ෬

Evening Prayer

Antiphon: God is abounding in patience and love.

Psalm 6:1–10 ✠ Psalm 118:121–28 ✠ Psalm 102:1–22

Scripture: 2 Peter 3:1–15

Reading: St. Anselm of Canterbury, archbishop, Doctor of the Church † 1109

Meditations 4

A biological father and mother usually possess a great loving devotion for those whom they have begotten. If they perceive that their offspring are afflicted by some distress or physical grief they willingly give themselves and their all, if the case demand it, to recover the safety of their own offspring. Many animals frequently do not fear to draw death down upon themselves on behalf of their own young, and so that their offspring might escape death they themselves run headlong into death. What is the source of this truth? From whence does this natural loving devotion derive if not from the one who is the fountain of love and loyalty, who wishes that none may perish, nor rejoices in the loss of the dying? Therefore, our Creator, the fountain of loving devotion, the wellspring of mercy, greater than all sweetness and everything worthy of love, upon seeing us his creatures disfigured by the contagion of sin, and likewise bearing the wounds of many great offenses injuring us to the point of death, with much great and far surpassing attentiveness turned towards us to cure our sins, to heal our infirmities, to transform our leprous and sordid offenses, our thoughts which were empty and scattered like dust. Like a human or animal parent, he turned to take care of his children and offspring.

Day 19

Morning Prayer

Antiphon: Draw me into your inner chambers, O God.

Psalm 5:1–12 ✠ Psalm 22:1–6 ✠ Psalm 25:1–12

Scripture: Song of Songs 1:1–3 VULG

Reading: St. Hildegard of Bingen, abbess † 1179

Book of Divine Works 2.19

The King has led me into his chambers. We will rejoice and be glad in you; the memory of your breasts is better than wine. It is right to love you. This is to be understood in the following way: I, the soul of a believer, have followed the path of truth—the Son of God who has redeemed human beings through his humanity. I am secure for I was led by the One who is the ruler of the universe into the fullness of his benefits where I find utter satisfaction in virtues and faithfully progress from virtue to virtue. Therefore, all of us who have been redeemed by the blood of the Son of God will exult with all our physical being and our whole soul rejoices in you, O Holy Divinity, through whom we subsist. We recall the sweetness of the heavenly reward which is greater than all the sufferings and tribulations we endured in conflict over the truth. All of that has become as nothing ever since we tasted what you have laid out before us as a sign of your commands. And thus those who live uprightly in deeds of holiness love you with a true and perfect love, for you bestow every blessing upon those who love you and in the end endow them with eternal life. Meanwhile, Wisdom floods the chambers, that is, the minds of mortals, setting forth the justice of true faith through which God is made known. There this faith presses out all the chill and dankness of vice to such an extent that such things can neither germinate nor grow again. Concomitantly, faith presses out for itself all the virtues so that wine can be poured into a chalice and given to people to drink. Because of this believers should rejoice and be glad in true faith and an eternal reward, bearing the staff of the good deeds they have done. Thirsting for God's justice, they suck the holiness of God's breasts, and in so doing, never have enough; thus they will forever be refreshed by contemplating the Divinity, for holiness outshines all human intellect.

Evening Prayer

Antiphon: Love is a flash of fire, a flame of God's very self.

Psalm 15:1–11 ✠ Psalm 107:1–6 ✠ Psalm 83:1–12

Scripture: 1 Corinthians 3:10–15

Reading: St. Hildegard of Bingen, abbess † 1179

Know the Way 2.1.7

A Vision: After the Other Creatures, Humanity Was Created from Earthy Mud

After that this [divine] flame stretched forth some of its fire to a little clod of muddy earth which was lying at the bottom of the atmosphere. This means that after all the creatures were created, the Word of God, in the strong will of the Father and because of the supernal sweetness of love, saw the poor and fragile material out of which the weak frailty of humanity, both bad as well as good, was to be produced. It was insensible and weighed down, not yet roused by the breath of life. Then this flame warmed the clod so that a body and blood was formed. The flame inundated it with warmth because the earth is the fleshly material of human nature. And the divine flame nourished the clod with vigorous sap just as a mother gives milk to her children. And it breathed into it so that a living human being was raised up.

Day 20

Morning Prayer

Antiphon: Come into the presence of God.

Psalm 64:1–13 ✠ Psalm 15:1–11 ✠ Psalm 30:1–24

Scripture: 4 Esdras 1:22–30 VULG

Reading: St. Gertrude the Great of Helfta, nun † 1302

The Herald of God's Loving-Kindness 3.72.1–2

Another time, praying for the persons who were commended to her, and remembering one of them with particular affection, Gertrude said to the Lord, "Most good and gracious Lord, grant my request in the sweetness of your paternal affection, for the one for whom I pray." The Lord responded, "I regularly grant your requests when you pray for her." Gertrude asked, "Then why does she incessantly beg me for prayers in pleading terms, speaking nothing but of her misery as if she had never received the slightest consolation from you?" . . .

The Lord responded, "I have placed her and the others very near me, where she cannot lack purifying trials. She is like the self-indulgent daughter who in her affection for her mother wishes to sit on the same seat as her mother and at the same level, but is inconveniently made to sit with the other daughters who have chosen seats appropriate for their own station, in the presence of their mother. Otherwise, the affectionate gaze of the mother would not be able to fall upon this child as directly as upon the daughters seated directly in front of her."

Evening Prayer

Antiphon: God is love, indescribable love.

Psalm 18:1–14 ✠ Psalm 18:129–36 ✠ Psalm 30:1–24

Scripture: 1 John 4:7–17

Reading: Bl. Angela of Foligno, Franciscan mystic † 1309

Memorial 7

In yet many other ways the soul knows that God enters into it, in ways which cannot be doubted. I shall mention two of these.

One manner is an unction which suddenly so rejuvenates the soul and renders all of the members of the body docile and in one accord with the soul, that nothing can touch it or offend it; nothing great or small can disturb it. At the same time the soul feels and hears God speaking to it. Moreover, in this great and completely ineffable unction, the soul understands with the utmost certitude and clarity that God is in it, and that neither a saint in paradise nor an angel could cause such an experience. And this is so ineffable that it deeply disconcerts me that I cannot think of anything with which to compare it. May God forgive me, for I greatly desire to relate all I know, but I would wish to speak only to manifest the goodness of God, if it be found pleasing.

Another manner in which the soul realizes that God is within it is through an embrace with which God encompasses the soul, an embrace like none a mother has ever given her child. Nor can anyone else on earth be conceived of who could embrace with so much love, which even comes close to the indescribable love with which God embraces the soul. God firmly draws the soul close with so much tenderness and love, that I don't believe anyone on earth who has not experienced this, could possibly believe it.

Day 21

Morning Prayer

Antiphon: God answers prayer according to God's loving wisdom.

Psalm 72:1–28 ✠ Psalm 137:1–8 ✠ Psalm 118:169–76

Scripture: Sirach 35:13–24

PRAYING—WITH THE SAINTS—TO GOD OUR MOTHER

Reading: St. Birgitta of Sweden, founder of the Bridgettine Order † 1373

Fifth Book of Revelations, Fifteenth Interrogation 25–29

[God told Birgitta], Now as to why my friends, petitioning me in their prayers, are not always heard by me, I reply: I am like a mother who, while seeing her child requesting something contrary to his own well-being, defers listening to the petition, all the while suppressing his tears with some indignation. Indeed, such indignation is not anger, but rather great mercy. Thus I, God, do not always hear my friends because I myself see, better than they themselves see, the things that are more useful for their well-being. Did not Paul and others pray effectively, yet they were not heard? But why? Because my friends, even in the midst of their abundant virtues, they themselves have weakness and things that need to be purged. Thus they are not heard so that they might be all the more humble and fervent towards me and be all the more lovingly defended and preserved by me while facing temptations to sin. Therefore it is a token of great loving tenderness that the prayers of my friends are not always granted, for the sake of their greater merit and for the proving of their constancy.

Evening Prayer

Antiphon: God calls everyone into salvation.

Psalm 21:1–11 ✠ Psalm 141:1–7 ✠ Psalm 85:1–17

Scripture: Matthew 20:1–16

Reading: St. Birgitta of Sweden, founder of the Bridgettine Order † 1373

Fifth Book of Revelations, Fifteenth Interrogation 62–65

[God told Birgitta], Now as to why one is called at the beginning and another person is called around the end, I reply: I am like the mother who perceives in her children the hope of life and gives stronger things to some and lighter things to others. She sympathizes with those for whom there is no hope, and does as much as she can for them. But if the children grow weaker due to their mother's medicine, what need is there to keep on trying? This is the way I deal with human beings. To the one whose will is foreseen as more fervent and whose humility and stability are more constant, this one received grace in the beginning, and it will continue to the end. Another, who in the midst of all his bad deeds still tries and attempts to do better, deserves to be called toward the end. But the one who is ungrateful, does not deserve to be admitted to his mother's breasts.

Thematic Readings for Non-Feast Days

Day 22

Morning Prayer

Antiphon: Heed your Mother's instruction.

Psalm 91:1–15 ✠ Psalm 2:1–12 ✠ Psalm 118:65–72

Scripture: Proverbs 1:1–8

Reading: St. Birgitta of Sweden, founder of the Bridgettine Order † 1373

Fifth Book of Revelations, Sixth Interrogation 12–15

[God told Birgitta], As to why unfavorable things happen to the just, I answer: My justice is that everyone should obtain what one seeks. But no one is just who does not desire to suffer unfavorable things for the sake of obedience and the perfection of righteousness, and who does not do good to one's neighbor out of divine love. My friends consider what I, their God and Redeemer, have accomplished for them and what I have promised to them. At the same time they attentively perceive the wickedness in the world, and as a precaution, more eagerly seek to obtain, for my honor and their own salvation as well as for the avoidance of sin, the unfavorable things of the world rather than their prosperity. And so I permit tribulations to happen to them. If some of them suffer with too little patience, I do not allow this to happen without a purpose; and I stand ever ready by their side in the midst of tribulation. When a son is rebuked by his loving mother during his childhood, the boy does not know enough to thank his mother because he does not know how to assess the reason for being reproved; but when he has reached the age of discretion, he thanks her, because through his mother's instruction he has been dissuaded from wrongdoing and has become accustomed to good behavior and discipline. I treat my chosen ones in a similar fashion.

℘ 📖 ℜ

Evening Prayer

Antiphon: Pray in the secret chamber of your heart where God intimately dwells.

Psalm 118:49–56 ✠ Psalm 7:1–17 ✠ Psalm 16:1–15

Scripture: Matthew 6:5–8

Reading: St. Teresa of Avila, nun and foundress, Doctor of the Church † 1582

The Way of Perfection 31.9–10

Notice very carefully this comparison which seems very appropriate in my opinion: the soul is like an infant that still nurses when lying at its mother's breasts, and the mother, without her baby's attempting to suckle, puts the milk in its mouth in order to provide it delight. The same applies here, for without the effort of the intellect the will is loving, and the Lord desires that the will, without thinking about things, should understand that it is with him and that the intellect does nothing more than swallow the milk which His Majesty places in its mouth, so as to enjoy its sweetness. The will knows that it is the Lord who is granting this favor, and it rejoices in its enjoyment; yet it doesn't desire to understand how it enjoys the favor or even what it enjoys, but forgets itself at the time, knowing that the One who is present shall not forget to see to what is appropriate for the will. Now if the will should depart to combat with the intellect, thereby sharing its experiences by drawing the intellect after itself, the will cannot do so at all, but will be forced to let the milk slip from its mouth and thus lose that divine nourishment.

Herein lies the difference between this prayer of quietude and that prayer in which the entire soul is united with God, for then the soul doesn't even experience the process of swallowing this divine food; without its understanding how, the Lord places the milk within it.

Day 23

Morning Prayer

Antiphon: God leads us on our journey with tender care.

Psalm 107:1–6 ✠ Psalm 76:13–20 ✠ Psalm 102:1–23

Scripture: Deuteronomy 1:29–31 LXX

Reading: St. Teresa of Avila, nun and foundress, Doctor of the Church † 1582

Conceptions of the Love of God 7.9

Perhaps it will appear that such persons make little progress in their lives and that to remain in their own little corner enjoying their delight is what is most important. It belongs to the Lord's providence, in my opinion, that these beginners do not realize where these other souls are along the journey, for their initial fervor would make them want to leap forward towards these others. But such a move would not befit them, for they are not yet weaned and for some time they still need to be nourished with the milk I mentioned at the beginning. Let them remain close to those divine breasts, and when they are strong enough, the Lord will take care of them to lead them on farther. If they advanced now, they would not accomplish the good that they think, but would only harm themselves.

Evening Prayer

Antiphon: Pray without ceasing, inspired by the Holy Spirit.

Psalm 118:57–64 ✠ Psalm 1:1–6 ✠ Psalm 34:1–28

Scripture: Ephesians 6:10–18

Reading: St. Teresa of Avila, nun and foundress, Doctor of the Church † 1582

Interior Castle 4.3.10

There is one strong warning I must give to those who find themselves in this state [of the prayer of quietude]: namely, that they guard themselves very carefully against occasions for offending God. For as yet, the soul is not yet weaned but is like a child beginning to nurse at the breast. If it turns away from its mother's breasts, what can be expected for it except death? I am very much afraid that this will happen to anyone to whom God had granted this favor and who then withdraws from prayer—unless the person does so for some very exceptional reason—but unless one returns quickly to prayer, one will go from bad to worse. I know there is a great amount of fear in this matter and I have been deeply grieved by certain people I know, in whom I have witnessed what I am describing. They left the One who with so much love wanted to be their friend and demonstrate it by deeds.

Day 24

Morning Prayer

Antiphon: Firmly attach yourself to God, O my soul.

Psalm 118:145–52 ✠ Psalm 7:1–17 ✠ Psalm 72:1–28

Scripture: Jeremiah 17:7–10

Reading: St. Robert Bellarmine, archbishop, Doctor of the Church † 1621

Commentary on the Psalms 130.2

As a weaned child is towards its mother, so reward in my soul. Not satisfied with having confessed to God, the searcher of hearts, that he always had the greatest abhorrence of pride, the psalmist confirms this by an oath or imprecation so as to make his words more thoroughly believed by everyone. Therefore he says, *If I was not humble-minded* about myself, *but exalted in my soul*, thus looking down upon others; *as a weaned child is towards its mother*, namely, as a recently weaned child, lies crying and weeping on its mother's lap or breast, having been deprived of that sweet milk to which it was so habituated; *so reward in my soul*, that is, may my soul be deprived of the sweetness of divine consolation, my special, if not only delight! Only those who have been filled with the same Spirit and have tasted just how sweet God is, can appreciate the amount of punishment the holy prophet imprecates upon himself.... *My good is to adhere to God* my supreme happiness, *the God of my heart*, my share, my inheritance, my portion, my all; with whom alone I am content, and ever will be. When David, then, in his humility and simplicity of spirit, like a suckling child, placed all his happiness in the milk of divine love, he could not have wished upon himself a greater calamity than to be in the state of an infant prematurely weaned, who refuses any type of consolation having been torn from its mother's breasts.

PRAYING—WITH THE SAINTS—TO GOD OUR MOTHER

Evening Prayer

Antiphon: God gives birth to us by the Word of Truth.

Psalm 138:1–14 ✠ Psalm 102:1–23 ✠ Psalm 90:1–16

Scripture: James 1:13–18 NT

Reading: St. Peter Canisius, priest, Doctor of the Church † 1597

Autobiography 1.2

I firmly believe that at that stage [of my life] you gave birth in my heart to the spirit of reverence and pious solicitude, that you preserved me so well, O Lord, that in what followed, my youthful frivolity ventured less into the beaten tortuous paths out of reverence for you the Divine Master. You began to pierce my flesh with fear of you and then I began to fear your judgments. Much later, no doubt thanks to your angel, my guardian angel, I began to delight in the sacred paintings and objects and in the rites of the church. I gladly assisted the priests during Mass, and I played the role of priest as a youth, imitating their manner of chanting, celebrating the liturgy, and praying. By imitating I relived the lives of my elders, and that's the folly of children, I suppose, but often it also prefigures in a way a person's future, and supplies to the attentive eye a witness to your marvelous ways and your providence. Now truly it happens especially with children when they are able to combine that which is childish with what is noble, they thereby withdraw from childishness, and bit by bit are led *from milk to solid food*. But the wisdom of this world cannot understand by what paths you, the Supreme Wisdom, consent to follow, for by your words you accommodate yourself to our capacity, which is that of an infant. And each day provides proof that you communicate the gifts of your graciousness to children in a manner different than that in which you bless the mature and the developed.

Day 25

Morning Prayer

Antiphon: God will help us along the path to eternal life.

Psalm 5:1–12 ✠ Psalm 91:1–15 ✠ Psalm 90:1–16

Scripture: Genesis 28:10–19

Reading: St. Thérèse of Lisieux, nun, Doctor of the Church † 1897

Counsels and Remembrances 1

Sister Thérèse of the Child Jesus told me: "You make me think of a little child who begins to stand up, but who doesn't know how to walk yet. Determined to climb to the top of the stairs to find her mother, the child lifts her little foot to tackle the first step. But it's all for naught. She falls back time and again without advancing. Now listen, be this little child, by practicing all the virtues. Without fail, lift your little foot to climb the stairway of holiness, and don't even think that you can scale the first step! No, but the Good God only asks of you, your good will. From the top of this stairway, God looks upon you with love. Soon, moved by your unsuccessful attempts, God will personally descend and embrace you, forever carrying you into the kingdom where you will never leave."

Evening Prayer

Antiphon: I am friend, sister, mother; I am everything you wish.

Psalm 140:1–5 ✠ Psalm 88:1–28 ✠ Psalm 26:1–14

Scripture: Mark 10:35–45

Reading: St. John Chrysostom, bishop, Father and Doctor of the Church † 407

Homilies on Matthew 76.5

Would not Christ have every right to turn away from us and punish us when he offers himself to us in everything and yet we reject him? Surely this is perfectly clear to everyone. For if you wish to adorn yourself, he responds, "Take *my* adornment. If you want to arm yourself, Take *my* weapons. If you wish to clothe yourself, Take *my* garment. If you are you hungry, Eat at *my* table. If you want to make a journey, Follow *my* way. Do you want to be an heir? Take *my* inheritance. Are you in search of a homeland? Enter the city which I have built and established. Are you interested in building a home? Build it in my dwellings. And I don't demand that you pay for what I offer; rather, I owe pay to you for this very thing, if you are willing to use all my blessings. What could match this generosity? I am father, brother, bridegroom, dwelling, nursing mother, clothing, root, foundation. I am everything you wish; you stand in need of nothing. I shall be your servant, for I came to serve, not to be served. I am friend, member, head, brother, sister, mother; I am all things. Only be my friend."

Day 26

Morning Prayer

Antiphon: God is our sister in intimacy, speaking to us as an intimate friend.

Psalm 129:1–8 ✠ Psalm 118:17–24 ✠ Psalm 132:1–3

Scripture: Wisdom 8:16–21 LXX

Reading: St. Mechtild of Hackeborn, nun † 1299

PRAYING—WITH THE SAINTS—TO GOD OUR MOTHER

Book of Special Grace 4.50

Because there was a devout person who was mourning very much, the servant of God, [Mechtild of Hackeborn], moved with compassion, asked the merciful Lord to support that person with the consolation of the Holy Spirit. The Lord replied, "Why is this soul so distraught? I have created her for myself and have given myself to her in everything she wished. I am her father regarding creation; I am her mother in redemption; I am her brother when it comes to sharing the kingdom; I am her sister concerning sweet communion."

Evening Prayer

Antiphon: God calls us sister and desires our friendship!

Psalm 133:1–3 ✠ Psalm 132:1–3 ✠ Psalm 118:137–44

Scripture: John 15:9–15

Reading: St. Alphonsus Liguori, bishop, Doctor of the Church † 1787

How to Converse Continually and Familiarly with God 6–9

Accustom yourself to speaking intimately with God, one on one, with familiarity and love, as if to your best friend who loves you dearly. It is a great mistake, as we have already noted, to be afraid and to approach God like an ashamed and sniveling servant, trembling with terror before his master. It's an even greater error to believe that conversing with God is nothing but tedious and wearisome. Absolutely not! *Having converse with Her involves no bitterness, and associating with Her, no tedium.* Ask people who love God with a genuine love and they will tell you that in the troubles of their lives, they experience no greater or more genuine relief than in loving and intimate conversation with God.

This relationship does not demand that you constantly think of God at the expense of your activities, or even your relaxation. It only requires that, without neglecting your other obligations, you treat God the way that you would those whom you love, and vice versa, in any other situation.

Your God is ever at your side, in fact, within you: *In whom we live, and move, and have our being.* There is no royal doorkeeper you need to go through, announcing you, so that you can speak with God. On the contrary, God delights that you interact on an intimate basis. Discuss all your affairs with God, your plans, your troubles, your fears, and anything else that concerns you. But above all, like I said, speak with God as to a friend with an open heart, for God can hardly speak to the soul that does not speak to God.

If a soul is not accustomed to speaking with God, she will hardly recognize God's voice speaking to her. On this account the Lord complains, *"Our sister is immature.... What shall we do for our sister when her days of courtship begin?* Our little sister is but a child when it comes to my love. How can I speak to her if she doesn't understand what I say?" Yes, God wishes to be feared as an almighty and terrible Master by those who despise divine grace; but on the other hand, God wishes to be treated like the dearest and most affectionate friend by those who love him. That is why God desires that we often converse with familiarity, and without any hesitation.

Of course it's true that the greatest reverence is always due God, but when you experience the grace of feeling the Divine Presence and the desire to speak with God as to the One who loves you more than anyone else, then express your feelings with total freedom and intimacy. *She hastens to make Herself known, in anticipation of our desires.*

Day 27

Morning Prayer

Antiphon: God wishes to be our wife, even though she is beyond our state.

Psalm 142:1–12 ✠ Psalm 118:57–64 ✠ Psalm 127:1–6

Scripture: Hosea 2:19–20, 23 LXX

Reading: St. Macarius the Great, Desert Father of the Church † 391

Spiritual Homilies 7.1

Picture, if you will, a young woman in the prime of her life, fairer, wiser and wealthier than all other women, taking for her husband a poor, base, grotesque man, clothed in torn rags. She removes the filthy tatters from him and clothes him with regal garments, placing a diadem on his head, and enters into union with him. Eventually the poor fellow becomes frightened and exclaims, "Am I, who am so miserable and poor and common and lowly, to have such a marriage bestowed upon me?"

This is exactly what God has done to poor wretched Man. God has given him to taste of another realm, of other delicious food, showing him glorious things and royal beauties both unspeakable and heavenly. Thus the man, comparing those spiritual delights against the things of this world, throws it all away, and whether he sees a king, or powerful rulers, or the wise, he fixes his focus upon the heavenly treasure. Because God is love, humanity has received the heavenly and divine fire of Christ. Humanity is at rest and rejoices, and is there transfixed.

Evening Prayer

Antiphon: Come take Wisdom as your wife.

Psalm 1:1–6 ✠ Psalm 18:1–14 ✠ Psalm 118:145–52

Scripture: Wisdom 8:2–8 LXX

PRAYING—WITH THE SAINTS—TO GOD OUR MOTHER

Reading: St. John of the Cross, priest, Doctor of the Church † 1591

Ascent of Mount Carmel 1.2.1–4

We can say there are three reasons why this journey made by the soul to union with God is called "night." The first deals with the starting point from which the soul proceeds, for it needs to gradually deprive itself of desire for all the worldly things it possesses, by denying them to itself. This denial and deprivation are, as it were, a night to all the human senses. The second reason has to do with the means, or the path along which the soul must journey to attain this union, namely faith, which is also as dark as night to human understanding. The third deals with the goal to which it travels, namely God, who is a dark night to the soul in this life. These three nights must pass through the soul, or rather, the soul must pass through them, so that it may attain divine union with God.

In the book of the holy Tobit these three types of night were represented by the three nights which, as the angel commanded, were to pass before the young Tobias should be united with his bride. On the first night he commanded him to burn the heart on the fish in the fire. This heart signifies the human heart that is attached to worldly things, which, in order that one may begin to journey towards God, must be burned and purified from all that is creaturely, in the fire of God's love. And in such a purgation the devil takes flight, for he has power over the soul only as long as it is attached to corporeal and temporal things.

On the second night the angel instructed him that he would be admitted into the company of the holy patriarchs, who are the fathers of the faith. By passing through the first night which is the privation of all sensory objects the soul immediately enters into the second night, and lives in faith alone, not excluding love, but other knowledge acquired by understanding, as we shall mention later, something that does not belong to the senses.

On the third night the angel told Tobias that he would obtain the blessing, which is God. God, by means of faith, which is the second night, continually communicates himself so secretly and intimately to the soul that God becomes another night for the soul. This divine communication is much more obscure and darker than those others, as we shall soon point out. Now, when this third night has passed, which is the complete accomplishment of the spiritual communication of God ordinarily done in great darkness of the soul, next there follows the soul's union with the Bride, She who is the Wisdom of God.

Day 28

Morning Prayer

Antiphon: We may, by analogy, contemplate our Creator.

Psalm 8:1–9 ✠ Psalm 88:1–28 ✠ Psalm 103:1–34

Scripture: Wisdom 13:1–9

Reading: Bl. John Paul II, pope † 2005

Catechism of the Catholic Church 41–43

Because our knowledge about God is limited, our language about God is equally limited. We can only employ names for God by taking creatures as our starting point, and according to our limited human ways of knowing and thinking.

All creation bears a certain likeness to God, especially humanity created in the image and likeness of God. The myriad perfection of creatures—their truth, their goodness, their beauty—all reflect the infinite perfection of God. Therefore we can name God by taking his creatures' perfections as our starting point, "for from the greatness and beauty of created things, by analogy, we can contemplate their Creator."

God transcends all creation. Consequently we must continually purify our language of everything within it that is limited, bound by images, or imperfect, if we are not to confuse our concept of God—"the ineffable, the incomprehensible, the invisible, the ungraspable"—with our human representations. Our human expressions always fall short of the mystery of God.

Understandably, when talking about God like this, our language is using human modes of expression; notwithstanding, it really does attain to God himself, although incapable of expressing God in his infinite simplicity. In fact, we must bear in mind that "between Creator and creature no similitude can be expressed without inferring an even great dissimilitude"; and that "regarding God, we cannot grasp what God is, but rather only what God is not, and how other beings are in relation to him."

Evening Prayer

Antiphon: God transcends both fatherhood and motherhood.

Psalm 130:1–3 ✠ Psalm 26:1–14 ✠ Psalm 21:1–23

Scripture: John 1:15–18 PESH

Reading: Bl. John Paul II, pope † 2005

Catechism of the Catholic Church 239

When calling God "Father," the language of faith primarily indicates two ideas: that God is the primary source and transcendent authority of everything; and at the same time is goodness and loving solicitude for all his children. God's parental tenderness can likewise be expressed through the image of motherhood, which powerfully signifies God's immanence as well as intimacy between Creator and creature. Thus the language of faith draws on the human experience of parents, who are in a certain fashion the first representatives of God for human beings. But this experience likewise tells us that human parents are fallible and can disfigure the face of fatherhood and motherhood. It is important, therefore, to remember that God transcends the human distinction between the sexes. He is neither man nor woman: he is God. Also he transcends human fatherhood and motherhood, all the while being their origin and standard.

✠

God Almighty

Day 1

Morning Prayer

Antiphon: Manna is white and sweet to the taste.

Psalm 5:1–12 ✠ Psalm 76:13–20 ✠ Psalm 4:1–8

Scripture: Exodus 16:31–35

Reading: St. Clement of Alexandria, priest, Father of the Church † ca. 215

Christ the Educator 1.6.41.1–3

After giving birth, milk is supplied to the infant. Breasts that once were admirably uplifted and pointed towards the husband, are now pendulous and point towards the child. They learn to offer the babe this most agreeable nourishment, wrought by nature for its convenient and salutary nourishment. Unlike perpetual well-springs, the breasts are not always engorged with milk ready to be drunk, but they transform the elements within them into milk, and cause it to flow. Well-adapted to and wholesome for the little one beginning to ingest its consistency and to grow, this nourishment is the result of a labor ordained by God, the Nursing Mother and the Father of all who are born, as well as born again. This food is similar to the manna that rained down from the heavens upon the ancient Hebrews, the celestial nourishment of angels. In fact, even to this day, wet nurses call the first flow of milk by the same name: manna. Although women who have given birth and become mothers flow with milk, the Lord, the fruit of the Virgin, did not bless their breasts or acclaim them nourishers. No, because the all-loving and philanthropic Father has rained down the Word; it is he himself who has become the spiritual nourishment of the virtuous.

Evening Prayer

Antiphon: God Almighty loves us in a feminine manner.

Psalm 6:1–10 ✠ Psalm 118:153–60 ✠ Psalm 145:1–10 TNK

Scripture: 1 John 4:7–16

Reading: St. Clement of Alexandria, priest, Father of the Church † ca. 215

Who Is the Rich Man That Shall Be Saved? 36.1—37.2

All the faithful, then, are good and godlike, worthy of their title which they wear like a diadem around their head. . . . These the Word calls *light of the world*, and *salt of the earth*. This is the seed, the image and likeness of God, his true offspring and heir, as if sent here on some kind of foreign mission by the Father's great dispensation and suitable arrangement. For God's sake the visible and invisible things of the universe have been created, some for service, others for discipline, while others for instruction about him; all being held together as long as the seed remains, and when it is harvested, these things will be quickly dissolved.

What else is necessary? Behold the mysteries of love! Then you shall have a vision of the womb of the Father, whom the Only-Begotten declared. God in God's very self is love, and for love's sake became visible to us. And while the ineffable aspect of God is Father, the aspect that has loving sympathy for us manifests itself as Mother. The Father, by the act of loving, became feminine, and the great proof of this is the One whom God gave birth to from himself. Now the fruit that is born of love is love.

Day 2

Morning Prayer

Antiphon: God our Creator rears us like a mother.

Psalm 41:1–11 ✠ Psalm 8:1–9 ✠ Psalm 102:1–22

Scripture: Hosea 11:1–4 TNK

Reading: St. Cheremon, Desert Father of the Church † ca. 400

In Cassian, *Consolations* 3.13.14

Now let us seek in human affairs a comparison for the incomparable mercy of our Creator, not that we presume to find anything of equal loving tenderness, but at least a certain resemblance to the indulgent graciousness. Picture a loving and caring nursing mother who, for a long time, carries a small child in her bosom so that she might eventually teach it to walk. At first, she lets it crawl, then she stands the child up and supports it with her right hand so that it learns to place one foot in front of the other. Next she leaves him for a moment, only to grasp him as soon as she sees that he is teetering, steadies him when he wobbles, picks him up once he's fallen down, and either stops him from falling or allows him to fall gently, lifting him up after a stumble. But once she has raised him to boyhood or to the vigor of adolescence and young manhood, she makes him carry burdens and do some work which will not oppress him but rather exercise him. She also lets him fight with his rivals. How much more the heavenly Father of all knows whom to carry in the bosom of his grace and whom to strengthen in his presence for virtue's sake by having them exercise free will, yet aiding them in their endeavors, hearing their pleas, not abandoning them when they seek help, and sometimes rescuing them from unseen dangers.

Evening Prayer

Antiphon: We must be born again of God in order to enter heaven.

Psalm 15:1–11 ✠ Psalm 118:161–68 ✠ Psalm 131:1–3 TNK

Scripture: John 3:1–6 NT

Reading: St. Cyril of Alexandria, Patriarch, Father and Doctor of the Church † 444

Commentary on Luke 11

He said to them, "When you pray, say, 'Our Father who art in heaven . . .'"
O superb liberality! O incomparable gentleness, befitting God alone! God bestows his own glory upon us; raises slaves to the dignity of freedom; grants that God be called Father, constituting us in the class of children. Through him we have received this, as the wise John bears witness writing about him, *To all those who received him, he granted the power to become children of God.* We are transformed to the status of sonship through a spiritual birth, not by a corruptible seed, but rather by the living and enduring Word of God, as Scripture says, *By willing it he gave birth to us by the Word of Truth so that we might be a kind of first-fruits of his creation,* as one of the apostles affirms. And Christ himself became the visible passageway, saying, *Unless one is born of water and Spirit, then one will not be able to enter into the reign of God.*

Day 3

Morning Prayer

Antiphon: The children of God are called gods.

Psalm 54:1–16 ✠ Psalm 83:1–12 ✠ Psalm 81:1–8

Scripture: Isaiah 44:21–24

Reading: John of Dalyatha, monk, Father of the Church † ca. 780

Homily 19

Glory to You, O Father and Lord of all creation, You who have given us a new mother, [Repentance], in view of a new birth, in order that we might be perfectly (re-)born from Your own Womb; so that when our inexperience infects us with every kind of filth, she might bathe us, purify us, beautify us, and like an attentive governess, wrap in the folds of her garment those who have been birthed by her, until, cherished, enlightened and well loved, they might make their way to you to become gods and royal heirs, children of your Lordship.

Evening Prayer

Antiphon: We have been cleansed by a new birth, thanks to God's maternal love.

Psalm 18:1–14 ✠ Psalm 120:1–8 ✠ Psalm 138:1–14

Scripture: 1 John 4:7–12

Reading: St. Hildegard of Bingen, abbess † 1179

Know Your Way 2.2.4

In this fashion the love of God has appeared in our midst: God sent the Only-Begotten Son into the world so that we might live through him. In this is love, not that we have loved God, but that God first loved us and sent his Son as a propitiation for our sins. What does this mean? That because God loved us in this fashion, another salvation has arisen than what we had in the beginning, when we were heirs of innocence and holiness; for the heavenly Father manifested his love in our dangers even though we warranted punishment, by sending his Word through human birth to be the one alone in the darkness of the world who was full of holiness by means of heavenly virtue. There the Word brought to completion all good things, and by his gentleness brought back to life those who had been expelled because of their uncleanness of sin thus being unable to return to the holiness they had lost. What does this mean? That through this fountain of life came the sweet embrace of God's maternal love, which has nourished us into life and is our help in the midst of dangers, even the most profound and sweetest love, preparing us for repentance.

Day 4

Morning Prayer

Antiphon: We are all nursed at the breast of God our mother.

Psalm 64:1–13 ✠ Psalm 118:169–76 ✠ Psalm 51:1–5 TNK

Scripture: Song of Songs 7:11—8:2

PRAYING—WITH THE SAINTS—TO GOD OUR MOTHER

Reading: St. Hildegard of Bingen, abbess † 1179

Know Your Way 2.6.35

Who will give you to me as my brother, sucking the breasts of my mother, that I may find you outdoors and kiss you, and no one will despise me? What does this mean? With groans, devotion and certain faith the people of the Church declare: "Who will be merciful to me a miserable person in tribulation and give me, you, the Bridegroom of the Church?" You whom I call my brother because of your incarnation, you who suck the mercy and truth that nourish humanity from the Divinity, she who is my mother in my creation, naturally giving me life with invigorating growth.

Evening Prayer

Antiphon: God's grace, like milk, causes us to grow and be transformed.

Psalm 21:1–11 ✠ Psalm 121:1–9 ✠ Psalm 103:1–34

Scripture: 2 Corinthians 3:12–18

Reading: St. Hildegard of Bingen, abbess † 1179

Book of Divine Works 4.105

A human being is endowed with intelligence and sensitivity; intelligence because of understanding everything and sensitivity because of sensing what lies within human grasp. God fills the whole flesh of humanity with vitality when God breathed the spirit of life into it. Hence a human being chooses whatever pleases it in the knowledge of good and evil, and rejects whatever is displeasing. However, God sees what a human being has in mind. If a person proposes something which is not of God, then God turns away and at once such people succumb to those who first devised evil and thus wished to destroy heaven; something that does not affect God. For it would be unbecoming if God were to destroy God's very self. If, however, a person were to sigh out the name of the Father and call upon God with genuine desire, the protection of the angels rushes to that person's aide so that he is no longer impeded by the Enemy. If one asks for the good greatly desiring it, immediately God will send milk, at first in a gentle manner, but then God will flood that person with streams of grace, in this way the person will rise from virtue to virtue.

Day 5

Morning Prayer

Antiphon: God, our true mother, will never forget us.

Psalm 72:1–28 ✠ Psalm 118:9–16 ✠ Psalm 131:1–3 TNK

Scripture: Isaiah 66:9–13 VULG

Reading: St. Albert the Great, bishop, Doctor of the Church † 1280

Commentary on Isaiah 49:15

Even if she should forget (Isa 49:15). This response is the Lord's consolation, first by way of a simile, second by way of explanation where it says, *Your builders have come* (v. 17). The simile is twofold, namely human fondness and a display of fondness. Human fondness relates to two things: human relations and the superabundance of divine tenderness. Therefore it says, *Even if,* according to customary human fondness, *a woman should forget,* due to feebleness let's say, affected by weakness in any direction due to *her infant,* who itself, because of its tender and innocent age deserves loving-kindness and fondness. *More than the love of women, as a mother loves her only child, did I love you* (2 Sam 1:26). *Her bowels were moved deeply for her child* (1 Kgs 3:26). *Lest she not have mercy on the child of her womb,* to whom she gave birth, whom she suckled and fed. *For our destitution was sufficient for us that we might see our son* (Tob 5:25). *My son, have pity upon me who carried you in my womb for nine months, and suckled you with my milk for three years, and nourished you and raised you to your present age* (2 Mac 7:27). The mother, however, is mentioned more often than the father, because no matter how moved the father might be, he remains steadfast, whereas the mother is moved by compassion.

And if she should forget . . . I, however, shall not forget you, that is, divine tenderness is incapable of forgetting us. As God says, *I have remembered you, pitying your youth* (Jer 2:2). *May my tongue cleave to my palate if I remember you naught* (Ps 136:6). While it might seem as if God has forgotten us because of the trials we experience to some extent and then feel forsaken, to this charge God responds, *For a brief moment I have forsaken you, but with great mercy I will gather you back* (Isa 54:7), and, *Hide yourself for a brief moment until the indignation passes by* (Isa 26:20). Thus God says, *I, however, shall not forget you,* in other words, I am more than a mother; I have formed you and carried you from eternity in the light of my foreknowledge. *You who are carried in my womb and borne in my bowels* (Isa 46:3). *The Lord your God has carried you, like a human being carries its child, in all your paths, wherever you wandered* (Deut 1:31). Thus our Lord has formed us in God's womb of foreknowledge, borne us in tender attentiveness, and was stretched out in the throes of giving birth through the passion of our redemption. *You will be like a child to the Most High, and God will be more tender to you than a mother* (Sir 4:11). *As one whom a mother caresses, so shall I comfort you* (Isa 66:13).

Evening Prayer

Antiphon: Come and cuddle in the bosom of God.

Psalm 118:49–56 ☩ Psalm 26:1–14 ☩ Psalm 130:1–3

Scripture: Matthew 23:37–39 NT *Alternate translation*

Reading: St. Albert the Great, bishop, Doctor of the Church † 1280

Commentary on the Psalms 26:10

Yet the Lord will receive me (Ps 26:10). God has become father and mother for me. *Call no one on earth your father, for one is your Father who is in heaven* (Matt 23:9). God indeed is our father because he provides things for us like a father does his children. *Is not he your father, who created you, fashioned you, and established you?* (Deut 32:6). *And now, O Lord, you are our father, and we are clay; you are our maker, and we are all the work of your hands* (Isa 64:8). *And you shall be called by a new name, one which the mouth of the Lord shall declare* (Isa 62:2). Again, it is the father's duty to give commands. *I will do everything that you have commanded me, father* (Tob 5:1). Such is God in both the Old and New Testaments. It is the father's duty to lead his child. Thus God says, *You shall call me father and shall not cease walking after me* (Jer 3:19).

God properly acts as mother in four ways: To contain her offspring in her womb, *Listen to me, you who have been carried within my womb, who have been borne in my bowels* (Isa 46:3); To incubate and cuddle, indeed God does so—*How often I wanted to gather your children together like a mother hen gathers her chicks beneath her wings* (Matt 23:37); To suckle her young with milk, *As to little ones in Christ, I provided you milk, not solid food* (1 Cor 3:1–2); and finally, To nourish her offspring so that they mature, *I have nourished children and raised them* (Isa 1:2), etc.

Day 6

Morning Prayer

Antiphon: Like a mother, you have helped everyone in need.

Psalm 91:1–15 ☩ Psalm 24:1–22 ☩ Psalm 118:73–80

Scripture: Genesis 43:1–14 TNK

Reading: St. Gertrude the Great of Helfta, nun † 1302

Spiritual Exercises 7

As if accompanied by Mercy and Love you will appease the Father with these words, saying them with your heart and mouth:

O Sweet Mercy of God, full of loving-kindness and clemency, behold I am miserable, suffering sorrow and anguish of heart, I seek refuge in your loving and kind counsel because you are all my hope and trust. You have never despised a miserable person. You have shunned no sinner, even the most abject. You have not rejected anyone seeking refuge in you. You have never passed anyone by who was in distress, without showing compassion. Like a mother, you have always brought help to everyone in need. In accordance with your name, you have stood with loving-kindness beside everyone who invokes you.

Evening Prayer

Antiphon: Like a mother, you cuddle the frightened child in your bosom.

Psalm 118:57–64 ✠ Psalm 24:1–22 ✠ Psalm 112:1–9

Scripture: James 1:1–6

Reading: St. Gertrude the Great of Helfta, nun † 1302

Spiritual Exercises 7

As if accompanied by Mercy and Love you will appease the Father with these words, saying them with your heart and mouth:

O Cherishing Love, worthy of honor, behold me, a miserable human being, driven around by the most powerful wind of my thoughtlessness and terrified by thunderclaps of my conscience regarding my sins: I take refuge beneath the shelter of your loving-kindness because I know all too well that there is no hope for me but in you, and apart from you will find no rest. Like a mother you cuddle the lost child in your bosom.

Day 7

Morning Prayer

Antiphon: God allows unpleasant things to happen.

Psalm 107:1–6 ✠ Psalm 60:1–8 ✠ Psalm 54:1–16

Scripture: Nehemiah 9:26–31 TNK

Reading: St. Gertrude the Great of Helfta, nun † 1302

The Herald of God's Loving-Kindness 3.63.1

As it ordinarily happens that the injuries one receives from a friend are heavier to bear than those from an enemy, as it says, *If my enemy had reviled me I could have borne it . . .* , our saint [Gertrude], realizing that a sister who was quite spiritual and to whom she was attached with deep devotion and friendship wasn't reciprocating with the expected friendship, and even, almost out of spite for what was done for her, twisted things around, our saint thus, in the consternation that she experienced, sought refuge in the Lord. Now the Lord, consoling her with great care, told her, "Don't be upset, my daughter, I allowed that to happen for your greater spiritual good. For, in order to enjoy your company more often in which I take great delight, like a mother who has a child whom she tenderly loves and wishes to have at her side at all times, . . . likewise, desiring that you always stay by my side, I allow your friends to cause you some unpleasant experiences so that you don't become completely attached to any creature and that you passionately return to me, knowing that in me you can find the fullness of all joy and friendship without any change."

Evening Prayer

Antiphon: Save me O God in your mercy from my lukewarmness.

Psalm 138:1–14 ✠ Psalm 118:17–24 ✠ Psalm 50:1–19

Scripture: Revelation 3:14–22

Reading: St. Gertrude the Great of Helfta, nun † 1302

Spiritual Exercises 7

As if accompanied by Mercy and Love you will appease the Father with these words, saying them with your heart and mouth:

O Sweet Loving-Kindness of God. O dear Loving Liberality of God. You open your bosom to all; you are the refuge of the poor. O Loving-Kindness what do you suggest? Whither shall I flee from the face of the frigid blast, since I am not able to withstand the bitterness of winter? The lukewarmness of my soul has already frozen with frost the furrows of my heart. Ah, shelter me beneath your shoulders and hide my nakedness that puts me to shame. Then I shall warm myself beneath your pinions, and find hope forever beneath your wings.

O Loving-Kindness, O Tenderness, do not abandon me in my anxiety. Do not turn your face away from my sobbing and crying. May your charity compel you to patiently listen to me. Ah, open your bosom where I may repose for awhile and pour out my soul in your presence. I am certain that because of your goodness and your intrinsic loving-kindness that you do not despise the desolate, nor disdain the afflicted. Oh how favorable is your conduct with those in misery. Oh how agreeable are the scents of your perfumes to those on the verge of fainting away.

You raise the stricken; you deliver those in bondage. You despise no one in tribulation; you are attentive to the needs of everyone in a maternal and merciful manner. You console those in despair with loving-kindness. You come to everyone in dire need with great clemency.

Day 8

Morning Prayer

Antiphon: God tests us in order to strengthen us.

Psalm 118:145–52 ✠ Psalm 11:1–8 ✠ Psalm 16:1–15

Scripture: Exodus 15:22–27

Reading: St. Gertrude the Great of Helfta, nun † 1302

The Herald of God's Loving-Kindness 3.30.38

One day when Gertrude was tired, overcome by physical exhaustion, she said to the Lord: "What good am I, Lord, and what would you ever want to use me for?" The Lord replied: "As a mother consoles her children, I too, will console you," adding, "Haven't you ever seen a mother pacifying her child?" And as she remained silent, not recalling any memory, the Lord reminded her that about six months ago she had seen a mother playing with her child. The Lord especially pointed out three things which she had formerly overlooked. First, the mother often asked her little child to give her a hug, and the little one, despite his lack of development, struggled to lift himself up towards her. The Lord remarked that so too, the soul of the saint must make every effort to lift itself up in contemplation in order to arrive at the joy of God's infinitely tender love. Second, the mother tested the will of the child by asking: "Do you want this? Do you want that?" all the while not giving him either one of the two. So too, God at times tests people, allowing them to fear certain afflictions which they will never experience, nevertheless, God is perfectly satisfied if they intended to accept them, thus becoming worthy of an eternal reward. Third, no one else but the mother alone can interpret the utterances of this infant still too young to form words. Likewise, God alone understands the intention of the person, and judges accordingly, not like people who only judge by external appearances.

Evening Prayer

Antiphon: Do not be puffed up with self-importance.

Psalm 140:1–5 ✠ Psalm 17:1–31 ✠ Psalm 131:1–3 TNK

Scripture: 1 Corinthians 4:14–21

Reading: St. Catherine of Siena, religious, Doctor of the Church † 1380

Dialogue 72

I didn't want to remain silent about how ordinary people are misguided in their need for loving sensations, in the little bit of good they do perform (that is, what little virtue they exercise in times of consolation); nor regarding that spiritual self-love that yearns for consolations my servants wish to experience: how deceived these people are in their selfish love of pleasure that holds them back from knowing the truth of my affection or discerning where sin exists. Let alone about how the devil exploits their own sin to deceive them unless they keep to the path I have described to you.

I have told you all of this so that you and my other servants may walk on the path of virtue for love of me and for no other reason. They are misguided whose love is imperfect, who love me for my gifts and not for myself the giver. They often are deluded. Whereas the soul who has entered in truth into the house of self-knowledge, practicing perfect prayer and rising above the imperfect love that goes along with imperfect prayer (in the manner I described for you when I spoke about prayer), such a soul receives me experiencing affectionate love. She seeks to draw to herself the milk of my sweet tenderness from the breast of the teaching of Christ crucified.

Day 9

Morning Prayer

Antiphon: I am the mother of all virtue.

Psalm 129:1–8 ✠ Psalm 21:1–23 ✠ Psalm 24:1–22

Scripture: Sirach 24:4, 22–31 VULG

Reading: St. Catherine of Siena, religious, Doctor of the Church † 1380

Dialogue 96

I've told you about the fruit produced from the third kind of tears. Next comes the fourth and last, the stage of unitive tears which is not separate from the third, as I mentioned before, rather they are joined together just like love for me and love of neighbor; the one complements the other. But the soul has grown so much by the time she reaches the fourth stage that she not only endures all things with patience but gladly longs for suffering to such an extent that she spurns every sort of amusement, no matter what the source, simply in order to conform herself to my Truth, Christ crucified.

Such a soul receives the fruit of spiritual tranquility, an experiential union with my gentle Divine Nature in which she savors milk, just as an infant when quieted rests on its mother's breast, taking its mother's nipple in its mouth, and drinks her milk through her flesh. In such a manner the soul who has reached this final stage rests on the breast of my Divine Love and takes into her mouth, moved by holy desire, the flesh of Christ crucified. In other words, she follows his teachings and his footsteps, because she has learned in the third stage that it is impossible to follow after me, the Father. For no pain can befall me, the Eternal Father, but it can befall my beloved Son, the gentle and most loving Word. But you cannot walk without pain; you must attain proven virtue through suffering. So the soul rests on the breast of Christ crucified who is my love, and thereby drinks in the milk of virtue. In this virtue the soul experiences the life of grace and tastes within her very self my Divine Nature that gives the virtues their sweetness. This is the truth: the virtues were not sweet to her before, but now they are because they are practiced in union with me, Divine Love. In other words, the soul has no concern for her own benefit other than for my honor and the salvation of souls.

See then, gentle daughter, how sweet and glorious is this state in which the soul experiences such union at love's breast that her mouth is never without the breast nor the breast without milk.

Evening Prayer

Antiphon: The Holy Spirit convinces us about holiness and truth.

Psalm 133:1–3 ✠ Psalm 50:1–19 ✠ Psalm 142:1–12

Scripture: John 16:4–15

Reading: St. Catherine of Siena, religious, Doctor of the Church † 1380

Dialogue 96

See then, gentle daughter, how sweet and glorious is this state in which the soul experiences such union at love's breast that her mouth is never without the breast nor the breast without milk. Consequently, such a soul is never found without Christ crucified nor without me, the Eternal Father, whom she finds when she tastes the Supreme Eternal Deity. O who can fathom the powers with which that soul is filled! Her memory is filled with incessant remembrance of me as she lovingly imbibes my blessings. It's not so much my blessings per se, but my loving affection in granting them to her, especially the blessings of creation, for she clearly sees that she is created in my image and likeness.

At the first stage, she recognized the punishment that follows ingratitude for this blessing, thus she raised herself from her wretched state through the blessings of the blood of Christ in which I recreated her by grace. I washed away from her soul the leprosy of sin and thus she found herself in the second stage in which she tasted the sweetness of being in love with me, and experienced disgust for the sin in which she beheld how displeasing she had been to me that I had taken out her punishment on the body of my Only-Begotten Son.

Subsequently, she experienced the coming of the Holy Spirit who convinced and shall continue to convince the soul about Truth. When does the soul receive this light? After she has recognized, thanks to the first and second stages, my blessings dwelling within her. Then she receives the perfect light, understanding the truth about me, the Eternal Father: that in love I had created her to grant her eternal life. This is the truth, and I have demonstrated it to her in the blood of Christ crucified. Once the soul has come to know this, she loves it and shows her love by sincerely loving what I love and hating what I hate. Thus she finds herself in the third stage of love of neighbor. Thus the memory, with all imperfection in the past, is filled at the breast because she has remembered and retained within herself all my blessings.

Day 10

Morning Prayer

Antiphon: God withdraws from us for a time for our own good.

Psalm 142:1–12 ✠ Psalm 26:1–14 ✠ Psalm 37:1–22

Scripture: Wisdom 9:17—10:6 LXX

Reading: St. Catherine of Siena, religious, Doctor of the Church † 1380

Dialogue 70

Sometimes spiritual self-centeredness harms people in yet another way. If their desire and seeking are only for consolations and visions, then they shall succumb to spiritual bitterness and weariness when they are deprived of these. They subsequently think they have lost grace when I sometimes withdraw from their spiritual awareness. But I do often grant my servants spiritual consolations and visions, but as I previously told you, I sometimes withdraw from the soul and then return. I depart not by way of grace but withdraw experiential feelings in order to bring the soul to perfection. But this only sends such souls into bitterness and they think they are experiencing hell when they feel themselves removed from pleasure and feel the pains and torments of many temptations.

They should not be so ignorant or allow themselves to be deceived by spiritual selfishness that does not know the truth. Instead they should know me dwelling within them, know that I am that Ultimate Good who sustains their good will in time of conflict so that they do not turn their backs simply for the sake of experiencing pleasure. Therefore they should humble themselves, regarding themselves as unworthy of spiritual peace and tranquility. And this is exactly why I do withdraw from them: to humble them and to make they know my charity dwelling within, when they discover it in the good will with which I sustain them in times of trial. I want them to receive not only the milk of sweet tenderness that I poured out before their souls, but also to fasten themselves to the breast of my Truth so that they may receive milk along with the flesh. In other words, I want them to draw to themselves the milk of my love by meditating on the flesh of Christ crucified, namely his teachings out of which I have built a bridge for you to reach me. This is why I withdraw myself from them.

Thematic Readings for Non-Feast Days

Evening Prayer

Antiphon: God is better than father or mother; God is the best of all lovers.

Psalm 1:1–6 ✠ Psalm 102:1–22 ✠ Psalm 26:1–14

Scripture: James 5:7–11

Reading: St. Alphonsus Liguori, bishop, Doctor of the Church † 1787

How to Converse Continually and Familiarly with God 1–2

The holy Job was dumbfounded when considering that our God is so bent on doing good for us that God's heart has no greater urgent concern than to love us and make God's self loved by us. Thus speaking to God, Job exclaimed, *What is a human being, that you make so much of him, or that your heart has any feelings for him?* Accordingly, see how mistaken it would be to think that relating with God with great confidence and familiarity would be a lack of respect for God's infinite majesty. Assuredly, devout souls, you ought to respect God with all humility, and humble yourselves in the divine presence, especially when you remember your ingratitude and the offenses you committed in the past. But all this should not prevent you from relating to God with the most tender and intimate love, possible.

True, God is infinite Majesty, but at the same time, God is infinite goodness and unbounded love. You have in God the most sublime master that you can imagine, but you also have in God the greatest lover that you could ever wish for. God does not disdain our bold familiarity, but rather is overjoyed that you would interact with God with the same confidence, freedom, and affection with which little children interact with their mothers.

Behold how God invites us to sit at his feet! Behold the loving caresses that he promises us: *As nurslings you shall be carried at her breasts, and fondled upon her lap; as a mother speaks lovingly to her child, even so I shall comfort you.* Just as a mother delights in placing her child within her lap, there feeding and caressing it, with the same affection our loving God rejoices to interact with those souls who have given themselves entirely to God and placed all their hopes in God's goodness.

Realize that you have neither friend nor brother, father nor mother, spouse nor lover, who loves you more than your God does. Divine grace is that immense treasure by which we, lowly creatures and servants, become beloved friends of our very Creator. *For to human beings She is an infinite treasure; those who gain this treasure, win the friendship of God.*

✠

PRAYING—WITH THE SAINTS—TO GOD OUR MOTHER

God the Second Person: Wisdom

Day 1

Morning Prayer

Antiphon: Wisdom is her own Person.

Psalm 5:1–12 ✠ Psalm 118:17–24 ✠ Psalm 89:1–17

Scripture: Proverbs 8:22–25 VULG

Reading: Tertullian, Father of the Church † ca. 240

Treatise against Praxeas 6.1–2

 The power and constitution of the Divine Consciousness is demonstrated in Scripture under the name of Sophia, Wisdom. For what is wiser than the Reason or Word of God? Listen, therefore, to Wisdom herself, constituted as a second person: *At the first the Lord created me as the beginning of his ways, with his works in mind, before he made the earth, before the mountains were set in place, even before all the hills he gave birth to me*, that is to say, establishing and conceiving in God's own Consciousness.

 Furthermore, observe the distinction between them by her companionship with God, *When he was preparing the heavens*, she says, *I was present with him; and when he made his strongholds upon the winds which are the clouds above, and when he made secure the fountains which are beneath the heavens, I was as at his side, as a fellow artisan; I was she in whose presence God delighted; and I, too, daily delighted in his Person.*

Evening Prayer

Antiphon: Wisdom is like a mother hen, depositing spiritual gifts.

Psalm 6:1–10 ✠ Psalm 118:25–32 ✠ Psalm 16:1–15

Scripture: Matthew 23:37–39 NT

Reading: St. Rabanus Maurus, archbishop † 856

Scriptural Allegories

 The mother hen is the Wisdom of God, as in the Gospel passage: *Like a hen gathers her chicks beneath her wings.* . . . The Wisdom of God brings the elect to salvation by granting spiritual gifts.

Day 2

Morning Prayer

Antiphon: Wisdom, as Sovereign, establishes rulers.

Psalm 41:1–11 ✠ Psalm 5:1–12 ✠ Psalm 112:1–9

Scripture: Proverbs 8:12–21 TNK

Reading: St. Gregory of Nyssa, bishop, Father and Doctor of the Church † ca. 395

Against Eunomius 3.1.28–30

    The discourse depicts Wisdom as uttering certain statements in her own person. Now the diligent student knows quite well what is said in the passage where Wisdom makes counsel her dwelling place, and summons to herself knowledge and understanding, and states that she possesses strength and prudence, while she is herself called intelligence, and that she proceeds in the paths of righteousness and has her conversations in the ways of just judgment, and declares that through her, sovereigns reign, and princes issue righteous decrees, and monarchs govern their own realm. Now everyone will note that the considerate reader will accept none of the quoted passages without hesitation according to the obvious meaning. For by her kings are promoted to their dynasty, and if through her monarchy possesses its strength, it necessarily follows that Wisdom is portrayed to us as the establisher of monarchy, and transfers to herself the blame of those who govern wickedly in their kingdoms. But we know sovereigns who in reality advance, under the guidance of Wisdom, to the rule that has no end; namely the poor in spirit whose possession is the Kingdom of Heaven, as the Lord promises, who is Wisdom.

Evening Prayer

Antiphon: We are children born of the Spirit of Wisdom.

Psalm 15:1–11 ✠ Psalm 118:33–40 ✠ Psalm 143:7–12 TNK

Scripture: Galatians 4:19–31

Reading: St. Peter Damian, cardinal bishop, Doctor of the Church † 1072

Concerning True Happiness and Wisdom 3

    Indeed, just as heavenly Wisdom creates heavenly-minded and legitimate children of the Church, so too, earthly understanding makes one earthly-minded and illegitimate. Regarding these Baruch says, *And the children of Hagar who eagerly sought after that understanding which is of this world, the merchants of Theman, the confabulators of fables and seekers of knowledge, they did not know the way of Wisdom, nor did they remember her paths.* Therefore, those who are filled with desire to pursue worldly knowledge while despising spiritual Wisdom, they are the children of Hagar, not of Sarah; and being bastards, they are judged by the law of Ishmael, not that of Israel. Now since the name Hagar means "stranger," they are not the children of Wisdom, but rather strangers and foreigners, but not among those regarding whom the Apostle says, *Now, therefore, you are no longer strangers and foreigners, but fellow citizens with the saints, and of the household of God*. Likewise, dearly beloved, if I may again invoke the words of the prophet, Learn where true Prudence resides. For she is to be found in her essence only in God from whom you must diligently seek her.

Day 3

Morning Prayer

Antiphon: Wisdom, our Mother, has conceived us in love.

Psalm 54:1–16 ✠ Psalm 118:41–48 ✠ Psalm 89:1–17

Scripture: Song of Songs 8:5–7

Reading: Theodoret of Cyrus, bishop, Father of the Church † ca. 460

Commentary on the Song of Songs 3

It was not long after passing them by that I found the one whom my soul loved. I laid hold of him. I had hardly bypassed the created nature to reach the angelic nature itself so as to find my Uncreated Beloved, my Benefactor, when by faith alone I happened upon him. I bypassed all beings with the confirmation of the goal itself, namely the Cause of the universe is above every beings and is perceived by no nature whether by the senses or the intellect, being essentially superior to them. In this fashion, then, I bypassed all beings, seeking to bring home the bridegroom I desired. *I did not let him go before I brought him into my mother's house and into the chamber of she who conceived me.* That is to say, I did not stop seeking my lover until I enshrined him in my mind which is the house of God's Wisdom, She who is the Cause of all creation, and rightly Mother. . . . This Wisdom conceived me having the most excellent intention for me before the foundation of the world; thus also for my sake my lover submitted to human nature in its complete entirety.

Evening Prayer

Antiphon: In God lies the Treasury of Wisdom.

Psalm 18:1–14 ✠ Psalm 118:49–56 ✠ Psalm 121:1–9

Scripture: Colossians 2:1–5

Reading: St. Peter Damian, cardinal bishop, Doctor of the Church † 1072

Concerning Divine Omnipotence 8.1–20

Therefore it is certain that God Almighty contains all of the ages in the treasury of his eternal Wisdom, so that nothing can happen or transpire without God's being cognizant of the transitions of time. Thus, immovable in this ineffable citadel of divine majesty, God contemplates in a simple and singular perception all things constituted under the purview of his presence; however remote it might be, neither the past passes away, nor the future does not dawn. Just as God's nature is always to exist, and to remain the same for all eternity, circumscribing all that transpires, God envelopes within God's self, the courses of all the ages. And just as God encompasses within God's self all the ages without their passing away, so too, God absolutely contains within God's self all the extremities of the universe without their extending beyond reach. Manifestly this is why God says, *I fill heaven and earth.* And this is why it is said about Wisdom, *I alone encompassed the heavens.* Concerning her again, Solomon said, *As She is One, She call do all things, and renews everything, while herself perduring*; and elsewhere, *If the heavens, and the heavens of the heavens cannot contain you, how much less this house that I have built for you*!

Day 4

Morning Prayer

Antiphon: Wisdom wishes to be our mistress.

Psalm 64:1–13 ✠ Psalm 120:1–8 ✠ Psalm 122:1–4

Scripture: Wisdom 8:16–21 LXX

Reading: Bl. Henry Suso, prior † 1366

The Life of Henry Suso 3

In Holy Scripture, Eternal Wisdom presents herself as a lovable and charming mistress who graciously displays her charms with the intention to please everyone and speaks tenderly in the guise of a woman in order to draw all hearts to herself. . . . She showed herself to [Henry] in this fashion. She floated high above him, enthroned on the clouds; she shone like the morning star and her radiance was like the dazzling sun. Her crown was eternity; her raiment, celestial bliss; her words, sweetness itself; her embrace, the fullness of every joy. She was far away, and yet near at hand; on high and yet below; she was present and nevertheless hidden. She allows one to converse with her, yet no one can grasp her. She exercises authority in the highest heavens while touching the depths of the abyss. She extends her power from one end to the other and governs all things sweetly. . . .

Henry interiorly held converse with himself and asked of his heart, thirsting for love, "O my heart, see, from whence pours out such love and all delight? Where does all sweetness, beauty, joy of heart and loveableness derive? Surely it can only come from the erupting fountainhead of the pure Godhead!" . . . She was towards him totally like a mother who holds in her arms her nursing infant, or upright on her knees, when he moves his head and when his little body bobs towards its tender mother showing the heartfelt joy in these grace-filled movements. Such was the interior state of the servant [Henry's] heart in the delectable presence of Eternal Wisdom, in the experiential outpouring.

He then thought, "O Lord, if I had married a queen, my heart would have rejoiced. But now! You are the Empress of my heart, the Dispensatrix of all graces. In you I have all the riches as well as power that I could ever want!"

Evening Prayer

Antiphon: Wisdom carries us most tenderly in her bosom.

Psalm 21:1–11 ✠ Psalm 11:1–8 ✠ Psalm 131:1–3 TNK

Scripture: Sirach 4:1–11 VULG

Reading: St. Albert the Great, bishop, Doctor of the Church † 1280

Commentary on Isaiah 66.13

As one whom a mother caresses (Isa 66:13).

This holds true in the situations where God displays tender consolation like that of a mother, namely the Wisdom of God who is our mother par excellence, in whose womb we were formed. *I am the mother of pure love and reverence, of knowledge and holy hope* (Sir 24:24 VULG). This mother caresses us, and she more than any human mother. *You will be like a child to the Most High, and God will be more tender to you than a mother* (Sir 4:11). *If a woman,* that is to say mother, *were to forget her child, I will not forget you* (Isa 49:15). *Therefore I myself will console you. As a nursing mother cherishing her own children, so we in our love for you would have delivered to you not only the gospel of God, but our very souls as well* (1 Thess 2:7–8). This mode of being a mother is expressed in Isaiah where it says, *In his arms he will gather his lambs, and in his bosom he will carry them, those who are bearing young* (Isa 40:11). The affection of a mother likewise obtains in Matthew 23:37, *How often I wanted to gather together your children, like a hen gathers her chicks beneath her wings.* And, *Naomi took the child and placed him in her bosom and became his nurse* (Ruth 4:16). The name Naomi means tender or consoling and signifies Wisdom.

Thematic Readings for Non-Feast Days

GOD THE THIRD PERSON: THE HOLY SPIRIT

Day 1

Morning Prayer

Antiphon: The Holy Spirit dwells in humanity.

Psalm 72:1–28 ✠ Psalm 118:65–72 ✠ Psalm 103:1–34

Scripture: Job 32:6–9 TNK

Reading: Syrian hymn, mid to late second century

Odes of Solomon 28.1–7

> Like the wings of doves over their nestlings,
> and like the mouths of their nestlings towards their mouths;
> so too are the wings of the Spirit over my heart.
> My heart continually is refreshed and leaps for joy,
> like a baby who leaps for joy in its mother's womb.
> I trusted, thus I was at rest;
> because trustworthy is the One in whom I trusted.
> He has surely blessed me,
> and my head is near him.
> The dagger will not separate me from him,
> nor the sword.
> Because I am ready before destruction comes,
> and have been placed in his incorruptible wings.
> And immortal life embraced,
> even kissed me.
> And from it is the Spirit who dwells within me.
> And She cannot die because She is Life.

Evening Prayer

Antiphon: The Spirit ministers through women in the church.

Psalm 118:49–56 ✠ Psalm 131:1–18 ✠ Psalm 68:8–15 TNK

Scripture: 1 Timothy 3:1–13; Romans 16:1–2

Reading: Syrian liturgical practice, third century

PRAYING—WITH THE SAINTS—TO GOD OUR MOTHER

Syriac Version of the Didascalia 9

Now hear these things, O laity, you who are also the elect church of God. For the former people were likewise called a church; you, however, are the catholic Church, the holy and perfect, *a royal priesthood, a holy assembly, a people for inheritance*, the great Church, the bride adorned for the Lord God. Therefore those things which were formerly said, likewise fear now. Set aside oblations, tithes and first fruits for Christ, the true High Priest, and for his servants as well, and tithes of salvation to Him the beginning of whose name is the Decade. Hear, O catholic Church of God, that you were delivered from the ten plagues and thus received ten sayings, learned the Law, held fast the faith and believed in the Yod—the beginning of the Name; you are established in the perfection of God's glory. In place of the sacrifices of that time, now offer up prayers, supplications, and thanksgivings. In those days there were first fruits, tithes, oblations and gifts, but today the offerings are presented through the bishops to the Lord God, because they act as your high priests. But the priests and Levites now are the presbyters and deacons, the orphans and the widows. But the Levite and High Priest is the bishop. He is a servant of the word and mediator, but to you a teacher, and your father after God, who has begotten you through the water. This man is your chief and your leader and he is your mighty ruler. He guides in the place of the Almighty. Let him be honored by you as God is, because the bishop sits for you in the place of God Almighty. The deacon stands in the place of Christ, thus you should love him. And the deaconess shall be honored by you in the place of the Holy Spirit.

Day 2

Morning Prayer

Antiphon: Rebecca is a symbol of the Holy Spirit.

Psalm 91:1–15 ✠ Psalm 80:1–14 ✠ Psalm 143:7–12 TNK

Scripture: Genesis 28:1–5 TNK

Reading: St. Hippolytus, bishop and martyr, Father of the Church † 235

In Jerome, *Letter* 36.16

I promised that I would give you the allegorical significance of the text. Consequently, I will quote for you the words of the martyr Hippolytus.... According to him, Isaac is a figure of God the Father; Rebecca typifies the Holy Spirit; Esau stands for the ancient Hebrew people, as well as the devil; and Jacob represents the Church as well as Christ. The old age of Isaac depicts the consummation of the world. The dimming of his eyes signifies that in the world, faith disappeared and that the light of religion, formerly received by it, is overlooked. The summoning of his elder son: this is the acceptance of the Law by the Jews. The Father's delighting in his food and captured game stands for the people's being saved from their errors, caught by the just doctrine. The Word of God is the promise of the blessing and the hope of the future kingdom in which the saints will reign with Christ and celebrate the true Sabbath. Rebecca represents the fullness of the Holy Spirit.

Evening Prayer

Antiphon: Glory to the Spirit, she is sevenfold in majesty.

Psalm 118:57–64 ✠ Psalm 17:1–31 ✠ Psalm 142:1–12

Scripture: Revelation 5:1–14

Reading: St. Aphraates, priest, Father of the Church † ca. 350

Demonstrations 1.8–9

The prophet Zachariah also prophesied concerning this stone which is the Messiah. In fact, he said; *I saw a foundation stone of equity and love*. Why does he say "foundation," if not because He is with the Father from the foundation? He also says, "of love," for coming into the world, he said to his disciples, *This is my commandment, that you love one another*. Again he says, *I have called you my beloved friends*. And this is what the blessed Apostle says, *God has loved us in the love of his Son. The Messiah has truly loved us and gave himself up for us.*

Then the Prophet clearly explains what this stone is: *On this stone, behold, I open seven eyes*. And what are these seven eyes which are open on the stone if not the Spirit of God, She who dwells upon the Messiah with Her seven attributes, as the Prophet Isaiah declared: *The Spirit of God, She will rest and dwell upon him, the Spirit of Wisdom and of Intelligence, of Counsel and of Strength, of Knowledge and of the Fear of the Lord*. These are the seven eyes which are open on the stone; and these are the seven eyes of the Lord which survey all the earth.

Day 3

Morning Prayer

Antiphon: It is the Messiah who has conceived them and given birth to them out of his reflection (Aphraates *Demonstrations* 17.8).

Psalm 107:1–6 ✠ Psalm 118:73–80 ✠ Psalm 26:1–14

Scripture: 1 Corinthians 7:32–35

Reading: St. Aphraates, priest, Father of the Church † ca. 350

Demonstrations 18.10

In the Book of Moses we read: *A man will leave his father and mother, and unite himself to his wife; and they shall become one flesh*. Now this is truly a great and sublime prophecy. Does anyone really leave father and mother to accept a wife? This is the sense: When a man has not yet taken a wife, he loves and honors God his Father and the Holy Spirit his Mother, not having any other love. But when a man takes a wife, he departs from his Father and Mother, the ones just mentioned, for his mind is captivated by this world. His spirit, heart, and thoughts are dragged away from God by worldly matters which he begins to love and delight in *just as a man delights in the wife of his youth*. Thus is his love turned away from his Father and Mother.

Evening Prayer

Antiphon: The Holy Spirit illuminates our spirits so that we might see God in all things.

Psalm 138:1–14 ✠ Psalm 42:1–5 ✠ Psalm 35:5–12

Scripture: 1 Peter 3:18–22

Reading: St. Ephrem, deacon, Father and Doctor of the Church † 373

Hymns on the Nativity 1.41–51

> Adam anticipated the One who is the Lord of the cherubim
> who was able to make him dwell beneath the branches of the Tree of Life.
> Abel passionately desired for him to come in his lifetime,
> so he could see in place of the lamb that he sacrificed, the Lamb of God.
> Eve looked for him, even though the nakedness of women was great,
> so he would clothe them not in leaves, but in the glory
> that had been stripped away.
> The tower that many had erected prefigures the One who would descend
> to erect on earth a tower which ascends to the heavens.
> The ark as well, with its animals, prefigures the One
> who would build the holy Church in which souls are saved.
> In the days of Peleg the earth was divided into seventy tongues;
> this anticipated the One who would divide the earth by tongues
> among his Apostles.
> The earth which the flood engulfed cried out to her Lord silently;
> he descended and opened the baptismal font by which
> people are drawn up to heaven.
> Methuselah lived little less than a thousand years;
> he anticipated the Son who grants eternal life as inheritance.
> By means of a hidden symbol, the Divine Bounty was pleading on their behalf
> that their Lord would come in their generation and meet their needs.
> For the Holy Spirit who was in them by a silent contemplation
> interceded for them,
> and She moved them to see through Her, the Savior for whom
> they ardently yearned.

Thematic Readings for Non-Feast Days

Day 4

Morning Prayer

Antiphon: The Holy Spirit brooded over the waters and brought forth life.

Psalm 118:145–52 ✠ Psalm 3:1–8 ✠ Psalm 143:7–12 TNK

Scripture: Genesis 1:1–2 TNK

Reading: St. Basil the Great, bishop, Father and Doctor of the Church † 379

On the Six Days of Creation 2.6

How then did the Spirit of God move upon the waters? I will give you not my own personal opinion, but that of a Syrian who was as foreign to the wisdom of the world as he was at home in the knowledge of the true matters. He said, then, that the Syriac word was more expressive, and that because of its proximity to the Hebrew language it was closer to the meaning of the Scriptures. That is the signification of this word, "hovered" is, according to him, an interpretation for "brooded" and "made alive" the nature of the waters, as in the image of a bird that covers her eggs and warms them up, thus imparting to them a certain life force. Such is, to a certain extent, the Syrians say, the thought which is expressed in these words, "The Spirit hovered over the waters"; that is to say, she prepared the nature of the waters to produce living creatures. This is sufficient proof for those who ask if the Holy Spirit was removed from the creative activity.

Evening Prayer

Antiphon: Whoever is born of the Spirit is spirit.

Psalm 140:1–5 ✠ Psalm 4:1–8 ✠ Psalm 7:1–17

Scripture: John 4:21–24

Reading: St. Macarius the Great, Desert Father of the Church † 391

Collection of Homilies III 8.1

If anyone hasn't received grace from God nor exercised hope and received the gift of the Holy Spirit, then that person has rendered void the plan of God and denied by his actions all the Scriptures. If someone hasn't received the Divine Energies, that person is the plaything of illusions, remaining a stranger to the heavenly Church of the firstborn. That one has not come into communion with the spirits of the just and those who have attained perfection, nor been incorporated into the Jerusalem above. Such a person hasn't begun to adore the Father in spirit and in truth. In whomever God doesn't dwell, that person hasn't even begun to know God, for *Such is eternal life: that they know you, the one true God.* For *whoever is born of the Spirit is spirit, the birth deriving from God* protects that person, and *the Evil One cannot touch him.* . . . Without a mother a child does not come into the world and without intercourse a baby isn't conceived. Accordingly, without coming to birth through the Holy Spirit, no one can be born as a child of God; no one can enter into eternal life. *Those who are led by the Spirit of God, they are the ones who are the children of God.*

Day 5

Morning Prayer

Antiphon: The Spirit gives us revelations of God.

Psalm 129:1–8 ✠ Psalm 3:1–8 ✠ Psalm 62:1–11

Scripture: Ezekiel 8:1–4 TNK

Reading: St. Macarius the Great, Desert Father of the Church † 391

Collection of Homilies III 16.2

Certain birds, fearing the beasts that prowl on the ground, build their nests in a secluded and elevated spot, either on a roof or in a tall tree. The mother, circling overhead, brings to her hatchlings tender little morsels so that they can consume them, since they are themselves but little babies. Subsequently, at the appropriate time, she brings to the developing fledglings a type of food better suited to their stage of growth; and at the same time, once their wings sprout and develop, she teaches them bit by bit how to fly and hover around the nest, next how to soar around the tree, then how to glide from branch to branch, and finally how to fly a little farther in distance, until they reach adulthood and their wings are firmly developed. From that point onward, they fly from hill to hill and from mountain to mountain, gracefully and without difficulty, and with superb agility.

The same applies to the offspring of God who have been given birth to by the Holy Spirit through her own powerful means. First all, from the outset, the Spirit nourishes the children with spiritual milk, full of sweetness and heavenly affection touching their hearts. *I have given you milk to drink*, says the Apostle, *not solid food*; and Peter likewise exhorts, *As newborn infants, crave pure and spiritual milk.* Gradually, according to the progress and growth of the soul's regeneration, God provides the more solid food of the Spirit; and at the same time, the wings of grace—that is to say the power of the Spirit—increases in the soul with its progress in good works. Then the Divine Grace, the Good and Heavenly Mother, teaches the mind how to soar, at first around the nest of the heart, namely the thoughts, (that is to say, how to pray to God without mental distractions in the power of the Spirit). Next, the more solid the food is which is received by the soul from the Spirit of the Godhead, the farther and the higher it can soar, guided and sustained by the Spirit. And finally, once the soul has grown and attained the stature of spiritual maturity, the intellect gracefully flies from hillcrest to hillcrest and from mountain top to mountain top—that is to say, from this world here to the world above and from this dimension to the blessed and unfailing and infinite dimension. The mind soars with great and carefree abandon as well as agility, transported and directed by the wings of the Spirit towards visions and revelations concerning heavenly mysteries, towards ineffable spiritual contemplations which no fleshly tongue can express.

Evening Prayer

Antiphon: The Spirit empowers us to participate in the Divine Nature.

Psalm 133:1–3 ✠ Psalm 101:1–28 ✠ Psalm 81:1–8

Scripture: 2 Peter 1:3–8

Reading: St. Macarius the Great, Desert Father of the Church † 391

Collection of Homilies III 8.2

A perfect pearl of great price and regal qualities, worthy of a royal diadem, lacks nothing less than a king, and only a king is capable of wearing this pearl; it isn't befitting for another to bear such a pearl. In exactly the same manner, if someone isn't born by the royal and divine Spirit, doesn't become a heavenly and regal descendant, in short, a child of God, according to what is written: *To all those who have received him, he gave them the power to become children of God*, then it is impossible to bear the heavenly and costly pearl, the image of the true light who is the Lord, because one hasn't been born a child of the kingdom. And those who possess and bear this pearl will live and reign with Christ forever; for such is the meaning of the Apostle: *Just as we have borne the image of the earthly, so too shall we bear the image of the heavenly.* Christ is borne in the soul in an ineffable light, he is only known in truth by those who bear him, and is only seen by the eyes of the soul. For the non-initiated it is impossible to know the things of the Spirit, or even acquire faith, inasmuch as the heavenly image of the Anointed One hasn't been formed within, however, such a person will know by experience from the truth the sweet anointings of the Lord.

Glory to the One who so loved the human race and judged them worthy to become participants in his being, as Peter declared: *So that you might participate in the Divine Nature.* Since such great goods and divine charisms have been promised us, let us earnestly beg that we too may become participants just as the Apostle said: *My little children to whom I give birth all over again in order that Christ might be formed in you.* Woe to those who haven't searched for and found the spiritual realities and ineffable good gifts because not being born of the Spirit, they could not enter into the kingdom, for thus has declared the Lord.

PRAYING—WITH THE SAINTS—TO GOD OUR MOTHER

Day 6

Morning Prayer

Antiphon: The Spirit, like a mother bird, trains us for celestial things.

Psalm 142:1–12 ✠ Psalm 56:1–11 ✠ Psalm 60:1–8

Scripture: Wisdom 9:17—10:6 LXX

Reading: St. Macarius the Great, Desert Father of the Church † 391

Collection of Homilies III 16.2

The children of God become superior and transcendent to the wiles of wickedness when they are empowered by the Spirit and are habituated to a heavenly way of life; they no longer fear the ferocity of unclean spirits. Just as baby birds growing up, with their wings reaching full development, no longer fear the attack of wild animals or people since their way of life is spent mostly in the air, and just as no single human being understands the social habits of birds, likewise no human being who is filled with the spirit of this world fully understands the language of the Spirit. Only the children born of the Spirit of grace understand the language of their Mother, as the Apostle declares, *We communicate spiritual matters to those who are spiritual. But the mundane person does not accept the things which are from the Spirit of God.*

༄ 📖 ༂

Evening Prayer

Antiphon: The Spirit gives us rebirth so we can understand the things of God.

Psalm 1:1–6 ✠ Psalm 8:1–9 ✠ Psalm 143:7–12 TNK

Scripture: 1 Corinthians 2:9–16

Reading: St. Macarius the Great, Desert Father of the Church † 391

Collection of Homilies III 22.2

No human being knows *the thoughts of God unless the Spirit of God* dwells within him. *As for us, we have not received the spirit of this world but the Spirit who comes from God, so that we might know the things that God has graciously bestowed upon us. These are the things we talk about.* Therefore, let us seek the Lord and he will guide us and personally teach us; and we will understand the mysteries of God as much as it is possible for a human being to understand such things, not as God does. To us it belongs to learn how, for a person given birth to by the Spirit, how necessary it is to withstand the evil spirits and learn to seek help from the Lord and to fight against the Adversary.

Thematic Readings for Non-Feast Days

Day 7

Morning Prayer

Antiphon: The Spirit gives birth to us and forms us in the spiritual life.

Psalm 5:1–12 ✠ Psalm 112:1–9 ✠ Psalm 9:1–10

Scripture: Judith 16:13–14 LXX

Reading: St. Macarius the Great, Desert Father of the Church † 391

Collection of Homilies III 22.3

Just as a mother who has an infant loves it and embraces it with deep affection, enfolding it in her bosom, so too, the Spirit comes into the soul and embraces it in her bosom with much comforting and joy. By means of a powerfully divine energy such a person is absorbed by the Spirit, seized and captivated by the captivation of celestial mysteries, thus a divine mindset is formed within. Then the Spirit disperses all of the matters accumulating in the soul through negligence, throwing out all the seduction of the idols which had a hold on the soul and body, thus cleansing them. Now this person becomes totally dizzy and drunk with love, joy, and deep humility.

Evening Prayer

Antiphon: The Word of God warms, comforts, and nourishes the children of the Spirit. (Macarius *Collection of Homilies III 27.1*)

Psalm 6:1–10 ✠ Psalm 118:73–80 ✠ Psalm 30:1–24

Scripture: Luke 12:8–12 PESH

Reading: St. Macarius the Great, Desert Father of the Church † 391

Collection of Homilies III 27.1

Our beloved brothers and sisters are hungry and thirsty for the Word of Truth and with much love they desire to hear the message. And although we ourselves are without instruction, they receive with joy the Word of God which they desire and cherish, and because of this the Holy Spirit rejoices when her word is proclaimed in this world. For example, even if a child is an infant, unable to speak the language of its mother, the mother herself comes down to the same level as her child and speaks with it using goo-goos and gah-gahs. The mother rejoices when the infant coos back to her; she eagerly watches for any sound of affection. The same applies to us in comparison with the Lord's infinite and incomprehensible glory, not to mention power and knowledge; we are but mere babes incapable of worthily describing or expressing the mysteries of the Spirit. However, the Grace of the Spirit, Mother of the saints, likewise rejoices when one utters in this world the word regarding her. For the children who are born of the Spirit find their comfort and joy only in that word which has given birth to them.

Day 8

Morning Prayer

Antiphon: Let us become like doves, children of the Dove of Love.

Psalm 41:1–11 ✠ Psalm 54:1–16 ✠ Psalm 68:8–15 TNK

Scripture: Song of Songs 6:8–10

Reading: St. Gregory of Nyssa, bishop, Father and Doctor of the Church † ca. 395

Song of Songs 15

My dove, my perfect one is one; she is the one of her mother; she is the chosen one of her who gave birth to her. Surely we are not ignorant of the mother of the dove, for the tree is recognized by its fruit. With regard to humanity, we do not doubt that [Christ] was born from a human being; thus by seeking the mother of the chosen dove we will perceive her as none other than that dove already mentioned, for the nature of the parents is recognized in the child. Because *what is born of the Spirit is spirit*, the offspring is a dove. In fact, the mother is the Dove which alighted from heaven at the Jordan, just as John testifies. This is the Dove that the young maidens proclaim blessed. This is She whom the concubines and queens praise. For a path towards that blessedness lies open to everyone from every rank. For this reason the Song declaims, *The daughters saw her, and bless her; the queens and concubines praise her.* By nature everyone is drawn to desire what they bless and praise. Accordingly, the daughters praise the Dove and totally desire to become doves themselves.

Evening Prayer

Antiphon: O God, receive them in the outstretched arms of your Spirit, and into the blessed womb of your Light (Macarius *Collection of Homilies* III 6.3).

Psalm 15:1–11 ✠ Psalm 83:1–12 ✠ Psalm 56:1–11

Scripture: John 14:19–26 PESH

Reading: St. Macarius the Great, Desert Father of the Church † 391

Collection of Homilies III 27.4

It isn't true, as some claim who are led astray by misleading teachings, that Man is dead once and for all, and is thus incapable of accomplishing anything good.... Amongst all living creatures and even irrational beasts, whether quadrupeds or birds, according to an innate order nature safeguards the tenderness and behavior towards young, as well as the relationship and love of offspring for their mothers. Thus, to take our example from the birds, the swallow builds its nest in the heights, in an elevated spot, thereby protecting herself against reptiles, and there she nourishes and raises her offspring. The young are not receptive to the voice of any human, animal or anything else, nor distracted by them; but they listen only to the voice of their mother. Likewise they bob up and down and squawk seeking her. And the swallow, flittering back and forth according to instinct, brings home food to her young and gives it to them regurgitated so as to soften it, in order that her babies might nourish themselves naturally and easily.

It is the same for souls who, still remaining in the childhood of this world, are prey to passions and unable to accomplish the achievements of life because of the power of evil which clings to them. They begin to cry and seek for the help given by God and they subject themselves to suffering in the desire for eternal life, summoning by their tears and their cries the Heavenly Mother, the Holy Spirit, no longer being satisfied with anything of this world, but having their rest only in the participation in the Spirit and their hunger for food. Then the most excellent and Heavenly Mother, the Grace of the Spirit, comes to the souls of those who sought her; she raises them in her arms of life and warms them by means of spiritual and heavenly nourishment, namely the milk which is delicious, desirable, holy, spiritual and pure. She does this so that they might experience and know the Heavenly Father, growing each day by the progress of spiritual maturation, until they arrive at the perfect stature and come to *the unity of the faith and the knowledge of the Son of God* according to the word of the Apostle; then these souls obtain participation in eternal life.

Day 9

Morning Prayer

Antiphon: The sanctifying Spirit gives birth to us.

Psalm 54:1–16 ✠ Psalm 112:1–9 ✠ Psalm 68:1–15 TNK

Scripture: Wisdom 1:4–7 LXX

Reading: St. Gregory of Nyssa, bishop, Father and Doctor of the Church † ca. 395

Against Those Who Defer Baptism

Give the Dove time to fly to you, the Dove which Jesus the first time brought down from heaven by way of figure. She is without guile, meek, and very fertile. When she finds a person cleansed, like kindling wood well dried out, she builds her nest in him, and enflames the soul like a mother bird brooding over her eggs so that they hatch. She then gives birth to many young and rejoices over her offspring. These children are good actions, solemn discourses, faith, godly reverence, righteousness, prudence, chastity, and purity. These are the offspring of the Spirit, and our possessions.

PRAYING—WITH THE SAINTS—TO GOD OUR MOTHER

Evening Prayer

Antiphon: The Spirit instructs us in the mother tongue of all truth.

Psalm 18:1–14 ✠ Psalm 11:1–8 ✠ Psalm 118:81–88

Scripture: John 16:12–16 PESH

Reading: St. Gregory of Nyssa, bishop, Father and Doctor of the Church † ca. 395

On the Christian Mode of Life

    The grace of the Holy Spirit is given with the understanding that there is to be an increase and augmentation of what is received. It is necessary that the soul which has been born again by the power of God be nurtured by the Spirit in proportion to its intellectual development, sufficiently refreshed by the water of virtue and the abundance of grace. The physical nature of the newborn does not remain in the tenderness of age, but when it is nourished by food its body grows, according to the law of nature, in proportion to what was given. Accordingly, it is appropriate for the recently born soul whose participation in the Spirit restores to its nature its ancient beauty, having destroyed the sickness which follows due to disobedience, not to remain forever like a child, inactive, laying around, sleeping unmoved in the state of its birth, but to nourish itself with its own food, and, in proportion to what its nature craves, to rear itself by every virtue and exercise so that it strengthens itself through the power of the Spirit.

Day 10

Morning Prayer

Antiphon: The Spirit proceeds from God through the Word.

Psalm 64:1–13 ✠ Psalm 50:1–19 ✠ Psalm 103:1–34

Scripture: Isaiah 11:1–3 TNK

Reading: Synesius of Cyrene, bishop, Father of the Church † ca. 414

Hymn 2.1–10, 85–116

> It is You, at the break of dawn; it is You, in the glow of morning,
> it is You, in the fullness of day, even at the dusk of a holy day,
> at the start of a night divine, it is You that I praise O Creator!
> Healer of souls and healer of bodies, O Dispenser of wisdom!
> Likewise I praise the Son, the First-Born, the Primal Light.
> O Glorious Son of the ineffable Father,
> it is to You, O Blessed One that I sing at the same time
> that I laud the Father Almighty, and after You,
> that other Offspring born by the Father:

the Life-Giving Will, the Principal Arbitrator,
the Holy Spirit—Focus of the Begetter, Locus of the Begotten.
She is Mother; she is Sister; she is daughter;
she who gave birth to the hidden Root.
So that there might be an effusion from the Father towards the Son,
She the Effusive Being is brought forth.
She holds her place at the center, God issuing forth from God,
even through God the Son.
And through this sublime Effusion of the Father Immortal,
the Son in his turn, is likewise brought forth.

Evening Prayer

Antiphon: The Holy Spirit has been poured out into our hearts.

Psalm 21:1–11 ✠ Psalm 88:1–28 ✠ Psalm 138:1–14

Scripture: Romans 5:1–5

Reading: St. Augustine, bishop, Father and Doctor of the Church † 430

Commentary on the Psalms 143

The grace of the New Covenant which was veiled under the Law is now revealed in the Gospel. We have removed the veil and have seen what was hidden; we have seen it in the grace of our Lord Jesus Christ. . . . Now what did David do? He received grace. For the Law without grace cannot be fulfilled; *For the fulfillment of the Law is love.* And where is this love? See if it does not come from grace. *The love of God,* says the Apostle, *is poured out in our hearts by the Holy Spirit who is given to us.* Therefore grace causes the Law to be fulfilled and grace is signified by milk, for milk in the flesh is gratuitous—the mother doesn't seek to receive but satisfies herself with giving. The mother freely gives milk and is saddened if the child ceases to receive.

Day 11

Morning Prayer

Antiphon: The sound of the turtledove has been heard in our land.

Psalm 72:1–28 ✠ Psalm 12:1–6 ✠ Psalm 83:1–12

Scripture: Song of Songs 2:10–14

Reading: Theodoret of Cyrus, bishop, Father of the Church † ca. 460

PRAYING—WITH THE SAINTS—TO GOD OUR MOTHER

Commentary on the Song of Songs 2

The sound of the turtledove has been heard in our land. He once again calls the sound of the turtledove the teaching of the All-Holy Spirit. For this reason the Blessed David in the psalm mentions *Upon the wine vats,* after having said, *How desirable are your tabernacles, Lord of Hosts! I long for them and my soul faints for the courts of the Lord. My heart and my flesh rejoiced in the Living God.* Then he instructs about the cause of rejoicing, *For a sparrow found herself a home and a turtledove a nest in which she can raise her young.* And explaining he continued, *Your altars, O Lord of Hosts.* He teaches us that the young are those who obtained rebirth through the washing; their dwelling and nest are the divine altars upon which they are nourished, fed, grow their feathers, gradually reaching maturity. The grace of the Holy Spirit is like a mother who gives birth to them, here figuratively called a turtledove.

Evening Prayer

Antiphon: Without rebirth from the Spirit, we are spiritually dead.

Psalm 118:49–56 ✠ Psalm 24:1–22 ✠ Psalm 103:1–34

Scripture: John 3:1–6 NT

Reading: St. Cyril of Alexandria, Patriarch, Father and Doctor of the Church † 444

Commentary on John 2.1

Most assuredly I tell you, unless a person be born from above, that person cannot see the reign of God.

Now the will of the Father is that a human being become a partaker of the Holy Spirit, that the citizen of earth be born again into an unaccustomed and foreign life and be recognized as a citizen of heaven. By calling the rebirth by means of the Spirit "from above," he clearly shows that the Spirit derives its essence from God the Father. . . . *How can a person be born again when old? Can he enter a second time into his mother's womb, and be reborn? Jesus answered* . . . . Nicodemus is consequently shown to still be earthly-minded, and therefore no way receives *the things of the Spirit of God,* for he considers this most awesome and illustrious mystery to be foolishness. Upon hearing mention of a birth both from above and spiritual, he imagines the physical womb experiencing again birth pangs for what is already born, and does not rise above the law of our nature, taking into account things divine. . . .

Unless one be born of water and Spirit, it is impossible to enter into the Reign of God. Since [Nicodemus] did not understand as he ought, namely what the need of being born from above signified, [Christ] instructs him with a clearer teaching and provides for him the bare knowledge of the mystery. For when our Lord Jesus Christ refers to the rebirth through the Spirit as being from above, he shows that the Spirit is of an essence above all essences, through whom we become partakers of the Divine Nature, as becoming first fruits of the One who proceeds from it essentially, and through whom and in whom we are refashioned according to the Archetypal Beauty, and thus reborn into newness of life, and remolded for divine adoption.

Day 12

Morning Prayer

Antiphon: The Bride of Christ is born of the Holy Spirit.

Psalm 91:1–15 ✠ Psalm 13:1–7 ✠ Psalm 118:89–96

Scripture: Song of Songs 7:10—8:2

Reading: Theodoret of Cyrus, bishop, Father of the Church † ca. 460

Commentary on the Song of Songs 7–8

For my part, everything from new to old that my mother gave to me I kept for you, my Beloved; the commandments of the Old Covenant and the counsels of the New Covenant which I received from my mother who is the grace of the Spirit. . . .

Therefore, I am amazed and exclaim, *Who will bring you, my beloved, to be nursed at my mother's breasts? Drawn by this loving-kindness of yours, when I encounter you outside I shall kiss you, and they will not despise me. I shall take you to myself and lead you into my mother's house, even the chamber of she who conceived me. I will give you some spiced wine to drink and some juice from my pomegranates.* Intoxicated with love for you, not simply in the wedding chamber and in the bridal suite, but in the marketplace and in public as well, when I find you I shall embrace you and kiss you! Those who see will not blame me for doing so, knowing the flame of my love. Then taking you to myself from there, *I shall lead you into my mother's house, even into the chamber of she who conceived me.* Now what is the house of the All-Holy Spirit of whom the bride was born, if not the divine Temple?

Evening Prayer

Antiphon: Jesus grew strong in the power of the Holy Spirit.

Psalm 118:57–64 ✠ Psalm 14:1–5 ✠ Psalm 117:8–26

Scripture: Titus 3:4–8

Reading: Theodoret of Cyrus, bishop, Father of the Church † ca. 460

Commentary on the Song of Songs 7–8

For my part, everything from new to old that my mother gave to me I kept for you, my Beloved; the commandments of the Old Covenant and the counsels of the New Covenant which I received from my mother who is the grace of the Spirit. . . .

Who brings you, my beloved, to be nursed at my mother's breasts? When I encounter you outside, I shall kiss you, and they will not despise me. I shall take you to myself and lead you into my mother's house, even the chamber of she who conceived me. You will teach me. I will give you some spiced wine to drink and some juice from my pomegranates. This means that in his humanity he received every grace from the Spirit, as Scripture says, *The child Jesus grew and became strong in the Spirit, and the favor of God rested upon him.* So the bride, overwhelmed by the unspeakable loving-kindness, means *You were nursed at my mother's breasts.*

Now in order to preserve the sequence and appropriateness of the thoughts, let us begin a little further up and outline the meaning by way of summary. I received from my mother, the bride said, not only new things but old as well; and I will keep them for you. But out of your loving-kindness for humanity you took on our nature and nursed at the same breast as I in order to show through this your brotherliness. You were nursed, not from need, but to teach me that I should be suckled and from what type of nourishment I should draw grace. The reason you received baptism was not to wipe away the filth of sin, for you had not committed any sin, nor was deceit found in your mouth, nor to receive the grace of the All-Holy Spirit, for you were indeed full of grace, but to reveal to me the nature of the gifts of baptism and the manner in which I can be nursed at the grace of the Spirit. The reason the Holy Spirit descended in the form of a dove was not to provide you with what you did not possess, for you were already full of the Spirit's graces, but to reveal to me what the gift of baptism imparts.

Day 13

Morning Prayer

Antiphon: We have received the promised Holy Spirit.

Psalm 107:1–6 ✠ Psalm 118:97–104 ✠ Psalm 50:1–19

Scripture: Song of Songs 8:4–7

Reading: Theodoret of Cyrus, bishop, Father of the Church † ca. 460

Commentary on the Song of Songs 8

Now what is the house of the All-Holy Spirit of whom the bride was born, if not the divine Temple? . . . The bridegroom finds it expedient to say, *Under the apple tree I awakened you; there she who gave birth to you was in labor with you.* For believing the proclamation about our Savior, we approached the divine baptism and by approaching we obtained rebirth. Now the history of the Acts bears witness that the grace of the Spirit was in labor pains for us. When the most divine Peter spoke to the crowd and proposed teaching about the Savior to those present, the writer records that upon hearing his message, they felt compunction and said to Peter, *What shall we do in order to be saved?* and he replied to them, *Believe, and let each of you be baptized in the name of Our Lord Jesus Christ, and you will receive the promise of the Holy Spirit.* Accordingly the bridegroom says to the bride, *Under the apple tree I awakened you; there she who gave birth to you was in labor with you.* The repetition is not without purpose; wishing to point out who her mother is, he reminds her of her birth.

Evening Prayer

Antiphon: The Holy Spirit maternally protects us.

Psalm 138:1–14 ✠ Psalm 35:5–12 ✠ Psalm 120:1–8

Scripture: Revelation 7:9–17

Reading: St. Sahdona, bishop, Father of the Church † ca. 630

Book of Perfection 3.13

The person who embodies the renunciation of Christ whom he loves, rejoices in his company; he finds consolation in mixing with his friends, and his sorrow vanishes in the joy of our Lord. By spiritually contemplating the angels in God's light and the throngs of saints, he loses sight of what he loves according to the flesh. Such a person *forgets his father, his mother and his brothers*, for he is joined by love to the illustrious Father whose paternity endures for eternity, without beginning, and such a person has become a brother of the Son who exists since forever and who *doesn't blush to call us his brothers*, and he has merited the tender affection of the Most Holy Spirit, who maternally places us *beneath the shelter* of her holiness, and who gained for us by her *tender mercies the filial adoption.*

Day 14

Morning Prayer

Antiphon: Eve's coming from the side of Adam indicates the procession of the Holy Spirit.

Psalm 118:145–52 ✠ Psalm 3:1–8 ✠ Psalm 118:105–112

Scripture: Genesis 2:18–23

Reading: St. Anastasius of Sinai, abbot, Father of the Church † ca. 700

Sermon on the Making of Man 1.1

Let us once again have recourse to the beginning of the account. From this very deep resource we seek our origin, namely, how God fashioned the persons of our ancestors and leaders, that is, of Adam and Eve and the son who came forth from them, not according to the likeness of rational beings, that is, of angels, or again according to the correspondence of ensouled beings. Furthermore, we seek why God brought into existence Adam in an uncaused and unbegotten fashion, and the second human being, his son, being begotten from him, and why God brought Eve into existence, neither in a begotten nor even in an uncaused fashion, but rather in an apportioned manner, or more exactly, by means of procession from the essence of the uncaused Adam. This procession is an ineffable coming forth.

Accordingly, these three, as Methodius teaches, are our chief primogenitors, the consubstantial persons of all humanity, who typologically came into being as images of the Holy and consubstantial Trinity. The uncaused and unbegotten Adam possesses the type and image of the Uncaused and Almighty Cause of all, our God and Father. The beginning of Adam's son prefigures the image of the begetting of the Word, the Son of the God. The procession of Eve indicates the processional Person of the Holy Spirit. On this account, God did not breathe into Eve the breath of life, because she is a type of the breath and life of the Holy Spirit, and because, through the Holy Spirit, she is the expectation of the reception of God, who truly is the breath and life of all beings.

From this it is perceived and marveled at that the unbegotten Adam possesses no one like him in humanity who is unbegotten and uncaused, and similarly the procession of Eve is not paralleled; thus they exist as true types of the Unbegotten Father and of the Holy Spirit. Moreover, their begotten son is like all human beings, being begotten children and brothers and sisters, just as he possesses his type according to the image and likeness of Christ, the Begotten Son, who, having become a human being, is the firstborn, without seed, among many brothers and sisters.

Evening Prayer

Antiphon: The Word empowered us to be born children of God by the Spirit.

Psalm 140:1–5 ✠ Psalm 101:1–28 ✠ Psalm 17:1–31

Scripture: John 1:9–14 NT

Reading: St. Bede the Venerable, priest, Father and Doctor of the Church † 735

Homily on the Gospels 1.8

Let us look at what it says, *to as many as accepted him he gave them the power to become children of God*. The Evangelist says, *to as many as accepted him*, because, *God is not a respecter of persons, but in every nation whoever fears him and works justice is accepted by him*. Following this verse, the Evangelist indicates how those who believe can become children of God, and how much difference there is between this generation and that according to the flesh. *Who were not born of blood*, he says, *nor of the will of the flesh, nor of the will of man, but of God*. Indeed, the carnal generation of each one of us derives its origin from blood, that is, from the nature of male and female and by marital intercourse. But truly, spiritual generation is provided for by the grace of the Holy Spirit. Distinguishing it from the carnal, the Lord said, *Unless someone is born again of water and the Spirit, that person cannot enter into the kingdom of God*. What *is born of the flesh is flesh; what is born of the Spirit is spirit*. But unless anyone doubt that a human being can become a child of God and co-heir with Christ, the Evangelist provides an example, that the Son of God himself deigned to become a human being and dwell among humans, so that by existing as a partaker of human frailty he might grant to human beings to be partakers of his divine power.

Day 15

Morning Prayer

Antiphon: Glory to you, O Holy Spirit, Creator and Giver of Life!

Psalm 129:1–8 ✠ Psalm 18:1–14 ✠ Psalm 103:1–34

Scripture: Job 33:1–6 TNK

Reading: John of Dalyatha, monk, Father of the Church † ca. 780

Letter 51.10–11

You, O Most High Good, you dwell in all those who love you. They find you wrapped in ineffable radiance, in the glorious splendor of your Beauty, in the strength of your Nature, in the sublime knowledge which surpasses their knowledge of you. Everyone who loves you, finds you whole and entire with everything which is yours. In each of them you are entirely present in utterfulness, even though no one is able to entirely possess you. Glory to your Infinite Totality which contains all the created totalities, without their being able to total your completeness.

You are the Father of rational creatures born of your Spirit who is called Generatrix, in the feminine, because she has given birth to them in this world in order that they might in turn give birth to their world. But he is also called Generator, because he must beget for this world living rational creatures who will no longer beget. Just as it is from their mother that little ones nourish themselves and thanks to her grow to maturity, so too, those who have been birthed by your Spirit nurse on the milk of Life flowing from your Breast, in the world without end.

Evening Prayer

Antiphon: The Spirit has spoken through the prophets.

Psalm 133:1–3 ✠ Psalm 76:13–20 ✠ Psalm 102:1–22

Scripture: Matthew 3:1–17

Reading: St. Gregory of Narek, monk and priest † 1003

Prayers 33.4

> O Holy Spirit, by your Intermediary, He has revealed to us
> the Trinity of Persons in the unity of the Divine Nature;
> among these Persons You are recognized as One of Them,
> O Incomprehensible One.
> Through you and your Intermediary the first descendants of the Patriarchs,
> known as the "seers,"
> they have recounted with an illuminated language,
> the events both past and future,
> the deeds that happened and those which have not yet come to pass.
> You were proclaimed Spirit of God by Moses,
> you who hovered over the waters,
> O infinite Power.
> With an enveloping and formidable protection, full of solicitude,
> you stretched forth your wings as a sign of compassionate aid
> in favor of your newly born offspring,
> through which you revealed the mystery of the baptismal font.

Day 16

Morning Prayer

Antiphon: Let us suck upon the maternal sweetness of the Spirit.

Psalm 142:1–12 ✠ Psalm 18:1–14 ✠ Psalm 118:97–104

Scripture: Isaiah 60:14–16

Reading: St. Hildegard of Bingen, abbess † 1179

Know Your Way 2.3.25

> *And the children of those who afflicted you will come and bow down before you, everyone who slandered you will worship before your footsteps.* What does this mean? O you who are supernal peace and the purest sun, through you the living root will burst forth, rebirth through the Spirit and water, and those who were laying prostrate under the weightiest curse in the filth of vile impurity, they will come eagerly to acknowledge you; and bowed down in this manner, at last they will arise to truth and justice. How? They will suck upon the maternal sweetness of the true faith, not clearly knowing it by sight but grasping at it by means of faithful belief.

Evening Prayer

Antiphon: The Holy Spirit nurses us at the breast of Divine Love.

Psalm 1:1-6 ✠ Psalm 22:1-6 ✠ Psalm 131:1-3 TNK

Scripture: Luke 14:28-33

Reading: St. Catherine of Siena, religious, Doctor of the Church † 1380

Dialogue 141

My goodness endows the souls of the just more fully with spiritual riches when for love of me they stripped off material possessions because they have renounced the world and all its pleasures, even their own wills. These are the ones who enrich their souls, enlarging them in the bottomless reservoir of my love by abandoning all care not only for worldly riches but for themselves as well. Then I become their spiritual benefactor and in a material manner I exert a particular providence beyond the general one: my mercy, the Holy Spirit, becomes their servant. . . .

In fact, such a soul has the Holy Spirit as her mother who nurses her at the breast of Divine Love. The Holy Spirit has liberated her, as her master, releasing her from the slavery of self-love, for where the fire of love burns the water of selfish desire cannot enter to extinguish this sweet fire in the soul. This servant, I mean the Holy Spirit, whom I in my providential care have imparted to her, clothes her, nourishes her, inebriates her with tenderness and the ultimate riches.

Day 17

Morning Prayer

Antiphon: The Holy Spirit hovered over the waters, giving birth to all creatures.

Psalm 5:1-12 ✠ Psalm 56:1-11 ✠ Psalm 118:113-20

Scripture: Genesis 1:1-2 TNK

Reading: St. Lawrence of Brindisi, priest, Doctor of the Church † 1619

Commentary on Genesis 1

It says that the Spirit of God hovered over the waters, that is, moved over the surface fashioning things by its artistic will, indeed all things, giving birth to all creatures on the earth whether animal or plant, or anything similar. From the moisture they began to be formed and nourished, and that which was supple and malleable the Spirit subjected to its operation so that all things might be formed. . . .

Indeed, the Doctors of the Church Basil, Jerome, and Ambrose, as well as Diodorus constantly make this assertion regarding the Holy Spirit. In fact, regarding the Hebrew word *merahepheth*, notes Jerome, "we can say also means incubated, or brooded, as a bird warms her eggs giving them life." From this we know that it doesn't pertain to the spirit of the world, but rather to the Holy Spirit who is the creator of life for all creation from the beginning. Regarding this Diodorus says, "In the manner that a bird broods over her eggs with her wings so that her eggs stir to life, so the Holy Spirit hovered over the surface of the waters so that she caused them to produce that which can procreate." Basil states that the same was related to him by a Syrian scholar, and Ambrose in his *Hexameron* adduced this from the Syriac language.

Evening Prayer

Antiphon: The Holy Spirit also serves as the wet nurse of souls.

Psalm 6:1–10 ✠ Psalm 118:129–136 ✠ Psalm 22:9–11 TNK

Scripture: Luke 16:19–31

Reading: St. Catherine of Siena, religious, Doctor of the Church † 1380

Dialogue 151

Who would not have concluded that poor Lazarus was completely miserable and the rich man was basking in great happiness and contentment? But that was not the case, for that rich man for all his wealth suffered more pain than poor Lazarus tormented by his leprosy, because the rich man's selfish will thrived from which all suffering flows, whereas in Lazarus this will was dead and his will was so alive in me that he experienced refreshment and consolation in the midst of his suffering. He had been cast out by others, most especially by the rich man, and was neither cleansed nor looked after by them, but I myself provided that animals lacking reason should lick his sores. Now you see how at the end of their lives Lazarus enjoyed eternal life while the rich man suffered in hell. Thus the rich are left sad while my precious poor are happy. I hold them to my breast and give them the milk of great consolation; because they leave everything they possess me totally. The Holy Spirit becomes the wet nurse of their souls and their little bodies in whatever situation arises.

God Almighty Eternally Gives Birth to the Second Person

Day 1

Morning Prayer

Antiphon: God was never lacking Reason.

Thematic Readings for Non-Feast Days

Psalm 41:1–11 ✠ Psalm 118:137–144 ✠ Psalm 30:1–24

Scripture: Isaiah 45:9–12 TNK

Reading: St. Hippolytus, bishop and martyr, Father of the Church † 235

Against Noetus 10

God, while existing alone and having nothing contemporaneous with God's Self, decided to create a universe. Mentally conceiving the universe, God willed it, and by speaking, made it. What comes into being is at once in God's presence, just as he willed it, completed as he desired. For us, then, it is enough simply to know that there was nothing contemporaneous with God, except himself. Although God existed alone, God was manifold; for God did not lack Reason, or Wisdom, or Power, or Counsel; but everything was in God, and God was the All. When God willed, and as he willed in the times determined by him, God manifested his Word through whom he made everything. When God wills, he acts; when he thinks, his work is completed; when he gives utterance, he manifests; when he fashions, he displays wisdom. For everything that has come into existence he forms through Word and Wisdom, creating by Word and establishing them by Wisdom. He made them, therefore, as he willed, for he was God.

Now as the Author, and Counselor, and Artisan of things that are being formed, God gave birth to the Word. This Word which God possesses within God's Self, and which is invisible to the universe which is being created, God makes visible. By uttering what was previously a sound, and by light giving birth to light, God sent forth into creation, as its Lord, his very Mind, which previously was visible to himself alone. And the One who was invisible to the universe which is coming into existence, God makes visible, so that through the Word's appearance the universe might be able to perceive it and be saved.

Evening Prayer

Antiphon: The ancient apostolic faith declares the Eternal Word was born of God Almighty.

Psalm 15:1–11 ✠ Psalm 4:1–8 ✠ Psalm 2:1–12

Scripture: Acts 17:16–34

Reading: St. Justin Martyr, Apostolic Father of the Church † 165

First Apology 21–23

Now when we say that the Word, who is the first offspring of God, was engendered without any sexual union and that Jesus Christ our Teacher was crucified and died, and resurrected ascending into heaven, we are propounding nothing new and different from what you yourselves claim regarding the children of Zeus. For you know how many children your respected writers assign to Zeus: Hermes, the interpreting word and teacher of everyone, Asclepius, who, although he was a physician, was struck by lightning and ascended into heaven, and Dionysius as well, who was torn from limb to limb, and Hercules, who embraced the fire in order to escape his sufferings, etc. . . .

And when we assert that the Word of God was born of God in a peculiar manner, unlike ordinary generation, as we stated above, this is nothing extraordinary compared to your claim that Hermes is the angelic word of god. . . .

That this may be made clear to you, we shall set forth the following arguments to prove: [first] that whatever assertions we make, because we learned them from Christ and the Prophets who went before him, they alone are true, and are more ancient than all your writers, and that they should be believed, not because we profess the same as these authors, but because we declare the truth; and [second] that Jesus Christ alone is properly the Son who has been born by God, being God's Word and First-Born and Power, and having become human according to God's good pleasure, he taught us these things for the conversion and restoration of humanity.

Day 2

Morning Prayer

Antiphon: If you can't explain earthly matters, how can you explain spiritual matters?

Psalm 54:1–16 ✠ Psalm 8:1–9 ✠ Psalm 130:1–3

Scripture: Job 38:1–11 TNK

Reading: St. Hippolytus, bishop and martyr, Father of the Church † 235

Against Noetus 16

These are testimonies concerning the incarnation of the Word, and there also are very many others. But let us keep our focus on the subject at hand, brothers and sisters, namely, that it really was the Father's Power, which is the Word, that came down from heaven and not the Father himself. For he explicitly says, *I came out from the Father, and have come.* What is the subject of "I came out from the Father" if not the Word? And what has been given birth to, if not spirit, which is the Word? But you will ask me, "How is he born?" In your own case you can provide no explanation of how you were born, even though every day you see what causes a human being, and so you cannot provide an accurate explanation of the "*dispensation*" concerning his generation. Furthermore, you do not have it within you to know the skilled and indescribable artistry of the Maker, but can only see to see, understand, and believe that human beings are a work of God. Yet here you are seeking an explanation of the birthing of the Word, whom God the Father gave birth to according to his good pleasure, as he willed!

Is it not enough for you to learn that God created the universe? And yet you also boldly try to find out what God made it out of as well? Is it not enough for you to learn that the Son of God was revealed to you for your salvation, if you simply believe?

And yet you curiously inquire on all sides how he was spiritually born? No more than two human beings have been entrusted with an account of his birth, even according to the flesh, yet you dare to discover the account of his spiritual birth! Why this is an explanation that the Father reserves to himself, one which he will reveal later to the saints and those worthy of beholding his face. Let the words that have been spoken by Christ suffice for you: *what is born of the Spirit is spirit*. Accordingly, speaking through the Prophet God indicates the birth of the Word, that indeed he has been born, but reserves the explanation, to reveal it only in the time determined by himself, thus saying, *From the womb before the daystar I have given birth to you.*

Evening Prayer

Antiphon: The Word is the Firstborn of God.

Psalm 18:1–14 ✠ Psalm 118:153–60 ✠ Psalm 109:1–7

Scripture: John 1:1–8

Reading: St. Hippolytus, bishop and martyr, Father of the Church † 235

Refutation of All Heresies 10.33.1–2, 11

This God, being One and Over All, mentally conceived the Word first and gave birth to it, not Word in the sense of one spoken, but rather the indwelling rational thought of the God who is All. God gave birth alone to the Word from existence, for the Father himself was existence itself, out of whom the one born, the Word, was the cause of all things that are produced. The Word carried within himself the will of the Progenitor, not ignorant of the Father's mind. For simultaneously with his procession from the Progenitor, being his first-born, the Word possesses a voice within himself, the ideas conceived in his Father's mind. Therefore when the Father ordered the universe to come into existence, the Word completed it sequentially, for God's pleasure. . . . All these things the Word of God directs, the First-Born child of the Father, the voice of dawn *before the daystar*.

Day 3

Morning Prayer

Antiphon: My heart has uttered a most excellent Word.

Psalm 64:1–13 ✠ Psalm 44:1–17 ✠ Psalm 109:1–7

Scripture: Sirach 24:1–11 VULG

Reading: Tertullian, Father of the Church † ca. 240

Treatise against Praxeas 7.1–32

When God says, *Let there be light*, this is when Word itself assumes its own form and ornamentation, its own sound and utterance. This is the perfect birth of the Word, when it proceeds forth from God. It was first established by God for the purpose of thought under the name of Wisdom, *The Lord established me as the beginning of his ways*; then gave birth to me for the purpose of activity, *When he prepared the heavens I was present with him*. Thereby Wisdom established God as Father, from whom Wisdom proceeded, established as Son, the First-Born, as born before all things, and Only-Begotten as alone born from God, in a true sense from the womb of his own heart, just as the Father himself bears witness, *My heart has disgorged a most excellent Word*. For ever more, God delights in him, who reciprocally rejoices in God's presence, *You are my son, today I have given birth to you*, and, *Before the morning star I gave you birth*. So likewise, the Son in his own person, under the name of Wisdom, acknowledges the Father, *The Lord established me as the beginning of his ways, with his works in mind; before all the hills, he gave birth to me*.

Evening Prayer

Antiphon: Study the Scriptures for they are the words of life.

Psalm 21:1–11 ✠ Psalm 109:1–7 VULG ✠ Psalm 44:1–17

Scripture: Acts 17:10–12

Reading: Tertullian, Father of the Church † ca. 240

Treatise against Praxeas 11.1–3

It will be your duty, however, to produce your proofs from the Scriptures as plainly as we do when we prove that God reckoned his own Word, his Son. For if God calls him Son, the Son will be none other than the one whom God brought forth from out of himself. And if the Word came forth from God's very Self, he will be Son, not the one from whom he came forth; for he did not himself come forth from himself! Furthermore, you, who proclaim that the Father and the Son are one and the same, really do make the same Person the one who came forth and the one who brought forth. Now if God were able to do that, God certainly didn't do it! Or else bring forth the proof which I demand, like my clear citations, namely, find the Scriptures that demonstrate the Father and the Son to be identical, just as we, for our part, demonstrate the Father and Son to be distinct, I say distinct, not separate. I, for my part, set forth the following statement of God, *My heart has disgorged a most excellent Word*. Against this passage do you object that God somewhere else said, "My heart has disgorged myself as a most excellent Word," in such a manner that he is both the Disgorger and the Disgorged, the Producer and the Produced, since he himself is both Word and God? Take note, I myself allege that the Father said to the Son, *You are my son, today*

I have given birth to you. If you want me to believe that he himself is both Father and Son, show me some other passage stating, "The Lord said to himself, I am my own son, today I have given birth to myself," or on the other hand, "Before the morning star I have given birth to myself."

Day 4

Morning Prayer

Antiphon: The Eternal Son was born a second time so we can see God.

Psalm 72:1–28 ✠ Psalm 118:161–68 ✠ Psalm 26:1–14

Scripture: Exodus 33:18–23

Reading: St. Gregory the Illuminator, Catholicos, Father of the Church † ca. 332

Armenian Catechism 382

    He came and became a human being so that mortals would be able to see God. No one has seen God's essence, neither angels nor archangels, neither seraphim nor cherubim, nor the multitudes of heavenly angelic hosts. But the Son, hidden in the flesh, showed and revealed God to the mature in mind and understanding in order that they might be filled with the splendor of God's light. *Whoever has seen me, has seen my Father.* He came and fulfilled the promises, from the holy Virgin. And the first birth is from the Father before unmeasured ages, an eternal and everlasting birth, from an eternal and everlasting Father before all else.

Evening Prayer

Antiphon: Distinctions of male and female are abolished in baptism.

Psalm 118:49–56 ✠ Psalm 4:1–8 ✠ Psalm 24:1–22

Scripture: Galatians 3:23–28

Reading: St. Aphraates, priest, Father of the Church † ca. 350

Demonstrations 6.6

    Winter is near—summer has gone.
    The Sabbath rest comes—labor has ceased.
    The night is conquered—Light reigns.
    Death has lost its sting—swallowed up by Life.
    Those who must return to Sheol—cry and grind their teeth—
    but those who are going to the Kingdom rejoice;
    they exult and exalt with praise. . . .
    Those who shall have preserved their sanctity

will find their rest in the sanctuary of the Most High.
All those who are single-hearted,
the single Son from the womb of the Father, will cause to rejoice.
There will no longer be any male or female, any slave or free,
but all will be the children of the Most High.

Day 5

Morning Prayer

Antiphon: Eternal Wisdom is engendered by the Eternal One.

Psalm 91:1–15 ✠ Psalm 25:1–12 ✠ Psalm 2:1–12

Scripture: Proverbs 8:22–31 TNK

Reading: St. Hilary of Poitiers, bishop, Father and Doctor of the Church † 367

On the Trinity 4.21

    Wisdom, whom you yourself confess to be Christ, will contradict you saying: *When he established certain fountains under heaven, when he made strong the foundations of the earth, I was with him forming it. I was there with him and he delighted in me. Every day I rejoiced in his presence, all the time, when he rejoiced after the completion of the world, and he rejoiced in the sons of men.* Every pretext is hemmed in and every type of error is constrained to confess the truth. Wisdom, who was engendered before the ages, is in the presence of God. And she is not only close to him, but she ordains as well. Therefore, she is by his side as organizer. Understand the duty of ordering and arranging. The Father, by the very fact that he speaks, accomplishes it; the Son, by the fact that he executes what is said that must be accomplished, orders it. The distinction between the Persons has been made in such a way that the work may be referred to either one of them. To say, "*Let us make,*" places the command and the execution on an equal level; thus the words that are written, *I was by his side like an organizer,* truly mean that God was not alone in the operation.

    Wisdom rejoices before him who, as she indicated, shares his joy with her. *Every day I rejoiced in his presence, all the time, when he rejoiced after the completion of the world, and he rejoiced in the sons of men.* She made known the reason for her own joy. She rejoices because the Father rejoices, and rejoices regarding the completion of the world and the sons of men. In fact, it is written, *And God saw that it was good.* She rejoices that her works are pleasing to the Father which she completed in obedience to his command. For his own joy come from that, she affirms, that the Father rejoiced at the completion of the world and in the sons of men. It says, *in the sons of men,* because in the one Adam the entire human race had already begun to exist. Thus it isn't a solitary Father who speaks to himself when creating the world, for Wisdom is with him, collaborates, and rejoices that through her co-operation the work has been brought to realization.

Evening Prayer

Antiphon: God doesn't come from nothing.

Psalm 118:57–64 ✠ Psalm 89:1–17 ✠ Psalm 109:1–7

Scripture: John 1:15–18 NT

Reading: St. Hilary of Poitiers, bishop, Father and Doctor of the Church † 367

On the Trinity 6.16

God doesn't come from anything other than God. God doesn't come from nothing since he comes *from himself*; this indicates, in effect, the nature from which proceeds his birth. It can't be he himself since when it is said, *from himself* it refers to the birth of the Son issued from the Father. Consequently, after the indication that he is *from the womb*, I ask if it is possible to believe that he was born from nothing, since by reference to terminology regarding bodily functions, the true nature of the birth is revealed? Certainly God was not composed of bodily parts when he commemorated the birth of the Son, saying, *From womb, before the daystar I gave you birth*. He spoke in this fashion in order to enlighten our understanding while confirming the ineffable birth of the Only-Begotten Son from himself, from his own true Divinity. This was to impart to the faculties of our human nature the knowledge of the faith regarding the Divinity in a manner adapted to our human nature. By saying *from the womb*, God wanted thus to teach that it was not a creation out of nothing, but a natural birth of the Only-Begotten from his very self.

Day 6

Morning Prayer

Antiphon: Glory to the ewe who bore our iniquities!

Psalm 107:1–6 ✠ Psalm 50:1–19 ✠ Psalm 39:5–17

Scripture: Isaiah 53:1–7 TNK

Reading: St. Ephrem, deacon, Father and Doctor of the Church † 373

Hymns on the Nativity 3:2–3

> Thanks to the Wellspring sent for our salvation.
> Thanks to the One who repealed the Sabbath for its fulfillment.
> Thanks to the One who rebuked leprosy so that it disappeared.
> Fever also saw him and swiftly departed.
> Thanks to the Compassionate One who bore our misery.
> Glory to your coming that saved humanity.
> Glory to That One who came to us through his First-Born.

Glory to That Silent One who spoke by means of his Voice.
Glory to That Sublime One who was made visible through his Dawn.
Glory to That Spiritual One who was most pleased that his Child should be embodied.

Evening Prayer

Antiphon: Who can probe the deep things of God?

Psalm 138:1–14 ✠ Psalm 27:1–9 ✠ Psalm 118:169–76

Scripture: Luke 1:26–45

Reading: St. Ephrem, deacon, Father and Doctor of the Church † 373

Hymns on Virginity 31.1

> O Christ, you have given life to creation by your birth
> which manifestly took place from a womb of flesh.
> O Christ, you dazzled comprehension by your birth
> which brilliantly shone from all eternity from the Hidden Womb.
> I am in awe by you in two regards: The wandering find life in you,
> but scrutinizers go astray in you.

Day 7

Morning Prayer

Antiphon: I will sing to my well-beloved.

Psalm 118:145–52 ✠ Psalm 44:1–17 ✠ Psalm 109:1–7

Scripture: Isaiah 5:1–4

Reading: St. Athanasius, Patriarch, Father and Doctor of the Church † 373

Discourse against the Arians 4.24

> But truthfully, much is said regarding the Son in the Old Testament, as in the second Psalm, *You are my son, today I have given birth to you*; and in the ninth title, *To the end concerning the hidden things about the Son, a Psalm of David*; and in the forty-fourth, *To the end concerning the things that shall be changed for the sons of Korah, for understanding, a song about the Well-Beloved*; likewise in Isaiah, *I will sing to my Well-Beloved a song of my Well-Beloved regarding my vineyard. My Well-Beloved has a vineyard.* Now who is the Well-Beloved if not the Only-Begotten Son? As also found in the Hundred and Ninth Psalm, *From the womb, before the daystar, I gave birth to you*, about which I will speak later; and in the Book of Proverbs, *Before all the hills existed, he gave birth to me*; and in the Book of Daniel, *And the appearance of the fourth is like*

Thematic Readings for Non-Feast Days

a Son of God; and many other texts. For if antiquity is derived from the old testimonies, then the Son must be ancient, who is clearly mentioned in the Old Testament in numerous passages. . . .

[As scripture says,] *My heart uttered a good Word*. Now if the phrase "from the womb" pertains to a human being, so too, "from the heart." For if the womb is a human organ, likewise the heart is physical. But if the phrase "from the heart" refers to something eternal, then "from the womb" is also eternal. And if *the Only-Begotten* resides *within the womb*, then the Well-Beloved dwells within the womb. Now the *Only-Begotten* and the *Well-Beloved* are one and the same, as in the text *This is my well-beloved Son*.

☙ 📖 ❧

Evening Prayer

Antiphon: The Only-Begotten eternally dwells in the Womb of God.

Psalm 140:1–5 ✠ Psalm 2:1–12 ✠ Psalm 109:1–7 VULG

Scripture: John 1:15–18 PESH

Reading: St. Ephrem, deacon, Father and Doctor of the Church † 373

Commentary on the Diatessaron 1.2

The Word, having been begotten, possesses a form according to which he was uttered. He clearly said that he did not come from himself, but that he was begotten, that he wasn't Father, but Son. He said in fact, *God, whom no one has ever seen, the Only-Begotten, who is in the womb of his Father, has made him known*. And, *I am leaving, having come from the Father*. And if you declare that it is impossible that "He Who Is" was begotten, you accuse the Scriptures of lying, for it says, "He Was," as well as, *He was begotten from his womb*.

Day 8

Morning Prayer

Antiphon: It is customary for Scripture to signify in a human fashion what is beyond humanity.

Psalm 129:1–8 ✠ Psalm 3:1–8 ✠ Psalm 109:1–7

Scripture: Job 10:8–12

Reading: St. Athanasius, Patriarch, Father and Doctor of the Church † 373

Discourse against the Arians 4.27

Because there are some who are uninstructed, denying the being of the Son, and making little significance of the words: *From the womb, before the morning star, I gave birth to you*, as if this referred to Mary, asserting that *before the morning star* he was born of Mary, because to say *womb* could not refer to his relationship with God, it is necessary to say a few words on the matter. If then, because the word "womb" is a human designation, and therefore is alien to God, clearly "heart" likewise has a human signification. It necessarily follows that what has a heart also must have a womb. Since both are human, we must deny both, or seek to understand both. For as a word is from the heart, so is an offspring from the womb. And just as when the heart of God is spoken about, we do not conceive of it as being human, accordingly, if the Scripture says *from the womb*, it is not necessary to take it in a corporeal sense. For it is customary for divine Scripture to speak and signify in a human fashion what is beyond humanity. Consequently, concerning the fashioning of creation, it says, *Your hands made me and fashioned me*, and, *He commanded, and they were created*. Suitable then is its significance about each matter, attributing to the Son "proper identity" and "genuineness of birth," and to creation "the beginning of being." For God makes and creates everything, whereas the Word, or Wisdom, is born from God's very self. Now "womb" and "heart" clearly designate "proper identity" and "genuineness," for we likewise possess genuine birth from the womb, but our works we make by the hand.

Evening Prayer

Antiphon: Before the dawn of creation, you gave birth to me.

Psalm 133:1–3 ✠ Psalm 101:1–28 ✠ Psalm 109:1–7 VULG

Scripture: John 1:15–18 NT

Reading: St. Athanasius, Patriarch, Father and Doctor of the Church † 373

Defense of the Nicene Creed 3.13

Divine Scripture, which knows better than anyone the nature of everything, says through Moses, *In the beginning God created the heaven and the earth*; however, regarding the Son it doesn't interject another, but the Father himself declares, *From the womb before the daystar, I have given birth to you*, and again, *You are my son, today I have begotten you*. And the Lord testifies about himself in the Book of Proverbs, *Before all the hills, he gives birth to me*. Likewise, John remarks concerning things originated and created, *All things were made by him*, but when preaching about the Lord, John states, *The Only-Begotten Son, who dwells within the womb of the Father, has declared Him*.

Day 9

Morning Prayer

Antiphon: The Eternal Word is the natural Offspring of God.

Psalm 142:1–12 ✠ Psalm 118:9–16 ✠ Psalm 109:1–7

Scripture: Isaiah 66:9–13 VULG

Reading: St. Cyril of Jerusalem, bishop, Father and Doctor of the Church † 386

Catechetical Lectures 11.4–5

Again, upon hearing the term "son," do not hear it in an improper sense, but as truly offspring, a natural child, without beginning and not being advanced from servitude to that of adopted status, but an Offspring engendered from all eternity by an inscrutable and incomprehensible birth. Likewise, when you hear the term "first-born" do not think of this in a human manner, for among people the first-born have other siblings. . . .

He was born of the Father from the beginning, being above all beginning and all succeeding ages, Offspring of the Father, in all things like the One who gave birth, eternal of an eternal Father, Life born of Life, Light of Light, Truth of Truth, Wisdom of Wisdom, Sovereign of Sovereign, God of God, and Power of Power. . . .

For who shall describe his generation? God is Spirit, and being spirit and incorporeal, gave birth spiritually, an inscrutable and incomprehensible birth. For the Offspring himself says of the Father, *The Lord said to me, "You are my child; today I have given birth to you."* Now "today" is not recent, but eternal; "today" is timeless, before all ages. *From the womb before the daystar, I gave birth to you.*

☙ 📖 ❧

Evening Prayer

Antiphon: To deprive the One who grants to everyone the prerogative of parenthood, of similar dignity, would be irreverent.

Psalm 1:1–6 ✠ Psalm 26:1–4 ✠ Psalm 109:1–7 VULG

Scripture: John 14:6–11

Reading: St. Cyril of Jerusalem, bishop, Father and Doctor of the Church † 386

Catechetical Lectures 7.1–3

Concerning God being the First Principle, we spoke at sufficient length yesterday; by "sufficient," I mean not according to the dignity of the subject matter (for that is utterly impossible for perishable nature), but as much as our human frailty permitted. . . . Let us now resume the saving doctrines of the true faith, combining with the dignity of God as First Principle that of Paternity, and believing in "One God, Father."

For it is necessary not simply to believe in One God, but devoutly to accept as well that he is Father of the Only-Begotten, of our Lord Jesus Christ.

For thus we shall raise our thoughts higher than those of the Jews, who, while doctrinally professing that God is One . . . , do not admit that God is also the Father of our Lord Jesus Christ. In so doing they contradict their own Prophets who in the Divine Scriptures declare, The Lord said to me, *You are my Son; today I have begotten you.* Even to this day, they *rage and conspire together against the Lord and his Christ*, considering it possible to gain the friendship of the Father without devotion to the Son, not knowing that *no one comes to the Father except through the Son*, who says: *I am the Door*, as well as *I am the Way*. How will someone who dismisses the Way that leads to the Father and denies the Door be deemed worthy of admittance to God? Likewise they contradict what is written in the Eighty-Eighth Psalm, *He shall say of me, "You are my Father, my God, the Helper of my salvation." And I will make him the first-born, the highest of the kings of the earth.* For, if they persist in asserting that these words were spoken regarding David, or Solomon, or any of their successors, let them demonstrate how *"his throne,"* that they consider to be foretold in the prophecy, is *as the days of heaven*, and *like the sun before God, and as the moon established forever.* How are they not confounded by what is written: *From the womb before the daystar I have begotten you*, and, *He shall endure as long as the sun, and like the moon from generation to generation?* To refer these texts to a mere mortal is proof of complete and utter lack of sense. . . .

For our part, we embrace the devout teaching of our faith, worshipping One God, the Father of Christ; for to rob the One, who grants to everyone the prerogative of parenthood, of similar dignity, would be irreverent.

Day 10

Morning Prayer

Antiphon: His coming forth is from the beginning, from all eternity.

Psalm 5:1–12 ✠ Psalm 29:1–12 ✠ Psalm 109:1–7

Scripture: Micah 5:1–3

Reading: St. Cyril of Jerusalem, bishop, Father and Doctor of the Church † 386

Catechetical Lectures 11.19–20

Tell me first what He is who gave birth, and then learn what was born. But if you cannot conceive of the nature of the One who has given birth, don't busy yourself with how he gave birth.

For godly devotion it is enough for you to know, as we have said before, that God has only one Son, a single One, birthed according to God's nature; who did not begin to exist when he was born in Bethlehem, but is born before all ages. For listen to what the Prophet Micah says, *And you, Bethlehem, house of Ephrata, you are not the least among the thousands of Judah, for out of you shall come forth my leader who shall tend my people Israel. And his coming forth is from the beginning, from the days of eternity.* Therefore, do not become fixated on his coming forth from Bethlehem in the present age; rather, worship him as being eternally born from the Father. Do not admit anyone who speaks of a beginning of the Son in time, but acknowledge his timeless beginning, namely the Father. For the Father is the origin of the Son, timeless, incomprehensible, without beginning. The Father is the wellspring of the streams of righteousness, even of the Only-Begotten, who gave birth to him as he alone knows.

Evening Prayer

Antiphon: Only the One who begot knows the begotten, and Scripture attests that the Only-Begotten is God.

Psalm 6:1–10 ✠ Psalm 30:1–24 ✠ Psalm 21:1–23

Scripture: 1 John 5:1–6

Reading: St. Cyril of Jerusalem, bishop, Father and Doctor of the Church † 386

Catechetical Lectures 11.7, 13

Therefore he is Son of God by nature, not by adoption, born of the Father. *And whoever loves the One who begot, loves also the One begotten of him*; but whoever despises the Begotten in turn heaps insults upon the Begetter. So when you hear of God "begetting," don't succumb to bodily functions, nor understand a corruptible birthing, so as not to fall into impiety. *God is Spirit*, and the birthing is of a spiritual order. For corporeal beings give birth to corporeal beings, and the generation of bodies necessitates an interval of time. But there is no interval of time in the birth of the Son from the Father. Regarding natural generation, what is born is born imperfect; but the Son of God was born perfect; for what he is now, this is what he is from the beginning, born without beginning. We are so born as to pass from the ignorance of infancy to the exercise of reason. Your own generation as human is imperfect, for growth comes by progression. Do not imagine this to be the case here, nor charge with infirmity the One who gave birth. For if She gave birth to something imperfect, even though it were to acquire perfection in the course of time, you would be charging with infirmity She who gave birth; since what time bestowed afterwards, in your view, the Progenitor did not bestow from the very beginning. . . .

Do not be ashamed to confess your ignorance, for you share it with the angels. Only the One who begot knows the begotten, and the begotten knows the One who begat. The One who begot knows what he begot, and the Scriptures attest that the one who is begotten is God.

PRAYING—WITH THE SAINTS—TO GOD OUR MOTHER

Day 11

Morning Prayer

Antiphon: The Word has proceeded from God's generative womb.

Psalm 41:1–11 ✠ Psalm 44:1–7 ✠ Psalm 109:1–7

Scripture: Genesis 49:25–26 TNK

Reading: St. Ambrose, bishop, Father and Doctor of the Church † 397

The Patriarchs 11.51

 Jacob said, *From the womb, blessings of your father and your mother....* I believe it appropriate that we should understand this according to the spiritual mystery, as both begettings of the Lord Jesus: one according to the divinity and the other according to the humanity, because he was begotten from the Father before the ages. And for this reason the Father says, *My heart has uttered a good Word*, because the Word has proceeded from the profoundly intimate and incomprehensible substance of the Father and is always in him. Accordingly, the Evangelist also says, *No one has ever seen God, except the only-begotten Son, who is in the womb of the Father, he has revealed him.* Therefore, *the womb of the Father* is to be understood in a spiritual sense, as the secret innermost dwelling of the Father's love and nature, in which the Son always dwells. Consequently, the womb of the Father is the spiritual and secret interior from which the Son has proceeded as from a generative womb.

ଛ 📖 ଓ

Evening Prayer

Antiphon: God has never been devoid of Wisdom.

Psalm 15:1–11 ✠ Psalm 30:1–24 ✠ Psalm 89:1–17

Scripture: 1 Corinthians 1:17–25

Reading: St. Gregory of Nyssa, bishop, Father and Doctor of the Church † ca. 395

Against Eunomius 3.1.48–49

 After recounting these and similar matters, [Solomon] proceeds to his teaching regarding the dispensation in regards to humanity, why the Word became flesh. For it is clear to everyone that God who is over all creation has no created or imported element within himself, neither power, nor wisdom, neither light, nor reason, neither life, nor truth, or any of the other things that are contemplated in the fullness of God's bosom. All of these things, the Only-Begotten God is, Who is in the womb of the Father; thus the designation "creation" cannot properly be applied to any of those things contemplated within God.... For if the Wisdom of God was created, and Christ is the Power of God and the Wisdom of God, that would mean God possesses Wisdom as something alien to God's nature, subsequently received as a product, and not what God first possessed. But surely the One who has his being in the womb of the Father does not allow us to conceive of the Father's womb as ever void of himself.

Day 12

Morning Prayer

Antiphon: Surely the womb of God has not been empty.

Psalm 54:1–16 ✠ Psalm 31:1–11 ✠ Psalm 118:17–24

Scripture: Wisdom 9:13–18

Reading: St. Ambrose, bishop, Father and Doctor of the Church † 397

The Mystery of the Incarnation of Our Lord 1.2.11, 13

[Regarding] the mystery of the Lord's Incarnation . . . [some people] do not know how to distinguish rationally between the human nature and the divine. God's nature is simple, whereas a human being consists of a rational soul and a body. . . .

Therefore let us beware lest we separate the substance of the hidden nature of the Only-Begotten Son from the *bosom of the Father* and from, as it were, the paternal *womb*. And by these words on which is constructed the truth of the Incarnation which was assumed, let us consider how to render judgment regarding the divine generation, lest it likewise be said to one of us: *If you offer correctly, but do not divide correctly, you have sinned; be still*, that is, if we do not know how to distinguish that which is proper to the eternal divinity from the Incarnation; if we confound the Creator with the Creator's own works; if we declare that the Author of time began after time; for it is impossible that the One, through whom all things exist, be one of all of those things.

Evening Prayer

Antiphon: The Eternal Word of God is wrapped in human language.

Psalm 18:1–14 ✠ Psalm 34:1–28 ✠ Psalm 109:1–7 VULG

Scripture: Matthew 13:33–35

Reading: St. Jerome, priest, Father and Doctor of the Church † 420

Homilies on the Psalms 36

For if the Son assumed a human body he necessarily takes upon himself human language. Christ is human, and truly human; we declare this because of the Incarnation. Since, if he is human because of his physical nature, you see a body and are not scandalized; why then is it shocking if he speaks in human terms? If, however, the baseness of a body scandalizes you, if the Cross, the injuries, the blows, and the scourging, and all the brutalities of the Cross, if you find that scandalous, return to the beginning, and do not be scandalized; for the Father says to the Son, *From the womb before the daystar I have begotten you.* Are you shocked if Our Lord and Savior who truly assumed a human nature speaks in a human fashion when God the Father who did not assume human nature speaks like a human being: "*From the womb before the daystar I have begotten you*? I do not have a womb, but I cannot indicate my paternity in any other way than to use human language: *From the womb before the daystar I have begotten you.* 'From the womb,' that is to say, from my substance."

Day 13

Morning Prayer

Antiphon: God truly gives birth from the womb, from the Divine Nature.

Psalm 64:1–13 ✠ Psalm 35:5–12 ✠ Psalm 109:1–7

Scripture: Jeremiah 2:26–29

Reading: St. Jerome, priest, Father and Doctor of the Church † 420

Homilies on the Psalms 36

Listen, Eunomius; listen, Arius: Is the Lord a creature, a fashioned product, does the craftsman beget his own work? Does the craftsman call his work his son? A carpenter makes a bench; did he beget it from his womb? Hardly! What does he say? I made you with my hands. However, when the womb is mentioned a son is signified and not an adopted one; even though the adopted are also called sons. *To as many as received him he gave the power to become sons of God.* Psalm 109, however, explicitly states that God truly begets from the womb, from his nature, from his own bowels, from his very substance. *From the womb* means from the depths of the heart of his Divinity. Everything whatsoever the Father is by Divine Nature, he has given to the Son whom he has begotten: *From the womb before the daystar, I have begotten you.*

୨୦ 📖 ଓ

Evening Prayer

Antiphon: God the Son is equal to the Father, born equal, not born less. What the One is, the Other who was born, is likewise (Augustine, *Sermon* 140.5).

Psalm 21:1–11 ✠ Psalm 37:1–22 ✠ Psalm 109:1–7 VULG

Scripture: John 1:1–5

Reading: St. Augustine, bishop, Father and Doctor of the Church † 430

Sermon 135.4

The Father engendered what he himself is. If the Father engendered something other than what he himself is, then he did not engender a genuine Son. The Father declares to the Son, *From the womb, before the daystar, I have given birth to you*. What does *before the daystar* mean? The daystar signifies time. Therefore, before time, before every possible thing called "before," before everything that doesn't exist, and before everything that does exist. Consequently, the Gospel doesn't say, "In the beginning God made the Word," as when it says, *In the beginning God made heaven and earth*; or, "In the beginning the Word was born"; or, "In the beginning God gave birth to the Word." Rather, what does it say? Was, was, was. You hear "was," so believe it! In the beginning was the Word, and the Word was with God, and the Word was God. Whenever you hear "was," don't search for time, because he always was.

Therefore, he that always was, was always with the Son as well, because God is powerful enough to engender apart from time. He said to the Son, *From the womb, before the daystar, I have given birth to you*. What does *from the womb* mean? Did God have a womb? Are we to envision God as a composition of bodily parts? God forbid! So why did he say *from the womb*, if not to make us understand that God generated from his own substance? Thus what came forth *from the womb* is the same as the one who gave birth. Surely if the one who gave birth was one thing, and what came out of the womb was something else, it would be a monster, and not an offspring!

Day 14

Morning Prayer

Antiphon: Not by separation according to physical terms is the Divine Offspring born.

Psalm 72:1–28 ✠ Psalm 38:1–13 ✠ Psalm 109:1–7

Scripture: Wisdom 7:21–26 LXX

Reading: St. Cyril of Alexandria, Patriarch, Father and Doctor of the Church † 444

Commentary on John 1.10

For just as from the beauty of creatures is the power of the Creator of the universe proportionately seen . . . so will the Only-Begotten be shown superior in glory and more resplendent, surpassing all perception, beyond the power of sight, and known as God. . . .

[The Evangelist] says [the Only-Begotten] *is in the bosom of the Father* so that you may perceive him being in and of God as it is said in the Psalms, *From out of the womb, before the daystar, I gave birth to you*. For just as when it says, *from out of the womb*, it means from out of him truly and genuinely, using a likeness of things belonging to our nature (for what is born of human beings proceeds from out of the womb); so too, when the Evangelist says *in the bosom* he wishes to clearly signify nothing less than the Son being birthed from the womb of the Father. This is, as it were, by some divine shining forth and ineffable coming forth into his own Person, while containing him. Yet not by some surgical removal, nor by division in physical terms, is the Divine Offspring born of the Father. In fact, the Son somewhere says that he is in the Father and again the Father is in him. For the very divinity itself of the Father's essence naturally passes into the Son, in whom the Father is manifested. Furthermore, the Father has the Son rooted in himself indistinguishably in identity of essence, engendered from himself, yet not by division or extension, but inhering and forever co-existing. In this fashion, rather, with godly devotion we should correctly recognize the Son to be in the bosom of the Father.

Evening Prayer

Antiphon: Faith pertains to the things we cannot see or prove.

Psalm 118:49–56 ✠ Psalm 39:5–17 ✠ Psalm 109:1–7 VULG

Scripture: Hebrews 11:1–6

Reading: St. Cyril of Alexandria, Patriarch, Father and Doctor of the Church † 444

Dialogues on the Trinity 2

An object of comprehensive investigation is no longer faith. *An object of hope that one sees, no longer is hope. How can one wait expectantly for what one sees?* as the very wise Paul noted. Likewise, to draw a parallel with hope, the faith that one examines which is no longer beyond investigation, can no longer be faith. What one reveres by faith is totally free of proof. Thus, in my opinion, the same holds true for those who approach God and must believe that God exists, not belaboring it with investigation. Similarly, it is necessary to have the belief and disposition that God is Father and that he has engendered, but leave the "how" aside, without digging into the matter which is inaccessible. Absolutely no one, I think, would dream of laughing at those who have wisely judged it suitable to concede victory to the one who is by far superior.

Now one can posit that the mode of divine birth surpasses every intellect. Notwithstanding, one can learn that God the Father proclaims to the Word, born from out of himself, *From the womb, before the morning star, I have given birth to you.* That the birthing, so to speak, is authentic and the Son has been born from the same essence of the Father, the expression *from the womb* demonstrates this perfectly. It is a salient example, paradigmatic of our own life. Speaking of the birthing as *before the morning star* indicates without a doubt the mode of birth that is enshrouded in obscurity and incomprehensibility like the deepest darkness.

Day 15

Morning Prayer

Antiphon: What is born possesses the same nature as the mother: God from God.

Psalm 91:1–15 ✠ Psalm 41:1–11 ✠ Psalm 109:1–7

Scripture: Wisdom 7:27—8:1 LXX

Reading: Theodoret of Cyrus, bishop, Father of the Church † ca. 460

Commentary on the Psalms 109

From the womb before the daystar I have given birth to you. Here, as well, he had revealed the magnificence of [Christ]'s divinity. The Lord, who had already declared, *Sit at my right hand*, confesses the oneness in essence and proclaims the sameness of nature. The phrase *before the daystar* indicates existence before any time and before the ages. The words *from the womb* teach the sameness of essence. "For you are born," God says, "of no other source than my nature; *womb* obviously to be taken in a figurative fashion. For just as human beings give birth from a womb, and what is born possesses the same nature as the bearers, so too, you are born of me and manifest in yourself the essence of the bearer."

Evening Prayer

Antiphon: Anything illuminated becomes full of light.

Psalm 118:57–64 ✠ Psalm 42:1–5 ✠ Psalm 35:5–12

Scripture: Ephesians 5:8–14

Reading: St. Quodvultdeus, bishop, Father of the Church † 450

On the Creed 1.3.15–18, 20

The omnipotence of the Father is in the Son and the omnipotence of the Son is in the Father, since the Father is never without the Son, nor the Son without the Father. We simply are not able to explain that divine birth by which the Son proceeded from the Father and by which God was born of God, without beginning, without time, without a mother, without any lack of permanence, or any diminishment in himself. The Prophet declares, *But concerning his birth, who will recount it?* Truly, who can comprehend or discourse on how he who always exists in the Father was born and yet never departs from him? As I have said, we cannot properly recount it; nevertheless, we must prepare our hearts for this very Son, so that by illuminating and directing us by faith he may lead us to the splendor of his truth, lest we remain in the darkness of our incredulity. . . . Thus, just as God was born from God, and light from light, and day from day, so too, Omnipotence was born from the Omnipotent.

PRAYING—WITH THE SAINTS—TO GOD OUR MOTHER

Day 16

Morning Prayer

Antiphon: A shoot shall arise out of Jesse.

Psalm 107:1–6 ✠ Psalm 49:7–22 ✠ Psalm 44:1–17

Scripture: Isaiah 11:1–3 TNK

Reading: St. Maximos the Confessor, monk, Father of the Church † 662

Scholia on Letter 9 of Dionysius

Regarding the bodily image of God's womb. The womb of God is referred to in *From the womb before the daystar [I gave birth to you]*. The Word voiced in air is found in *I have emitted from out of my heart a good Word*. And regarding the Spirit being breathed forth, *And by the spirit of his mouth*. Regarding bosom, *The Only-Begotten who dwells within the bosom of the Father*. Regarding a sapling, according to the form of a plant, *She is a Tree of Life*, and *From a shoot, my Son, will arise*, and *Jacob shall bud and blossom*, attributed to Christ who is the fruit of salvation filling the earth, and like analogies. Note therefore, this is how one speaks about the womb of God, and the emitting of the Word, and similar things.

Evening Prayer

Antiphon: God has no form and dwells in unapproachable light.

Psalm 9:1–10 ✠ Psalm 24:1–22 ✠ Psalm 118:137–44

Scripture: 1 Timothy 6:13–16

Reading: St. John of Damascus, priest, Father and Doctor of the Church † 749

The Orthodox Faith 1.8

For since God is outside of time and without beginning, unaffected, unchanging, incorporeal, alone, and without end, God gives birth without time and without beginning, unaffectedly, unchangingly, and without any need of a sexual partner; nor does God's incomprehensible birth have beginning or end. It is without beginning, because God is immutable. The birthing is without process, because God is unaffected and incorporeal. It is likewise without a sexual partner because God is incorporeal and only one God without need of any other. It is unending and unceasing, because God is outside of time and without end, ever the same; for what is without beginning is without end.

Thematic Readings for Non-Feast Days

Day 17

Morning Prayer

Antiphon: The Speaker, the Word, and the Message are One.

Psalm 118:145–52 ✠ Psalm 50:1–19 ✠ Psalm 32:1–22

Scripture: Judith 16:13–15 LXX

Reading: St. Thomas Aquinas, priest, Doctor of the Church † 1274

Against the Gentiles 4.11

We must also consider that what is begotten, as long as it remains in the begetter, is said to be "conceived." Now God's Word is begotten by God in such a manner that he does not depart from God but remains within him, as stated above. Rightly, therefore, may the Word of God be described as conceived by God. Thus in Proverbs 8, the Wisdom of God declares, *The depths did not yet exist and I already was conceived.*

There is, however, a difference between the conception of God's Word and physical conception which we observe in animals. Now the offspring during the time of conception and enclosure in the womb does not yet possess its final perfection and is unable to subsist on its own apart from its begetter; thus when an animal is physically begotten, the conception of the begotten offspring is necessarily one thing and the delivery another. In the latter the offspring begotten is even spatially separated from its begetter by being brought forth from the womb. God's Word, however, existing in God the Speaker, subsists perfectly in him and is distinct from God the Speaker; for no spatial distinction is necessary when, as previously stated, there is only a distinction of relationship. Consequently, regarding the generation of the Word of God, conception is the same as birth. In this regard Wisdom has declared, *I was already conceived*, and a few words later, *before the hills I was brought forth.*

༄ 📖 ༃

Evening Prayer

Antiphon: Children were believed to dwell in the loins of their forefather.

Psalm 138:1–14 ✠ Psalm 53:1–7 ✠ Psalm 109:1–7 VULG

Scripture: Hebrews 7:1–10

Reading: St. Anselm of Canterbury, archbishop, Doctor of the Church † 1109

Monologion 42

Now I would like to conclude, if I may, that the One is truly Father and the Other truly Son, but I realize that it is necessary not to neglect asking oneself if the title of Father and Son is proper to them rather than applied like that of Mother and Daughter since there is no distinction of sex in them. For, if it is fitting that the One be Father and his child be Son because the One and the Other is Spirit, why isn't it befitting by a similar line of reasoning, that the One be Mother and the Other, Daughter, since the One and the Other is Truth and Wisdom? Is it because in the case of natures which possess a distinction of sex, the better sex is that of the father or of the son, and the lesser that of the mother or of the daughter? Such is naturally the case among many species, but regarding certain ones it is the contrary; in certain types of birds, for example, the feminine sex is always greater and stronger, the masculine being lesser and weaker.

Nevertheless, isn't it certainly more befitting that the Supreme Spirit be called Father rather than Mother for the reason that the first cause and principle of any child is always the father? For, if the paternal cause always precedes in a certain manner the maternal cause, it is very incongruous to apply the name of mother to the parent with whom no other cause is in accompaniment nor precedes it in the begetting of a child.

Day 18

Morning Prayer

Antiphon: The Word originates from within the Speaker.

Psalm 129:1–8 ✠ Psalm 44:1–17 ✠ Psalm 109:1–7

Scripture: Isaiah 66:9–13 VULG

Reading: St. Thomas Aquinas, priest, Doctor of the Church † 1274

Against the Gentiles 4.11

Regarding the physical generation of animals first an offspring is conceived, then it is delivered, and finally it obtains a presence to the parent being at once associated with and distinct from the parents. In the divine generation, all these things are simultaneous, for the Word of God is at once conceived, brought forth, and present. And because what is born proceeds from a womb, just as the generation of God's Word to indicate his perfect distinction from the Generator is called *birth*, it is called for a like reason *generation from the womb*. Thus we read in a Psalm, *From the womb, before the daystar I have begotten you*. Nevertheless, because the distinction between the Word and the Speaker is not the type that prevents the Word from being in the Speaker (as already stated)—just as the distinctiveness of the Word is indicated by calling him *brought forth* or *begotten from the womb*—so to show that this distinction does not prevent the Word from being in the Speaker, John says, that he is *in the bosom of the Father*. . . . The characteristics that belong distinctly to the father or to the mother in physical generation, are all attributed to the Father by Sacred Scripture in the generation of the Word; thus the Father is not only said *to give life to the Son*, but also *to conceive*, as well as *to give birth*.

Evening Prayer

Antiphon: Wisdom is proved right by her children.

Psalm 140:1–5 ✠ Psalm 118:25–32 ✠ Psalm 81:1–8

Scripture: Luke 7:31–35 NT

Reading: St. Thomas Aquinas, priest, Doctor of the Church † 1274

Against the Gentiles 4.12

Now that wisdom resides in God must surely be said by reason of the fact that God knows himself; but since he does not know himself by any external mode but by his own essence—indeed God's very act of understanding is his essence—the wisdom of God cannot be a habit, but is God's very essence itself. Now from what has been said it is evident that the Son of God is the Word and conception of God understanding himself. It follows, then, that the same Word of God, as wisely conceived by the Divine Mind, is rightly said to be "conceived or begotten Wisdom"; and so the Apostle gives to Christ the title: *the Wisdom of God.*

Day 19

Morning Prayer

Antiphon: Wisdom is the effulgence of God's glory.

Psalm 142:1–12 ✠ Psalm 44:1–17 ✠ Psalm 109:1–7

Scripture: Wisdom 7:21–26 LXX

Reading: St. Thomas Aquinas, priest, Doctor of the Church † 1274

Commentary on the Psalms 44:2

My heart has emitted a good word. According to this exposition Christ is praised by the Father in three ways: first, one describes his emanation; second, his power—*I myself say*; and third, his operation—*my tongue.*

Regarding his emanation from the Father the verse sets forth four things:

1. First of all his procession is natural since it says, *has emitted.* This is an emanation from superabundance. Likewise, the procession of the Father in relation to the Father is a divine emission, since it proceeds from the fullness of Divine Nature: *The Father loves the Son and has committed everything into his hands.*

2. Second, it sets forth the mode of his emanation, for it is not by a corporeal means nor by another nature, but through a spiritual mode. *My heart*, not as if it were from out of nothing, or coming from another essence, but from my heart: *From the womb before the daystar I have given birth to you.*

3. Next, it sets forth the property of the One who proceeds, for it is the Word; *In the beginning was the Word*.

4. Finally, it sets forth the perfection of the One who proceeds, for he is *good*, as possessing all the goodness of divinity; *No one is good, except God alone*.

Evening Prayer

Antiphon: You rightly call me Teacher and Lord.

Psalm 133:1–3 ✠ Psalm 60:1–8 ✠ Psalm 109:1–7 VULG

Scripture: John 13:12–17

Reading: St. Thomas Aquinas, priest, Doctor of the Church † 1274

Lectures on the Gospel of John 11.215, 218

The Evangelist mentions the proficient Teacher of this wisdom when he adds, *it is the Only-Begotten Son who is in the bosom of the Father*. He shows the competence of this Teacher in three ways: by a natural likeness, by a singular excellence, and by a most perfect consubstantiality. . . .

Although the Son knows in a unique fashion, he would lack the ability to teach if he were not able to know completely. Thus the Evangelist adds a third point, namely, his consubstantiality to the Father, when he says, *who is in the bosom of the Father*. Now "bosom" is not to be understood here as referring to the fold in human garments; rather it indicates the hidden recesses of the Father. For what we bear in hidden places, we carry in the bosom. The hidden things of the Father are his unsurpassed power and knowledge, since the divine essence is infinite. In that bosom, therefore, that is, in the hidden most recesses of the paternal nature and essence—which transcend all the power of any creature—resides the Only-Begotten Son; thus he is consubstantial with the Father.

What the Evangelist signifies here by "bosom," David expressed by "womb," saying: *From the womb, before the daystar*, that is, from the innermost and hidden recesses of my essence, incomprehensible to every created intellect, *I gave birth to you*, consubstantial with me, so the same nature, virtue, power, and knowledge.

Day 20

Morning Prayer

Antiphon: The Offspring is in the image and likeness of the Parent.

Psalm 5:1–12 ✠ Psalm 68:1–32 ✠ Psalm 109:1–7

Scripture: Genesis 5:1–3

Reading: St. Robert Bellarmine, archbishop, Doctor of the Church † 1621

Commentary on the Psalms 109.4

From the womb, before the daystar, I begot you; you shall possess such a principality because I, your Almighty Father, *begot you* not as I did all created things out of nothing, but *from the womb*, from my own womb, as my true, natural, and consubstantial Son, and that *before the daystar*, before I created the stars, before any creature whatsoever, even before all ages. . . . *From the womb*, the holy Fathers [of the Church] quite rightly use this expression as a proof of the divinity of Christ; for if he were a creature, he could not be said to be born from the womb since no one can declare that a house, or a chair, or any manufactured product is born from the womb. Furthermore, God nowhere says that the heavens or the earth were born from the womb. Besides, by the womb is to be understood the "secret and intimate essence of God"; and although a womb belongs to a mother alone and not to a father; nevertheless, it is properly said "born from the womb of God the Father," thus indicating most clearly the consubstantiality of the Son with the Progenitor. Clearly a son is from the mother's substance as well as from that of the father; accordingly, because God has no need of a wife to beget and give birth to a Son, he is rightly said to be "born from the womb of God the Father," as Isaiah says, *Shall not I, who cause others to bring forth children, myself bring forth, declares the Lord? Before the daystar* indicates the eternity of the Son who was born before the creation of the daystar, and thus before all created things. But the daystar is named, for God himself is the Uncreated Light, *the True Light that enlightens all human beings* and angels.

Evening Prayer

Antiphon: In the Resurrection, we shall behold God face to face and be immersed in the Divine Life.

Psalm 26:1–14 ✠ Psalm 66:1–7 ✠ Psalm 79:1–19

Scripture: Colossians 1:9–12

Reading: St. Francis de Sales, bishop, Doctor of the Church † 1622

Treatise Concerning the Love of God 3.12

O Holy and Divine Spirit, eternal Love of the Father and of the Son, be propitious to my immaturity. Then, Theotimus, our understanding shall behold God, yes I declare it, it shall see God *face to face*, contemplating by means a view of true and real presence, the Divine Essence herself, and in her infinite beauties: all power, all goodness, all wisdom, all justice, and the rest of the profundity of perfections.

This understanding shall see clearly then, the infinite knowledge which God the Father had from all eternity of his own beauty, and wishing its full expression in himself, he pronounced and eternally declared the Word, the Verbum, or the most unique and infinite speech and diction, which, comprising and representing all the perfection of the Father, can be only one true God self-same, without division or separation. Then we shall truly see that eternal and wondrous generation of the Word and Divine Son, by which he was eternally born to the image and likeness of the Father. . . .

O Theotimus, what joy, what exultation to celebrate this eternal birthing which is manifested *in the splendor of the saints*, to celebrate it by beholding it, and to behold it by celebrating it!

Day 21

Morning Prayer

Antiphon: Your word is burning within me; I cannot contain it.

Psalm 41:1–11 ✠ Psalm 44:1–17 ✠ Psalm 69:1–5

Scripture: Jeremiah 20:9; 23:29

Reading: St. Robert Bellarmine, archbishop, Doctor of the Church † 1621

Commentary on the Psalms 45.1

David says, *My heart has uttered a good word*; this means my mind, out of the fullness and abundance of the divine light and celestial revelations, my mind has delivered to others this psalm containing a *good word*, that is, an exceedingly gracious and saving word for all humanity. To understand the text fully, we must first go into some details. Note the term the prophet utilizes, *has uttered*, which when translated literally means "belched forth," indicating that this psalm was not composed by himself, nor left to his own discretion; but like the wind that is involuntarily released from the stomach, he was obligated to utter the word whether he wanted to or not. . . . In describing the divine emanation of this *good word* from the heart of David, it relates to the production of the Eternal Word and attempts to lead us by the hand to an understanding of the generation of the Divine Word, produced not as children are normally produced by generation, nor by election, nor by adoption from out of many, but born from the fullness of the Father's heart, the very Word of his most perfect Mind, his Only Word, and therefore supremely excellent and good. Thus the expression *good word* may be uniquely applied to him: *My heart has uttered a Good Word*.

✠

RELATIONSHIPS IN THE TRINITY CAN BE EXPRESSED IN FEMININE TERMS

Day 1

Morning Prayer

Antiphon: God defies human understanding but is three equal Persons.

Psalm 54:1–16 ✠ Psalm 15:1–11 ✠ Psalm 22:1–6

Scripture: Genesis 17:1–4, 15–21 TNK

Reading: Syriac hymn, mid to late second century

Odes of Solomon 19.1–5

> A cup of milk was offered to me,
> and I drank it in the sweetness of the Lord's gentleness.
> The Son is the cup;
> and he who was milked is the Father;
> and she who milked him is the Holy Spirit;
> because his breasts were full,
> and it was necessary that his milk not be released without purpose.
> The Spirit of Holiness opened her womb,
> and mixed the milk of the two breasts of the Father,
> and gave the mixture to the world without their knowing it.
> and those who have received it are in the perfection of the Right Hand.

Evening Prayer

Antiphon: We believe in One God who is a Divine Triad.

Psalm 1:1–6 ✠ Psalm 32:1–22 ✠ Psalm 109:1–7

Scripture: Matthew 3:13–17

Reading: St. Dionysius of Rome, pope, Father of the Church † 268

Dionysius of Rome's *Epistle* as found in Athanasius, *Defense of the Nicene Creed* 26

Next I have reason to turn to those who divide and cut God into pieces, thus destroying that most sacred doctrine of the Church of God, the Divine Monarchy. They resolve the One God into three particular powers and divided substances, even into three godheads. I am informed that some of your catechists and teachers of the Divine Word take the lead in this belief, being diametrically opposed, as it were, to Sabellius's opinions, for Sabellius blasphemously affirms that the Son is the Father and vice versa. But these others in some fashion preach three gods, dividing the Holy Monad into three substances altogether foreign to each other and totally separate. For it is necessary that with the God of the universe is united the Divine Word, and that the Holy Spirit fondly reposes and dwells within God; thus must the Divine Trinity be necessarily gathered up into one and brought together under one head, as into one summit, I mean the God of the universe, God Almighty.

For it is the teaching of the irreverently-minded Marcion to sever and to divide the Divine Monarchy into three sources, a diabolical instruction, a doctrine that is not of Christ's true disciples and lovers of the Savior's teachings. For these disciples know very well that a Trinity is clearly preached by the Divine Scripture, and that neither the Old nor the New Testaments preach three gods.

Not less to be censured are those who hold the opinion that the Son is a product, and imagine that the Lord came into existence as one of the things which came to be; whereas the divine oracles bear witness to a befitting birth suitable to him, but not to any fashioning or production. It is blasphemy then, and not to the ordinary degree but the highest, to say that the Lord is any type of handiwork [of God]. For if he became Son, then once he did not exist; but he always was, since, of course, he exists in the Father, as he himself says, and since Christ is Word, Wisdom, and Power, which, as you know, the Divine Scriptures say are attributes of God. If then the Son came into being, then at one time these attributes did not exist; therefore, there was a time when God was without them. This is totally absurd! But why discourse more on these matters to you, men full of the Spirit and well aware of the absurdities which come to light if one says the Son is a product. . . .

O foolhardy people! Is the Word a product, who is *the First-Born of every creature*, who is *born from the womb before the daystar*, who spoke as Wisdom, *Before all the hills, you gave birth to me*? And in many passages of the divine oracles the Son is said to have been born, but nowhere to have come into existence. These texts clearly convict of misconception those who presume to call his divine and ineffable birth a "product."

Therefore, neither may we divide into three godheads the wondrous and divine Monad, nor disparage with the title "creature" the dignity and supreme majesty of the Lord; but we must believe in God the Father Almighty, and in Christ Jesus his Son, and in the Holy Spirit, and maintain that the Word is united with the God of the universe. For he says, *I and the Father, we are one*, and *I am in the Father and the Father is in me*. For thus, the Divine Triad and the holy preaching of the Monad will be preserved.

Day 2

Morning Prayer

Antiphon: In the Scriptures, several places God says "Let us."

Psalm 64:1–13 ✠ Psalm 70:1–24 ✠ Psalm 118:33–40

Scripture: Isaiah 44:6–8

Reading: St. Gregory the Illuminator, Catholicos, Father of the Church † ca. 332

Armenian Catechism 259

The Lord God is singular in essence and there is none before him. No other Creator of the universe, both visible and invisible, exists except the Only-Begotten Son who was born from the Father, and the Spirit exists as well, of the same who is from the being of the same. In the beginning this world was made by God, created by the singular power of the Almighty will, one essence of united thought, will, and nature of the consubstantial Trinity.

Evening Prayer

Antiphon: We profess faith in Three Divine Persons sharing the same characteristics.

Psalm 6:1–10 ✠ Psalm 32:1–22 ✠ Psalm 109:1–7 VULG

Scripture: John 15:16–26 PESH

Reading: St. Anastasius of Antioch, Patriarch, Father of the Church † 599

Oration on the Holy Trinity 1.12

We profess there to be only One God, the Holy Trinity, in which nothing discordant exists, nor do we recognize any such thing among the Persons, let alone utter it. As God has borne witness regarding the Begotten Son, *I have given birth to* him *from the womb before the daystar, from the womb* signifying in the recesses of the hidden and ineffable essence, and again as the Holy Spirit said regarding him, *The Spirit shall rest upon me.* Likewise our Savior Jesus, one in being with the Paraclete, said, that the Spirit *proceeds from the Father.*

Day 3

Morning Prayer

Antiphon: In your Light, we see Light.

Psalm 72:1–28 ✠ Psalm 35:5–12 ✠ Psalm 109:1–7

Scripture: Isaiah 63:7–10

Reading: St. Jerome, priest, Father and Doctor of the Church † 420

Homilies on the Psalms 36

From the womb before the daystar, I have given birth to you. Before the daystar— this literary form in Greek is called synecdoche, and by the grammarians "the part signifies the whole." Therefore, when *before the daystar* is said, it names one creature but signifies all creation. When scripture says, *before the daystar,* let us understand this as if it said: before the moon, before the sun, before every created thing. *From the womb before the daystar I have given birth to you. Before the daystar*! Before the daystar that is seen in the world, True Light was born! Thus another psalm says, *In your Light we see Light.* This statement is addressed to the Father: O Father, in the Light of the Son we see Light: The Holy Spirit. *From the womb before the daystar I have given birth to you.*

☙ 📖 ❧

Evening Prayer

Antiphon: The personal properties distinguish the Divine Persons.

Psalm 15:1–11 ✠ Psalm 32:1–22 ✠ Psalm 109:1–7 VULG

Scripture: Hebrews 1:1–9 NT

Reading: St. John of Damascus, priest, Father and Doctor of the Church † 749

The Orthodox Faith 1.8

It is only in these personal properties—being unbegotten, being born, and procession—that the three Divine Persons are distinguished from one another, being indivisibly divided, not by essence, but by the distinguishing characteristic of their proper subsistence. . . .

And thus we speak of individual subsistences so as to avoid conceiving of the Divine Nature as having any composition, for composition is the beginning of disintegration. Furthermore, we say that the three Persons dwell within one another so as not to introduce a whole multitude of gods. By the three Persons, we understand that there is no composition or confusion. By the Persons having the same essence and dwelling within one another and by their being the same in will, operation, power, authority, and movement—so to speak—we recognize the indivisibility and the unity of God. For there is really One God: God [Almighty], the Word, and God's Spirit.

Day 4

Morning Prayer

Antiphon: The origins of Adam, Seth, and Eve reflect a divine mystery.

Psalm 91:1–15 ✠ Psalm 3:1–8 ✠ Psalm 8:1–9

Scripture: Tobit 8:4–8

Reading: St. John of Damascus, priest, Father and Doctor of the Church † 749

The Orthodox Faith 1.8

The birthing is an action belonging to God's nature and proceeding from God's essence. It is without beginning and is eternal, so that the Progenitor experiences no change and is not a first God and then a later God, receiving no augmentation. . . .

The Word is called Only-Begotten because he alone, was born alone, out of the Father alone. For there is no other birthing like the begetting of the Son of God, nor is there any other Son of God. Consequently, although the Holy Spirit proceeds from out of the Father, this is not birthing, but procession. This is another mode of existence, and just as incomprehensible and unknowable as the begetting of the Son. Wherefore, the Son has all things whatsoever the Father has, except the quality of being unbegotten, and this exception does not signify any difference in essence or dignity, but rather a mode of existence. Now just as Adam was unbegotten (because God fashioned him), and Seth was begotten (because he is Adam's son), Eve was not begotten because she proceeded from Adam's side. Nevertheless, they do not differ from each other according to nature because they are all human; but they only differ in the mode of coming into existence.

Evening Prayer

Antiphon: God Almighty heals and vivifies by the Divine Word and Wisdom—the Holy Spirit (Theophilus of Antioch. *To Autolycus* 1.7).

Psalm 18:1–14 ✠ Psalm 32:1–22 ✠ Psalm 109:1–7

Scripture: John 14:19–26 PESH

Reading: St. John of Damascus, priest, Father and Doctor of the Church † 749

The Orthodox Faith 1.12

Whenever I think of the relation of the three Persons to one another, I know that the Father is Super-Essential [Self-luminous] Sun, [the Heavenly Sphere], Well-Spring of Goodness, Unfathomable Depth of Being, of Reason, of Wisdom, of Power, of Light, of Divinity, the birthing and emitting Source of Good concealed within itself. Therefore, the Father himself is Mind, Unfathomable Depth of Reason, Progenitor of the Word, and through the Word, Emitter of the Revealing Spirit. And to state matters succinctly, the Father has no Reason, Wisdom, Power, or Will other than the Son, who is the only Power of the Father and the Primordial Energy behind the creation of all things. As a perfect Person born of a perfect Person, in a manner which he alone knows, he is the One who is the Son and is so called.

Now the Holy Spirit is a power of the Father revealing the hidden things of divinity, who proceeds from the Father through the Son, in a manner which the Spirit alone knows, but not by birth. Wherefore the Holy Spirit is the Perfecter of the creation of the universe. Consequently, whatever pertains to the Father such as Cause, Well-Spring, and Progenitor, must be ascribed to the Father alone. And whatever pertains to the Son as caused, birthed Offspring, Reason, Primordial Energy, Will, and Wisdom, must be ascribed to the Son. And whatever pertains to the caused, proceeding, revealing, and perfecting Power must be ascribed to the Holy Spirit. The Father is the

Well-Spring and Cause of the Son and the Holy Spirit, Progenitor of the only Son and Emitter of the Holy Spirit. The Son is Offspring, Word, Wisdom, Power, Image, Radiance, and totally characteristic of the Father. The Holy Spirit is not an offspring of the Father, but is the Spirit of the Father as proceeding out of the Father. For without the Spirit there is no impulse. And the Holy Spirit is the Spirit of the Son, but not from him, but as proceeding through the Son from the Father; for the Father alone is Cause.

Day 5

Morning Prayer

Antiphon: What Wisdom is and how she came to be, I will tell you, and will not hide any mysteries from you, but will trace her steps from the beginning of her origin, thus establishing knowledge of her in full light (Wis 6:22 LXX).

Psalm 107:1–6 ✠ Psalm 112:1–9 ✠ Psalm 118:41–48

Scripture: Wisdom 6:12–20 LXX

Reading: St. John of Damascus, priest, Father and Doctor of the Church † 749

The Orthodox Faith 1.8

We believe in the Father, the origin and cause of all, born of no one, who alone is uncaused and unbegotten, maker of all, and by nature Father of his one and only-begotten Son, our Lord and God and Savior Jesus Christ, and by nature the Emitter of the Most Holy Spirit. We also believe in one Son of God, the Only-Begotten, our Lord Jesus Christ, who was born of the Father before all ages, Light born from Light, true God from true God, begotten, not made, one in essence with the Father, through whom all things came into existence. When we say that he was before all the ages, we mean that his birth is without time or beginning, for the Son of God was not brought into being out of nothing. The Only-Begotten is the effulgence of God's glory, the very character of the Father's being, the living Wisdom, the Power, the subsistent Word, the essential, perfect and living Image of the invisible God. Indeed, he was always with and in the Father, being eternally born from God without beginning. For the Father never existed when the Son did not, but the Father and the Son brought forth from him, simultaneously existed together, for a father could not be called a father without a child. Surely, if God did not have a Son, then God was not Father; and if God subsequently had a Son, subsequently becoming Father without having previously been Father, then God experienced change from not being Father to becoming Father. This is the most heinous of all blasphemies! For it is impossible to speak of God as lacking natural generative power, and the power of generating means the power to generate from oneself, that is, of one's own being, offspring similar in nature to oneself.

✠

The One, Holy, Catholic, and Apostolic Faith

Day 1

Morning Prayer

Antiphon: Go and learn the meaning of the words (Matt 9:15).

Psalm 118:145–52 ✠ Psalm 72:1–28 ✠ Psalm 1:1–6

Scripture: Jeremiah 23:3–36

Reading: St. Athanasius, Patriarch, Father and Doctor of the Church † 373

Defense of the Nicene Creed 5.21

    Therefore, if they, like the others, object that the terms [of the Nicene Creed] are strange, let them consider the sense in which the Council wrote, and anathematize what the Council [of Nicaea] anathematized; and afterwards, if they are able, let them censure the wording. But I know very well that if they have the mindset of the Council, they will totally accept the wording in which it was set forth. However, if they wish to baulk about the sense, everyone must recognize that it is fruitless to discuss the wording with them, when they are only seeking an occasion for impiety. This then was the reason for these expressions; but if they still grumble that such words are unscriptural, that very complaint is a reason why they should be cast out, as arguing in circles and not possessing a sound mind. Furthermore, let them blame themselves in this matter, for they set the example, beginning their assault against God with words not in Scripture. Nevertheless, if anyone is interested in finding out the truth, let them know, that, even if the expressions are not in the Scriptures in so many words, all the same, as was said before, the wording contains the sense of the Scriptures. The expressions convey the meaning to those who have perfect hearing for right worship.

    Now it's up to you to ponder this matter, and for the ill-instructed to listen well. I have already demonstrated, and it should be believed as true, that the Word is from the Father, is the only Offspring proper and natural to him. From whence may one conceive the Son to exist, who is the Wisdom and Word, in whom all things came into existence, if not from God himself? Notwithstanding, the Scriptures teach us about this, since the Father says through David, *My heart uttered a good Word*, and *From the womb, before the daystar, I gave birth to you*. And the Son testifies about himself to the Jews, *If God were you Father, you would love me, for I come forth from the Father*, and again, *Not that anyone has seen the Father, except the one who is from God, he has seen the Father*. Likewise, *I and my Father are one*, and, *I am in the Father and the Father is in me*, which is equivalent to saying, I am from the Father, and inseparable from him. Also, when John said, *The Only-Begotten Son, who resides within the womb of the Father, has declared Him*, he spoke about what he had learned from the Savior. For what does *in the womb* signify, if not the Son's genuine birth from the Father?

Evening Prayer

Antiphon: We believe.

Psalm 21:1–11 ✠ Psalm 25:1–12 ✠ Psalm 109:1–7

Scripture: 1 Timothy 6:11–16

Reading: Second Ecumenical Council (Constantinople I) 381

Nicene-Constantinopolitan Creed, Latin text

 We believe in one God the Father Almighty, maker of heaven and earth, of all things visible and invisible, and in one Lord Jesus Christ, the Son of God, the Only-Begotten, born of the Father before all ages, God of God, Light from Light, True God from True God, born not made, one in being with the Father, that is one substance with the Father, through whom all things were made, who for us human beings and for our salvation came down and was incarnate from the Holy Spirit and the Virgin Mary, became human and was crucified for us under Pontius Pilate and was buried, and on the third day rose and ascended into heaven and is seated at the right hand of the Father; he is coming again with glory to judge the living and the dead, whose kingdom will have no end; and in the Holy Spirit, the Lord and Giver of Life, who proceeds from the Father, with the Father and the Son is worshipped and glorified, who spoke through the Prophets; in one, holy, catholic, and apostolic church; we confess one baptism for the remission of sins, we expect the resurrection of the dead and the life of the world to come. Amen.

Day 2

Morning Prayer

Antiphon: He is the only Son of God, born of the Almighty before all ages.

Psalm 129:1–8 ✠ Psalm 25:1–12 ✠ Psalm 2:1–12

Scripture: Wisdom 2:12–20

Reading: St. Cyril of Jerusalem, bishop, Father and Doctor of the Church † 386

Catechetical Lectures 11.1–2

 Regarding the creedal words: "the Only-Begotten Son of God, born of the Father before all ages, through whom all things were made."

 In yesterday's sermon we gave sufficient expression, as far as we could, regarding the hope we have in Jesus Christ. But we must not merely believe in Christ Jesus nor accept him as one of the many who are improperly called christs. For they were figurative christs, anointed ones, but he is the true Christ, not having been raised to the priesthood by way of advancement among men, but eternally possessing the dignity of the priesthood from the Father. And for this reason, the Faith, guarding against our supposing him to be one of the ordinary anointed ones, adds to the profession of our faith: "in One Lord Jesus Christ, the Only-Begotten Son of God."

Again, upon hearing the term "son," do not imagine him as an adopted child, but a natural son, an Only-Begotten Son, having no sibling. For this very reason, he is called "Only-Begotten," because in the dignity of the divinity and concerning his birth from the Father, he has no sibling.

Evening Prayer

Antiphon: Mary is the mother of God Incarnate.

Psalm 118:49–56 ✠ Psalm 25:1–12 ✠ Psalm 72:1–28

Scripture: Luke 1:1–4, 26–38

Reading: Third Ecumenical Council (Ephesus) 431

Formula of Union, Greek Text

We will briefly state what we are convinced about and profess regarding the God-bearing Virgin and the manner of the Incarnation of the Only-Begotten Son of God, not as an addition but in the manner of a full statement, just as we have received and possess it from the beginning from the Sacred Scriptures and from the Tradition of the Holy Fathers, adding nothing whatsoever to the Creed set forth by the Holy Fathers of Nicaea. For, as we have just declared, that Creed is sufficient both for the knowledge of godly worship and for the refutation of all heretical false teaching. We will speak not presuming to approach the unapproachable, but we confess our weakness and thus preclude those who would reproach us for investigating matters beyond the human intellect.

We confess, accordingly, that our Lord Jesus Christ, the Only-Begotten Son of God, perfect God and perfect man composed of a rational soul and a body, born before all ages from the Father according to divinity, the same in the last days, for us and for our salvation, was born of Mary the Virgin according to his humanity, one and the same, one in essence with the Father in divinity and one in essence with us in humanity. Because a union of two natures occurred, we therefore confess one Christ, one Son, one Lord.

Day 3

Morning Prayer

Antiphon: If you wish to remain Catholic, believe that God gave birth to the Word.

Psalm 142:1–12 ✠ Psalm 25:1–12 ✠ Psalm 109:1–7

Scripture: Proverbs 30:4–5

Reading: St. Augustine, bishop, Father and Doctor of the Church † 430

Sermon 140.2, 5

Hold onto this firmly and steadfastly if you wish to remain Catholic: God the Father gave birth to the Son beyond time, and caused him to be born of the Virgin in time. The first birth transcends time, the second illuminates all time. Each birth, however, is awe-inspiring; the former without a mother, the latter without a father. When God generated the Son, he generated him from himself, not from a mother. When the mother generated the Son, as a virgin she generated, not from a man. He was born of the Father without a beginning; of his mother he was born today with a definite beginning. Born of the Father he made us; born of a mother he remade us. He was born of the Father in order that we might have being; he was born of his mother so that we might not perish. . . .

What does the Catholic faith profess? . . . That God the Son is equal to the Father, born equal, not born less.

Evening Prayer

Antiphon: Born of God outside the limitations of time, the Word bestows on us eternal life.

Psalm 118:57–64 ✠ Psalm 109:1–7 VULG ✠ Psalm 2:1–12

Scripture: Philippians 2:6–11

Reading: St. Augustine, bishop, Father and Doctor of the Church † 431

Sermon 214.6

He, though, who *in the form of God did not consider it robbery to be equal to God,* and *through whom we were created,* in order *to seek and to save that which was lost, emptied himself, taking the form of a slave, being made in human likeness, was found in condition as a man.* And so we believe that "he was born of the Holy Spirit and of the Virgin Mary." And so, each of his births are awe-inspiring, both that of his divinity as well as that of his humanity. The first is from the Father without a mother; the second is from a mother without a father. The first is outside of all time, the second at *the acceptable time*; the first eternal, the second opportune; the first without a body *in the womb of the Father,* the second with a body that did not violate his mother's virginity; the first without any sexuality, the second without any virility.

Thematic Readings for Non-Feast Days

Day 4

Morning Prayer

Antiphon: Heresies make the light of truth shine brighter.

Psalm 5:1–12 ✠ Psalm 72:1–28 ✠ Psalm 25:1–12

Scripture: Sirach 3:21–24

Reading: St. Augustine, bishop, Father and Doctor of the Church † 430

Sermon 51.11

Now regarding the mysteries which lie hidden here, nobody content with a simple faith would probe them, because if no one pried into such matters then no one would discover them, if it were not for these critical objectors pounding at the door. When heretics hurl their objections, the little ones become greatly disturbed; and when disturbed they start asking questions. Their questioning is like a beating of their heads against the mother's breasts, that they might yield as much milk as is sufficient for her little ones. Then, because they are disturbed, they search for answers, and those who know and have learned these things because they have investigated them and God has opened to their knocking, they in turn, open on their part, to those who are disturbed. And so it turns out that those very objectors prove themselves useful for the discovery of truth even though they raise their objections to lead people astray into error. Consequently, the quest for truth would be conducted less diligently if it were not for the lying adversaries it has. *For*, Scripture says, *there must also be heresies*; and as though we asked why, it immediately adds, *in order that those who are genuine might be made manifest among you*.

Evening Prayer

Antiphon: God always was and always shall be.

Psalm 138:1–14 ✠ Psalm 1:1–6 ✠ Psalm 88:1–28

Scripture: John 1:1–18

Reading: St. Bede the Venerable, priest, Father and Doctor of the Church † 735

Homily on the Gospels 1.8

And wondrously, blessed John, at the beginning of his Gospel, sublimely imbues us with the faith of believers concerning the Savior's divinity, and he forcefully overcomes the heretics' lack of faith. Now there were heretics who said, "If Christ was born, there was a time when he was not." John convicts them of falsehood when in the very first words he had said, *In the beginning was the Word*. He did not say, "In the beginning the Word began to exist," in order to demonstrate clearly that the Christ's coming into existence was not from time, but rather that he existed at the emergence of time, and in order that by this wording he could show that the Word was born of the Father without any temporal beginning. . . .

And there were others who accepted that Christ was God, but made from the time that Incarnation took place, not eternal and born from the Father before the ages. Thus certain persons of this type are recorded to have said, "I do not envy Christ's being made God, for I, too, if I so choose, can become just as he is." The Evangelist refutes their perverse idea when he said, *He was in the beginning with God.* That is, this Word, which is God, did not come into existence from time, but in the beginning was God with God. In the same manner they were enemies of truth who did not deny that Christ already existed before his birth from the Virgin, but notwithstanding they did not believe that he was God, born from the Father, but believed he was created by the Father, and thus was less than the Father because he was a creature. The evangelic proclamation condemns them as well when it says, *All things were made through him, and apart from him nothing was created.* Now since no creature was made apart from him, it is perfectly clear that the One through whom every creature was created is not himself a creature.

Day 5

Morning Prayer

Antiphon: To be a true and perfect Catholic one must believe the Word was born of the Father.

Psalm 5:1–12 ✠ Psalm 1:1–6 ✠ Psalm 109:1–7

Scripture: Proverbs 8:22–31 TNK

Reading: St. Peter Damian, cardinal bishop, Doctor of the Church † 1072

Letter 81

First of all, therefore, whoever wishes to be a true and perfect Catholic must believe in God the Father Almighty, the maker of all that is seen and unseen. Such a person must also believe in God's only-begotten Son, namely, the Word, God's Power and Wisdom, through whom all things were created. The Word was not created, but begotten before all ages. . . .

We do not believe whatsoever that in Christ the Son of Man is other than the Son of God. Indeed, from the very moment of the Lord's incarnation God passed into man and man into God, so that both the One who was born of the Father before all ages is at once truly the Son of Man and a true human being, and the One who at the end of the ages was born of the Virgin is truly both the Son of God and beyond all doubt true God. Therefore we correctly profess two births regarding Christ: one from the Father without any beginning or passage of time, everlasting and co-eternal in all things with the One who Engendered; and the second birth was that from the substance of his mother in the course of time. Consequently, in Christ divinity and the human condition coalesced so that the Word of God might become flesh, and flesh might pass into God, in order that the one Emmanuel should spring from both substances and be the proper Mediator between God and humans.

Evening Prayer

Antiphon: Believe by faith what you profess in the Creed.

Psalm 138:1–14 ✠ Psalm 25:1–12 ✠ Psalm 2:1–12

Scripture: Colossians 1:25–28

Reading: St. Peter Canisius, priest, Doctor of the Church † 1597

A Sum of Christian Doctrine 1.9

In the Creed it says: "I believe in Jesus Christ." This shows forth the second Person in the Godhead: "Jesus Christ true God and true man"; properly called by the name "Jesus" meaning Savior of his people, and "Christ," that is, Anointed by the Holy Spirit, and *full of all grace and truth*, Messiah, King, and our High Priest, who *holds the primacy in all things* and *in whom does bodily dwell the whole fullness of the Godhead*. Furthermore it shows him to be the only Son of God, born of the Father, begotten from all eternity, natural, one in being, and altogether equal to him according to divinity.

Day 6

Morning Prayer

Antiphon: The believers were of one heart and one mind (Acts 4:32).

Psalm 5:1–12 ✠ Psalm 25:1–12 ✠ Psalm 132:1–3

Scripture: Romans 15:1–6

Reading: Pope Eugene IV and the Seventeenth Ecumenical Council (Florence) 1439

Session 8 Council, 22 November 1439

Eugenius, bishop, servant of the servants of God, a record for perpetual memory. Let all people everywhere who go by the name of Christian: *Exult in God our helper, rejoice in the God of Jacob!* Behold the Lord once again, *mindful of his mercy*, has deigned to remove from his church another stumbling block which has endured for more than nine centuries. *The One who makes peace in highest heavens and is peace on earth for people of good will*, has granted in his ineffable mercy that most longed for union with the Armenians. . . .

In the first place, therefore, we give them the holy Creed issued by the hundred and fifty bishops in the Ecumenical Council of Constantinople, with the addition "and the Son," which, for the sake of declaring the truth and from urgent necessity, was legally and reasonably added to that Creed, which runs as follows:

I believe in one God the Father Almighty, maker of heaven and earth, of all things visible and invisible, and in one Lord Jesus Christ, the Son of God, the Only-Begotten, born of the Father before all ages, God of God, Light from Light, True God from True God, born not made, one in being with the Father, that is one substance with the Father, through whom all things were made, who for us human beings and for our salvation came down and was incarnate from the Holy Spirit and the Virgin Mary, became human and was crucified for us under Pontius Pilate and was buried, and on the third day rose and ascended into heaven and is seated at the right hand of the Father; he is coming again with glory to judge the living and the dead, whose kingdom will have no end; and in the Holy Spirit, the Lord and Giver of Life, who proceeds from the Father and the Son, with the Father and the Son is worshipped and glorified, who spoke through the Prophets; in one, holy, catholic, and apostolic church; I confess one baptism for the remission of sins, I expect the resurrection of the dead and the life of the world to come. Amen

We decree that this holy Creed should be either sung or read during the mass at least on Sundays and major feasts, as is the Latin custom, in all Armenian churches.

Wisdom Delighted in the Children of the Earth and Became Incarnate in Christ Jesus

Day 1

Morning Prayer

Antiphon: Wisdom is embodied in Christ.

Psalm 41:1–11 ✠ Psalm 76:13–20 ✠ Psalm 39:5–17

Scripture: Sirach 24:1–9 LXX

Reading: St. Cyprian, bishop and martyr, Father of the Church † 258

Testimonies against the Jews prologue; 2.1

Cyprian, to his [spiritual] son Quirinus, greetings. It was befitting, my beloved son, that I obey your spiritual desire, which begged with urgent petitions those divine teachings through which the Lord has designed to teach and instruct us by the Sacred Scriptures, that, being led out of the darkness of error and enlightened by the pure and shining light, we maintain our way of life through the savings sacraments. And indeed, just as you have requested, so our discourse has been composed. This treatise has been compiled as an abridged compendium, so that what was written should not be copiously scattered about, but as far as my poor memory recalled, I might recollect all that was necessary, into selections and connected headings, under which I may appear not to have treated the subject, so much as to have gathered material for others. . . . I have composed two books of moderate and equal length. . . . The second book contains the sacrament of Christ, that the one has come who was announced according to the Scriptures.

Second Book Chapter One: Christ is the First-Born, the very Wisdom of God, by whom all things were made.

According to Solomon in the Book of Proverbs: *The Lord established me as the beginning of his ways, with his works in mind, before the world, he founded me. In the beginning, before he made the earth, and before he constituted the abysses, before the fountains of water sprang forth, before the mountains were set into place, and before all the hills, the Lord gave birth to me. He made the regions and the uninhabitable places, as well as the uninhabitable limits under the heavens. When he prepared the heavens, I was present with him; and when he set his seat apart. When he made the clouds above the strong winds, and when he put into place the firm fountains under heaven, when he founded the fortified foundations of the earth; I was at his side, ordering them. I was She in whom he delighted. Furthermore, daily I rejoiced before his presence in every time, when he rejoiced in the completed earth.* Also the same [concerning Wisdom] in Ecclesiasticus: *Out of the mouth of the Most High I went forth, first-born before every creature . . . .*

Evening Prayer

Antiphon: Wisdom incarnate was rejected just like the prophets she had sent.

Psalm 140:1–5 ✠ Psalm 79:1–19 ✠ Psalm 2:1–12

Scripture: Luke 11:47–51 NT

Reading: St. Ephrem, deacon, Father and Doctor of the Church † 373

Paschal Hymn 1.11–15

> The Conqueror descended to be beaten, not by Satan
> —for he conquered that one; he throttled him.
> He was conquered by his "crucifiers."
> He had conquered by means of his justice, but was conquered due to his goodness.
> He conquered the Strong One and was conquered by the weak.
> They crucified him who handed himself over who was conquered
> in order to conquer.
> He overcame in the midst of his temptations, and was overcome,

thanks to his tenderness.
He vanquished Satan in deserted places when he provoked Him.
He was vanquished by Satan in inhabited places when that one crucified Him.
When He was killed, He killed him in order to conquer him by his own defeat.
Wisdom who makes all things perfect, who discourses with her children,
questioned the ignorant and disputed with the scribes.
She imparted intelligence to everyone. She has sown in every one the truth.
The Wisdom of God descended into the midst of fools.
She made them wise through her instruction; she illuminated
them with her explanations.
In payment for her help, they buffeted and struck her.

Day 2

Morning Prayer

Antiphon: Wisdom dwells in Christ, God made flesh.

Psalm 54:1–16 ✠ Psalm 80:1–14 ✠ Psalm 118:65–72

Scripture: Proverbs 9:1–6, 11 TNK

Reading: St. Gregory of Nyssa, bishop, Father and Doctor of the Church † ca. 395

Against Eunomius 3.1.43–45, 46

Since therefore Solomon did not claim mere human wisdom for himself when he said, *God has taught me wisdom*, and elsewhere saying, *all my words have God speaking in them*, referring to God all that is spoken by himself, it is profitable in this section of Proverbs to examine the prophecy that is mingled in with this Wisdom. We affirm that in the preceding part of the book where he says that *Wisdom has constructed for herself a house*, he foreshadows through this saying the construction of the Lord's flesh. For the true Wisdom did not dwell in another's lodging, but built for herself that dwelling place out of the Virgin's body. Here Solomon adjoins to his discourse the unity composed of both elements, I mean that of the house and that of Wisdom who constructed the house, namely of the humanity and of the divinity that was cemented with a human being. . . . Thus we may see in this passage Solomon prophetically moved, and delivering in its fullness the mystery of the Incarnation.[1]

---

1. The play on words here is beautiful. The Greek word for house is *oikos* and the term Gregory uses here for "incarnation" is *oikonomia*, from the same root, literally meaning household management, regularly translated as "dispensation" [of grace], a word earlier Fathers used to refer to the incarnation.

Evening Prayer

Antiphon: Wisdom assumed our human weakness so that we might be healed.

Psalm 133:1–3 ✠ Psalm 80:1–14 ✠ Psalm 118:73–80

Scripture: Matthew 23:37–39 NT

Reading: St. Augustine, bishop, Father and Doctor of the Church † 430

Questions on the Gospels 1.36

As the Lord said to Jerusalem, *How often I wanted to gather your children together, like a hen gathers her young beneath her wings, but you would not!* This species of animal displays great affection for her children, so that affected by their feebleness she in turn becomes feeble, and if any dangerous animal approaches, she protects her brood beneath her wings, against any evil assault. Such is our Mother, the Wisdom of God, who assumed the weakness of our humanity, as the Apostle says, *The weakness of God is stronger than men*, thus she protects our weakness and resists the devil, so that we might not be taken captive.

Day 3

Morning Prayer

Antiphon: Wisdom broods over us like a loving mother.

Psalm 64:1–13 ✠ Psalm 81:1–8 ✠ Psalm 35:5–12

Scripture: Genesis 1:1–2 TNK

Reading: St. Augustine, bishop, Father and Doctor of the Church † 430

On the Literal Meaning of Genesis 1.18.36

Let us remember, above all, as I have said on numerous occasions, that God does not operate under the constraints of time, or by motions of body or soul, as do human and angelic beings, but rather God operates by the eternal, unchanging, and fixed exemplars of his coeternal Word and by a kind of brooding action, as it were, of his equally coeternal Holy Spirit. The Greek and Latin translations say regarding the Holy Spirit that the Spirit *was stirring above the waters*; however, in Syriac, a language close to Hebrew (the following interpretation is said to be expounded on by a Christian scholar of Syria), the meaning is not *was stirring above*, but rather *was brooding over*. This action is not like someone nursing a swelling or flesh wound with the appropriate application of either cold or hot water, but rather like that of a bird brooding over her eggs. The mother aids in the development of her young by the warmth of her body, by means of an affection similar to love. Thus we must not regard the Genesis account in a human fashion, as if the utterances of God were subject to time throughout the various days of divine operation. For Divine Wisdom herself, assuming our weak human nature, has come to gather the children of Jerusalem under her wings, as a hen gathers her brood, not so that we might always remain little children, but rather that, being infants regarding malice, we may cease being children in spirit.

Evening Prayer

Antiphon: Wisdom makes visible the Way to God Almighty.

Psalm 1:1–6 ✠ Psalm 83:1–12 ✠ Psalm 118:97–104

Scripture: John 14:1–9

Reading: St. Augustine, bishop, Father and Doctor of the Church † 430

Confessions 7.18.24

I searched for the path to gain the strength I needed to enjoy you, but I did not discover it until I embraced the Mediator between God and humanity, the man Christ Jesus, who is God above all and blessed forever. I hadn't embraced you even though Christ called out, explaining, *I am the Way, the Truth, and the Life*, nor did I experience him yet as the food which, although I was still too weak to eat it, had been mingled with our nature. For this very reason *the Word became flesh* in order that your Wisdom, through whom you created the universe, that she might become milk adapted to our infancy.

Day 4

Morning Prayer

Antiphon: Wisdom descended from the throne of God to be with us.

Psalm 72:1–28 ✠ Psalm 118:81–88 ✠ Psalm 88:1–28

Scripture: Wisdom 9:1–4, 9–11 LXX

Reading: St. Augustine, bishop, Father and Doctor of the Church † 430

On the Trinity 4.20.27–28

The Son is the Father's Word which is also called his Wisdom. So what's so amazing about his being sent, not as if he were unequal to the Father, but sent because he *is a pure outflowing of the glory of God Almighty*? Now in this case what flows out, and that from which it flows, are one and the same substance. It's not like water flowing out from some hole in the ground or some rock, but like light flowing from light. Accordingly Scripture says regarding Wisdom *She is the effulgence of eternal light;* now this surely means Wisdom is the light of Eternal Light. . . .

So she is sent by the One from whom she flows. Thus the person who loved and desired this Wisdom prayed, *Send her out from your holy heavens, and send her from the throne of your Glory to be present with me and labor with me*, that is, to teach me to labor not in vain. Her labors are the virtues. Now her being sent to be with human beings is one thing, and her being sent to be a human being is another. *For she enters into holy souls and makes them friends of God and prophets*, just as she likewise fills the holy angels and works through them whatever pertains to their ministries and functions. But *when the fullness of time came* she was sent, not to fill angels nor even to become an angel, . . . nor to accompany human beings or to dwell in them, since she had already been like this with the patriarchs and prophets of old; no, it was so that the Word might become flesh, that is, become a human being. . . . So the Word of God is sent by the One whose Word he is, sent by the One from whom he is born.

Evening Prayer

Antiphon: Strip off your old self and be renewed in the image of your Creator.

Psalm 6:1–10 ✠ Psalm 84:1–13 ✠ Psalm 118:81–88

Scripture: Colossians 3:1–11

Reading: St. Augustine, bishop, Father and Doctor of the Church † 430

Tractate on the Gospel of John 21.1

We are mortals bearing flesh, walking around in this life. And although we are born again of the seed of the Word of God, nevertheless we are made new in Christ in such a manner that we are not yet completely stripped of the old Adam. For, what there is in us, the mortal and *corruptible part that weighs down the soul*, appears to be of Adam, and evidently is so; but what there is in us, the spiritual part that lifts up the soul, this is from God's gift and mercy, who sent his only Son to have a share with us in our death, and to lead us to his own immortality. This one we have for our master, that we might not sin; and as our Defender, if we have sinned, confessed, and been converted; and as an Intercessor on our behalf, if we desire any good thing from the Lord; and as the Giver of all blessings with the Father, because the One God is Father and Son. But he spoke these things as a human being to humans; hidden God and manifest human being, so that he might make them gods who are manifestly mere humans; and Son of God, made Son of man, that he might make mortal children to be children of God. By what skill of his Wisdom he does this, we perceive in his own words. For he speaks to the little ones as someone little: however, in such wise little, that he is likewise great; and although we are little, in him we are great. Therefore, he speaks as one cherishing and nourishing those who suck at the breast and who grow by loving.

PRAYING—WITH THE SAINTS—TO GOD OUR MOTHER

Day 5

Morning Prayer

Antiphon: Wisdom has become totally intimate by assuming our human nature.

Psalm 91:1–15 ✠ Psalm 39:5–17 ✠ Psalm 118:89–96

Scripture: Wisdom 8:16–21 LXX

Reading: St. Cyril of Alexandria, Patriarch, Father and Doctor of the Church † 444

Commentary on Luke 18:29

Solemnly I assure you, there is no one who has left home, or wife, or brothers and sisters, parents or children, for the sake of the Kingdom of God, who shall not receive a bountiful return in this age and life everlasting in the age to come. Befitting of God is this declaration, holy and wondrous the decree. See how he raises up everyone who hears to hope, promising not merely the fullness of gracious gift which is conferred upon the saints, but likewise confirming his promise by an oath when he begins his declaration with the word "solemnly," which functions as part of an oath. Not only does he include within his promises anyone who disregards wealth, but those as well, he states, who leave father or mother, or wife or siblings, or home all for the sake of the Kingdom of God....

Each of us who has believed in Christ and loved his name, if one has left a house shall receive the mansions that are above; and if one abandoned a father, shall acquire the Father who is in heaven. If one has been forsaken by brothers, Christ shall receive him into the brotherhood. If he has left a wife, he shall receive as intimate companion Wisdom who comes down from above, from God's presence, and by her he shall bring forth beautiful offspring. And if he leaves mother, he shall receive *the Jerusalem above, who is free and is our mother.*

Evening Prayer

Antiphon: Wisdom identifies with our weakness so we can identify with God's glory.

Psalm 15:1–11 ✠ Psalm 85:1–17 ✠ Psalm 118:97–104

Scripture: Luke 13:34–35 NT

Reading: St. Bede the Venerable, priest, Father and Doctor of the Church † 735

Exposition on the Gospel of Matthew 4.23

How often I wanted to gather your children together as a mother hen gathers her chicks beneath her wings. The Lord sets forth this animal as an analogy because of the great affection she bears for her young; she feels their weakness and she herself becomes weakened. When various difficulties arise, she protects her chicks beneath her wings; she fights against the bird of prey. This is how our mother, the Wisdom of God, acts, who became weak by assuming human flesh, thus protecting our weakness; she stands in the way of the devil so that he might not snatch us. And because she strove with such feeling against the bird of prey, she put an end to the devil by her power.

Day 6

Morning Prayer

Antiphon: Wisdom is the Tree of Life we can now grasp in Christ Jesus.

Psalm 107:1–6 ✠ Psalm 89:1–17 ✠ Psalm 118:105–12

Scripture: Proverbs 3:13–19 TNK

Reading: Oecumenius, Father of the Church † early sixth century

Commentary on the Book of Revelation 12.7.4–5

The text reads, *On the other side of the river was a fruitful tree of life producing fruit every month.* Now the Lord is the Tree of Life according to what the writer of Proverbs remarks concerning Wisdom. The text says, *She is a Tree of Life to all those who lay hold of her.* And the wise Paul instructed us, *Christ is the Power of God and the Wisdom of God* thereby teaching that not only are the saints made rich by Christ's gifts of grace, but they also possess Christ dwelling within them and with them, something which is the culmination of the highest state of blessing. She, the Tree of Life, that is Christ, brings to perfection for the saints unceasing fruits and gifts, so that honor super-abounds upon honor and they are never lacking the divine flow of bounty. *And the leaves of the tree,* the text says, *were for the healing of the peoples.* The life-giving leaves are those who are dependent upon Christ and adhere to Christ, namely, the patriarchs and matriarchs, prophets and prophetesses, male and female apostles, evangelists, martyrs and confessors, and all those who according to the seasons celebrate the sacred rituals of the Gospel, pastors of the church, and every righteous person. All of these have now found healing for their souls, and all good things will continue to be supplied to the saints.

Evening Prayer

Antiphon: Wisdom is eternal but became temporal as well by taking on flesh.

Psalm 18:1–14 ✠ Psalm 110:1–9 ✠ Psalm 118:113–20

Scripture: John 1:1–14

Reading: St. Rabanus Maurus, archbishop † 856

Commentary on Sirach 1.1

All wisdom is from the Lord God and remains with him forever, even before the ages. The writer begins this book [of Sirach] talking about the eternal Wisdom of God, she who is Christ, who always was with the Father before all ages. This is in accordance with the Gospel of John which commences with the verses: *In the beginning was the Word and the Word was with God and the Word was God. He was in the beginning with God*. Therefore *all wisdom is from God*, she who is Christ who is the fountain of life and *the true light that enlightens everyone coming into this world*. The Word was born of God the Father *and through him all things were made, and nothing was made apart from him*.

Day 7

Morning Prayer

Antiphon: Wisdom gives birth to us so we can become children of God.

Psalm 118:145–52 ✠ Psalm 113A:1–9 ✠ Psalm 118:121–28

Scripture: Sirach 24:1, 10–22 LXX

Reading: St. Thomas Aquinas, priest, Doctor of the Church † 1274

Summa Theologiae IIaIIae.45.65

Peacemaking is well suited to Wisdom. The statement *They shall be called the children of God* indicates the reward. Now human beings are called children of God inasmuch as they participate in the likeness of the Only-Begotten and natural Son of God, according to Romans, *Those whom he foreknew . . . to be made conformable to the image of his Son*, who is Wisdom Begotten. Thus by receiving the gift of Wisdom a person enters into the state of being a child of God.

Consequently: 1) It belongs to love to possess peace, but it belongs to wisdom to make peace by setting things in right order. Likewise, the Holy Spirit is called the *Spirit of adoption* inasmuch as we receive from the Spirit, the likeness of the natural Son who is Wisdom Begotten. 2) The text refers to Uncreated Wisdom who first unites herself with us by the gift of love and reveals mysteries to us flowing from that love. The knowledge of these mysteries is infused wisdom, a gift, which is not the cause of love, but its great effect.

Evening Prayer

Antiphon: Born from time eternal, produced in womb virginal (Peter Damian, *Opera* IV).

Psalm 21:1–11 ✠ Psalm 4:1–8 ✠ Psalm 113B:9–19

Scripture: Romans 8:31–39

Reading: St. Peter Damian, cardinal bishop, Doctor of the Church † 1072

Concerning Divine Omnipotence 17.21–36

Above all, concerning everything that we have said, don't let this one point escape you, namely, that God, the Creator of all things, is co-eternal with all power as well as all knowledge, and that in the womb of his Wisdom, God encompasses, establishes, and sustains forever all the passages of time, the past, the present, and the future, without allowing anything novel to arise, nor anything, in passing, to pass into oblivion.

Now what is this Power by which God can accomplish all things? What is this Wisdom by which God knows all things? Let us ask the Apostle. *Christ*, he responds, *is the Power and the Wisdom of God*. There certainly is the true eternity, the true immortality; there the eternal today that never passes away; there this present, perpetually fresh and established with a stability so persistent that it cannot diminish, and or ever fade away.

☦

Christ is our Mother

Day 1

Morning Prayer

Antiphon: We are contained in the bowels of Christ our mother.

Psalm 129:1–8 ✠ Psalm 120:1–8 ✠ Psalm 83:1–12

Scripture: Isaiah 51:1–3 TNK

Reading: St. Justin Martyr, Apostolic Father of the Church † 165

Dialogue with Trypho 135

When Scripture says, *I am the Lord God, the Holy One of Israel, who has made known Israel, your king*, will you not understand that Christ truly is the everlasting King? For you are aware, are you not, that Jacob, the son of Isaac, never was a king? Therefore, Scripture again explains to us what king is meant by Jacob and Israel: *Jacob is my Servant, I will uphold him; and Israel is my elect, my soul shall receive him. I have bestowed upon him my Spirit, and he shall bring forth judgment to the nations. He shall not cry out, nor shall his voice be heard without. The bruised reed he shall not break, and the smoldering wick he shall not extinguish, until he shall bring judgment to victory. He shall shine out and shall not be discouraged until he has established judgment on the earth. And in his name, shall the nations trust*. Then is it in Jacob the patriarch that you yourselves and the nations shall trust? Or is it not in Christ? Since Christ is designated by Israel and Jacob, likewise, we, who have been quarried out from the bowels of Christ, we are the true Israelitic race.

Evening Prayer

Antiphon: Christ is all things to and for us.

Psalm 118:49–56 ✠ Psalm 121:1–9 ✠ Psalm 101:1–28

Scripture: 1 Peter 1:3–5 NT

Reading: Post-Apostolic writing ca. 190

Acts of Peter 39

[Peter's alleged dying words:] Because you have divulged and made all of this known to me, O Word of God, you whom I even now call the Tree of Life, I give you thanks, not with lips riveted shut, nor with this tongue which pours forth both truth and falsehood, nor with this voice which makes itself heard in an earthly fashion, but I give you thanks, O King, with this inner voice enveloped in silence, which doesn't resound outwardly, which isn't spoken by physical organs, which doesn't enter into carnal ears, nor is heard by corruptible flesh. It is a voice which doesn't exist in this realm, which isn't spoken upon the earth, a message which isn't found in books, which doesn't belong to one without belonging to another. It is with this voice, Christ Jesus, that I give you thanks. It is with this silent voice with which the Spirit interiorly moves me to love you, to converse with you, to behold you. You are only made intelligible through the Spirit. You are a father to me, a mother to me, a brother to me, a friend, a servant, a steward. You are all, and everything exists in you.

Day 2

Morning Prayer

Antiphon: Christ becomes all things for our sake.

Psalm 142:1–12 ✠ Psalm 123:1–8 ✠ Psalm 118:137–44

Scripture: 1 Enoch 5:7–9 Ethiopic

Reading: St. Macarius the Great, Desert Father of the Church † 391

Spiritual Homilies 31.4

When God notices the earnestness with which you seek him, then God appears with a self-manifestation to you.... For when God first sees your diligent search and how totally and unceasingly you are waiting with expectation, then God teaches you and grants you authentic prayer and genuine love. In short, God's very self becomes all things in you: paradise, a tree of life, pearl, crown, architect, cultivator, sufferer, one impervious to suffering, human, God, wine, living water, lamb, bridegroom, warrior, armor; Christ becomes all things in every situation. And just as the baby doesn't know how to take care of itself, or look out for itself, but looks only to its mother, waiting until she is moved with compassion and lifts it up, accordingly, faithful souls always place their hope only in the Lord, ascribing all righteousness to God.

Evening Prayer

Antiphon: As a mother, Christ accommodates to our stage of spiritual growth.

Psalm 118:57–64 ✠ Psalm 124:1–5 ✠ Psalm 130:1–3

Scripture: Luke 4:38–41

Reading: St. Gregory of Nyssa, bishop, Father and Doctor of the Church † ca. 395

On the Making of Man 25.6–7

For since the wonder of the resurrection was great and beyond belief, beginning with inferior instances of the miraculous power, he gradually accustoms our faith for the greater. For a mother who nurses her infant with solicitude, supplies milk from her breast to its mouth while it is still tender and soft; and yet when the infant begins to grow and sprout teeth she gives it bread, not hard but soft since it cannot chew, so that the tender and untrained gums may not be bruised by rough food. She softens the food with her own teeth and makes it palatable and suitable for the capabilities of the digester. Then as its capabilities increase with growth she gradually causes the baby to advance, accustomed to soft food and then to more solid nourishment. In like fashion, the Lord, nourishing and fostering with miracles the infancy of the human mind, like some baby not yet grown, displays a prelude of the power of the resurrection in the case of a desperate disease. The prelude, though it was a great achievement, was not yet such a matter that the declaration of it would not be believed; for by *rebuking the fever* which was fiercely gripping Simon's mother-in-law, he produced such a great removal of the malady enabling her who was already considered at death's door, to *minister* to those present.

Day 3

Morning Prayer

Antiphon: The Incarnate Word of God is our virgin mother!

Psalm 5:1–12 ✠ Psalm 124:1–5 ✠ Psalm 118:73–80

Scripture: Jeremiah 18:13–14 *Vetus Latina*: "What great things the Virgin of Israel has done! The breasts shall not fail from the rock, nor snow from Lebanon, nor shall the water decline which is borne by the strong wind." This earliest Latin translation was based off of the LXX: "Who has heard of such exceedingly stupendous things as what the Virgin of Israel has done? The nourishing breasts shall not fail to flow from rocks, or snow from Lebanon. Nor will the water violently pushed by the wind, turn aside."

Reading: St. Ambrose, bishop, Father and Doctor of the Church † 397

Concerning Virgins 1.5.21–22

And what is virginal chastity if not purity free from vile contagion? And whom can we appraise as its author if not the immaculate Son of God, whose flesh did not experience corruption, whose divinity experienced no contagion? Consider then how great are the merits of virginity. Christ was before the virgin; Christ was from the Virgin—indeed, born of the Father before the ages, but born of the Virgin for the ages. The former was of his own nature, the latter is for our benefit. The former always was, the latter he willed.

Contemplate another merit of virginity: Christ is the spouse of the virgin, and if one may say so, Christ is of virginal chastity, for virginity is of Christ, not Christ of virginity. Christ is, therefore, the virgin who was espoused, the virgin who carried us in her womb, the virgin who gave birth to us, the virgin who nursed us with her own milk, of whom we read: *What great things the virgin of Jerusalem has done! The breasts shall not fail from the rock, nor snow from Lebanon, nor shall the water decline which is borne by the strong wind.* Who is this virgin who is watered by the fountains of the Trinity, from whose rock waters flow, whose breasts don't fail, and whose honey is poured forth? This is the Trinity who waters her Church: Father, Christ, and Spirit.

Evening Prayer

Antiphon: Christ is both our bridegroom and our bride.

Psalm 138:1–14 ✠ Psalm 125:1–6 ✠ Psalm 18:1–14

Scripture: Acts 9:1–9

Reading: St. Augustine, bishop, Father and Doctor of the Church † 430

Commentary on the Psalms, Second Discourse on Psalm 30 2.1.4

It is Christ who is speaking here through the prophet; yes, I dare to declare: Christ is speaking. The prophet will propound certain things in this psalm which may appear impossible to apply to Christ, to that excellency of our Head, above all to that Word who in the beginning was God dwelling with God. Likewise, certain other things will be said which seem incongruous with the One who took the form of a servant, the servile form he took from the Virgin. Nevertheless, it is Christ speaking, because in Christ's members Christ speaks. And in order that you may know that Christ the Head and his Body are one, he himself said when speaking about marriage: *The two shall be in one flesh. Therefore now they are not two, but one flesh.* But does He say this, perhaps,

Thematic Readings for Non-Feast Days

of any marriage whatsoever? Listen to the apostle Paul: *And they shall be two in one flesh. This is a great mystery; but I speak in Christ and in the Church.* Therefore while in reality there are two, from them one certain person arises, from Head and Body, from bridegroom and bride. Now the marvelous surpassing unity of this person Isaiah the prophet also commends; for Christ, prophesying likewise speaking through him, declares: *As a bridegroom he has bound me with a crown, and as a bride she has adorned me with ornaments.* He calls himself both bridegroom and bride. Why bridegroom and why bride, if not because they shall be two in one flesh?

Day 4

Morning Prayer

Antiphon: Christ displays the loving patience of a true parent.

Psalm 41:1–11 ✠ Psalm 125:1–6 ✠ Psalm 88:1–28

Scripture: Sirach 4:12–21 VULG

Reading: St. Peter Chrysologus, archbishop, Father and Doctor of the Church † 450

Sermon 31.1

Goodness is the mother of all the virtues; malice is the origin of the vices. Glory is the companion of the virtues; confusion follows on the heels of the vices. Thus vices are deliberately concealed whereas virtues are openly brought to light. That is why Christ, the light of all virtues, acted openly, spoke with clarity, disclosed himself as God, displayed loving patience as Parent, and disciplined as Lord.

Evening Prayer

Antiphon: Christ comes as a mother to heal our illnesses.

Psalm 140:1–5 ✠ Psalm 126:1–5 ✠ Psalm 118:153–60

Scripture: Mark 2:15–17

Reading: St. Peter Chrysologus, archbishop, Father and Doctor of the Church † 450

Sermon 29.5

The healthy have no need of a doctor, but the sick do. I have not come to call the righteous, but sinners. And who was not diseased? For the very nature of the human species was so sick. Therefore the Lord came for all, in order to cure all, having found all to be ill. But surely he deserved to die who had contempt for the doctor, refused to question himself and admit that he was sick.

But the Lord makes apparent the meaning of his metaphor, saying: *I have not come to call the righteous, but sinners.* Now the Lord is not rejecting the righteous, rather the arrogant. He is referring to those who, while not being righteous, boast that they are. And where were those righteous when, the prophet declared, *There was no one who practiced justice, no not one*? In order to recognize their illness, let them receive the doctor and thus be cured. Let them admit that they are sinners and recognize Christ as their Parent and Table Companion, so that pardon might be liberally bestowed, and that later as Judge he might not render an unending sentence due to their obstinacy.

Day 5

Morning Prayer

Antiphon: God sees within the heart as a mother knows how to do.

Psalm 54:1–16 ✠ Psalm 118:161–68 ✠ Psalm 7:1–17

Scripture: 1 Samuel 16:1–7

Reading: St. Peter Chrysologus, archbishop, Father and Doctor of the Church † 450

Sermon 32.4

But they were silent. And considering them from all angles with anger, [Christ] was deeply saddened by their blindness of heart. It says, *considering from all angles*, not simply, *considering*; in other words, not merely looking at the surface as humans do, but as God, perceiving external forms, internal hearts, minds, and intentions, as well as past, present, and future. *Considering them from all angles with anger, [Christ] was deeply saddened.* As Lord, Christ is angered, as Parent—deeply saddened, as human—hurt, and as God—deeply moved.

Evening Prayer

Antiphon: The One who is and was our God before the ages wanted to be our Parent throughout these last ages in order to save us with loving-kindness.

Psalm 133:1–3 ✠ Psalm 127:1–6 ✠ Psalm 26:1–14

Scripture: John 7:25–29

Reading: St. Peter Chrysologus, archbishop, Father and Doctor of the Church † 450

Sermon 49.1–2

As soon as the Holy Evangelist notes that the Lord endured or experienced human things, a literalistic interpretation hurls everything into confusion like a tidal wave. For feeble minds are not capable of hearing, discerning, and interpreting the mysteries regarding the Lord's flesh, as today's reading demonstrates, which says: *And Jesus left there and went off to his homeland.* From whence does he come? Where does he go, he who is contained and confined in no place? To what homeland does he journey, who fashioned and possesses the whole world? As the Prophet declares: *Yours are the heavens and yours is the earth; you founded the earth and its fullness.* Surely it is not for himself, but for you that Christ comes and goes, until such time as he allow you to come in who were once expelled, recalling you from exile, leading and carrying you back who were cast out. For this reason, Jesus went off to his homeland, not to return to his homeland, but for you to return to your homeland which Adam had ceased to possess.

He went off to his homeland. If he was born, how can he not be a human being? If a human being, then how not a citizen? If a citizen, who should be surprised that he has homeland? But here he is speaking in the fashion of humanity, not according to the status of divinity; because the One who is and was our God before the ages, wanted to be our Parent throughout these last ages in order to save with loving-kindness those whom God created with power; and by sharing their experiences, receives back those who were alienated by conviction and decree.

Day 6

Morning Prayer

Antiphon: As a loving parent, the Incarnate Word persuades us.

Psalm 64:1–13 ✠ Psalm 118:169–76 ✠ Psalm 102:1–22

Scripture: Hosea 11:1–4 TNK

Reading: St. Peter Chrysologus, archbishop, Father and Doctor of the Church † 450

Sermon 50.2–3

It states, *he entered into the boat*. Christ always enters the boat of his Church, calming the waves of the present age, so that he might transport in tranquility those who believe in him across to his heavenly homeland and make citizens of his own City those whom he made sharers in his humanity. Therefore, Christ does not need the ship, rather the ship needs Christ, because without a heavenly Pilot the ship of the Church is unable to circumnavigate through the sea of this world with so many and great dangerous turning points, and sail to its heavenly harbor. We have said these things, dear brothers and sisters, insofar as they pertain to a spiritual understanding. Now let us proceed with the historical narrative.

It reads: *He entered into the boat, and crossed the sea and came to his own city.* The Creator of the universe and Lord of the world, after he confined himself in human flesh for our sake, began to have a human homeland, began to be a citizen of a Jewish city, began to have parents, himself the Parent of all parents, so that love might invite, endearment attract, affection encompass, and his humanity sweetly persuade those whom sovereignty had caused to flee, fear had driven away, and sheer power had exiled.

Evening Prayer

Antiphon: Perfect love transcends the limited categories of masculine and feminine.

Psalm 1:1–6 ✠ Psalm 131:1–18 ✠ Psalm 118:9–16

Scripture: Galatians 3:23–28

Reading: St. Maximos the Confessor, monk, Father of the Church † 662

Centuries on Love 2.30

Whoever is perfect in love and has attained the peak of detachment knows no distinction between one's own and another's, between faithful and unfaithful, between slave and free, or indeed between masculine and feminine. But having transcended the tyranny of the passions and looking steadfastly into the one nature of human beings, that person regards all equally and is equally disposed towards all things. For in that person there is neither Greek nor Jew, neither male nor female, neither slave nor free, but Christ is all and in all.

Day 7

Morning Prayer

Antiphon: O Divine Mother, kiss me with your comforting kiss.

Psalm 72:1–28 ✠ Psalm 132:1–3 ✠ Psalm 118:17–24

Scripture: Song of Songs 1:1–4 LXX

Reading: St. Gregory of Narek, monk and priest † 1003

Commentary on the Song of Songs prologue; 1

He prepared you from the womb; your mother was the most beautiful among women.
The *womb* refers to the baptismal font, and it is the Church which is called *Mother* Sion, because 'Sion is called mother, and a child was born in her.'
A body shall be born for him without fault and without blemish, by another Providence; that is to say, by the Holy Spirit. The Apostle, likewise, declares, *Born again, not of corruptible seed, but of the incorruptible, living and eternal; Word of God.* . . .
The Song of Songs, which is Solomon's The name *Solomon* means *peace*. In this fashion he symbolizes Christ, for 'He is our peace,' as the Apostle declares.
Now since we have been born by a new form of generation, we implore our Parent to kiss us with maternal love, to bring us near to the divine mouth, so that when She kisses us, we may drink from her mouth that which her all-holy mouth uttered: 'If anyone is thirsty, come to me and drink.'

Thematic Readings for Non-Feast Days

Evening Prayer

Antiphon: I prefer no one over you, Lord, and willingly pick up my cross.

Psalm 6:1–10 ✠ Psalm 136:1–6 ✠ Psalm 118:25–32

Scripture: Matthew 10:37–39

Reading: St. Gertrude the Great of Helfta, nun † 1302

The Herald of God's Loving-Kindness 3.42.2

The Lord said, "Whoever will associate their pains and adversities with the spiritual bouquet of my Passion—ever mindful to imitate the example of my Passion—by arranging their lives and pressing themselves close to me—truly that one is 'a fragrant sachet resting between my breasts,' so that, through my special affection, everything which I merited through my patience and other virtues, I will add to their own merits." Gertrude asked, "My Lord, how will you receive such a vibrant sentiment, since no one is so deeply moved before the image of your Cross?" The Lord responded: "I will welcome it with satisfaction, but, nevertheless, whoever is moved by an image and does not follow me by imitating the examples of my Passion, I will have towards them the dispositions analogous to those of a young daughter with regard to her mother who dresses her up according to her own tastes and vanity without once taking into account her daughter's own preferences, even at times in opposition to her wishes. To the extent that the mother refuses what the daughter desires, she being less grateful for anything she receives, since she perceives that her mother bedecks her with all sorts of ornaments more for her own glory and not out of any genuine tenderness for her daughter. Accordingly, any sentiment, honor, and respect rendered to the image of my Cross cannot completely satisfy me, as long as one does not make any effort to imitate the examples of my Passion."

Day 8

Morning Prayer

Antiphon: Christ embroiders the pattern of holiness upon our souls.

Psalm 91:1–15 ✠ Psalm 137:1–8 ✠ Psalm 44:1–17

Scripture: Proverbs 31:10–31

Reading: St. Anthony of Padua, priest, Doctor of the Church † 1231

Sermons for the Fourth Sunday after Easter 4.4

Christ is also called am embroiderer. No matter what the cloth, embroidering is done with a needle. Observe that a needle has two parts: the point and the eye. The point signifies the divinity, the eye—the humanity. The Lord himself speaks of this needle in the Gospel, *The camel cannot pass through the eye of the needle.* The camel with the hump on its back represents the rich man laden with riches and thus he is incapable of passing through the eye of the needle, that is to say, the poverty of Jesus Christ. Or, to interpret it another way, the eye is the tender mercy God displayed in his first coming; the point being the penetrating justice with which he will pierce us in the final judgment. With this kind of needle our embroiderer will stitch for the faithful soul a beautiful tunic, sewn with the distinctive and richly variegated colors of the virtues. As it says in the Book of Proverbs, *She has sewn a garment for herself, fine linen and purple are her vestment.* A garment, namely a vestment, usually interweaves a variety of colors; the fine linen of chastity and the purple of the Lord's Passion are the befitting vestment for the faithful soul.

Evening Prayer

Antiphon: Divinity joined with humanity, did what humanity could not do alone.

Psalm 15:1–11 ✠ Psalm 39:5–17 ✠ Psalm 88:1–28

Scripture: Romans 5:12–21

Reading: St. Catherine of Siena, religious, Doctor of the Church † 1380

Dialogue 14

Human nature was able to atone for its sin only by virtue of the Divine Nature. In this fashion the infection of Adam's sin was removed, leaving only its telltale sign, that is the inclination to sin and every type of physical defect—like the scar that remains after a person's wound has been healed. Now Adam's sin prevailed with a deadly infection, but the Great Physician came, my only-begotten Son, and cured your sickness by drinking the bitter medicine you could not swallow because you were too weak. He did as the wet nurse who herself drinks the medicine that the baby must swallow, because she is big and strong while the baby is too frail to endure the bitterness. My only-begotten was your wet nurse, uniting the greatness and strength of divinity with your nature in order to drink the bitter medicine of his death on the Cross and thereby heal and impart life to you who were babies debilitated by sin.

Day 9

Morning Prayer

Antiphon: There is nothing the saints need that God herself is not for them.

Psalm 107:1–6 ✠ Psalm 147:1–7 ✠ Psalm 118:33–40

Scripture: Deuteronomy 32:12–14 TNK

Reading: St. Nicholas Cabasilas, monk and priest † ca. 1391

Life in Christ 1.4

Now the Savior is ever present in every manner with those who live in him so that he supplies their every need and is all things for them, not allowing them to look to anything else whatsoever or to seek anything else from elsewhere. There is nothing the holy ones need that he is not himself, for he gives birth to them, nourishes them, and causes them to grow. He is their light and breath and by means of himself he fashions an eye for them and, in addition, provides them light enabling them to see himself. He is one who nourishes and is himself the food.

Evening Prayer

Antiphon: God enables us to pray, carried along in the arms of love.

Psalm 18:1–14 ✠ Psalm 7:1–17 ✠ Psalm 118:41–48

Scripture: Romans 8:18–27

Reading: St. Francis de Sales, bishop, Doctor of the Church † 1622

Consoling Thoughts 1.21

And we, like little children of our heavenly Father, can advance in two ways: first, by the steps of our own will conformed to his, always holding with the hand of our obedience that of his divine will and following it wherever it may lead. This is what God requires of us by manifesting his will, for when he wishes that I do what he commands, he wills that I have the ability to accomplish it. And secondly, we can also advance with Our Lord without having any self-will, simply allowing ourselves to be carried along, according to his Good Pleasure, like an infant in the arms of its mother, by an admirable contentment which one can call union, or more so the unity of our will with God's.

Day 10

Morning Prayer

Antiphon: Like a mother, you guide my steps.

Psalm 118:145–52 ✠ Psalm 8:1–9 ✠ Psalm 3:1–8

Scripture: Hosea 11:1–4 TNK

Reading: St. Faustina Kowalska, nun † 1938

PRAYING—WITH THE SAINTS—TO GOD OUR MOTHER

Divine Mercy in My Soul 249, 264

Jesus, I trust in you; I place my trust in the ocean of your merciful love. You are a Mother to me. . . .

O my Jesus, keep me near to you! See how weak I am! I cannot advance one step forward by myself; so you, Jesus, must constantly stand by me like a mother beside her helpless child—and even more so.

☦

GOD PROVIDES US WITH LIFE-GIVING MILK

Day 1

Morning Prayer

Antiphon: El Shaddai, God the Breasted One, provides for us with maternal compassion.

Psalm 129:1–8 ✠ Psalm 9:1–10 ✠ Psalm 118:65–72

Scripture: Genesis 43:1–14 TNK

Reading: St. Clement of Alexandria, priest, Father of the Church † ca. 215

Christ the Educator 1.6.34.3—36.1

Now we have come to the point where we must provide a defense for this childlikeness of ours by interpreting the text from the Apostle: *I provided you with milk to drink, as little children in Christ, not with solid food, for you were not yet ready for it. Indeed, nor are you ready now.* Now it seems to me that we need not understand this passage as applying to the Jews. In fact, I will parallel it with another verse from Scripture: *I will lead you forth to a good land, flowing with milk and honey.*

The juxtaposition of these two scriptural texts causes a considerable difficulty to arise if one wishes to apprehend their significance. If the childhood characterized by the milk is the beginning of faith in Christ, and the milk is disparaged as infantile and imperfect, then how can the future repose of the perfect and enlightened, characterized by the solid food, be esteemed as the milk of children? Perhaps the word *as* which signifies a comparison, really indicates some such metaphor—without a doubt we need to read the passage as such: *I have provided you with milk to drink in Christ,* then, after a short pause, resuming, *as little children,* in order to make understood by this pause in the reading, the following meaning: "I have instructed you in Christ, who is the simple, true, and natural spiritual nourishment." That, in fact, is what life-giving milk truly is by nature, readily flowing from breasts of tender love.

Consequently, the whole passage can be understood in this manner: Just as nursing mothers nourish newborn babies with milk, so too, I have instilled you with the Word which is the milk of Christ, feeding you, drop by drop, spiritual nourishment.

Therefore, perfect milk is a perfect form of food and brings to perfection that which is without repose. For this reason, then, milk had been promised with the honey for the time of eternal repose. And naturally, once again the Lord promises the just with milk in order to clearly demonstrate that the Word is at the same time both *Alpha and Omega, the beginning and the end*—the Word being symbolized by milk.

Evening Prayer

Antiphon: The Lord is the milk of the flock.

Psalm 21:1–11 ✠ Psalm 8:1–9 ✠ Psalm 79:1–19

Scripture: Acts 20:17–32

Reading: St. Clement of Alexandria, priest, Father of the Church † ca. 215

Christ the Educator 1.6.37.2–3

If human wisdom is the chief boast of knowledge, as one might consider it, then take heed to the Scriptural command: *Let not the wise boast in their wisdom, nor the strong in their strength, but let those who boast, boast in the Lord.* We, however, are those who are *taught by God*, and we boast in the name of Christ. Why then should we not suppose that the Apostle spoke about the milk of the little ones in the following sense: according to the good shepherd, the leaders of the Church are the shepherds and we, we are the sheep; when the Apostle said that the Lord is the milk of the flock, isn't he merely preserving the natural connection of his allegorical language? Once again, undoubtedly, the passage: *I gave you milk to drink, not solid food, because you were not yet able*, can be adapted to this meaning, if we take *solid food* to be essentially the same as milk. Either way, it is the same Word, whether fluid and soothing as milk or consistent and compact as solid food.

Day 2

Morning Prayer

Antiphon: Milk and honey are showered upon us.

Psalm 142:1–12 ✠ Psalm 118:97–104 ✠ Psalm 20:1–14

Scripture: Sirach 24:1–3, 18–22 LXX

Reading: St. Clement of Alexandria, priest, Father of the Church † ca. 215

Christ the Educator 1.6.45.1–2

We are nursed with milk at the breast, nourishment from the Lord, as soon as we are born; and as soon as we are born again we are favored with the good news concerning the hope of [eternal] rest, even that heavenly Jerusalem in which, as it is written, *milk and honey are showered* upon us. Through the symbol of these material nourishments, we are given a pledge of the sacred nourishment. For solid food is done away with, as the Apostle says, but the nourishment that we receive from milk leads directly to heaven, rearing us up to be citizens of heaven and members of the angelic choirs. Now since the Word is the overflowing Wellspring of Life and called the Stream of Oil, then assuredly Paul can employ a similar figure of speech and call him "milk," further saying, *I have given you to drink.* For we imbibe the Word, the nourishment of Truth.

Evening Prayer

Antiphon: Our Nursing Mother provides the drink of immortality.

Psalm 118:49–46 ✠ Psalm 11:1–8 ✠ Psalm 131:1–3 TNK

Scripture: 1 Peter 1:10–12

Reading: St. Clement of Alexandria, priest, Father of the Church † ca. 215

Who Is the Rich Man that Shall Be Saved? 23.2–4

Hear the Savior, "I gave you new birth, you who were ill-born by the world for death. I set you free; I healed you; I redeemed you. I will provide you with life unending, eternal, and celestial. I will show you the face of God, the good Father. *Call no man your father on earth. Let the dead bury the dead, but you, follow me.* For I will lead you up to a rest and enjoyment of ineffable and indescribable good things, *which eye has not seen and ear has not heard, nor have they entered into the human heart, which angels long to look into, and see what good things God has prepared for the saints and the children who love him.* I am your Nursing Mother, giving myself as food, of which whoever tastes no longer experiences the trial of death, and day to day giving the drink of immortality. I am the Teacher of most heavenly instructions."

Day 3

Morning Prayer

Antiphon: God adapts to us the pure spiritual milk.

Psalm 5:1–12 ✠ Psalm 12:1–6 ✠ Psalm 118:73–80

Scripture: Deuteronomy 32:12–14 TNK

Reading: Origen, Father of the Church † 254

Against Celsus 4.18

Regarding the nature of the [Divine Word who is God], just as the quality of food changes into milk in the nursing mother so as to adapt to the nature of the infant, or as nourishment is prepared by the doctor in regard to the good health of the sick person, or is adapted to the vital strength of someone stronger, so too, God appropriately changes for human beings, in relation to the needs of each one, the power of the Word to whom naturally belongs the property of nourishing the human soul. The Word becomes for one, as the Scripture says, *a pure spiritual milk*, for another who is weak, like a *vegetable*; and for someone who is full-grown, *solid food*. Surely, the Word does not lie about its own nature when it nourishes each person according to the capability of reception.

Evening Prayer

Antiphon: Let us sing praise to the gift of heavenly milk, the Word Incarnate.

Psalm 118:57–64 ✠ Psalm 12:1–6 ✠ Psalm 4:1–8

Scripture: Luke 11:27–28

Reading: St. Clement of Alexandria, priest, Father of the Church † ca. 215

Hymn to Christ the Educator

> Gather your children together, ask of their childlike candor,
> a holy hymn of praise and sincere songs of joy,
> canticles sung by pure lips, to You, O Christ, their Teacher. . . .
> O Word, Eternal Source, O Time never spent,
> Divine Light Eternal, and Well-Spring of Mercy,
> Artisan of Virtue at work in holy lives,
> we sing hymns of praise to God.
> Ah, Christ Jesus, O Heavenly Milk,
> flowing from sweet breasts of the well-graced Virgin-Bride,
> from abundant storehouses of wisdom, released through life's travails;
> As for us little children with tender mouths agape,
> always suckling the breast of the maternal Word of God,
> imbibing the dew of the Spirit, content and warmly satisfied,
> we, with simple praises, celebrate without delay
> the majesty of Christ, paying this holy tribute
> with harmonious voices in one accord for the lesson of life well taught.
> Let us now form a veritable chorus in honor of the All-Powerful Servant,
> a choir stirred by tranquility.
> O offshoot of Christ, O people of Wisdom,
> let us glorify, one and all, the God of Peace!

PRAYING—WITH THE SAINTS—TO GOD OUR MOTHER

Day 4

Morning Prayer

Antiphon: The heavenly manna has become celestial milk.

Psalm 41:1–11 ✠ Psalm 76:13–20 ✠ Psalm 102:1–23

Scripture: Numbers 11:4–12 TNK

Reading: St. Gregory of Nyssa, bishop, Father and Doctor of the Church † ca. 395

On the Life of Moses 2.137, 140

There is another matter worthy of contemplation without rushing past it. After those who walk in virtue had crossed the sea, after the water had been sweetened, after that splendid encampment by the springs and palm trees, and after their drinking from the rock, their supplies from Egypt became depleted. And so when the foreign food which they had packed out of Egypt has run out, there showered from above food which was simultaneously variegated and uniform. In its appearance it was uniform, but in quality it was variegated, for it adapted itself to each person's form of desire....

This unearthly bread, then, is the Word, it adapts its power through myriad forms, suitable to those who eat. The Word knows not only how to be bread, but how to become milk and meat and vegetables and whatever else might be suitable to and desired by the recipient. So teaches Paul, the divine Apostle, who sets such a table as this for us preparing his message as solid dressed meat for the more mature and as vegetables for the weaker and as milk for those who are babies.

Evening Prayer

Antiphon: God's maternal love is transformative.

Psalm 138:1–14 ✠ Psalm 13:1–7 ✠ Psalm 118:81–88

Scripture: 1 Thessalonians 2:7–8

Reading: St. Augustine, bishop, Father and Doctor of the Church † 430

Commentary on the Psalms, Second Discourse on Psalm 30 2.1.9

For you are my strength and my refuge; and for your name's sake you will be my leader and nourish me. Not for any merit of my own, but for your name's sake so that you may be glorified, not because I am worthy. *You will be my leader* so that I never stray away from you; *and nourish me* that I might be able to digest the food with which you feed the angels. The one who has promised us heavenly food, here below has nourished us with milk, exercising maternal compassion. For just as a mother nursing her infant transfers from her flesh the very same food which otherwise would not be suitable for the baby (the little child actually receives what it would have eaten at table, but the food transferred through the flesh is adapted to the little one), accordingly the Lord, so as to transform her Wisdom into milk for our sake, came to us clothed in flesh. Therefore it is the Body of Christ which says, *and you will nourish me.*

Day 5

Morning Prayer

Antiphon: El Shaddai, God the Breasted One, blesses you.

Psalm 54:1–16 ✠ Psalm 14:1–5 ✠ Psalm 68:8–15 TNK

Scripture: Genesis 49:25–26 TNK

Reading: St. Ambrose, bishop, Father and Doctor of the Church † 397

The Patriarchs 11.50–51

And he blessed him with the blessing of heaven from above, and with the blessing of a land having all things. For He made all things subject to the Son, heavenly things according to the blessing of heaven, earthly things according to the blessing of the earth, so that he would have dominion over both humans beings and angels. And therefore, in that contemptible body, so to speak, *You prevailed because of the blessing of breasts and womb, the blessings of your father and mother.* Jacob said the *breasts*, or the two Testaments, in one of which Christ was foretold and in the other revealed. And befittingly he said *breasts*, because like children nourished on spiritual milk, the Son nurtured us and offered us to God.

Evening Prayer

Antiphon: The divine breasts waft with the perfume of heavenly virtues.

Psalm 140:1–5 ✠ Psalm 118:89–96 ✠ Psalm 40:9–13 TNK

Scripture: Hebrews 5:11–14

Reading: St. Gregory of Nyssa, bishop, Father and Doctor of the Church † ca. 395

Song of Songs 1

Your breasts are sweeter than wine and the perfume of your ointments above all fragrances. These words signify, in our opinion, a meaning which is neither insignificant nor unimportant. For through the comparison of milk flowing from the divine breasts with the joy we experience from wine, we learn that all human wisdom and knowledge about the universe, as well as power of observation and comprehension of the imagination cannot compare with the simple nourishment of the divine teachings. For milk flows from the breasts and is the food of infants; whereas wine, with its potency and capacity to warm, is the enjoyment of the more mature. Nevertheless, the perfection of the wisdom of this world is far inferior compared with the childlike instruction of the Divine Word. Therefore, the divine breasts are better than human wine, and the perfume of the divine ointments is lovelier than all of other aromatic fragrances. The following seems to me to be the meaning: We understand the perfumes as virtues—wisdom, temperance, righteousness, fortitude, and the like. Now if we anoint ourselves with these perfumes, each of us, according to one's capacity and choice, will have a good fragrance.

Day 6

Morning Prayer

Antiphon: To Abraham, Isaac, and Jacob I appeared as El Shaddai, God the Breasted One (Exod 6:3 TNK).

Psalm 64:1–13 ✠ Psalm 14:1–5 ✠ Psalm 68:8–15 TNK

Scripture: Isaiah 42:10–16 TNK

Reading: St. Augustine, bishop, Father and Doctor of the Church † 430

Commentary on the Psalms 67.22

He subsequently calls this mountain *the mountain of God, a big-breasted mountain, a mountain full of curds, a plump mountain*. But here what else would he call plump if not big-breasted? For there likewise is a mountain called by that title, namely, Selmon. But what mountain should we understand by *the mountain of God, a big-breasted mountain, a mountain full of curds*, if not the very Lord Christ? For another prophet says concerning the Christ, *There shall be manifest in the last times the mountain of the Lord prepared on the top of the mountains*. He himself is *the mountain full of curds* because of the babes to be nourished with grace as with milk; *a big-breasted mountain* to strengthen and enrich them by the excellence of the gifts. For even the milk itself out of which curds are made, signifies grace in a marvelous manner because it flows out of the overflowing abundance of the mother's bosom, and out of a sweet compassion for little babies it is poured forth.

Evening Prayer

Antiphon: The milk of grace is efficacious for spiritual growth.

Psalm 133:1–3 ✠ Psalm 118:89–96 ✠ Psalm 130:1–3

Scripture: 1 Corinthians 3:1–2 NT

Reading: St. Bernard of Clairvaux, abbot, Doctor of the Church † 1153

Sermons on the Song of Songs 9.5, 6

Now let us see what this esteem for the Bridegroom's breasts means. [*For your breasts are better than wine, sweetly smelling of the finest ointments.*] . . . When the Bride said, *Your breasts are better than wine*, she meant, "The milk of grace that flows from your breasts is more efficacious for my spiritual progress than the biting reprimands of my superiors. Not only *are your breasts better than wine*, but *sweetly smelling of the finest ointments* as well. In fact, you do not refrain from nourishing with the milk of interior delights those who are close to you, but you just as well effuse the pleasing perfume of good repute to those who are absent. Thus *you receive a good testimony* from those who are near you as well as *from those who are outside*. You have, as I profess, milk within and ointments without, for you would have no one to be refreshed by your milk, if you did not at first draw them by your perfume."

Day 7

Morning Prayer

Antiphon: You have nursed me from your breasts.

Psalm 72:1–28 ✠ Psalm 118:97–104 ✠ Psalm 130:1–3

Scripture: Song of Songs 1:1–4 LXX

Reading: St. Bernard of Clairvaux, abbot, Doctor of the Church † 1153

Sermons on the Song of Songs 9.4

The text continues, *For your breasts are better than wine, sweetly smelling of the finest ointments*. As to who spoke these words, the author doesn't say, so we are free to attribute them to the person whom we think they best suit. For my part, I can see reasons to assign them either to the bride, to the bridegroom, or to bride's companions. At first I'll show how fittingly they belong to the bride. . . . In her attempt to excuse her temerity she turns to the bridegroom and declares, *For your breasts are better than wine, sweetly smelling of the finest ointments*. This is as if to say, "If I appear to be '*highminded*,' you are the cause, O my Bridegroom! You have nursed me from your breasts with the milk of sweetness, with such an indulgence that all fear is banished, not by my temerity, but by my love for you."

Evening Prayer

Antiphon: God acts as our nursemaid.

Psalm 1:1–6 ✠ Psalm 188:104–12 ✠ Psalm 22:9–11 TNK

Scripture: 4 Esdras 1:22–30 VULG

Reading: St. Aelred of Rievaulx, abbot † 1167

Mirror of Charity 2.12.29–30

> Whereas *the beginning of wisdom is the fear of the Lord*, the consummation of wisdom is the love of God. Its commencement is in fear; its perfection is in love. Here is work, there reward. The former leads up to the latter, yet it does not attain itself except through itself. Upon the spirit which is often afflicted by fear, weighed down by grief, cast down by despair, absorbed in sadness, and corroded away by acidic weariness, there falls a drop of marvelous sweetness dripping from the balsam trees of that fatly rich and milky mountain, as if it were carefully overflowing in a most peaceful manner. At the splendor of its radiantly divine light the whole fog of irrational sensations is dissipated. At its pleasantly sweet taste, all bitterness is put to flight, the heart is dilated, the spirit enriched and its capacity to ascend is enhanced in a marvelous manner. Thus lukewarmness is driven out by fear, and fear is seasoned by the taste of divine sweetness. Lest the spirit stay sluggish at the lowest levels, fear rouses it; lest it fade away by laboring, desire nourishes it. Without a doubt, instructed by the alternation of these two, the spirit totally absorbed by ineffable charity, no longer grows fatly rich with love, but burning for the ardently desired embraces of the one who is the fairest of all the sons of men, begins to want to be dissolved and to be with Christ, daily saying with the Prophet: *Alas for me, that my sojourn is prolonged*. And so the Lawgiver bestows a blessing, administering the wine of compunction along with the fear of himself to those who are just beginning, and milk from the breasts of his consolation to those who are making progress. And when they are weaned from this milk, upon entrance into his glory, they shall be made to feast.

Day 8

Morning Prayer

Antiphon: Hasten earnestly to the maternal breasts of Jesus.

Psalm 91:1–15 ✠ Psalm 118:113–20 ✠ Psalm 131:1–3 TNK

Scripture: Hosea 1:10; 2:1, 14 VULG

Reading: St. Aelred of Rievaulx, abbot † 1167

Mirror of Charity 2.19.59

> Therefore, do you see, I asked, that your fervent conversion and your strict manner of life are, as it were, the fruit of those tears? That was their purpose, they brought it about bit by bit, or rather, through them God worked. Is it any wonder then that, as I already said, they have ceased now that their business is accomplished? Now you must undergo trials for the sake of Christ, you must exercise the virtue of patience, chastise the insolence of your carnal desires by repeated vigils and fasts, suffer temptations, and turn your soul away from all earthly cares. But especially, you must mortify your

self-will by practicing the virtue of obedience. And in all this, whenever your soul is exceedingly tired, hasten earnestly to the maternal breasts of Jesus through devotional prayer. Drawing forth for yourself from their abundance, the milk of wondrous consolation, you will say with the Apostle, *Blessed be God who consoles us in all our tribulations.*

Evening Prayer

Antiphon: The Beloved leaned upon Christ's breast.

Psalm 6:1–10 ✠ Psalm 101:1–28 ✠ Psalm 130:1–3

Scripture: John 13:19–25

Reading: St. Aelred of Rievaulx, abbot † 1167

Rule of Life for a Recluse 31

"Who is that?" I ask you, "Who is reclining on Christ's breast and laying his head in his bosom? Happy whoever it might be. Oh, I see, 'His name is John.' O John, make known what sweetness is there, what grace and tenderness, what light and devotion you are imbibing from that fountain! Certainly all the treasures of wisdom and knowledge are to be found there, the fountain of mercy, the dwelling of loving piety, the honeycomb of eternal sweetness! . . ."

O virgin soul, exult now! Draw near and do not put off laying claim for yourself to some portion of this sweetness. If you are not able to take possession of all of it, leave John to the breast from whence he will become inebriated with the wine of gladness in the knowledge of Christ's divinity, while you run to the breast of his humanity, nourishing yourself on the newly squeezed milk. . . .

Hurry, do not delay! Eat the honeycomb with your honey; drink your wine with your milk. The blood is turned into wine so that you might become intoxicated; the water changed into milk so that you might be nourished.

Day 9

Morning Prayer

Antiphon: We have received the two breasts of God's covenantal love.

Psalm 107:1–6 ✠ Psalm 17:1–31 ✠ Psalm 118:121–28

Scripture: Baruch 4:4–8, 30 LXX

Reading: St. Thomas Aquinas, priest, Doctor of the Church † 1274

PRAYING—WITH THE SAINTS—TO GOD OUR MOTHER

Exposition on the Song of Songs 1

Solomon, who was inspired by the Divine Spirit, composed this little book regarding the wedding of Christ and the Church, and did it in the form of a nuptial hymn between Christ and the Church, namely the song regarding the bridal chamber. Thus fittingly is this little book called the Song of Songs because it is more excellent than all other songs. Just as one says King of kings, and Lord of lords, and Solemnity of solemnities, so too one says Song of Songs due to its excellence and dignity. Furthermore, in this most obscure book, nothing is commemorated in person with such an almost theatrical style in which it was composed.

Therefore it says, *Let him kiss me with the kisses of his mouth*. The voice desiring this represents the future community of Christ, and seems to say, "Because all of the things that he promised to me by the prophets about his coming, have come to pass, *let him kiss me with the kisses of his mouth*, that is, let he himself speak to me." *Because your breasts are better than wine*. . . . The breasts of Christ signify the sweetness of the Gospel with which he wishes to suckle with milk the infancy of our belief. Wine, on the other hand, represents the austerity of the Law. But the breasts of Christ are better than wine because the sweetness of the Gospel is better than the austerity of the Law.

Evening Prayer

Antiphon: The good deeds of the saints clothe the Bride in milk-white linen.

Psalm 15:1–11 ✠ Psalm 22:1–6 ✠ Psalm 118:129–36

Scripture: Revelation 19:1–9

Reading: St. Aelred of Rievaulx, abbot † 1167

Rule of Life for a Recluse 25–26

The end of the Law is love, flowing from a pure heart, a good conscience and unfeigned faith. In these you should glory; in these you should delight; within, not without, in true virtues, not in paintings and statues. White linen cloths should cover your altar; their whiteness will commend chastity and display simplicity. Think about what work, what poundings it took to rid the linen of the earthly color in which it grew and to bring about such whiteness so that it might adorn an altar, cover Christ's Body. We are all born with the color of earth, for, *In iniquity was I conceived, and in sin my mother conceived me*. . . .

Let these be the thoughts the furnishings of your oratory bring to mind, instead of feasting your eyes on tasteless changing trappings. Let it be sufficient for you to have on your altar an image of our Savior hanging on the Cross. This will bring to mind his Passion for you to imitate. His outstretched arms will invite you to embrace him; in these you shall find delight. His naked breasts will pour forth for you the milk of sweetness which will console you.

Day 10

Morning Prayer

Antiphon: We are sustained by the divine milk of God's maternal love.

Psalm 118:145–52 ✠ Psalm 112:1–9 ✠ Psalm 24:1–22

Scripture: Isaiah 66:9–13 VULG

Reading: St. Teresa of Avila, nun and foundress, Doctor of the Church † 1582

Conceptions of the Love of God 4.4

When this most wealthy Bridegroom desires to enrich and endow the soul more, he changes it into himself to such an extent that, just as a person swoons from intense pleasure and joy, it appears to the soul that it is left suspended in those divine arms, drawn to that sacred side and those divine breasts. It doesn't know how to do anything other than rejoice, sustained by the divine milk with which the Bridegroom is nourishing it, and making it better so that he might endow it and it might merit more each day.

Awakening from that sleep and celestial intoxication, it remains as though stupefied and dazed, seized by a holy insanity, and thus in my opinion, can truly say these words: *Your breasts are better than wine.* While it was in that state of intoxication, the soul thought it impossible to ascend higher, but now that it saw itself in a loftier state and completely inundated in the countless grandeurs of God, being sustained in this manner, she makes a subtle comparison and says: *Your breasts are better than wine.*

Evening Prayer

Antiphon: Crave spiritual milk; taste and see that the Lord is good!

Psalm 18:1–14 ✠ Psalm 25:1–12 ✠ Psalm 118:97–104

Scripture: 1 Peter 1:25—2:3 NT

Reading: St. Teresa of Avila, nun and foundress, Doctor of the Church † 1582

Interior Castle 7.2.6

With the passage of time, [the soul's life in Christ] becomes more evident through its effects, for by some secret aspirations the soul clearly understands that it is God who endows it with life. These aspirations come so frequently in such a vibrant manner that they in no way can be doubted. Though they are indescribable, the soul experiences them quite vividly. Yet the feeling is so overwhelming that at times the soul cannot but help the loving exclamations they cause: O Life of my life! Sustenance that sustains me! And things of that sort. For from those divine breasts, where it appears that God is forever sustaining the soul, there flows streams of milk which bring comfort to all who dwell in the castle. It seems that the Lord desires in some fashion that these others enjoy all that the soul enjoys and from the full-flowing river, where this tiny spring is swallowed up, a spurt of that fluid will sometimes be directed towards the sustenance of those others.

Day 11

Morning Prayer

Antiphon: O my soul, be intoxicated with God's love!

Psalm 129:1–8 ✠ Psalm 118:137–44 ✠ Psalm 30:1–24

Scripture: Isaiah 66:9–13 TNK

Reading: St. Teresa of Avila, nun and foundress, Doctor of the Church † 1582

Conceptions of the Love of God 4.4–5

 Just as an infant doesn't understand how it grows or gets its milk, since often without its suckling or doing anything the milk is placed in its mouth, likewise here the soul is totally ignorant and doesn't know how or from where that exceedingly great blessing came from, nor can comprehend it. But it does know that it is the greatest blessing it has ever tasted in life, even if all the delights and pleasures of the world were added together and compared to it. It realizes that it is nourished and made better yet doesn't know how it deserved this. It is instructed in great truths without seeing the Master who teaches it; fortified in the virtues and favored by the One who so well knows how to comfort and has the power to do so. The soul doesn't know what to compare this grace to, except for the great love a mother has for her child, nourishing and caressing it.

 This comparison is appropriate, for the soul is so elevated and incapable of using its understanding that it is somewhat like an infant who receives and delights in a caress without having the intelligence to understand where it comes from. For in the slumber caused by the divine intoxication the soul is not so completely incapacitated that it is unable to understand or function at all; it realizes that it is near God, and thus with reason its exclaims, *Your breasts are better than wine!*

Evening Prayer

Antiphon: How sweet is the consolation of God's maternal love!

Psalm 21:1–11 ✠ Psalm 25:1–12 ✠ Psalm 118:153–60

Scripture: 2 Corinthians 1:3–5

Reading: St. Francis de Sales, bishop, Doctor of the Church † 1622

Introduction to the Devout Life 4.13.2

Sometimes tender and delightful affections are, nevertheless, quite beneficial and useful. They excite the soul's appetite, strengthen the spirit, and add a holy joy and cheerfulness to an eager devotion, rendering our actions lovely and agreeable even on the outside. This delight that one experiences in divine matters is what made David exclaim, O Lord, *how sweet are your words to my palate, sweeter than honey to my mouth!* Certainly, the least amount of consolation from devotion that we receive is worth more in every way than the most excellent worldly amusements. The breasts and the milk, that is, the favors of the Divine Spouse, are sweeter to the soul than the most expensive wine of earthly pleasures. The person who has tasted this sweetness regards all other consolations as gall and wormwood.

Day 12

Morning Prayer

Antiphon: God carried me like a mother and gave me her milk to drink.

Psalm 142:1–12 ✠ Psalm 27:1–9 ✠ Psalm 118:161–68

Scripture: Numbers 11:4–12 TNK

Reading: Syriac liturgical text, mid to late second century

Odes of Solomon 35.1–7

> The sprinkling of the Lord overshadowed me with rest,
> and a cloud of peace he set over my head,
> that it might guard me always,
> and it became my salvation.
> All were disturbed and disquieted,
> and smoke and judgment belched forth from them.
> But I was tranquil in the Lord's company,
> more than shade was he to me,
> and more than a foundation.
> I was carried like a child by its mother;
> and he gave me milk,
> the dew of the Lord.
> And I grew strong by his favor,
> and was at rest in his perfection.
> And I extended my hands in the ascent of myself,
> and I directed myself towards the Most High,
> and I was kept safe near him.

Evening Prayer

Antiphon: Crave the milk of everlasting life.

Psalm 118:49–56 ✠ Psalm 29:1–12 ✠ Psalm 118:169–76

Scripture: 1 Peter 1:25—2:3 NT

Reading: St. Anthony of Padua, priest, Doctor of the Church † 1231

Sermons for the Sunday in the Octave of Easter 1.12

You should desire milk, namely what Augustine refers to when saying, "The bread of angels has become milk for little ones." "Milk [*lac*] derives its name from its color because it is a white liquid and the Greek word for white is *leuchos*. The substance of this liquid is produced from blood. Now after birth whatever blood hasn't been consumed in the womb as nourishment flows by a natural transference into the breasts where it becomes white and acquires the characteristics of milk." From here it will become food for the newborn. "For the matter out of which generation happens is the same matter from which one is fed. Milk is blood transformed and digested; there is nothing corrupt about it." In the blood, which bears a dreadful appearance, the wrath of God is seen; in the milk, which is sweet to the taste and of a most pleasant color, the mercy of God is signified. The blood of wrath was transformed into the milk of mercy in the breast, that is, in the humanity of Jesus Christ.

God as Maternal Bird or Animal

Day 1

Morning Prayer

Antiphon: Let us hide in the shelter of your wings.

Psalm 5:1–12 ✠ Psalm 35:5–12 ✠ Psalm 62:1–11

Scripture: Sirach 2:1–18

Reading: St. Clement of Alexandria, priest, Father of the Church † ca. 215

Exhortation to the Greeks 10

Do you not know that this is true above everything else, that the good and godly, since they have held in high esteem what is good, shall obtain the good reward; while, on the other hand, the wicked shall receive punishment according to their deeds? . . . For God grants life freely, but wicked custom after our departure from this world, brings on the sinner unavailing remorse along with punishment. . . . Now seeing these things, do you persist in blindness and refuse to rise your sights to the Master of All, the Lord of the universe? Will you not escape and break out of these prisons and fly to the mercy that comes from heaven? For God, out of his great love for humanity still stays close to humanity; just as when a mother bird flies coming to one of her young that has fallen out of the nest, and if a serpent should open its mouth to swallow the little bird, "the mother flutters round about, uttering cries of grief for her beloved offspring." Now God the Father seeks the creature and heals its falling away, and pursues the serpent, and restores the nestling to strength again, and incites it to fly up to the nest.

Evening Prayer

Antiphon: We are fledglings of God.

Psalm 118:57–64 ✠ Psalm 31:1–11 ✠ Psalm 16:1–15

Scripture: John 21:1–14

Reading: St. Clement of Alexandria, priest, Father of the Church † ca. 215

Christ the Educator 1.5.12.1–2; 1.5.14.2–4

Education is the training of children, as the word pedagogy itself clearly means. It remains to us, however, to consider who the children are suggested by Scripture, and to specify their Pedagogue, that is to say Teacher. We are the children. Scripture celebrates us quite often and in many different ways, describing us in numerous figures of speech, thereby introducing variety to the simplicity of the faith. For example, in the Gospel it says, *Standing on the shore, the Lord said to his disciples* (they were fishing), *Children, don't you have any fish?* He refers to those who already held the position of disciples, as children. . . .

Now when he says *Let my lambs be placed on my right*, he symbolically signifies the simple; they belong to the category of children, like the lambs, and not like the adults, known as sheep. And he reckons the lambs as deserving first place, thus praising, before all other human qualities, gentleness, simplicity of mind, and innocence. And whenever he mentions *young suckling calves*, he again figuratively alludes to us, and the same with *as innocent and gentle as doves*. By Moses, he commands *two young birds, a pair of pigeons or of turtledoves to be offered for sin*; thus meaning that the sinlessness of such gentle birds, their innocence, as well as their unruffled nature are very pleasing to God, letting it be understood that similar can sanctify similar. Furthermore, the timidity of the turtledoves typifies the fear we should have towards sin.

That he refers to us as fledglings is shown in Scripture, *As the hen gathers her chicks under her wings*. In this sense we are the Lord's little chicks, a name that marvelously and mystically describes the simplicity of soul belonging to childhood.

PRAYING—WITH THE SAINTS—TO GOD OUR MOTHER

Day 2

Morning Prayer

Antiphon: God carries us on her wings.

Psalm 41:1–11 ✠ Psalm 118:9–16 ✠ Psalm 62:1–11

Scripture: Deuteronomy 32:9–11 TNK

Reading: St. Clement of Alexandria, priest, Father of the Church † ca. 215

Christ the Educator 1.7.53.3; 1.7.55.2—56.1

With great clarity through [the Prophet] Hosea, the Word has spoken concerning himself, *I am your Pedagogue,* [your Instructor]. Now pedagogy is godly reverence and education in the service of God, instruction in the knowledge of truth and a sound formation that leads to heaven. . . .

Our Instructor is the holy God, Jesus, the Word directing all humanity. God's very self, loving humanity, is our Instructor. Somewhere in a canticle the Holy Spirit says about him, *He provided sufficiently for the people in the desert, in the midst of thirst and burning heat, and parched land, he lead them around and instructed them and guarded them as the apple of his eye. As an eagle protects her nest, displaying her fond care for her young, spreading her wings out, and carrying them upon her back; the Lord alone led them; there was no strange god within their midst.* From my point of view, Scripture clearly is depicting the Instructor of children and describing the guidance given.

Evening Prayer

Antiphon: The Lord protects us beneath her wings like a hen, her chicks.

Psalm 138:1–14 ✠ Psalm 118:17–24 ✠ Psalm 60:1–8

Scripture: Matthew 23:37–39 VULG

Reading: St. Hilary of Poitiers, bishop, Father and Doctor of the Church † 367

Commentary on Matthew 24.11

During the time when the Lord took a body and offered his help to everyone, being known as a human being, he often wanted to call them together by the preaching of the Prophets. But it was in vain and practically for nothing that he displayed such affection. Like a hen which gathers her chicks, he wanted to keep them under his wings. That is to say, in the present time, becoming as a mother bird, earth-bound and domestic, like one of those for her little ones, he procures by means of his wings— which are really his body— a protection affording the warmth of immortal life. He directs them to fly in a type of new birth. Amongst chickens, the manner of being born is different than that of living, for they are at first enclosed in the eggshell which evokes

Thematic Readings for Non-Feast Days

the image of a bodily barrier; next, warmed by the assiduous care of their mother, they break forth so that they can fly. Such is the manner of this domestic and somewhat earth-bound Bird who wanted to gather them together about himself, thus causing those who had already seen the light of day according to the rule of natural birth, to be reborn by means of a regeneration thanks to the warmth of the One Who reanimates them, so that they might soar towards the Kingdom of Heaven on his corporeal wings.

Day 3

Morning Prayer

Antiphon: We shall escape evil like a sparrow and take refuge under God's wings.

Psalm 54:1–16 ✠ Psalm 83:1–12 ✠ Psalm 62:1–11

Scripture: Proverbs 26:2

Reading: St. Hilary of Poitiers, bishop, Father and Doctor of the Church † 367

Homilies on the Psalms 56.3

David begins the psalm, *Have compassion on me, have compassion on me: for in you my soul places its trust.* He asks for compassion because he trusts in the Lord. He teaches by this that the compassion of God is placing one's hope in God, so that they might believe. And the tender mercies of God that effect a movement in whomever, causes one to say, *And I will take refuge in the shadow of your wings until adversity passes by.* By nature birds defend their weak young by sheltering them under their wings, or by flapping their wings, and even by outrageous behavior. We recognize this especially in a mother hen that gathers her brood between her wings either sheltering them or protecting them. The Lord recalls such a practice as an example of his tender care, saying, *How often I wanted to gather your children, like a mother hen who gathers her chicks beneath her wings, but you would have none of it!*

Evening Prayer

Antiphon: God guards us like an eagle does her brood.

Psalm 140:1–5 ✠ Psalm 102:1–23 ✠ Psalm 16:1–15

Scripture: Matthew 23:37–39 PESH

Reading: St. Jerome, priest, Father and Doctor of the Church † 420

Commentary on Matthew 4.37

Jerusalem, Jerusalem, you who kill the prophets and stone those who were sent to you, how often I wanted to gather your children as a mother hen gathers her chicks under her wings, but you would have none of it. Jerusalem refers not to the stones and buildings of the city but to its inhabitants. He laments with paternal affection. Like we read elsewhere that he was moved to tears upon seeing Jerusalem. These words, *how often I wanted to gathered your children*, testify that all of the former prophets were sent by him. This comparison with the mother hen gathering her chicks under her wings, parallels the canticle in Deuteronomy where we read, *As an eagle protects her nestlings and guards her brood, spreading her wings, God took them and bore them up on his pinions.*

Day 4

Morning Prayer

Antiphon: God guards us like a mother bear and a lioness.

Psalm 64:1–13 ✠ Psalm 103:1–34 ✠ Psalm 62:1–11

Scripture: Hosea 13:5–8 LXX

Reading: St. Gregory of Nyssa, bishop, Father and Doctor of the Church † ca. 395

Against Eunomius 2.298–300, 304

Each one of these [many] titles contains neither the nature nor the divinity of the Only-Begotten, nor the character of being. Notwithstanding, he is given many names, and the appellation is legitimate; for it is right to believe that there is nothing idle or meaningless in the divine utterances. . . . We ourselves make the following claim: as our Lord provides in various ways for human life, each variety of benefit is suitably identified by one of such titles, the providential care and operation observed therein conforming to a type of name. Such a title, in our estimation, is denoted "conceptually." Now if that is not pleasing to our controversialists, let each do as he prefers. Nevertheless, it's only the person who is ignorant of the scriptural figures of speech who will oppose what we say. If one were educated in the divine appellations, one would surely know that "Curse," and "Sin," and "Frantic Cow," and "Lion's whelp," and "She-bear robbed of her cubs," and "Leopardess," as well as similar names, are applied to the Lord by the Scriptures according to the various concepts. . . . Thus it is clear that the Divinity is assigned names with various connotations corresponding to the variety of activities, named in such a way that we may understand.

Evening Prayer

Antiphon: The wings of God were outstretched on the Cross.

Psalm 133:1–3 ✠ Psalm 118:25–32 ✠ Psalm 16:1–15

Scripture: 1 Peter 2:21–25

Reading: St. Jerome, priest, Father and Doctor of the Church † 420

Homilies on the Psalms 68

With his pinions he will conceal you. Who will conceal you? The God of heaven, of course, just as a mother hen conceals her chicks and an eagle her nestlings. Likewise in the song in Deuteronomy it says that God carried the people of Israel upon his shoulders, and like the eagle protected them. The same text may be interpreted as referring to the Savior because on the Cross he protected us with his "wings." *And under his wings you will find refuge.*

Day 5

Morning Prayer

Antiphon: Like mother birds hovering over their young, God shields us.

Psalm 72:1–28 ✠ Psalm 34:1–28 ✠ Psalm 62:1–11

Scripture: Isaiah 31:4–5 TNK

Reading: St. Augustine, bishop, Father and Doctor of the Church † 430

Commentary on the Psalms, Second Discourse on Psalm 90 1.5

He will defend you between his shoulders and you will hope under his wings. He says this so that your protection may not be for yourself from yourself, so that you may not imagine that you can defend yourself; he will defend you and deliver you from the hunter's snare and from harsh words. The phrase *He will defend you between his shoulders* may be understood as referring to both in front and behind, for the shoulders surround the head. But the words, *you will hope under his wings* makes it clear that the protection of the expanded wings situates you between the shoulders of God, so that God's wings on this side and that, place you in the middle thus you will not fear lest anyone hurt you, only be careful never to leave that place where no enemy dares to approach. If a hen protects her chicks beneath her wings, how much more will you dwell in safety beneath the wings of God, even against the devil and his angels, the powers which circle about in the air like hawks to carry off the weak young ones.

For the comparison of the hen to the very Wisdom of God is not without warrant, for Christ himself, our Lord and Savior, spoke of himself as likened to a hen: *Jerusalem, Jerusalem, how often would I have gathered your children together, even as a hen gathers her chicks, and you would not.* What Jerusalem would not, let us be willing. She was carried off by the powers of the air when she fled the hen's wings, presuming on her own strength while she in fact was weak. Let us, confessing our weakness, seek refuge beneath God's wings who will be for us as a hen protecting her chicks. There is nothing demeaning in the name hen. Consider other birds, brothers and sisters; many hatch their eggs before our very eyes, warming their young, but none enfeebles herself with regard to her hatchlings as the hen does. We see swallows, sparrows, and storks outside their nests without being able to know if they have young or not; but we know the hen to be a mother by the feebleness of her voice, the outstretched ruffling of her feathers.

She totally changes from love for her chicks; because they are feeble, she enfeebles herself. Thus since we were weak, the Wisdom of God made herself weak when the Word became flesh and dwelt among us so that we might hope under her wings.

Evening Prayer

Antiphon: God humbled God's self and became weak for our sake.

Psalm 1:1–6 ✠ Psalm 118:33–40 ✠ Psalm 16:1–15

Scripture: Philippians 2:6–11

Reading: St. Augustine, bishop, Father and Doctor of the Church † 430

Commentary on the Psalms, Second Discourse on Psalm 90 2.2

But in what manner does God protect you? It says *He shall defend you between his shoulders*, that is, God will place you before his breast so that he may protect you under his wings if you will acknowledge your weakness so that as a weak fledgling you might fly beneath the wings of your mother, lest you be snatched away by a bird of prey. The powers of the air are birds of prey, the devil and his angels; they wish to seize upon our weakness. Let us fly beneath the wings of our Mother, Divine Wisdom, because Wisdom herself voluntarily became weak on our account when the Word was made flesh. Just as the hen enfeebles herself with regard to her chicks so that she might protect them with her wings, so too our Lord Jesus Christ, who, *being in the form of God, did not think it robbery to be equal with God* in order that he might experience weakness with us and protect us under his wings, *made himself of no reputation and took upon himself the form of a slave and was made in human likeness and found in the fashion of a human being.* Thus *under his wings you will place your hope.*

Day 6

Morning Prayer

Antiphon: Like a mother eagle, God delivered Israel.

Psalm 91:1–15 ✠ Psalm 76:13–20 ✠ Psalm 62:1–11

Scripture: Exodus 19:3–8

Reading: St. Jerome, priest, Father and Doctor of the Church † 420

Homilies on the Psalms 20

With his pinions he will conceal you. This same thought is found in Deuteronomy: As an eagle spreads its wings over its nestlings, so the Lord protects us. There the Lord is compared to an eagle protecting its young. We are justified in saying, therefore, that God protects us as a father, as well as like a hen protecting her chicks so that they won't be snatched away by a hawk. Notwithstanding, another interpretation is possible: *With his pinions he will conceal you.* He was lifted up on the Cross and stretches out his hands, and protects us. *And under his wings you will find refuge.*

Evening Prayer

Antiphon: The birds of the air have nests, but the Son of Man has nowhere to rest.

Psalm 6:1–10 ✠ Psalm 118:41–48 ✠ Psalm 16:1–15

Scripture: Matthew 8:18–20

Reading: St. Augustine, bishop, Father and Doctor of the Church † 430

Commentary on the Psalms, Second Discourse on Psalm 58 1.10

I am admonished to say something else here regarding the sublime nature of our Lord. For he became weak even to the point of death, and assumed the weakness of the flesh so that he might gather together the chicks of Jerusalem under his wings as a hen shows herself weak with her little ones. For have we not observed this thing in some bird at some time or another, such as in those which build their nests before our very eyes, like the house sparrows or the swallows our annual guests, so to speak, or like the storks and various sorts of birds which build their nests in plain view, and hatch eggs, feed babies, such as the very doves we see day to day? Have we not known, have we not carefully observed, have we not seen some bird become weak with her little ones? In what fashion does a hen exhibit this weakness? Surely I am speaking about a known fact, which in our sight is a daily occurrence; how her voice grows hoarse, how her whole body becomes scraggly? The wings droop, the feathers are rustled, and you see around the chicks some other languishing thing. This is maternal love which is found as weakness. Why was it therefore, if not for this, that the Lord willed to be a mother hen, declaring in the Holy Scriptures, *Jerusalem, Jerusalem, how often I willed to gather your children even as a hen her chicks under her wings, but you weren't willing*! However, he has gathered all peoples, like a hen her chicks. He has become weak for our sakes, receiving flesh from us, which is from the human species. He was crucified, despised, buffeted, scourged, hung on a tree, wounded with a spear. Unquestionably this pertains to maternal weakness and not to loss of majesty.

Day 7

Morning Prayer

Antiphon: Wisdom enfeebled herself like a hen, hidden from other birds.

Psalm 107:1–6 ✠ Psalm 35:5–12 ✠ Psalm 62:1–11

Scripture: Job 28:20–27 TNK

PRAYING—WITH THE SAINTS—TO GOD OUR MOTHER

Reading: St. Augustine, bishop, Father and Doctor of the Church † 430

Tractate on the Gospel of John 15.6–7

> The strength of Christ created you; the weakness of Christ recreated you. The strength of Christ caused what did not exist, to be; the weakness of Christ caused what did exist, to not cease to be. He established us by his strength; he sought us by his weakness. Therefore, being weak, he nourished the weak as a hen does her little chicks; in fact, he likened himself to this: *How often*, he said to Jerusalem, *I wanted to gather your children under my wings as a hen does her brood, but you would have none of it*. Now you see, brothers and sisters, how a hen becomes enfeebled with her chicks. No other bird who is a mother is known to act this way. We see sparrows of every sort building their nests before our very eyes; swallows, storks, doves, we observe them constructing their dwellings, yet unless we see them actually in their nests we do not recognize them to be parents. But the hen, in fact, becomes enfeebled in regard to her young, so that even if the chicks themselves are not following her, or you don't see her young, you nevertheless recognize her to be a mother. With her wings arching, her feathers ruffled, her voice hoarse, all her limbs drooping and abject, by this as I said, even if you don't see her brood, you nevertheless perceive her to be a mother. Thus was Jesus accordingly weak, fatigued from the journey. His journey is the assumption of human nature on our behalf.

෨ 📖 ଓ

Evening Prayer

Antiphon: The mother pelican sheds her blood to bestow life.

Psalm 15:1–11 ✠ Psalm 101:1–28 ✠ Psalm 16:1–15

Scripture: 1 Peter 1:17–21

Reading: St. Augustine, bishop, Father and Doctor of the Church † 430

Commentary on the Psalms, First Discourse on Psalm 101 1.8

> Let us contemplate the Lord himself, if it perhaps be he, and thus recognize him as the pelican in the wilderness. . . . Let us not skip over what is said, or even read of this bird, that is the pelican; not rashly asserting anything but not at the same time remaining silent about what has been left to be read and uttered by those who wrote about it. Give me an ear that if it be true, you may agree, and if false, you may not hold it. It is said that these birds kill their young with blows of their beaks, and mourn them for three days when killed by themselves in their nest. Next they say the mother deeply wounds herself and pours out her blood over her nestlings, drenched in this they revive. This may be true or it may be false, yet if it were true, behold how it agrees with the Lord who revived us by his blood. It accords with him in that the mother's flesh revives her young with her blood; it agrees quite well. For he calls himself a hen

brooding over her chicks, *O Jerusalem, Jerusalem, how often would I have gathered your children together, even as a hen gathers her chicks under her wings, and you would not.* For he possesses the authority of a father and the affection of a mother just as Paul is both father and mother, not through himself, but because of the Gospel: father where he says: *Although you have numerous instructors in Christ, you do not numerous fathers, for in Christ Jesus I have begotten you through the Gospel.* Paul is likewise mother when he says, *My little children, for whom I am in labor pains again until Christ is formed in you.* Therefore if this be true, then this bird bears a great likeness to the flesh of Christ by whose blood we are restored to life. But how does it accord with Christ that the mother pelican kills her own young? Does this not agree with it: *I will kill and I will revive; I will wound and I will heal?*

Day 8

Morning Prayer

Antiphon: Let us build our nest in the wood of the Cross.

Psalm 118:145–52 ✠ Psalm 37:1–22 ✠ Psalm 62:1–11

Scripture: Jeremiah 8:7–8

Reading: St. Augustine, bishop, Father and Doctor of the Church † 430

Commentary on the Psalms, First Discourse on Psalm 101 1.8

He ascended into heaven, became as a sparrow flying; that is, by ascending; *alone on the housetop*; which signifies in heaven. Therefore he is like the pelican by birth, as the owl by dying, and as the sparrow by ascending again: there in the wilderness, as one alone; here in the broken down walls, as someone killed by those who could not stand in the building; and here again watching and flying for our sakes alone on the housetop, there Christ intercedes for us. For our Head is like a sparrow and his body is like the turtledove. *For the sparrow has found for herself a house.* What house? In heaven where he intercedes for us. *And the turtledove a nest* signifies that the Church of God has found a nest in the wood of his Cross, where *she may lay her young*, her children. *I have watched and have become as it were a sparrow sitting alone upon the housetop.*

Evening Prayer

Antiphon: The mother hen tears the scorpion to shreds.

Psalm 18:1–14 ✠ Psalm 90:1–16 ✠ Psalm 16:1–15

Scripture: Luke 10:17–20

PRAYING—WITH THE SAINTS—TO GOD OUR MOTHER

Reading: St. Augustine, bishop, Father and Doctor of the Church † 430

Sermon 105.11–12

Let us be very sure we don't hear the words *Lift up your hearts*, to no avail. Why set our hearts upon the earth when we can see how the world is being turned upside down? I strongly urge you to put your hearts where you say you do, give an answer for your hope to those who mock and blaspheme the title "Christian." Let no one by his grumbling and discontentment deflect you from your hope of future blessings. Everyone who blasphemes our Christ because of the present adversities are the scorpion's tail. Let us place our egg, [our hope], under the wings of the hen of the Gospel, who cries out to that faithless and doomed city, *O Jerusalem, Jerusalem, how often would I have gathered your children together, even as a hen her chicks, and you would not!* Let it never be said of us, *How often have I wished, and you would not!* That hen, you see, is Divine Wisdom. She assumed flesh to accommodate herself to her chicks. Note the hen, ruffling her feathers, with wings arched and bending down, clucking in a coarse, tremulous, tired, and languid fashion, so that she might be on the same level as her little brood. So let us lay our egg, then, that is to say our hope, under the wings of this hen.

Perhaps you have seen how a hen tears a scorpion to shreds. O then that the Hen of the Gospel would tear into pieces and devour these blasphemers—creeping out of their holes and crawling on the ground, inflicting their horrible stings—and ingest them into her body so as to transform them into an egg!

Day 9

Morning Prayer

Antiphon: The Divine Majesty portrays herself as a bird.

Psalm 129:1–8 ✠ Psalm 3:1–8 ✠ Psalm 62:1–11

Scripture: Job 39:26—40:2

Reading: St. Cyril of Alexandria, Patriarch, Father and Doctor of the Church † 444

Commentary on Matthew 23:37

Concerning the hen gathering her chicks under her wings, this is said with regard to how the Divine Majesty manifests itself, especially in human form. For concerning God, Moses said, *He stretches out his wings to take them up*, and David said, *The children of humanity will hope in the covering of his wings*.

Evening Prayer

Antiphon: God offers us the egg of life as nourishment.

Psalm 21:1–11 ✠ Psalm 37:1–22 ✠ Psalm 56:1–11

Scripture: Luke 11:9–13

Reading: St. Peter Chrysologus, archbishop, Father and Doctor of the Church † 450

Sermon 55.6

If he asks for an egg, will he offer him a scorpion? It is an ordinary and customary thing that children regularly ask for an egg, and that parents don't deny an egg to the little ones who ask. But because Christ came to gather his own as a mother hen does her young, Christ furnished God's Word as an egg for the nourishment of the holy offspring of the Church.

Day 10

Morning Prayer

Antiphon: God shall renew your strength, and give you wings to soar.

Psalm 142:1–12 ✠ Psalm 102:1–22 ✠ Psalm 62:1–11

Scripture: Isaiah 40:28–31

Reading: Cassiodorus, monk, Father of the Church † ca. 580

Exposition on the Psalms 90:4

He shall overshadow you with his shoulders and under his pinions you shall trust. His truth shall encompass you as a shield. In this verse and the next two that follow, what most beautiful imagery the prophet employs to praise the Lord's acts of kindness towards the most holy person introduced earlier! He recounts the fitting rewards for the one whose character he previously approved. We must search out these rewards with great care, to see if by God's grace we can discover some worthy meaning. The Lord's shoulders are miraculous works by means of which the divine power is demonstrated as if by broad shoulder blades. His wings are the prophets' warnings, which if received with pure minds, lead faithful souls ever heavenward. Perhaps you may ask what this overshadowing might bestow? So that the sun does not scorch you by day, nor the moon by night? Or again, what do the Lord's wings bring about? The answer is the Lord's protection, which you should realize you experience like a mother's devotion in the midst of a world fraught with dangers. As the Scripture says elsewhere, *Jerusalem, Jerusalem, how often I wanted to gather your children together like a mother hen gathers her chicks beneath her wings.*

Evening Prayer

Antiphon: Look at the birds of the sky; God provides for them.

Psalm 118:49–56 ✠ Psalm 38:1–13 ✠ Psalm 16:1–15

Scripture: Matthew 6:25–34

Reading: Cassiodorus, monk, Father of the Church † ca. 580

Exposition on the Psalms 56:2

And in the shadow of your wings I shall hope, until iniquity passes by. Let us understand the exceeding pure holiness of this prayer. In the first verse, before everything else, he begged the Lord to have mercy on himself. In the second, he states why he should obtain what he asks for. In the third, how he can be delivered from the imminent persecution. Now the shadow of the wings is a mother's protection which nurtures young chicks by a display of affection as well as shields them from the threat of a storm. Because this defense reveals the great resourcefulness of a mother's devotion, such a comparison is frequently found embedded in the Sacred Scriptures, as the Lord in the Gospel says: *Jerusalem, Jerusalem, how often I wanted to gather together your children as a mother hen gathers her chicks beneath her wings, and you would not.*

Day 11

Morning Prayer

Antiphon: Do not soar like an eagle with pride; return to God.

Psalm 5:1–12 ✠ Psalm 39:5–17 ✠ Psalm 62:1–11

Scripture: Obadiah 1:3–4

Reading: St. Sahdona, bishop, Father of the Church † ca. 630

Book of Perfection 4.50–51

Let us not hesitate to follow the Lord, believing in him, hoping in his goodness. Let us approach the Lord so that he approaches us. Let us not avoid him so that he might reunite us to himself and gather us close to him, *like a mother hen gathers her chicks beneath her wings*. Let us make haste, therefore, lovingly to press close beneath his wings, *so that he might save* us *beneath his feathers* and *protect us under his pinions*. Let us love to dwell beneath his shadow and glory in his shelter.

ℰℴ 📖 ℭℜ

Evening Prayer

Antiphon: Like an eagle, God protects the followers of Christ.

Psalm 118:57–64 ✠ Psalm 42:1–5 ✠ Psalm 16:1–15

Scripture: Revelation 12:7–17

Reading: St. Anselm of Canterbury, archbishop, Doctor of the Church † 1109

Prayer to St. Paul 10.227–38

And you, my soul, dead through your own doing, run under the wings of Jesus, your mother, and bewail your woes beneath her feathers. Ask that your wounds may be tenderly cared for, and thus fostered, life might return. Christ, my mother, you gather together your chicks under your wings, this dead chick of yours, nestles beneath your wings. For your gentleness comforts the frightened; your sweet smell restores the despairing. Your warmth grants life to the dead; your touch justifies sinners. Recognize, O mother, your dead son by the sign of your Cross and the sound of your confession. Re-animate your little one; resuscitate your dead chick; justify your sinner. Let your terrified one be consoled by you; by himself despairing, let him be comforted by you; and in your unalienable grace of integrity let him be refashioned. From you flows the consolation for miseries; blessed be you for ages and ages. Amen.

Day 12

Morning Prayer

Antiphon: My brood had spurned me, but I will bring them back to life.

Psalm 41:1–11 ✠ Psalm 118:65–72 ✠ Psalm 62:1–11

Scripture: Isaiah 1:2 VULG

Reading: St. Peter Damian, cardinal bishop, Doctor of the Church † 1072

Letter 86

To what extent God was to love his own, the pelican demonstrates by its natural instinct. We are informed by those who have expended much effort in understanding the nature of animals, that this bird loves its offspring as no other, but the ungrateful fledglings do not reciprocate this love. As soon as the chicks begin to grow, together they begin attacking both parents. The parents strike back but because they are incapable of moderating their discipline, it's as if they turn the rod of correction into a sword, thus killing their brood with too many thrashings. On the third day, while the mother sits on her dead chicks, she pecks at their side with her beak and opens it, from which the mother's blood trickles down onto the dead fledglings and suddenly brings them back to life. These matters appear to be not so much a symbol as gospel truth. Through Isaiah the fashioner of human beings clearly stated, *I engendered children and raised them, yet they have rebelled against me.* God was likewise struck by his reprobate children, just as the pelican was by its chicks, as another passage of Scripture testifies, *The wicked have risen up against me without mercy; they sought to kill me. They did not refrain from spitting in my face, and with lances they wounded me.*

Now just as the pelican killed its young with repeated blows, God afflicted the perverse people with the grave calamity of captivity and war, as the prophet remarked, *You have struck them down, but they paid no attention; you pierced them to the heart, yet they refused to accept discipline.* But the pelican repaid the evil of her ungrateful fledglings with good, when they were restored to life by their mother's blood. Now the Wisdom of God, the Mother of all the living, opened her side as she hung on the Cross and thus, by pouring out her precious blood she restored to life those who had been slain.

Evening Prayer

Antiphon: God wishes to cherish us as a mother bird her young.

Psalm 138:1–14 ✠ Psalm 118:73–80 ✠ Psalm 60:1–8

Scripture: 4 Esdras 1:22–30 VULG

Reading: Bl. Guerric of Igny, abbot † 1157

First Sermon for Epiphany 6

Christ will cherish you as does the mother hen her chicks under her wings, if only you are willing. How often he wished to do so, but you were unwilling.

Day 13

Morning Prayer

Antiphon: The Wisdom of God became infirm to heal our infirmities.

Psalm 54:1–16 ✠ Psalm 56:1–11 ✠ Psalm 62:1–11

Scripture: Deuteronomy 32:9–11 VULG

Reading: St. Thomas Aquinas, priest, Doctor of the Church † 1274

Golden Chain on the Gospel of Matthew 23

O Jerusalem, Jerusalem, you that kill the prophets and stone those who are sent to you, how often would I have gathered your children together, even as a mother hen gathers her chicks beneath her wings, and you would not! As Chrysostom notes, . . . "regarding *How often would I have gathered you together* as if to say, No matter what, these your murders have not alienated me from you, but I would have taken you to me, not just once or twice, but many times over." The greatness of his love is shown by the comparison with a mother hen. And as Augustine remarks, "This species of bird has the greatest affection for its young, so much so that when they are sick the mother herself becomes infirm as well. And what you will rarely discover in any other animal, the hen will fight against any bird of prey, protecting its young beneath its wings." In like manner, our mother, the Wisdom of God, having become infirm as it were by assuming flesh—according to the saying of the Apostle: *The weakness of God is stronger than human beings*—protects our infirmity and resists the Devil so that he cannot carry us off as his prey.

Evening Prayer

Antiphon: Meditate upon the Cross that stretches across the heavens.

Psalm 140:1–5 ✠ Psalm 4:1–8 ✠ Psalm 16:1–15

Scripture: Colossians 1:15–20

Reading: St. Aelred of Rievaulx, abbot † 1167

Sermon 36.4–6

For indeed the Cross is erected, its head raised to heaven, its feet extended to earth, its arms stretched out in this fashion so that heaven and earth are placed together. Furthermore, if you lay the crucifix back, one part will grasp the east, the other the west, the third the south, the fourth the north. Therefore do you see in what mystery this kind of death of Christ is chosen? The Apostle himself clearly expounded: *He humbled himself*, he says, *and became obedient to death, even death on a cross*. And the very mystery sets forth, *Because of this*, he says, *God exalted him and gave him a name that is above every name, so that at the name of Jesus every knee must bend in heaven, on earth, and under the earth*. Therefore because through the Cross he had taken possession of heaven and earth, on the Cross he was positioned as if he embraced heaven and earth. Now it is true that his death happened not on earth, but above the earth, this being the case unless through his blessed Passion by means of earthly actions he was lifted up, for surely we know *the things which are above, not the things which are on the earth*? Since it is true that his arms were outstretched as he died, this is a sign of his marvelous loving care which is like a hen that gathers together her chicks under her wings and protects them from the danger of a rapacious bird. In the same way, he embraces us with maternal affection under the wings of his grace protecting us from the attack of abominable spirits; he does this to be our greatest guardian.

Day 14

Morning Prayer

Antiphon: God carries us on the eagle's wings of resurrection.

Psalm 64:1–13 ✠ Psalm 118:81–88 ✠ Psalm 62:1–11

Scripture: Exodus 19:3–8

Reading: St. Robert Bellarmine, archbishop, Doctor of the Church † 1621

Commentary on the Psalms 90:4

He will overshadow you with his shoulders and under his wings you will trust. The Prophet now speaks in his own right and confirms the word of the just, saying, "You were right to say, *I will trust in him, because he has delivered me from the fowler's snare*, for he really did deliver you and will always deliver you from every danger. For as long as you will be a fledgling, no match for your enemies, God will foster you under his wings like an eagle or a hen nurtures its offspring." . . . In the Holy Scriptures God has been compared to these two birds: the eagle and the hen. *As an eagle enticing her young to fly, and hovering over them* (Deut 32:11) and *How often I wanted to gather together your children like a mother hen gathers her young* (Matt 23:37). God was an eagle before the Incarnation and a hen afterwards; or if this is to refer to Christ alone, as God he is an eagle, and as man a hen; or, while Christ experienced temporal mortality he was a hen and after the Resurrection, an eagle. Scripture therefore says, *he will overshadow you with his shoulders*, that is, God like an eagle or a hen, will *gather you under his wings*, will overshadow with his shoulders so that you will have nothing to fear from the heat of the sun, or the driving wind and rain, or from birds of prey. Nestled *under his wings* in the greatest of safety, under God's care and protection, you will be able to trust in deliverance and safety.

Evening Prayer

Antiphon: The glory of the Most High will overshadow you.

Psalm 133:1–3 ✠ Psalm 118:89–96 ✠ Psalm 35:5–12

Scripture: Luke 1:26–38

Reading: St. Robert Bellarmine, archbishop, Doctor of the Church † 1621

Commentary on the Psalms 90:1

The one who dwells in the support of the Most High, shall abide under the protection of the God of Heaven. The second part of the verse, in which a reward is promised to those who put their trust in God, means that whoever truly trusts in the divine assistance shall not be disappointed in his hope, but shall be totally protected by the Lord. The several words in each part of the verse beautifully correspond with each other. The word *dwells* corresponds with abide under, *support* with protection; and the phrase *Most High* corresponds with God of heaven. The Hebrew term for protection signifies shade or shadow, signifying that God protects those who trust in him, as the mother hen gathers her chicks beneath the shadow of her wings.

✟

Thematic Readings for Non-Feast Days

Christ as the Woman Searching for the Lost Coin

Day 1

Morning Prayer

Antiphon: Whose image is on the coin? That of the royal heir.

Psalm 72:1–28 ✠ Psalm 49:7–22 ✠ Psalm 118:97–104

Scripture: Wisdom 2:21–24

Reading: St. Ephrem, deacon, Father and Doctor of the Church † 373

Hymns on Virginity 5.8

> By the oil lamp are found things which are lost in the dark,
> and by the Anointed One, likewise is found the soul which is lost.
> The oil lamp returned our lost things, and the Anointed as well, our treasures.
> The oil lamp found the coin, and the Anointed One, the image of Adam.

Evening Prayer

Antiphon: The Wisdom of God lights her lamp and searches for the lost coin.

Psalm 1:1–6 ✠ Psalm 18:1–14 ✠ Psalm 118:105–12

Scripture: Luke 15:8–10 NT

Reading: St. John Chrysostom, Patriarch, Father and Doctor of the Church † 407

On Luke 15:11

> The breasts of Christ produce an unending flow of love like honey. The brightly beaming Wisdom of Christ lights a lamp and sets it on the lamp stand of the Cross, illuminating the whole world to godliness. Using this lamp, the Wisdom of God searches for the one lost coin and having found it, she adds it to the nine coins, that is, to the angels. Beloved, it is now good to discuss who this woman is who possesses ten coins. She is the Wisdom of God; she possesses the ten drachmas. Of what sort? Add them up: angels, archangels, principalities, authorities, powers, thrones, dominions, cherubim, seraphim, and Adam the first-formed. This drachma, I mean Adam, consumed the wickedness of the devil and therefore was dragged down to the depths of life and was covered with grime by the hedonistic desires of sin. But humanity was found again by the Wisdom of God when she appeared. How did she find it, beloved? She came down from heaven, receiving the clay lamp of the body and joining it with the light of divinity, she then set it on the lamp stand of the Cross searching for the lost coin. Thus she brings it into the enclosure of the court and grazing ground of the angels.

PRAYING—WITH THE SAINTS—TO GOD OUR MOTHER

Day 2

Morning Prayer

Antiphon: Each coin is stamped with the royal visage.

Psalm 91:1–15 ✠ Psalm 118:113–20 ✠ Psalm 79:1–19

Scripture: Sirach 17:1–3

Reading: St. Cyril of Alexandria, Patriarch, Father and Doctor of the Church † 444

Commentary on Luke 15

Through the former parable in which the lost sheep signified the human race upon the earth, we learned that we are the creation of the God of the universe, since he brought into existence that which previously did not exist. *For he made us, and not we ourselves*, as it is written. *And he is our God, and we are the people of his pasture, the flock of his hand.* And through this second parable, in which that which was lost is compared to a drachma, again as one out of ten. Because it is out of a perfect number, and of a sum of total counting (for the number ten is also perfect, being the end of the series counting up from the first unit), it is manifestly clear that we are created in the royal image and likeness, namely in that of the God of the universe. For the drachma is the coin on which is stamped the royal visage. How can anyone doubt that we have fallen from such a state and been lost, and have been found by Christ, being transformed by holiness and righteousness, when the blessed Paul has written, *And all of us, with unveiled faces beholding the glory of the Lord as reflected in a mirror, are being transformed into that same image from one degree of glory to the next, for this comes from the Lord who is Spirit.* And he sends a message to the Galatians in these terms, *Children, of whom I once again in the pangs of giving birth, until Christ is formed within you.* Thus a search was made for that which had fallen, and why the woman lit the lamp, for we were found by the Wisdom of God our Father, She who is the Son, when the divine light shone within us, and intellectual Daystar arose, and the Sun of Righteousness had arisen, and the day dawned, according to the Scriptures.

Evening Prayer

Antiphon: The woman is Christ, the Wisdom of God.

Psalm 6:1–10 ✠ Psalm 35:5–12 ✠ Psalm 118:105–12

Scripture: Matthew 22:15–22

Reading: St. Romanos Melodius, deacon, Father of the Church † 556

Thematic Readings for Non-Feast Days

Hymn of the Resurrection 6.1–2, from the Byzantine Liturgy

> Hearing the parable of Christ in the Gospel written by Luke
> let us not overlook its significance;
> and guided by faith let us discover the meaning
> of the woman and the drachmas:
> of the one she lost and diligently sought,
> lighting a lamp, thoroughly sweeping her house.
> When she had found it she invited her neighbors:
> "Come, rejoice with me! I have found what I had lost."
> Now, therefore, let us beseech Christ:
> "You, O Lord, enlighten our souls,
> for you appointed a light,
> you who are the Resurrection and Life."
> The number of the drachmas is evident to everyone:
> ten, the total of everything the Lord possesses,
> the One who created the universe in Wisdom.
> The woman, as is known, is the Virtue and Wisdom of the Creator;
> She is the Christ—the Wisdom and Power of God.
> The ten drachmas are the principalities and authorities,
> the powers and thrones, the sovereignties,
> the angels and archangels, the cherubim and seraphim,
> and the first creature, humanity that she had lost,
> and sought after, and found in its fallen condition;
> She, the Life and Resurrection.

Day 3

Morning Prayer

Antiphon: The likeness to the Creator is restored.

Psalm 107:1–6 ✠ Psalm 50:1–19 ✠ Psalm 118:121–28

Scripture: Isaiah 46:3–5 VULG

Reading: St. Gregory the Great, pope, Father and Doctor of the Church † 604

Forty Gospel Homilies 34

> Or what woman, having ten silver pieces, if she were to lose one coin, does she not light a lamp and turn the house upside down, seeking diligently until she finds the coin she has lost? The shepherd [in the previous parable] and this woman have the same significance: God's very Self, the very Wisdom of God. And because a coin bears an image, the woman lost a silver piece when humanity, created in the image of God, by sinning withdrew from the likeness of its Creator. Wherefore the woman lights a lamp because the Wisdom of God appeared in human nature. A lamp is a light in a clay ves-

sel, and a light in a clay vessel is divinity in the flesh. Regarding this corporeal vessel of clay Wisdom herself says: *My strength is dried up like a clay vessel.* Now a clay vessel becomes firm and strong in fire; its strength was dried up like a clay vessel, because by the tribulations of the passion she strengthened the body she had assumed for the glory of the resurrection.

Once the lamp was lit she turns upside down the house, because as soon as her divinity began to illuminate the body, our whole consciousness was perturbed. A house is turned upside down when the human conscience is upset by considering its accused state. Now this term *turns upside down* does not differ from what is read in other manuscripts, namely, *thoroughly cleansed.* For unless a depraved mind is first turned over by fear, it is not thoroughly cleansed of its accustomed vices. Thus once the house has been turned inside out the coin is found, because when a person's conscience is upset, the likeness to the Creator is restored.

And when she found it, she calls together her friends and neighbors, declaring: "Rejoice with me, for I have found the silver coin which I had lost." Who are her friends and neighbors if not the heavenly powers, we previously mentioned. For they are as close to supernal Wisdom in proportion to how they draw near through the grace of uninterrupted vision. And while I am on the subject, I shouldn't carelessly omit to inquire as to why the woman who signifies the Wisdom of God had ten coins, of which she lost one, and found when she sought it out. The reason is that the Lord created the nature of angels and humans so that they might come to know God's self. Because God created the nature to last forever, without any doubt he created it in his own likeness. In truth, the woman possessed ten silver coins because there are nine orders of angels, but so that the number of the elect might be complete, humanity was created as a tenth. Humanity was not lost by its Creator after its sin, because Eternal Wisdom restored it by shining through the miracles in her human body with the light of the clay vessel.

Evening Prayer

Antiphon: Give back to God what belongs to God.

Psalm 15:1–11 ✠ Psalm 53:1–7 ✠ Psalm 118:105–12

Scripture: Luke 20:20–26

Reading: St. Hildegard of Bingen, abbess † 1179

Know Your Way 3.2.20

What woman having ten coins, if she loses one of them, does not light a lamp, sweep the house, and diligently search until she find it? And when she has found it she summons her friends and neighbors, declaring, "Rejoice with me, for I have found the coin which was lost." This means: The Holy Divinity had ten coins, that is to say the ten orders of the heavenly hierarchy, namely the chosen angels and humanity. She lost one coin when humanity fell into death by following the devil's seduction instead of the divine precepts. Hence the Divinity lit a burning lamp, clearly Christ, true God and true human, the most brilliant Sun of Justice. With him she swept the house, namely the Jewish people, and she diligently searched the Law for every signification which brings about salvation, and established a new sanctification, and thus found her lost coin, humanity, whom she had lost. Then she called together her friends, namely earthly deeds of justice, and her neighbors, that is the spiritual powers, and said, "Rejoice with me in great praise and joy, and build the heavenly Jerusalem with living stones, for I have found humanity, who had perished by the devil's deception!"

Day 4

Morning Prayer

Antiphon: Wisdom takes account of the affairs of God.

Psalm 118:145–52 ✠ Psalm 60:1–8 ✠ Psalm 112:1–9

Scripture: Sirach 24:1–9 LXX

Reading: St. Nicholas Cabasilas, monk and priest † ca. 1391

Life in Christ 1.6

Through the Sacred Mysteries (= Sacraments) we live in God. We remove our life from this visible world to the one which is not seen, by exchanging, not the place, but the manner of life and very life itself. For we ourselves were not moved towards God, nor did we ascend to God; rather, God himself came and descended to us. We did not do the seeking; rather, we were the object of the seeking. The sheep did not seek the shepherd, and the lost coin did not seek the master of the house; rather, it was he who stooped to earth and retrieved his image.

✠

SACRAMENTAL LIFE IN CHRIST: MYSTERY OF THE CHURCH

Morning Prayer

Antiphon: Our Mother is God who gives birth to Mother Church.

Psalm 129:1–8 ✠ Psalm 66:1–7 ✠ Psalm 118:121–28

Scripture: Isaiah 66:9–13 VULG

Reading: St. Gregory of Narek, monk † 1003

Commentary on the Song of Songs 8:5

The Bridegroom speaks to the Bride, saying, *Under the apple tree, I shall awaken you. There my mother bore you; there did she who bore you go into labor.*

First it is beneficial to examine the nature of the apple in order to understand the significance of *I awakened you under the apple tree*. The apple is a salutary food, very beneficial to the weak. It is even fit for rulers and delights the senses of those who taste it with a mixture of other scents. Our St. Gregory the Illuminator says this as well.

Now [the Bridegroom] likens the apple to the words of the Law and of the Prophets which were first delivered to us by the Holy Spirit on Mount Sinai through the mediation of Moses, and then over the course of time to develop through the Prophets. Now birds, by sitting on their eggs for an extended period of time transmit life to them, mediating their warmth at the disposition of the Creator. Similarly, our nature having been placed beneath the Law and the message of the Prophets for an extended period of time, was incubated by God the Father and the Son (who is referred to as our Bridegroom and Beloved), and was given birth to by the Mother of All, She who is his birther by nature, and ours by grace. This is why [the Bridegroom] uses the words *go into labor*; labor pertains to a *mother*. For this reason the Father is called Mother, Christ's mother and our mother as well. The Father, consequently, was in labor through the message of the Law and the Prophets, and through water and the Spirit gave birth to his children, the siblings of Christ. Thus there is indeed only One Mother, our Birther—the Father Almighty.

But Christ was born first. Subsequently by his baptism and through the coming of the Holy Spirit, he opened the heavens which were closed by Adam. Thus he bestowed upon us the same generation through the Holy Spirit.

Evening Prayer

Antiphon: The Church was formed from the side of Christ.

Psalm 18:1–14 ✠ Psalm 68:1–32 ✠ Psalm 4:1–8

Scripture: Ephesians 5:21–33

Reading: St. John Chrysostom, Patriarch, Father and Doctor of the Church † 407

How to Choose a Wife 3

For just as Eve, according to Scripture, was produced from Adam's side, so too, are we produced from Christ's side; for this is the meaning, *Of his flesh, and of his bones*. As we all know, Eve was produced from the side of Adam, and Scripture clearly declares that God caused a deep sleep to fall upon Adam, took one of his ribs from his side, and constructed the woman. But how can we demonstrate that the Church was constituted from the side of Christ? Scripture brings this to light. For when Christ was raised upon the Cross, had been nailed to it and died, *One of the soldiers came and pierced his side, and out flowed blood and water*; now out of that blood and that water the whole Church was constituted. And Christ himself bears witness to this when he says, *Unless one is born again from water and Spirit, it will be impossible to enter into the Kingdom of Heaven.* He refers to the blood [of life] as the Spirit [of life]. Indeed, we are born through the waters of baptism, and nourished through the blood. Do you see how we are from his flesh and from his bones? Do you see how from that blood and water we are given birth and nourished [like suckling babes]? For just as while Adam was asleep the woman was constructed out of him, so too, while Christ slept in death, the Church was formed from his side.

THE MYSTERY OF BAPTISM

Day 1

Morning Prayer

Antiphon: Milk and water share an intimate relationship.

Psalm 129:1–8 ✠ Psalm 69:1–5 ✠ Psalm 118:129–36

Scripture: Isaiah 42:10–16 TNK

Reading: St. Clement of Alexandria, priest, Father of the Church † ca. 215

Christ the Educator 1.6.49.2–3; 1.6.50.3–4

Milk is the wellspring of nourishment. By its presence, a woman is known to have truly given birth and become a mother, therefore bestowing on her a certain lovable charm. That is why the Holy Spirit through the Apostle, mystically places these words in the Lord's mouth, *I have given you milk to drink.* For if we have been born again, becoming members of Christ, then the One who gives us new birth nourishes us with his own milk, the Word. For anyone who has naturally given birth, immediately provides nourishment to the one who is born. In the same manner that the rebirth occurred, accordingly the nourishment must be spiritual. . . .

Now milk has a natural affinity with water, just as the spiritual and purifying washing has with spiritual nourishment. . . . Indeed, the Word has the same intimate relationship with the waters of baptism as milk does with water. For milk is the only liquid that absorbs water and is used as a purgative remedy when so mixed, just as baptism cleanses us from sin.

Evening Prayer

Antiphon: The breath of life blows upon the baptismal waters.

Psalm 21:1–11 ✠ Psalm 70:1–24 ✠ Psalm 118:137–44

Scripture: John 3:1–6 NT

Reading: St. Aphraates, priest, Father of the Church † ca. 350

Demonstrations 6.14

Now, my friend, we, too, have received the Spirit of the Messiah and the Messiah dwells in us, as it is written, for She, this Spirit, has said through the mouth of the prophet, *I will dwell with them and walk with them.* Therefore, let us prepare our temples for the Spirit of the Messiah and not grieve Her lest She depart from us. Remember the warning of the Apostle, *Do not grieve the Holy Spirit with whom you have been sealed unto the day of salvation.* Through baptism, in fact, we have received the Spirit of the Messiah, and, at the moment when the priests call upon the Spirit, She opens the heavens, descends, and She broods over the waters animating them; and those who have been baptized are clothed in Her. In fact, She, the Spirit, stays away from all those who are born of the flesh until they experience the rebirth through the waters; then they receive the Holy Spirit.

Day 2

Morning Prayer

Antiphon: The Spirit effects forgiveness of sins through baptism.

Psalm 142:1–12 ✠ Psalm 76:13–20 ✠ Psalm 56:1–11

Scripture: Nehemiah 9:13–17 TNK

Reading: Syriac spiritual manual *Liber Graduum*, mid fourth century

Book of Steps 12.1

Brothers and sisters, because we believe there is a secret stripping of the heart as it forsakes the earth and is raised to heaven, we should be stripped physically even of our belongings and inheritance, for then we shall be keeping the commandments of the One who bestows life upon all; then we shall realize that the person who is united to our Lord, constantly meditating upon him, enjoys a secret prayer of the heart. Let us pray not only with our body but with our heart as well, just as Jesus blessed and prayed in both body and spirit. The Apostles and Prophets likewise prayed in this manner.

We must not be fools who refuse to be persuaded by their parents. We must not forsake our spiritual parents and acquire for ourselves ones "of the flesh" who are not true, who instead will cause us to forget the truth of our Lord and his messengers. Instead, we know there is a secret fasting of the heart, a fasting from evil thoughts. But let us likewise fast openly, as our Lord and his messengers did, both the former and the latter. In truth, we know that the body is a hidden temple and that the heart is a hidden altar for ministry in the Spirit. Likewise, let us devote ourselves to that visible altar and approach that visible temple, so that constantly working in these, we may live forever and ever in what is free and mighty, the Church in heaven, and beside that altar which is adorned and set up in the Spirit; before which the angels minister with all the saints, and where Jesus serves as priest and effects the consecration before them and above them and on every side of them. Finally, we know that the "perfect" are baptized into Jesus Christ and are secretly purified; let us believe in and be sure of this visible baptism. Let us believe in the Spirit: that she is there and that she brings about the absolution and the remission of sins, because the one who believes in her, undergoes the baptism and does good deeds.

Evening Prayer

Antiphon: We are born of God, through the breaking of the baptismal waters.

Psalm 118:49–56 ✠ Psalm 79:1–19 ✠ Psalm 4:1–8

Scripture: John 1:1–18

Reading: St. Cyril of Alexandria, Patriarch, Father and Doctor of the Church † 444

Commentary on John 1.9

Who were born, not by blood, nor by the desire of the flesh, nor by the will of man, but by God.

The [Evangelist] says regarding those who through their faith have been called to adoption by God in Christ, they have stripped off the inferiority of their own status and are splendidly attired as if clothed in brilliant white raiment with the grace of the One who honors them, thus they advance to a status that transcends their nature. For they no longer are recognized as children of the flesh, but rather as offspring of God by adoption. Take note of what precaution the blessed Evangelist employs in his words. His caution was necessary, because he was wishing to say that those who have believed have been given birth to by God, but he did not intend anyone to believe that they were truly engendered from the very essence of God the Father. This would run the risk of making them completely like the Only-Begotten, or to say that the text, *I have given birth to you out of the womb before the daystar*, applied to him only in some relative sense; for doing so would bring the Only-Begotten down to the level of natural creatures, even though he is said to have been born by God. The Evangelist foresaw this necessary precaution. For having said that the power was given to become children of God by the One who is Son according to nature, thereby having implied they became children of God by adoption and grace, he could next say without any danger that they were *born of God*. He did so in order to bring to light the magnitude of the grace showered upon them, which was such that it brought together into intimate kinship with God the Father that which was alien, and transposed what was servile to the born privileged status of a lord, by means of God's ardent love.

Day 3

Morning Prayer

Antiphon: What is born of the Spirit is spirit.

Psalm 5:1–12 ✠ Psalm 80:1–14 ✠ Psalm 143:7–12 TNK

Scripture: Genesis 1:1–2 TNK

Reading: St. John Chrysostom, Patriarch, Father and Doctor of the Church † 407

Homilies on John, on 3:6

What is born of the flesh is flesh; and what is born of the Spirit is spirit.

    No longer is there an earthly mother, no longer pangs of birthing, nor the nuptial bed, and physical intercourse, rather the formation of our nature is from above, from the Holy Spirit and water. For the water achieves its purpose, becoming a means of birth for what has already been physically born. Just as the womb is to the embryo, so the water is to the believer, because one is molded and formed in the water. For from the very beginning God said, *Let the waters bring forth crawling creatures having life.* From the instant that the Lord came forth from Jordan's waters, the water no longer brings forth *crawling creatures having life,* but rather rational souls bearing the Holy Spirit.

    What is molded in the womb, however, needs the process of time, but this is not the case with water, since all comes about in an instant. Whereas physical life is perishable and has its inception from carnal corruption, and what has been born is slow in its formation. Such is the nature of bodies; they attain their completion in the process of time. But this is not so regarding what is birthed by the Spirit. Why? Because they are perfectly formed from the beginning. Yet when Nicodemus was totally disturbed upon hearing these things, see how Christ revealed to him the inexpressible meaning of this mystery, and made understandable what had previously been incomprehensible.

What is born of the flesh is flesh; and what is born of the Spirit is spirit.

Evening Prayer

Antiphon: The side of Christ is the womb of eternal life.

Psalm 118:57–64 ✠ Psalm 101:1–28 ✠ Psalm 41:1–11

Scripture: 1 Corinthians 10:1–17

Reading: St. John Chrysostom, Patriarch, Father and Doctor of the Church † 407

Baptismal Instructions 3:17–19

There came out from His side water and blood. Beloved, do not pass this mystery by without reflecting upon it, for I have yet another mystical exposition to give. I said that there was a symbol of baptism and the sacramental mysteries in that blood and water. It is from both of these that the Church is given birth *through the bath of regeneration and renewal by the Holy Spirit*, through baptism and the sacramental mysteries. Now the symbols of baptism and the mysteries issue forth from the side. It is from his side, therefore, that Christ has formed the Church, just as he formed Eve from the side of Adam.

And that is why Moses, in his account of the first man, has Adam say: *Bone of my bone and flesh of my flesh*, wishing to signify to us the Master's side. Just as at that time God took the rib of Adam and formed a woman, so too Christ gave us blood and water from his side and formed the Church. And just as then he took the rib from Adam when he was in the depth of sleep, so now he gave us blood and water after his death, first the water and then the blood. But what was then a deep slumber is now a death, so that you may learn that this death is henceforth only sleep.

Have you recognized how Christ unites the bride to himself? Have you noticed with what nourishment he nurtures us all? It is by the same nourishment that we have been formed and that we are fed. Just as a woman nurtures with her own blood and milk the offspring she has birthed, so too Christ continuously nurtures with his own blood those whom he has brought forth.

Day 4

Morning Prayer

Antiphon: What mother gave me birth through baptism? The Holy Spirit.

Psalm 41:1–11 ✠ Psalm 81:1–8 ✠ Psalm 118:153–60

Scripture: Song of Songs 7:14—8:5

Reading: St. Gregory of Narek, monk and priest † 1003

Commentary on the Song of Songs 7:13

For all these reasons [the Bride] said, *The mandrakes have exuded their scent, even to the gates. All the fruit, whether old or new, which my mother has given me, will be stored up for you, my Beloved.* These are the words of praise that the apostles and leaders have for the faithful in Christ whom they offer to him as *a people prepared*, now and at the Great Day of Judgment. They shall repeat the words of the prophet, *Behold me and the children whom God has given me.* These words are similar to those already said, *I have stored this up for you, my Beloved.* This renders an account of the people who will be presented to God. *Whether old or new* refers to the people from ancient times or recent. And as to the words *what my Mother has given me*, the *mother* is the Catholic church as well as the Holy Spirit who gave birth through the baptismal font and Christ who nourished us with his blood.

Evening Prayer

Antiphon: Birth through baptism is birth into the resurrected life.

Psalm 138:1–14 ✠ Psalm 83:1–12 ✠ Psalm 118:161–68

Scripture: 1 Corinthians 15:22–29

Reading: St. Nicholas Cabasilas, monk and priest † ca. 1391

Life in Christ 2.9

    The birth by Baptism is the beginning of the life to come, and the provision of new members as well as faculties is the preparation for the way of life. Yet it is impossible to be prepared for the future life if we do not receive the life of Christ here and now. He became *the father of the Age to come* just as Adam became the father of the present age, for it was Adam who began for humanity the life which is mired in corruption. Just as it is impossible to live this natural life without receiving the physical qualities of Adam as well as the human faculties requisite for this life, so too, no one can obtain that blessed world alive without being prepared by the life of Christ, and being formed according to that image. And in yet another fashion is the baptismal washing a birth. It is Christ who gives birth and we are those who are born; and for whoever is born, it is quite clear that the One who gives birth bestows his own life on that person.

The Mystery of Chrismation/Confirmation

Morning Prayer

Antiphon: Christ, the Anointed One, anoints us with sacred oil.

Psalm 54:1–16 ✠ Psalm 83:1–12 ✠ Psalm 22:1–6

Scripture: Deuteronomy 32:12–14 TNK

Reading: St. Gregory of Narek, monk and priest, † 1003

Commentary on the Song of Songs 8:5

    The Bridegroom speaks to the Bride, saying, *Under the apple tree, I shall awaken you. There my mother bore you; there did she who bore you go into labor.*

First it is beneficial to examine the nature of the apple in order to understand the significance of *I awakened you under the apple tree*. The apple is a salutary food, very beneficial to the weak. It is even fit for rulers and delights the senses of those who taste it with a mixture of other scents. Our St. Gregory the Illuminator says this as well.

Now [the Bridegroom] likens the apple to the words of the Law and of the Prophets which were first delivered to us by the Holy Spirit on Mount Sinai through the mediation of Moses, and then over the course of time to develop through the Prophets. Now birds, by sitting on their eggs for an extended period of time transmit life to them, mediating their warmth at the disposition of the Creator. Similarly, our nature having been placed beneath the Law and the message of the Prophets for an extended period of time, was incubated by God the Father and the Son (who is referred to as our Bridegroom and Beloved), and was given birth to by the Mother of All, She who is his birther by nature, and ours by grace. This is why [the Bridegroom] uses the words *go into labor*; labor pertains to a *mother*. For this reason the Father is called Mother, Christ's mother and our mother as well. The Father, consequently, was in labor through the message of the Law and the Prophets, and through water and the Spirit gave birth to his children, the siblings of Christ. Thus there is indeed only One Mother, our Birther—the Father Almighty.

But Christ was born first. Subsequently by his baptism and through the coming of the Holy Spirit, he opened the heavens which were closed by Adam. Thus he bestowed upon us the same generation through the Holy Spirit.

Evening Prayer

Antiphon: We have received the Anointing from God.

Psalm 140:1–5 ✠ Psalm 131:1–18 ✠ Psalm 140:1–5

Scripture: 2 Corinthians 1:20–22

Reading: St. Nerses IV, Catholicos † 1173

Jesus, Son, Only-Begotten of the Father 205–6

> You created me a human being, born from the earth,
> the last born of the children of Adam,
> being a child of the night,
> placed in the world of iniquity and full of evil.
> You once again gave birth to me without evil;
> you created me anew in the Holy Font;
> you anointed me with your heavenly oil
> so I might be adopted by your heavenly Father.

PRAYING—WITH THE SAINTS—TO GOD OUR MOTHER

The Mystery of the Eucharist

Day 1

Morning Prayer

Antiphon: The mother's blood is transformative and life-giving.

Psalm 64:1–13 ✠ Psalm 4:1–8 ✠ Psalm 22:1–6

Scripture: Genesis 49:25–26 TNK

Reading: St. Clement of Alexandria, priest, Father of the Church † ca. 215

Christ the Educator 1.6.39.1—40.2

    If then certain lovers of disputes wish to continue to maintain that milk represents the initial instructions as a sort of elementary food, while solid food represents spiritual knowledge, thereby placing themselves at the height of knowledge, let them understand that when they limit the name of nourishment to solid food, like the Body and Blood of Jesus, they are being carried away by their boastful "wise" enlightenment, in contradistinction to the simple truth. One certainly knows that blood is the first substance produced in a human being; some even go so far as to claim it constitutes the substance of the soul. Now this very blood, under the effect of a natural ripening and fermentation which takes place once the mother has given birth, transforms itself; reaching full bloom it loses its color and becomes old and white so as not to frighten the child.

    Furthermore, blood is the most fluid part of the flesh; in fact, it is a sort of liquid flesh. Yet milk, for its part, is more nourishing and finely broken down than blood. Now whether it is a matter of blood being supplied to the fetus directly through the mother's umbilical cord, or the case of the menstrual flow of blood—having been ordered by the All-Nursing and Generative God—to cut off from its normal course and naturally reroute itself to the already swollen breasts where the blood transforms itself because of the warm breath [in the lungs] so that it is furnishes the infant a desirable nourishment, in the end, it is blood which has been transformed.

    More than any other organ of the body, the breasts are the most responsive to motherhood. After childbirth, once the cord through which the blood formerly flowed to the fetus is cut off, there is an obstruction in the circulation and the blood surges towards the breasts. Now as the blood accumulates, the breasts begin to swell and the blood turns itself into milk. . . . In any case, one will not be able to find anything more nourishing, more delightful, or whiter than milk. And in every point, spiritual food is similar to it: delightful, because it derives from grace; nourishing, because it is life; and dazzling white, because it is the daylight of Christ. Therefore it has been clearly demonstrated that the Blood of the Word is like milk.

Evening Prayer

Antiphon: My blood is truly drink, the cup of life.

Psalm 140:1–5 ✠ Psalm 4:1–8 ✠ Psalm 15:1–11

Scripture: 1 Corinthians 3:1–2 NT

Reading: St. Clement of Alexandria, priest, Father of the Church † ca. 215

Christ the Educator 1.6.36.2–5

It is equally justifiable to take the Scripture [I gave you milk to drink . . .] in another sense: *For myself, brothers and sisters, I could not speak to you as spiritual people, but as beings carnally driven, as mere youths in Christ.* Thus it is possible to consider the *carnal* as those who are recently instructed in the faith and are as yet *babes* in Christ. For the Apostle calls *spiritual*, those who have already believed through the Holy Spirit, and *carnal*, those who are newly taught and not yet purified. He naturally refers to them as *carnal* because they still possess the carnal mindset of the pagans. *For since there still exists among you jealousy and discord, are you not carnal and your behavior all too human?* Therefore he remarks, *I gave you milk to drink*, which is to say, I poured out knowledge upon you, and by means of instruction I have nourished you to eternal life. The phrase *gave to drink* symbolizes a means of perfect participation, for only the mature are said to drink, whereas infants suck.

My Blood, declares the Lord, *is truly drink*. Perhaps, then, when the Apostle says, *I gave you milk to drink* this signifies the perfect happiness which one finds in the Word who is the milk, that is, the knowledge of the truth.

Day 2

Morning Prayer

Antiphon: The Word is everything to the newborn, both father and mother.

Psalm 72:1–28 ✠ Psalm 130:1–3 ✠ Psalm 21:1–11

Scripture: 4 Esdras 1:22–30 VULG

Reading: St. Clement of Alexandria, priest, Father of the Church † ca. 215

Christ the Educator 1.6.42.1–3

O wondrous mystery! There is one Father of the universe, one Word of the universe, one Holy Spirit everywhere the same. And there alone is one virgin who became a mother; I like to call her the Church. This mother alone, didn't have any milk, because she alone never became a woman. She is at once both virgin and mother: undefiled as a virgin, affectionate as a mother. Calling her children around her, she nurses them with a holy milk, the Word for infancy. For this reason she did not have any milk, because the milk was this beautiful and well-suited Child, namely the Body of Christ. She nurses, by means of the Word, the young brood which the Lord himself gave birth to through travails of his flesh, which the Lord himself wrapped in swaddling bands of blood, most precious. O holy child-birthing! O holy swaddling bands! The Word is everything to the newborn, both father and mother, tutor and nurse. *Eat my flesh*, he declares, *and drink my blood!* These are the well-adapted nourishments that he so generously supplies. He hands over his very flesh and pours out his very blood. Nothing is wanting for the children that they may grow.

Evening Prayer

Antiphon: Let us consume the Body and Blood of the Life-Giving Word.

Psalm 133:1–3 ✠ Psalm 15:1–11 ✠ Psalm 22:1–6

Scripture: Revelation 7:9–17

Reading: St. Clement of Alexandria, priest, Father of the Church † ca. 215

Christ the Educator 1.6.45.4–46.1; 1.6.47.2–3

The Lord said, *I have food to eat of which you do not know. My food is to do the will of the One who sent me.* You see here another kind of food, which figuratively, just like milk, represents the will of God. Besides, he also called the accomplishment of his sufferings, a "*cup*," in the sense that he alone had to drink it and drain it to the dregs. Just as the fulfillment of the Father's will was nourishment for Christ, so too, for us infants who suckle at the breast [*mastos*], that is the Word of Heaven, Christ himself is our food. Accordingly, the Greek verb *masteusai* "to suck," is a synonym for "to seek," for to the babes who seek the Word, the Father's breasts of love for humanity supply the milk. . . .

Thus via numerous ways is the Word figuratively portrayed: solid food, flesh, nourishment, bread, blood, and milk. The Lord is all these things for our refreshment, for those who have believed in him. Therefore, let no one think it strange that we speak figuratively of the blood of the Lord as milk. For isn't blood figuratively represented as wine when Scripture says, *he washes his garment in wine, his robe in the blood of the grape*? That means he will clothe the body of the Word with his own blood, just as he will suckle those who hunger for the Word with his own Spirit.

Day 3

Morning Prayer

Antiphon: Taste that the Lord is sweet.

Psalm 91:1–15 ✠ Psalm 130:1–3 ✠ Psalm 22:1–6

Scripture: Isaiah 66:9–13 TNK

Reading: St. Clement of Alexandria, priest, Father of the Church † ca. 215

Christ the Educator 1.6.42.3; 1.6.43.2—44.1

The Word is everything to the newborn, both father and mother, tutor and nurse. *Eat my flesh*, he declares, *and drink my blood!* . . . Listen to this interpretation: the flesh represents the Holy Spirit, for by the Spirit the flesh was created; and the blood suggests to us the Word, for as precious blood the Word has been poured over us for life. The union of the two is the Lord, nourishment for babes, the Lord: spirit and word. Our nourishment, which is the Lord Jesus, the Word of God, spirit made flesh, heavenly flesh made holy. This nourishment is the milk flowing from the Father, through whom alone, we infants are nourished. And he, the well-beloved Word, our Nursing Mother, has poured his blood out upon us, saving humanity. Therefore, having trusted in God, we fly to the "care-banishing breast" of the Father, which is the Word, in whom we find refuge. He alone, as is befitting, supplies to us babes the milk of love, and those alone are truly blessed who suck at this breast. With this in mind, Peter says, *Lay aside, therefore, all malice and all guile, hypocrisy, envy, and slander. As newborn babes, crave the spiritual milk so that thanks to it you may grow to salvation; if you have tasted that the Lord is sweet.*

Evening Prayer

Antiphon: His body became bread to give life to our mortality.

Psalm 1:1–6 ✠ Psalm 4:1–8 ✠ Psalm 103:1–34

Scripture: John 6:32–35

Reading: St. Ephrem, deacon, Father and Doctor of the Church † 373

Hymns on the Nativity 3.9

> Glory to That One who sowed his Light in the darkness,
> and the darkness was condemned by its vices that concealed its secrets.
> But the Light stripped off and removed from us the garment of filthiness.
> Glory to the Most High who mingled
> his Salt with our spirits, his Milk with our souls.
> His body became Bread to give life to our mortality.

Day 4

Morning Prayer

Antiphon: The Eucharist is the heavenly manna, the bread of angels.

PRAYING—WITH THE SAINTS—TO GOD OUR MOTHER

Psalm 107:1-6 ✠ Psalm 4:1-8 ✠ Psalm 22:1-6

Scripture: Wisdom 16:20-21

Reading: St. Augustine, bishop, Father and Doctor of the Church † 430

Commentary on the Psalms, Psalm 130 9

It is not without a reason, my brothers and sisters, that he speaks with such humility, *Lord, my heart is not lifted up, nor are my eyes raised on high; neither do I exercise myself in great things, nor in wonderful things above me. If I had not lowly thoughts but exalted my soul as someone taken from his mother's breast, such is the reward for my soul.* . . . I will explain this to you, beloved, as best I can. You know that our Lord Jesus Christ is the Word of God, according to these words of John, *In the beginning was the Word, and the Word was with God, and the Word was God. This one was with God in the beginning. All things were made through him, and without him nothing was made.* Therefore he is bread, from whence the angels draw life. Behold, the bread is prepared for you, but grow by means of the milk so that you may arrive at the bread. And how, you ask, do I grow by means of milk? That which Christ became for you on account of your weakness, this first believe, and steadfastly hold. Therefore as when a mother sees that her child is incapable of taking food, she nevertheless gives it food, namely sustenance that has passed through her flesh; for the bread upon which the infant feeds is the very same which the mother ate—the infant is not suited for eating at the dinner table but is suited for feeding from the breast. Therefore the bread is passed from the table through the mother's breasts so that the same sustenance might in turn reach the little infant. Accordingly, our Lord Jesus Christ when he was *the Word with the Father, through whom all things were made,* who, *being in the form of God, did not consider it robbery to be equal with God,* such as his angels might receive him according to their degree, and upon which the heavenly powers and virtues, namely intellectual spirits might feed, meanwhile humanity lay weak and enwrapped in flesh upon the earth, thus the heavenly bread could not reach humanity. Thus in order that humanity might feed upon the bread of angels, and so that the true manna might descend upon the truer People of Israel, *The Word was made flesh and dwelt among us.*

Evening Prayer

Antiphon: Let us approach the nipple of the Spiritual Cup.

Psalm 6:1-10 ✠ Psalm 15:1-11 ✠ Psalm 22:1-6

Scripture: 1 Corinthians 10:23-29

Reading: St. John Chrysostom, Patriarch, Father and Doctor of the Church † 407

Homilies on Matthew 82.5

Consider with what sort of honor you have been honored, from what sort of Table you are partaking. One which, when angels see it they tremble, and do not even dare to gaze upon it without awe on account of the brightness that radiates from it, with this sort of Table we are fed, with this we are compounded, and we are made one body and one flesh with Christ. *Who shall declare the mighty deeds of the Lord, and cause all his praises to be heard?* What shepherd feeds his sheep with his own limbs? And why do I say shepherd? There are often mothers that after the pangs of birth, hand over their children to other women to nurse them, but he does not permit this; rather, he himself nurtures us with his own Blood, and by every means possible intertwines us with himself.

. . . With each one of the believers does he mingle himself through the sacramental Mysteries, and to those whom he has given birth, he nourishes by himself and does not hand over to another. In so doing, he likewise persuades you again that he has taken your flesh. Let us not then be remiss, having been deemed worthy of so much, both of love and honor. Do you not observe infants, with how much eagerness they grasp the breast? with what earnest desire they firmly plant their lips upon the nipple? With the same desire let us also approach this Table, and the nipple of the spiritual Cup. Or rather, with much eagerness let us, like suckling babes at the breast, draw out the grace of the Spirit; let it be our sole angst, not to partake of this Nourishment.

Day 5

Morning Prayer

Antiphon: The Heavenly Manna is transformed to meet the needs of each recipient.

Psalm 118:145–52 ✠ Psalm 103:1–34 ✠ Psalm 131:1–18

Scripture: Nehemiah 9:18–21 TNK

Reading: St. Maximos the Confessor, monk, Father of the Church † 662

Centuries on Knowledge 1.100

The manna given to Israel in the wilderness is the Word of God which adapts those who eat it for every spiritual delight and which is *transformed to every taste according to the different desires of those who eat it*. For it possesses all the qualities of spiritual food. Thus for those who are born from above through the Spirit by an incorruptible seed it becomes authentic spiritual milk, and for those who are weak it is a medicinal herb to stimulate the passive faculty of the soul; for those who have trained the spiritual dimension of the soul by exercise, discerning good and evil, he gives himself as nourishment. The Word of God likewise has other infinite powers which cannot be described here on earth.

PRAYING—WITH THE SAINTS—TO GOD OUR MOTHER

Evening Prayer

Antiphon: You gave your Body and Blood for me, O Life-Giving Fount!

Psalm 15:1–11 ✠ Psalm 50:1–19 ✠ Psalm 22:1–6

Scripture: John 6:53–58

Reading: St. Nerses IV, Catholicos † 1173

Jesus, Son, Only-Begotten of the Father 748–54

> I who believe with all my soul and who adore you, the Only-Begotten,
> forgive me the faults that I have committed; may you not recall my past sins.
> Having fulfilled the words of Scripture and handed over your spirit to the Father,
> when the soldier pierced you with a lance a wellspring sprung
> from your sacred side:
> water to bathe in in the Holy Font, blood to drink in the Sacrament,
> because of the wound of she who was born from the side,
> through whom the first-formed man sinned.
> I who am mortal and born from sin, blood composed out of the dust,
> you have bathed me in the stream from your Side,
> and I, once again, am returned to my former state.
> Please don't let me remain in sin, but deign to wash me in your flow.
> If my petitions are not granted, at least let my sins be washed by my tears.
> Open my mouth to the stream of sacred Blood flowing from your side,
> like an infant at the breast who grasps its mother's nipple,
> so that I may drink with joy and exult in the Holy Spirit.
> May the taste of your Chalice become delicious,
> pure and perfect love of the Vine without admixture.

Day 6

Morning Prayer

Antiphon: A mother gives milk to her child, her very self.

Psalm 129:1–8 ✠ Psalm 79:1–19 ✠ Psalm 22:1–6

Scripture: Sirach 24:4, 22–31 VULG

Reading: St. Anthony of Padua, priest, Doctor of the Church † 1231

Sermons for the Second Sunday after Easter 2.3

> *I am the good shepherd.* Shepherd, or pastor, comes from the verb *pascere*, to feed. Every day Christ feeds us with his flesh and blood in the sacrament of the altar. . . .
>
> And so Jesus Christ feeds us each day with gospel teachings and the sacraments of the Church. In his arms outstretched on the Cross, he gathers us together. Thus John

says, *so that the children of God who are scattered might be gathered together into one*, and thus *he receives them into his bosom*. He lifts us to the bosom of his tender mercy as a mother with her child. In Hosea it says, *I was like a foster parent to the people of Ephraim; I carried them in my arms*. Christ nourishes us with his blood, as if it were milk. On Mount Calvary he was wounded for us with a lance in or under the breast so that he could supply us with his blood, as a mother gives milk to her child, and he has carried us in his arms, outstretched on the Cross.

Evening Prayer

Antiphon: Come to the Table!

Psalm 18:1–14 ✠ Psalm 4:1–8 ✠ Psalm 22:1–6

Scripture: Matthew 26:26–31

Reading: St. Nicholas Cabasilas, monk and priest † ca. 1391

Life in Christ 4.10

It is clear that we are personally invited to the Eucharistic Banquet in which we truly take Christ in our hands and receive him in our mouth by which we are commingled with him in soul, and united in body, and mingled in blood. And this is rightly so! For to those who receive the Savior and cling to him until the end, he himself is the Head that governs the body and they are members made fit for him. Consequently, the members should experience the same birth as the Head. That Flesh did not have its origin *from blood, nor from the will of the flesh, nor from the will of a man, but from God*, the Holy Spirit. *For that which was conceived in her*, it says, *is of the Holy Spirit*. Thus it is proper that the members likewise should be born in this way, since this birth of the Head was in fact the birth of the blessed members. For the birth of the Head, brought the members into existence, and if then, birth is the beginning of life so that to be born is to begin one's life, and Christ is the life of those who cling to him, then they were born of Christ when he entered this life and was born.

So tremendous, then, is the abundance of good things flowing from the Holy Table! It rescues from punishment; it wipes out the shame due to sin; it renews our youthful beauty; it binds us closer to Christ than any physical bond can. In short, of all the mysteries, the Eucharist perfectly perfects us in true Christianity.

Day 7

Morning Prayer

Antiphon: Christ nourishes us from his life-giving breast.

Psalm 142:1–12 ✠ Psalm 81:1–8 ✠ Psalm 18:1–14

Praying—With the Saints—To God Our Mother

Scripture: Isaiah 62:5–9

Reading: St. Gregory Palamas, archbishop † 1359

Homily 56

Christ has become our brother; uniting himself to our flesh and blood, he has assimilated himself to us.... He has bound himself to us, and in turn adapted us to himself, like a groom unites himself to the bride, by becoming a single flesh with us, through our communion with this Blood. Likewise, he has become our father through holy Baptism that conforms us to him, and he nourishes us from his own breast like a mother, full of tenderness, with her sucklings.... Come, says Christ, eat my Body, drink my Blood..., so that not only might you be in the image of God, but that you might become gods and sovereigns, eternal and celestial, by clothing yourselves in me, your Lord and God.

Evening Prayer

Antiphon: Jesus, Living Host, you are my Mother!

Psalm 21:1–11 ✠ Psalm 4:1–8 ✠ Psalm 22:1–6

Scripture: John 6:47–51

Reading: St. Faustina Kowalska, nun † 1938

Divine Mercy in My Soul 230, 249

Oh Jesus, Living Host, you are my Mother you are everything to me! With simplicity and love, with faith and trust, I will always come to you, O Jesus! I will share everything with you, just as a child does with its loving mother, my joys and sorrows—in a word, everything...

Jesus, I trust in you; I place my trust in the ocean of your merciful love. You are a Mother to me.

☥

The Mystery of Matrimony

Morning Prayer

Antiphon: God blesses the bonds of holy matrimony.

Psalm 5:1–12 ✠ Psalm 18:1–14 ✠ Psalm 127:1–6

Scripture: Tobit 8:4–8

Reading: St. Peter Chrysologus, archbishop, Father and Doctor of the Church † 450

Sermon 69.2

God was present to their desires, granted the prayers of individuals, responded quickly to what was asked, revealed what was hidden, predicted future events, uncovered what was sought after, conferred the kingdom, dispensed riches, regulated the rains, bestowed fertile lands, and with fecundity and honor blessed the bonds of holy matrimony with children. But God believed this to not be enough, if he were to demonstrate his deep affection for us by endowing us with prosperity, but not likewise endure our adversities. After all these signs, God entered the world in poverty, lay in a cradle: thus as a human being through his infant cries God implores, seeks, pleads for the very loving-kindness that he manifested to you. The Parent of All experienced you as parent, the One who is above everything, existed subjected to you.

Evening Prayer

Antiphon: Marriage reflects God's desire to be wedded to us.

Psalm 118:49–56 ✠ Psalm 18:1–14 ✠ Psalm 127:1–6

Scripture: Ephesians 5:21–33

Reading: St. Mechtild of Hackeborn, nun † 1299

Book of Special Grace 4.59

My dearest daughter in Christ, the Lover of your soul holds your hand in his right hand, holding each of your fingers in his, so that he might reveal to you how he operates in your soul and how you ought to follow him, imitating his example. . . .

The ring finger represents his faithful heart, which bears with tender care our worries, like the most faithful mother, raising our burdens and pains to his ineffable and faithful heart, protecting us from every evil.

THE MYSTERY OF RELIGIOUS PROFESSION (MALE)

Morning Prayer

Antiphon: Be wed to Wisdom and live in love.

Psalm 41:1–11 ✠ Psalm 49:7–15 ✠ Psalm 60:1–8

Scripture: Wisdom 8:16–21 LXX

Reading: St. Bernard of Clairvaux, abbot, Doctor of the Church † 1153

Letter 322

 To his very dear son in Christ, Hugh, *a new creature in Christ*, that he might be encouraged in the Lord, from Brother Bernard, called Abbot of Clairvaux.

 Upon hearing of your conversion, *we rejoiced and our hearts were filled with joy*. Why shouldn't men be glad and angels rejoice? Already it is a day of celebration, a day resounding in heaven with voices raised in praise and thanksgiving. A noble youth, genteel, has conquered the evil one, scorned the world, mortified his flesh, renounced the affection of his parents, and soared above the snares of the rich by taking wing. Where does such wisdom come from, my son? Not even among the ancients of Babylon was such wisdom found. According to, or contrary to the teaching of the Apostle, they were those who wished to become rich and so fell into temptation, the devil's snare for them. But the Wisdom of our Hugh is celestial, not terrestrial. *I give you praise, Father, that you have hidden this from the wise* and have revealed it to a child. You, also my son, ought to thank our Redeemer for this gift, and *keep the innocence of a child with the thoughts of grown men*. Do not allow the roughness of our monastic life to frighten your tender years. Remember, "the rougher the thistle, the softer the cloth." The sweetness of Christ will take away the inedible taste from the prophet's portion of the flour-cake. When you experience the venomous stings of temptation, fix your gaze on the Bronze Serpent raised on the staff, and suck the wounds of the Crucified as if they were breasts. He will be a mother to you, and you will be his son.

Evening Prayer

Antiphon: Those who prove victorious will be dressed in white robes.

Psalm 118:57–64 ✠ Psalm 49:7–15 ✠ Psalm 60:1–8

Scripture: Revelation 3:1–6

Reading: St. Peter Damian, cardinal bishop, Doctor of the Church † 1072

On the Perfection of Monks 1

 Call to mind what was said to the angel of the church of Sardis, *Be vigilant and strengthen the things that remain, that are about to die; for I do not find your works to be complete before my God.* Since the angel did not find his works to be completed before God, he testified that even those things which had been done well were on the verge of death. Consequently, if that which is dying within us is not kindled into life, what remains alive in us will soon be extinguished. Certainly one loses the benefit of the work one has done if the labor is not brought to completion. What benefit is it if a body begins to be formed in a mother's womb and does not attain the fullness of natural development? You know very well concerning what child it was said, *When a woman is in labor she experiences sorrow, because her hour has come; but as soon as she has given birth to a child, she no longer remembers the anguish, filled with joy that a human being is born into the world.*

The Mystery of Religious Profession (Female)

Morning Prayer

Antiphon: Be wed to Wisdom and live in love.

Psalm 44:1–17 ✠ Psalm 49:7–15 ✠ Psalm 60:1–8

Scripture: Wisdom 8:16–21 LXX

Reading: St. Melito of Sardis, bishop, Post-Apostolic Father of the Church † ca. 180

Hymn Papyrus Bodmer XII

> Hymn the Father, you holy ones;
> sing to your Mother, you virgins.
> —We hymn, we exalt God exceedingly, we the holy ones.
> You have been exalted by becoming brides and bridegrooms,
> for you have found your Bridegroom, Christ.

On Faith, fragment 15

> We have gathered from the Law and the Prophets those things which have been predicted about our Lord Jesus Christ, so that we may demonstrate to your Charity that he is perfect Mind, the Word of God who was born *before the morning star*. He is the Creator with the Father, the fashioner of Man, who was *all things in all*:

> among patriarchs a patriarch,
> in the Law a law,
> among the priests a chief of priests,
> among the kings a captain,
> among the prophets a prophet,
> among the messengers a messenger,
> in the utterance a Word,
> among the spirits a Spirit,
> in the Father a Son,
> in God a God,
> Ruler for ever and ever.

Evening Prayer

Antiphon: Those who prove victorious will be dressed in white robes.

Psalm 118:57–64 ✠ Psalm 49:7–15 ✠ Psalm 60:1–8

Scripture: Revelation 6:9–11

Reading: Bl. John Paul II, pope † 2005

Orientale Lumen 9

I would also like to recall the resplendent witness of nuns in the Christian East. This witness has presented us with an example of great value in the Church to what is specifically feminine, even going beyond the mentality of the time. Throughout recent persecutions, particularly in Eastern European countries, when numerous male monasteries were forcibly closed, female monasticism kept the torch of monastic life burning brightly. The nun's charism, with its own unique characteristics, is a visible sign of the motherhood of God which the Sacred Scriptures often recall.

The Mystery of Holy Orders

Morning Prayer

Antiphon: Offer yourself as a living sacrifice to God.

Psalm 54:1–16 ✠ Psalm 109:1–7 ✠ Psalm 131:1–18

Scripture: Hosea 2:19–20, 23 LXX

Reading: St. Faustina Kowalska, nun † 1938

Divine Mercy in My Soul 239

Prayer during the Mass on the day of the perpetual vows: Today I place my heart on the paten where your heart has been placed, O Jesus, and today I offer myself together with you to God—your Father and mine—as a sacrifice of love and adoration. Father of Mercy, look upon the sacrifice of my heart, but gaze upon it through the wound in the Heart of Jesus.

Union with Jesus on the day of perpetual vows: O Jesus, from now on your Heart is mine, and mine is yours alone. The very thought of your Name, Jesus, is the delight of my heart! Truly I would not be able to live for a moment apart from you, Jesus. Today my soul has lost itself in you, my only treasure. My love experiences no obstacles in giving proof of itself to its Beloved.

The words of Jesus during my perpetual vows: *My Bride, our hearts are joined together forever. Remember to whom you have consecrated yourself . . . I cannot put everything into words.*

My petition while we were lying prostrate under the pall: I begged the Lord to grant me the grace to never deliberately or consciously offend him by even the littlest sin or imperfection.

Jesus, I trust in you! Jesus, I love you with all my heart! When times are most difficult, you are my Mother.

Evening Prayer

Antiphon: You are a priest forever, according to the Order of Melchizedek.

Psalm 138:1–14 ✠ Psalm 109:1–7 ✠ Psalm 131:1–18

Scripture: Hebrews 10:1–14

Reading: St. Ephrem, deacon, Father and Doctor of the Church † 373

Hymn on the Resurrection 3.7–9

> The Royal Son, in his bold-facedness,
> came to marry the Church of his people.
> Just as he had proven his love and fidelity,
> He united her to himself, and himself to her,
> so that there would no longer be any separation.
> Thus she is seated in the Royal Palace,
> clothed in royal raiment.
> The month of Nisan celebrated the wedding,
> bedecked and bejeweled with flowers.
> Glory to You, O Lord of Nisan.
> In the month of Nisan the flowers rip open
> their buds and blossom forth.
> Their blossoms spring forth, fresh and naked,
> and become a crown for others.
> The month of Nisan is the Feast of Feasts,
> in it the Great High Priest ripped open his bosom,
> and the priesthood fled.
> It left the priesthood laying their naked
> and clothed our naked Lord.
> Blessed be the Just One who reclaimed what was his!
> It was in the month of Nisan that the Spirit saw
> the great high priest Caiaphas,
> from whom was torn away the priesthood,
> despoiled of the sacerdotal office.
> She tore open the Temple curtain.
> The Spirit went forth; She made all things come forth.

For the Sanctuary where the services were celebrated,
saw that it no longer had a priest to minister in it.
The True High Priest entered the Eternal Temple.
Blessed be he through whom worship is now resplendent!

The Mystery of Anointing of the Sick

Morning Prayer

Antiphon: God works through the hands of the doctor.

Psalm 64:1–13 ✠ Psalm 29:1–12 ✠ Psalm 22:1–6

Scripture: Sirach 38:1–15

Reading: St. Francis de Sales, bishop, Doctor of the Church † 1622

Consoling Thoughts 2.21

Often the remedies and medicines prescribed by doctors and pharmacists are rejected by the sick, but if they are offered by the hand of someone they love, love overcomes the fear, and they receive the medicine with joy. And in the case of a little sick child, without seeing its mother, simply by the knowledge it has of her desire, takes everything brought to it, eating it without taking any delight in it, because it doesn't enjoy eating or have the consolation of seeing its mother, but simply eats and swallows to do her will. My God, why doesn't the good pleasure of our Lord in a similar fashion always make bitterness palatable, pains delightful, and struggles desirable, even when God would be satisfied with it?

Evening Prayer

Antiphon: God's holy oil heals us.

Psalm 140:1–5 ✠ Psalm 102:1–22 ✠ Psalm 22:1–6

Scripture: James 5:13–16

Reading: St. Francis de Sales, bishop, Doctor of the Church † 1622

Consoling Thoughts 3.3

Take care of yourself very cautiously as long as your present illness continues. Don't be worried at all about not forcing yourself to do any kind of exercise, unless it's done gently. You get tired praying on your knees, then sit up. If you don't have the mental attention to pray for half an hour, then pray for a quarter, or only half that. I beg you to place yourself in the presence of God, and to suffer your sorrows before him. . . .

Don't hold back from complaining when you want to, but I ask that you tell your complaints to God with a filial attitude, as a tender child would towards its mother. For as long as it is done lovingly, there is no danger in complaining, or in begging for a cure, or in changing positions, or in seeking comfortability; only do so with love, resigning yourself into the loving arms of the most holy will of God. It's foolish to imagine that you don't make any acts of virtue well; for, as I previously told you, they do not cease to be good even though they are performed languidly and with great heaviness as if by force. You can only give God what you have, and during this time of affliction, you don't have any other good works you can do.

The Mystery of Last Rites

Morning Prayer

Antiphon: As a loving mother, God is with us at our hour of death.

Psalm 72:1–28 ✠ Psalm 21:1–23 ✠ Psalm 22:1–6

Scripture: Wisdom 2:23—3:9

Reading: St. Mechtild of Hackeborn, nun † 1299

Book of Special Grace 4.7

If a person wishes to offer me an acceptable gift, let him strive to exercise himself in these three things. First, let him try to be faithful to his neighbor whenever he or she is in need or in trouble, and, as much as possible, to lessen and excuse all that person's defects and sins. If the person shall do this, then I will be faithful in everything for which he might have a need, and I will overlook all his sins and failings, and make an excuse for him before my Father. Second, let the person strive to take refuge in me alone in all his tribulation, nor let him complain of his trouble to anyone, but to me alone let him open up with confidence every grievance of his heart. Such a person I shall never forsake in his time of need. Third, let the person endeavor to walk with me in truth, and then at his last hour, just as a mother receives her loving child, I shall receive him into my parental embrace, and he shall rest forever more.

Evening Prayer

Antiphon: May the God of peace, make you perfect and holy in body, soul, and spirit.

Psalm 133:1–3 ✠ Psalm 21:1–23 ✠ Psalm 22:1–6

PRAYING—WITH THE SAINTS—TO GOD OUR MOTHER

Scripture: 1 Thessalonians 5:23–24

Reading: Bl. Marguerite of Oingt, prioress † 1310

A Page of Meditations 47–49, 51–53

Sweet Lord, what shall I do in that hour when I shall not be able to help or take care of myself, when my mouth and eyes will be closed and my soul will be separated from my body? Then my enemies will be before and behind me; they will struggle so persistently that they will be able to tempt me. One will tempt me to go against the faith, another allure with vainglory, another will try to make me despair.

Sweet Lord, what shall I do and what will become of me in that terrible hour, that is, at my end and on the Day of Judgment? Sweet Lord, what shall I do then? In which hand will you set me, and in which place will you place me?

Sweet Lord, I beseech you and ask you because of your great mercy that you look at me in that hour with those benevolent eyes with which you looked at my master, the blessed Peter, and that you grant me the protection of your holy faith and the sign of your holy Passion. I beg of you that you give me such firm perseverance that I will be beyond all fear and all doubt. . . .

And I beseech you that you give me virtue and grace in that hour so that I can invoke and cry out to you and commend my soul to you as from a good heart; and I pray that you receive my soul through the hands of your holy angels.

And I beg of you, Sweet Lord, that you will not allow me to pass from this life before you have purified me completely.

Sweet Lord, I have no father or mother except for you, and you know that I love you with all my heart and that I desire nothing else than to be with you.

THE GRIEVING PROCESS

Morning Prayer

Antiphon: Mourn and honor the dead with faith in God's triumphant love.

Psalm 91:1–15 ✠ Psalm 37:1–22 ✠ Psalm 6:1–10

Scripture: Sirach 38:16–23

Reading: St. Francis de Sales, bishop, Doctor of the Church † 1622

Consoling Thoughts 3.11

As a gentle mother, leading her little child with her, helps it to walk, carries it when she sees the need, allows it to take a few steps by itself in areas less dangerous and quite level, sometimes taking it by the hand and steadying it, and sometimes lifting it up in her arms and carrying it for awhile, likewise our Lord has continual care for the conduct of his children. Sharing love with them, he makes them walk in his presence, holding out to them his hand in the midst of difficulties and carrying them himself in their trials which he sees would otherwise be unbearable. He has declared this through Isaiah, *I am you God, taking you by the hand, and saying to you: You have nothing to fear; I have helped you.* And this guidance, so full of sweetness, God maintains with regard to our souls since their inception into love until the time of final perfection, which is only effected at the hour of death. *Whoever perseveres to the end, shall be saved.*

Evening Prayer

Antiphon: God's maternal compassion consoles us.

Psalm 1:1–6 ✠ Psalm 101:1–28 ✠ Psalm 83:1–12

Scripture: 2 Corinthians 1:3–9

Reading: St. Francis de Sales, bishop, Doctor of the Church † 1622

Consoling Thoughts 4.4

O how my soul is pained for your heart, my dearest mother! For I seem to see this poor maternal heart all weighed down with an extreme anguish, an anguish, however, which we cannot blame or consider strange if one remembers how lovable this son of yours was. . . . My dearest mother, it is true, this dear son was one of the best that ever lived; everyone who knew him knew it and acknowledged it. But is this not a great part of the consolation that we ought to take now, my dearest mother? For, honestly, it seems to me that those whose lives are worthy of memory and esteem, live on even after their departure; since we find so much pleasure in recalling them to mind, and representing them to the minds of others who remain.

He has departed from this world to enter into that which is the most desirable of all, and to which we must all go, each in his own time, and where you will see him sooner than you would perhaps have seen him, if he had remained in this world. . . .

Let us not be grieved, we shall all be reunited soon. We incessantly go on and approach that place where our beloved departed are, and in two or three moments, we shall be there. Let us think only about making steady progress and to pursue every good which we saw in them. I beg of you, my dearest daughter, to place your heart at the foot of the Cross and accept the death and the life of all those whom you love, for love of the One who gave his life and accepted death for your sake. . . .

When you recommend your child to the Divine Majesty, simply say, "O Lord, I recommend to you, the child of my bowels, but more so the child of your bowels of mercy, born of my blood, but born again of yours."

The Mystery of the Final Resurrection

Prayer

Antiphon: Love is as strong as Death. The Spirit of God, the Spirit of Love, restores relationships.

Psalm 5:1–12 ✠ Psalm 60:1–8 ✠ Psalm 29:1–12

Scripture: Romans 8:1–11

Reading: St. Aphraates, priest, Father of the Church † ca. 350

Demonstrations 6.14

Regarding the one who will have preserved the Spirit of the Messiah in purity, this is what she will say concerning him when she returns to the Messiah, "The body in which I went and which I was clothed in the waters of baptism has kept me in holiness." The Holy Spirit will beseech the Messiah to resurrect the body which guarded her in a pure fashion. She, the Spirit, will seek also to be reunited with him in order that the body may be resurrected in glory. But the person who will have received the Spirit in the waters of baptism and grieved her, she will flee him even before he dies, and she will go away according to her condition, approaching the Messiah to lodge a complaint against this person who has grieved her.

When the moment of the final consummation will come and the moment of the resurrection approach, the Holy Spirit who will have been safeguarded in purity, she will receive a great impulsion corresponding to her condition. She will come before the Messiah; she will stand watch at the doors of the tombs, there where the people guarded her in purity, and she will await the cry.

When the watchers will have opened the doors of heaven before the King, then the trumpet will sound, the trumpets will blare, and the Spirit who awaits the cry, she will hear them. In all haste, she will open the tombs; she will resurrect the bodies and those who are buried in the graves; she will clothe again in glory the one who comes with her.

The Liturgical Calendar:
Fixed Feast Days

January 1 — The Solemnity of Mary, Mother of God

Morning Prayer

Antiphon: God is glorious in his holy ones.

Psalm 5:1–12 ✠ Psalm 80:1–14 ✠ Psalm 44:1–17

Scripture: Micah 5:1–3

Reading: From St. Maximos the Confessor, monk and Father of the Church † 662

Letter 13

Once again, we believe that the person of Christ is not divisible into two natures, into divinity and humanity. For just as when we speak of the two natures of Christ, we think of his divinity and humanity as a whole comprised out of parts, we speak of a union comprised of two natures and believe in a whole person in divinity and humanity. The "parts" of Christ of which he is constituted are his divinity and humanity. I repeat, through St. Cyril [of Alexandria] we have learned to believe in, speak about, and proclaim a 'single nature of the Word of God Incarnate' in a body possessing a rational and intellectual soul. And by "incarnate" we mean that he inhabited the being of our nature; that there is only one Christ who worked miracles and experienced the Passion; that there are two births: the one without a corporeal nature before the ages, born of the Father, and one in time, with a bodily nature, born of the Virgin Mary for our sakes. For this reason, we properly and truly confess her to be the Mother of God since God the Word who was born before the ages, was at the end of time born through her and made flesh.

Evening Prayer

Antiphon: Maternally compassionate and gracious is Yahweh,

slow to anger and abounding in steadfast love. (Psalm 103:8 TNK)

Psalm 133:1–3 ✠ Psalm 80:1–14 ✠ Psalm 44:1–17

Scripture: Micah 7:18–20 TNK

Reading: From St. Maximos the Confessor, monk and Father of the Church † 662

Letter 13

The person of Christ, which is singular and complete, is not divisible by any term according to his characteristics and properties into extremes. When I think of extremes I speak of God the Father from whom before the ages Christ was born in a divine fashion, and of the holy and glorious Virgin and Mother from whom the same was born in a human fashion for our sakes. . . . By recognizing the differences in the [divine and human] properties of Christ, the singular person of Christ is not divided.

January 6—The Solemnity of the Epiphany

Morning Prayer

Antiphon: Kings shall come and bow before you, offering gifts.

Psalm 5:1–12 ✠ Psalm 71:1–12 ✠ Psalm 80:1–14

Scripture: Isaiah 60:1–6

Reading: St. Augustine, bishop, Father and Doctor of the Church † 430

Sermon 199.3

One cannot believe that Christ's birth was determined by any sort of astrological decree, for the Magi saw the star in the East only after Christ had been born. This clearly demonstrates, therefore, that Christ was not born under its dominion, but rather that he himself appeared as the One having dominion over the star, for the star did not keep to its shining path in the celestial constellations, but instead pointed out to those who were seeking Christ the path to the very place where he had been born. Thus it wasn't the star that wondrously caused Christ to appear with life; on the contrary, Christ wondrously caused the star to appear. Nor did the star determine the miracles of Christ; rather, Christ determined the appearance of the star among the other miracles. He himself, when born of his mother, caused a new star to appear in the heavens to shine on earth, just as when born of the Father he fashioned the heavens and earth. . . . So let us celebrate with devout solemnity this day on which the Magi, who from among the Gentiles, having recognized the Christ, worshipped him.

Evening Prayer

Antiphon: We saw his star and have come to worship.

Psalm 133:1–3 ✠ Psalm 80:1–14 ✠ Psalm 71:1–12

Scripture: Matthew 2:1–12

Reading: St. Nerses IV, Armenian Catholicos † 1173

Jesus, Son, Only-Begotten of the Father 328–31

> First, by your Divine Spirit
> the soul of the Holy Virgin was sanctified,
> and the Power of your Heavenly Father,

covered her in its shadow.
Then, you, the Only-Begotten Son,
you freely descended into her bowels
you became flesh truly,
God and Man, the two forming but one.
You were born with our human body,
you who were born first of all by the Father without a body.
You have taken away the sorrows of the first-formed human,
whom you covered with leaves, thanks to your swaddling clothes.
O you, the Word, in the manger of speechless animals,
have become the food of those endowed with speech.
O you, the Light, manifested by the light of the star,
the Magi have come to adore you, thanks to its light.

January 25—Feast of Paul's Conversion

Morning Prayer

Antiphon: Although apostles, we were as gentle with you as a nursing mother with her children.

Psalm 5:1–12 ✠ Psalm 80:1–14 ✠ Psalm 118:169–76

Scripture: Acts 9:1–8

Reading: St. Anselm of Canterbury, archbishop, Doctor of the Church † 1173

Prayer to St. Paul 10.205–26

Then both of you [Christ and Paul] are mothers. For even if you are fathers, you are nevertheless mothers. For you have brought it about, you, O Christ, through yourself, and you Paul through him, that born to death, we might be reborn to life. Therefore you are fathers because of your effect; you are mothers because of your affect; fathers because of your authority, mothers because of your affability; fathers by your protection, mothers by your compassion. Thus you, Lord, are a mother, and you too, Paul. Even if you do not possess the equality in the quantity of your affection, yet in quality you are not unalike. Although regarding the greatness of your kindness you are not co-equal, nevertheless, in the will you are one of heart. Though you do not possess equal fullness of compassion, still in intention you are not discordant.

Why should I keep silent about what you have said? Why should I conceal what you have openly proclaimed? What reason is there to hide what you have done? You have revealed yourselves as mothers; I know myself to be your son. I give you thanks for having brought me forth as a son when you made me a Christian. You, O Lord, in yourself, and you, O Paul, through him. You by the teaching that you established, and you by the teaching which inspired you. You by the grace that you granted me; you by the grace which you received from him.

Paul, my mother, Christ also bore you, therefore place your dead son before the feet of Christ, your mother, because he is also Christ's son. What am I saying? Better yet throw him into the bosom of Christ's tenderness, since he is even more so his mother. Pray that he will bring back to life a dead son, who is not so much yours as his. Pray for your son, for you are his mother, that Christ might revive your son, for he is his mother as well. Do, Mother of my soul, what the mother of my flesh would do. If she were to hope, she would certainly pray as much as she could and would not cease until she had obtained what she could. Certainly if you so desire it, you cannot despair, and if you pray, you can obtain your request. Insist then that this dead soul which you gave birth to as alive might be restored to life; do not cease pleading until it is given back to you alive.

Evening Prayer

Antiphon: The maternal tenderness of God was displayed through Paul.

Psalm 133:1–3 ✠ Psalm 80:1–14 ✠ Psalm 84:1–13

Scripture: 1 Thessalonians 2:5–12

Reading: Bl. Guerric of Igny, abbot † 1157

Second Sermon for the Feast of Saints Peter and Paul 2–3

When Christ left them [and ascended to heaven], the celestial spirits rejoiced that the Only-Begotten had returned, being solicitous, however, for the newly adopted progeny, they appeared to have been moved with pity and petitioned, "Who will nourish them? You suckled them, but you weaned them before they were ready. You didn't raise them to become young men, nor bring the young maidens to full term of their growth. Who will nourish them? *Our sister is little and does not yet have breasts.* You said to Peter, *Pasture my sheep.* But he himself does not have enough milk in his breasts. His tender care will quickly cease to flow, for even still he fears more about his own hide than the souls of these little ones. He will readily abandon the sheep when tempted, he who when interrogated, denied you, his Shepherd, who are also theirs."

But then suddenly the Holy Spirit was sent from heaven, poured out like milk from the very breasts of Christ, and Peter was filled with abundant milk. And soon after, Saul was transformed into Paul, the persecutor became the predicator, the torturer—the mother, the butcher—the nurse; thus you see clearly that his [murderous] blood was transformed into sweet milk, his cruelty into tenderness. These two breasts [Peter and Paul], being attached to her chest, the Church glories that she is not only a fecund mother, but also a fortified city: *I am,* she exclaims, *a walled-city and my breasts are towers.*

February 2—Feast of the Presentation of the Lord

Morning Prayer

Antiphon: I have consecrated myself to you, O God.

Psalm 5:1–12 ✠ Psalm 26:1–13 ✠ Psalm 64:1–13

Scripture: Malachi 3:1

Reading: St. Nerses IV, Armenian Catholicos † 1173

Jesus, Son, Only-Begotten of the Father 334–36

> You who are the Law-giver, according to the Law
> you entered into the Temple to be offered there.
> And you who are the Ancient of Days,
> you were caressed as an infant, in the holy arms of the elder.
> I, who through sin, was born into sin,
> you have birthed me anew in your Holy Font.
> I have been stripped by the trickery of the Evil One;
> I have sunk again into the mire of my sins.
> Purify me once again by your birth,
> by offering me to the Father who is in heaven,
> Through the supplications of the Mother of God,
> and the prayers of Simeon the Elder.

Evening Prayer

Antiphon: Behold the Lord has suddenly entered his Temple.

Psalm 137:1–8 ✠ Psalm 83:1–12 ✠ Psalm 27:1–9

Scripture: Luke 2:22–40

Reading: St. Hippolytus, bishop, martyr, Father of the Church † 235

Commentary on Luke 2

> Now we proclaim that the Word of God was the first-born, coming down from heaven to the Blessed Mary, and was formed as a first-born human in her womb, so that the first-born of God might be manifested in this union with the first-born human. Now when they brought him to the Temple to present him to the Lord, they fulfilled the oblations of purification. For if the gifts of purification required by the Law were offered on his behalf, then in this wise he was made under the Law; but if the Word was not subjected to the Law as the slanderers imagine, he being the Law

itself, neither did God need sacrifices of purification, for God purifies and sanctifies everything in a single moment. However, since he took upon himself the constitution of a human being as he received it from the Virgin, and became under the Law, and was purified according to the demands of the first-born, it was not because he needed this ceremony that he underwent its cleansing, but in order that he might redeem from the bondage of the Law those who were sold under the judgment of its curse.

February 22—Feast of the Chair of St. Peter

Morning Prayer

Antiphon: You are Peter, and upon this rock I will build my church.

Psalm 5:1–12 ✠ Psalm 80:1–14 ✠ Psalm 60:1–8

Scripture: Deuteronomy 32:15–18 TNK

Reading: St. Francis de Sales, bishop, Doctor of the Church † 1622

The Consoling Thought of St. Frances de Sales, ed. Rev. Pere Huguet, trans. Fr. Pustet (New York: Fr. Pustet and Co., 1857), 137–38; unplaced to the 18th French edition

St. Paul has told us that every thing turns to good for those who love God. Every thing turns to their welfare, even their faults, and sometimes the most grievous faults. God permits those faults in order to heal a vain presumption, and to teach us what we are, and of what we are capable. David acknowledged that the adultery and homicide into which he had fallen served to keep him in continual distrust of himself. *It is a blessing for me*, he says to God, *that thou hast humbled me; I have been more faithful since to thy commandments.* The fall of St. Peter was a most useful lesson to him, and the humility with which it inspired him disposed him to receive the gifts of the Holy Ghost, and to become head of the Church, and preserved him amid the dangers of so eminent a position. St. Paul, during the period of his greatest success in the apostleship, preserved himself against pride and vanity, by remembering that he had been a blasphemer and a persecutor of the Church of God. A humiliating temptation, from which God would not deliver him, served as a counterpoise to the sublimity of his revelation.

If God knows how to draw advantage even from the greatest sins, who can suppose that he will fail to turn our daily faults to our sanctification? It is a remark made by the masters of spiritual life, that very often God leaves in the holiest souls some defects, which, notwithstanding all their endeavors, they cannot eradicate. He acts thus in order to make them feel their weakness; to show them what they could be without grace, to guard them from the inflation of vanity on account of His favors, to dispose them to receive other benefits with greater humility, to keep a holy self-hatred alive in their breasts, to withdraw them from the snares of self-love, to preserve their fervor and confidence towards Him, and to teach them the necessity of having continual recourse to prayer. The child that tumbles when it wanders a little distance from its mother, returns to her with greater tenderness, and from experience learns not to quit her in a hurry again. The lesson it has received on its own weakness and its mother's goodness, inspires it with a livelier affection for her.

Evening Prayer

Antiphon: Like newborn babes, crave pure spiritual milk, so that thanks to it, you may grow up into salvation, since you have tasted that the Lord is good.

Psalm 133:1–3 ✠ Psalm 80:1–14 ✠ Psalm 113A:1–9

Scripture: 1 Peter 1:3–5 NT

Reading: Homily of an Apostolic Father of the Church, second century

2 Clement 14:1–3

So then, brothers and sisters, by doing the will of God our Father we shall be members of the first Church, the spiritual one, that was created before the sun and the moon. But if we fail to fulfill the will of the Lord, we shall become as those mentioned in Scripture, *My house has become a den of thieves*. We must, therefore, choose to be members of the Church of Life in order to be saved. I don't suppose you're unaware that the living Church is *the Body of Christ*; for Scripture says, *God created humanity male and female*. Now the male represents Christ and the female the Church. Furthermore, the Sacred Books and the Apostles teach that the Church doesn't belong to the present, but existed from the very beginning. For she was spiritual, as was our Jesus, but was manifested in the last days so that she might save us. Now the Church, being spiritual, was manifested in the flesh of Christ to show us that if any of us guard her in the flesh and don't corrupt her, that person shall receive her again in the Holy Spirit, for this flesh is a copy of the Spirit.

MARCH 19—SOLEMNITY OF JOSEPH, HUSBAND OF MARY

Morning Prayer

Antiphon: I fostered them like one who raises an infant to his cheeks.

Psalm 5:1–12 ✠ Psalm 80:1–14 ✠ Psalm 102:1–22

Scripture: Hosea 11:1–4 TNK

Reading: St. Ephrem, deacon, Father and Doctor of the Church † 373

PRAYING—WITH THE SAINTS—TO GOD OUR MOTHER

Hymns on the Nativity 4.146–54

> Mary bore a mute babe
> but in him were concealed all our tongues.
> Joseph carried him, yet hidden in him
> was the Silent Nature older than anything else.
> He laid down like a little Child, yet hidden in him
> was the treasury of Wisdom that is sufficient for everyone.
> He laid down and he sucked Mary's milk,
> yet all creatures take suck from his blessings.
> He is the living Breast of life-giving breath;
> from his life the dead were suckled, and they came back to life.
> Without the breath of air no one can live;
> without the Power of the Son no one can exist.
> Upon the life-giving breath of the One who makes all alive
> depend the living beings above and below.
> As in truth he sucked Mary's milk,
> he has given suck: to the universe, life.
> As indeed he dwelt in his mother's womb,
> in his Womb dwells all creation.

Evening Prayer

Antiphon: Christ is the firstborn of many brothers and sisters.

Psalm 133:1–3 ✠ Psalm 80:1–14 ✠ Psalm 102:1–22

Scripture: Luke 2:41–52

Reading: St. Bede the Venerable, priest, Father and Doctor of the Church † 735

Homily on the Gospels 1.6

It happened, [the Evangelist] says, *that while they were there the days for her to give birth were fulfilled, and she gave birth to her first-born son.* He calls the Lord "first-born," not because we are to believe that the blessed Mother of God gave birth to other children after him, (it is true that she is commendable for her unique perpetual chastity with her husband, Joseph), but because he properly names him "first-born" since John says, *But to as many as received him he gave them the power to become children of God*. Among these children he rightfully holds the primacy, who before he was born in the flesh was Son of God, born without any beginning. He descended to earth, however, became a sharer in our nature, and lavished upon us a share in his grace, so that, as the Apostle remarks, *he should be the first-born of many brothers and sisters*.

March 25 — Solemnity of the Annunciation

First Evening Prayer

Antiphon: I have called my Fair One, my Beloved.

Psalm 133:1–3 ✠ Psalm 80:1–14 ✠ Psalm 102:1–22

Scripture: Luke 1:26–35 PESH

Reading: St. Ephrem, deacon, Father and Doctor of the Church † 373

Hymns on the Nativity 21.6–8

> The Power that governs the universe dwelt in a confined womb.
> While dwelling there, she held the reins of the universe.
> Her Parent was ready for his will to be accomplished.
> The heavens and all creation were filled by her.
> The Sun entered the womb, and in the height and depth
> its rays permeated.
> He dwelt in the vast wombs of all of creation;
> they were too small to contain the immensity of the Firstborn.
> How indeed did the small womb of Mary suffice?
> It's a wonder that it sufficed, if not, what perplexity!
> Of all the wombs that contained him, a single sufficed:
> the Womb of the Great One who engendered him.
> But the womb that did contain him, if it contained all of him,
> is somehow equal to the wonderful Womb of the Great One
> who gave birth to him.
> But who would dare say that a womb so constricted,
> weak, and abject, is equal to the womb of the Infinite Being?
> It is out of compassion that he dwelt there and since his nature is immense,
> he was not limited in the slightest.

Morning Prayer

Antiphon: Mary became the Tabernacle of God Most High.

Psalm 5:1–12 ✠ Psalm 80:1–14 ✠ Psalm 102:1–22

Scripture: Wisdom 6:12–20 LXX

Reading: St. Gregory of Nyssa, bishop, Father and Doctor of the Church † ca. 395

On the Three-Day Period of the Resurrection

The Holy Spirit came upon the Virgin and the Power of the Most High overshadowed her in order to constitute in her a New Man. He is called "New" because he is created in a divine manner and not according to human intercourse so that he might become a receptacle not made by human hands for God. For the Most High does not dwell in hand-crafted objects, I mean those things constructed by human beings. Now when Wisdom was constructing a house for herself, and by the overshadowing of her power the form had been molded within as if by the impress of a seal, then the divine power intermingled with both elements out of which the human nature is constituted, namely soul and body, having intermixed herself in each correspondingly. For since these two had experienced death because of disobedience, (since death is the alienation of the soul from real life, and for the body means corruption and decay), death had to be kicked out of the house by the insertion of life into both of these parts.

Second Evening Prayer

Antiphon: I am well-pleased with my handmaid.

Psalm 133:1–3 ✠ Psalm 80:1–14 ✠ Psalm 102:1–22

Scripture: Proverbs 9:1–6, 11 TNK

Reading: St. Augustine, bishop, Father and Doctor of the Church † 430

Sermon 225.2

Do not fear, Mary. You have found favor with God. You shall conceive and bear a son and name him Jesus. When the angel made this announcement to her, she asked, *How shall this happen, since I do not know man?* If she were planning to know a man, she would not be astonished. That astonishment testifies to her vow. *How shall this happen since I do not know man?* How shall it happen? And the angel replied, *The Holy Spirit shall come upon you.* There you have the answer to your question. *And the Power of the Most High shall overshadow you; and therefore the Holy One to be born of you shall be called the Son of God.* The angel spoke well in saying, *shall overshadow you*, to preserve your virginity from experiencing the heat of passion. And when she was pregnant, the Gospel says about her, *Mary was found to be with child by the Holy Spirit.* Therefore, the Holy Spirit brought about the flesh of Christ; and the only-begotten Son of God brought about his own flesh. How do we prove this? Because Scripture says: *Wisdom has built for herself a house.*

June 25 — Solemnity of the Birth of John the Baptist

Morning Prayer

Antiphon: You shall go before the Lord to prepare straight paths.

Psalm 5:1–12 ✠ Psalm 80:1–14 ✠ Psalm 84:1–13

Scripture: Luke 1:57–80

Reading: St. Ephrem, deacon, Father and Doctor of the Church † 373

Hymns on the Nativity 27.14–18

> The Greatest of all, entirely descended to unspeakable humiliation.
> He returned from that humiliation to seize the unlimited majesty
> of the Right Hand.
> It's a great wonder that from such height he did not proceed little by little
> to descend and embrace such smallness.
> [Rather] he flew from the Womb of Divinity to humanity.
> The sun, your sun, announces your mystery as if by mouth.
> In the winter, as your type, it descends to a low level;
> In summer, like you, it ascends on high and rules over all.
> Also the type of your conception, my Master, and that of John your Herald,
> the mystery of both your conceptions and births,
> by light and darkness are portrayed and revealed to the observant.
> The conception of John took place in Tishri
> (around October) when darkness prevails.
> Your conception took place in Nisan
> (around April) when the light reigns over darkness and subdues it.

Evening Prayer

Antiphon: I send my messenger ahead of you.

Psalm 133:1–3 ✠ Psalm 80:1–14 ✠ Psalm 113B:9–19

Scripture: Matthew 11:7–15

Reading: St. Peter Chrysologus, archbishop, Father and Doctor of the Church † 450

Sermon 89.5–6

> *In the days when Herod was king of Judaea*, it states, *there was a certain priest named Zechariah of the order of Abijah, and his wife was a descendant of Aaron; her name was Elizabeth. Furthermore, both of them were righteous in the eyes of God, and*

proceeded blamelessly according to all the commandments and precepts of the Lord.... Both of them, it says, *were righteous in the eyes of God.* This is a novel happiness; it is a unique marriage, when one mind dwells in two people, one holiness in two persons. What was separated by sex was united by mind, what was double in appearance was one in conduct; and virtue made the same those whom nature brought forth as different. *Both of them*, it says, *were righteous in the eyes of God.* To be pleasing according to human judgment, to be righteous in the eyes of human beings comes from superior human virtue and achievement. But in the eyes of God, who scrutinizes hearts, discerns thoughts, perceives the workings of the mind, to be righteous does not come from human achievement, but is a divine gift. If one is great who does not sin in the flesh, how much greater is the person who does not sin in the heart? Thus John was born of more than just the flesh of those who in the eyes of God sinned neither in heart nor body.

The evangelist added the following: *Proceeding blamelessly according to all the commandments and precepts of the Lord.* Proceeding—someone proceeds who does not stand in the paths of sinners, who realizes that he or she is a sojourner in this world, who without trepidation enters the mansions of the virtues albeit they are difficult to traverse. Such a person is a tireless traveler climbing the mountains of God's precepts and the high places of the commandments so as to enjoy completely the presence of God our Parent in the blessedness of the heavenly homeland.

June 29—Solemnity of Sts. Peter and Paul

Morning Prayer

Antiphon: We are God's co-workers while you are his cultivation, his construction.

Psalm 5:1–12 ✠ Psalm 80:1–14 ✠ Psalm 121:1–9

Scripture: 1 Corinthians 3:1–11

Reading: Bl. Guerric of Igny, abbot † 1157

Second Sermon for the Feast of Saints Peter and Paul 2–3

When Christ left them [and ascended to heaven], the celestial spirits rejoiced that the Only-Begotten had returned, being solicitous, however, for the newly adopted progeny, they appeared to have been moved with pity and petitioned, "Who will nourish them? You suckled them, but you weaned them before they were ready. You didn't raise them to become young men, nor bring the young maidens to full term of their growth. Who will nourish them? *Our sister is little and does not yet have breasts.* You said to Peter, *Pasture my sheep.* But he himself does not have enough milk in his breasts. His tender care will quickly cease to flow, for even still he fears more about his own hide than the souls of these little ones. He will readily abandon the sheep when tempted, he who when interrogated, denied you, his Shepherd, who are also theirs."

But then suddenly the Holy Spirit was sent from heaven, poured out like milk from the very breasts of Christ, and Peter was filled with abundant milk. And soon after, Saul was transformed into Paul, the persecutor became the predicator, the torturer—the mother, the butcher—the nurse; thus you see clearly that his [murderous] blood was transformed into sweet milk, his cruelty into tenderness. These two breasts [Peter and Paul], being attached to her chest, the Church glories that she is not only a fecund mother, but also a fortified city: *I am*, she exclaims, *a walled-city and my breasts are towers*.

Evening Prayer

Antiphon: God wishes to bring to us birth by the word of truth.

Psalm 133:1–3 ✠ Psalm 80:1–14 ✠ Psalm 18:1–14

Scripture: James 1:13–18 NT

Reading: Bl. Guerric of Igny, abbot † 1157

Second Sermon for the Feast of Saints Peter and Paul 2

The Bridegroom himself, *in the days of his flesh*, had engendered several children *by the word of truth* and as long as he remained with them he suckled them at the breasts of edification and consolation. Now the Bridegroom certainly has *breasts better than wine*, that is to say, better than the teachings of the Law or the joy of this world. The Bridegroom truly has breasts so that nothing should be lacking to him of all the duties and titles of loving-kindness. He is father by virtue of the natural creation and of the regeneration which comes through grace, and also by virtue of his authority regarding instruction and discipline. He is a mother as well in the gentleness of his affection, and a nurse because of the constant personal attention and solicitous care that maternal duty requires. These little ones, therefore, that he nourished were *like the first fruits of his creatures*, but only a first offering, and there remained a great deal of care and work to be done to bring them to perfection, *until Christ was formed in* them.

June 30—Synaxis of the Twelve Apostles (East)

Morning Prayer

Antiphon: You are part of a building that has the Apostles for its foundation.

Psalm 5:1–12 ✠ Psalm 80:1–14 ✠ Psalm 121:1–9

Scripture: Ephesians 2:11–22

Reading: St Ephrem, deacon, Father and Doctor of the Church † 373

PRAYING—WITH THE SAINTS—TO GOD OUR MOTHER

Hymn on the Crucifixion 3.16–17

> It is in you, O Sacred Place, that amazement took place,
> among the disciples, due to what they heard.
> Never have birth pangs seized a mother
> like they seized the Twelve.
> They wanted to keep quiet, but they couldn't.
> They wanted to speak, but they didn't dare.
> The sheep signaled the Lamb:
> Teach us! Who is the wolf?
> Take the leather satchels, he said.
> Then they took on the appearance of dead ones,
> laying inert in Sheol.
> He showed that he would be killed like a man,
> that he would not be able to nourish, even though a Nursing Mother.
> Then, however, he was resurrected so that they might learn
> that it is he who nourishes all flesh.
> Dead, he ceased to function, but alive, once again,
> he nourished, in order to show that he had been dead and made alive.

Evening Prayer

Antiphon: This mystery has been revealed through the Spirit to the holy Apostles.

Psalm 133:1–3 ✠ Psalm 80:1–14 ✠ Psalm 126:1–5

Scripture: Ephesians 4:1–13

Reading: St. Irenaeus, bishop, Post-Apostolic Father of the Church † 202

Against Heresies 3.24.1

The preaching of the Church is everywhere consistent, continuing in congruency, receiving testimony from the prophets, apostles and all of their disciples, just as I have demonstrated. This testimony encompasses "the beginning, the middle and the end," in short, the totality of the dispensation of God and the infallible operation ordained for the salvation of humanity, namely, our Faith. This Faith, which we have received from the Church, we preserve with great care and unceasingly by the Spirit of God. Such a deposit of great worth sealed in an excellent vessel, renews itself and the very vessel which contains it.

It is to the Church herself, in fact, that has been entrusted this "Gift of God," just as the breath of life was bestowed upon the first-formed human, this is so that all the members might partake of it and thereby be vivified. It is in her that has been deposited the communion with Christ, that is, the Holy Spirit, the down-payment of incorruption, the confirmation of our faith, and the ladder of our ascent to God.

For *In the Church* it is said, *God has established apostles, prophets, teachers* and all the other means by which the Spirit operates. . . . For there where the Church is, there also is the Spirit of God; and there where the Spirit of God is, there is the Church and every grace, for the Spirit is Truth. That is why those who exclude themselves from the Spirit, no longer nourish themselves from the breasts of their Mother with regard to true life; neither do they partake from the resplendent fountain which issues from the Body of Christ.

July 22—Mary Magdalene (Equal of the Apostles— East)

Morning Prayer

Antiphon: You are part of a building that has the Apostles for its foundation.

Psalm 5:1–12 ✠ Psalm 80:1–14 ✠ Psalm 121:1–9

Scripture: Ephesians 2:11–22

Reading: St. Peter Chrysologus, archbishop, Father and Doctor of the Church † 450

Sermon 80.6

And Jesus met them and said, May you be well! Christ met those women who faithfully hurried [from the Tomb], so that what they had believed by faith they might acknowledge by sight, and that he might by his presence strengthen those women who were in the throes of trepidation due to what they had heard. *Jesus met them, saying, May you be well!* Christ met them as Lord, greeted them as Parent, animated their affection, and thus checked their fear.

Evening Prayer

Antiphon: Christ appeared first to Mary of Magdala who went and told the apostles.

Psalm 133:1–3 ✠ Psalm 80:1–14 ✠ Psalm 85:1–17

Scripture: John 20:1–18

Reading: St. Francis de Sales, bishop, Doctor of the Church † 1622

Consoling Thoughts 1.15

It is very true that we need to have a great deal of confidence to abandon ourselves, without any reserve, to Divine Providence; but when we do completely abandon ourselves, Our Lord takes care of everything and guides everything. Now if we withhold something which we do not confide in him, he leaves us as if saying, "You consider yourself smart enough to handle that without me; you can do so. You'll see what will happen."

St. Mary Magdalene, who completely abandoned herself to Our Lord, remained at his feet and listened while he spoke. And when he stopped speaking, she ceased listening, but she never budged from his presence. Thus her soul, abandoned to Our Lord, rested in his arms like a child in its mother's bosom, who, when she puts it down to walk, walks until its mother picks it up again, and when she carries it, allows itself to be carried. The child doesn't have a care in the world where it is or is going, but it allows itself to be carried or led as its mother pleases. Likewise, the soul that loves the will and good pleasure of God in everything that happens to it, either allows itself to be carried or walks if need be, accomplishing with great care everything indicated by the will of God.

August 6—Solemnity of the Transfiguration

Morning Prayer

Antiphon: The glory of God shone through the humanity of Christ. Alleluia!

Psalm 5:1–12 ✠ Psalm 80:1–14 ✠ Psalm 8:1–9

Scripture: Matthew 17:1–8

Reading: St. Francis de Sales, bishop, Doctor of the Church † 1622

Consoling Thoughts 4.14

But you will say to me, "Since we shall converse with and listen to all those who will be in this heavenly Jerusalem, what shall we say? What shall we speak about? What will be the subject of our conversation?" God! I tell you, and what a subject! It will be about the mercy of God shown to us here below, by which he made us capable of entering into this joy of this blessed bliss in which the soul shall have nothing more to desire, for in this word bliss are summed up all sorts of goods, which are nevertheless only one Good which consists in the enjoyment of God.

But again, what shall we discuss in our conversation? We shall talk about the passion and death of our Lord. Do we not learn this in the Transfiguration when he speaks of nothing other than the summit of the sufferings he must experience in Jerusalem, nothing other than the death of the Divine Savior? Oh if we could comprehend something of the consolation the blessed shall experience when speaking of this death, how much our souls would delight in thinking about it! . . .

What shall we do, dear souls, what will become of us, I ask you, when we shall behold the most adorable and lovable heart of our Divine Master, through the sacred wound of his side, all aflame with the love he bears us, a heart in which we shall see our names written in letters of love? Oh, is it possible, we shall then say to our Divine

Savior, 'You have loved me so much that you have engraved my name in your heart and in your hands?' Notwithstanding, this is absolutely true. The prophet Isaiah, speaking in the person of our Lord, declares, *Even if a mother should happen to forget her child which she carried in her womb, yet I shall never forget you for I have engraved your name on my hands.* But our Lord, sweetly improving on these words, shall say to us, "Not only have I engraved your name on my hands, but on my very heart as well." A subject, indeed, of the greatest consolation, to see that we are so dearly loved by our Lord that he carries us always in his heart!

Evening Prayer

Antiphon: Behold the face of God and marvel.

Psalm 133:1–3 ✠ Psalm 80:1–14 ✠ Psalm 16:1–15

Scripture: 2 Peter 1:16–18

Reading: St. Maximos the Confessor, monk, Father of the Church † 622

Letter 14

One becomes a pure worshipper of this mystery by confessing the One above, who was born of the Father before all ages, and who was born below for our sakes at the end of the ages, of a mother, by assuming flesh endowed with a rational and intellectual soul. This is why we rightly and in truth believe that the Holy Virgin Mother of God, pregnant with the Word in place of any seed, carried in her womb and gave birth to what became incarnate from her, the same who worked miracles, who freely experienced human suffering, crucifixion, entombment, resurrection on the third day according to the Scriptures, and bodily ascension into heaven, from whence he had descended to us without a body.

August 15 — Solemnity of the Assumption of Mary

Morning Prayer

Antiphon: The virtuous one sought to please God, and so God displayed love.

The virtuous one was living among sinners, and thus has been taken up.

Psalm 5:1–12 ✠ Psalm 44:1–17 ✠ Psalm 80:1–14

Scripture: Sirach 44:16

Reading: Syro-Malankara Rite

PRAYING—WITH THE SAINTS—TO GOD OUR MOTHER

Vespers for the Presentation of Mary in the Temple

Praise to the Eternal Light which shone forth from the Eternal Light and sprang forth from the virgin's womb, the womb of his mother, the hope of life. To whomever magnifies and honors the memory of his mother in heaven and on earth, belongs glory, honor, and praise. . . . Therefore, we beseech you, O Full of Grace, since you have liberality of speech before Immanuel, born from you, ask for us that we may truly be born again through his living and eternal word. As flesh can only give birth to flesh, and it is the Spirit who gives birth to spirit, obtain for the Church, your Son's bride, those gifts and charisms of the Holy Spirit, which are her bridal garment.

Evening Prayer

Antiphon: Mary pondered and had faith, knowing that God had prepared a place for her.

Psalm 133:1–3 ✠ Psalm 80:1–14 ✠ Psalm 44:1–17

Scripture: Revelation 12:1–6

Reading: St. Bede the Venerable, priest, Father and Doctor of the Church † 735

Homily on the Gospels 1.7

Mary, however, preserved all these words, pondering them in her heart. Mary, maintaining the rules of virginal modesty, didn't wish to divulge to anyone the secret things which she knew about Christ, but she reverently waited for that time and place when he would want to divulge them. Although her mouth was silent, in her careful and vigilant heart she examined these secret matters. Now this is what the Evangelist says, *pondering in her heart*. She pondered those things which she has seen in relation to those matters which she had read were to take place. Now she saw that she herself was from the stock of David springing up in Nazareth and had conceived God's Son of the Holy Spirit. She had read in the Prophet, *A shoot shall sprout from the root of Jesse, and a nazareus will ascend from his root, and the Spirit of the Lord will rest upon him.* She also had read, *And you, O Bethlehem Ephrata, are a little one among the thousands of Judah; out of you shall come forth from me the one who is Ruler in Israel, and his coming forth is from the beginning, from the days of eternity.* She saw that she had given birth in Bethlehem to the Ruler of Israel, who was born from all eternity from the Father, God before the ages.

August 29—Beheading of John the Baptist

Morning Prayer

Antiphon: John bore witness to Christ in his life and his death.

Psalm 5:1–12 ✠ Psalm 80:1–14 ✠ Psalm 21:1–23

Scripture: 2 Kings 2:1–15

Reading: St. Aphraates, priest, Father of the Church † ca. 350

Demonstrations 6.13

>   Regarding John [the Baptist], our Lord testifies that he is the greatest of the prophets; but he received the Spirit by measure, since John had acquired a spirit of the same type as Elijah had received. Just as Elijah dwelt in solitude, so too did John. The Spirit of God, She drove him to dwell in the desert, in the mountains and in the caves.
>
>>   Elijah—the flying raven nourished him;
>>   John ate the flying locust.
>>   Elijah was girded with a leather cincture about his loins;
>>   John girded his loins with a leather belt.
>>   Elijah—Jezebel persecuted him;
>>   Herodias persecuted John.
>>   Elijah reprimanded Ahab;
>>   John reprimanded Herod.
>>   Elijah parted the Jordan;
>>   John opened baptism.
>>   Elijah—the double portion of his spirit rested on Elisha;
>>   John imposed his hands on our Savior who received the Spirit without measure.
>>   Elijah opened the heavens and ascended;
>>   John saw the heavens open and the Spirit of God,
>>   She descended and rested on our Savior.

Evening Prayer

Antiphon: The herald is summoned before an earthly king, to appear before the Heavenly King.

Psalm 133:1–3 ✠ Psalm 80:1–14 ✠ Psalm 109:1–7

Scripture: Matthew 14:3–12

Reading: St. Ephrem, deacon, Father and Doctor of the Church † 373

Hymns on the Nativity 21.1–2

> Regarding the birth of the First-born, on his feast day let us speak forth.
> On his day he proffered hidden means of help.
> If the impure [Herod] on his own feast in commemoration of his birth
> offered a gift of anger, a head upon a platter
> how much more will the Blessed One grant blessings
> to the one who sings on his feast.

September 8—Feast of the Birth of Mary

Morning Prayer

Antiphon: I am the mother of fair love.

Psalm 5:1–12 ✠ Psalm 39:5–10, 17 ✠ Psalm 21:3–5, 9–11, 22–23

Scripture: Sirach 24:4, 22–31 VULG

Reading: Bl. Guerric of Igny, abbot † 1157

Second Sermon on the Nativity of Mary 1

> I am the mother of fair love, and of reverence, and of knowledge, and of holy hope. Perhaps you'll remember that last year when I commented on the beginning of this text which we read today, I applied it to the Blessed Mother of God, not improperly, I believe. Nevertheless, I did not reject the interpretation according to which all of this reading properly pertains to her Son, who is the Wisdom of God.

Evening Prayer

Antiphon: There is an appointed time for every matter under heaven: a time to give birth.

Psalm 4:1–8 ✠ Psalm 39:5–10, 17 ✠ Psalm 21:3–5, 9–11, 22–23

Scripture: Genesis 3:9–20

Reading: St. Hippolytus, bishop and martyr, Father of the Church † 235

Sermon on Elchana and Anna

> Tell me, O Blessed Mary,
> what was conceived by you in your womb,
> and what was borne by you in your virginal matrix?
> For it was the Word,
> the First-born of God,

who descended from heaven to you,
and was formed in your womb
as a first-born human,
so that the First-born Word of God
might be shown to be united
with a first-born human.

SEPTEMBER 14—FEAST OF THE EXALTATION OF THE CROSS

Morning Prayer

Antiphon: Wisdom is a Tree of Life.

Psalm 5:1–12 ✠ Psalm 80:1–14 ✠ Psalm 3:1–8

Scripture: Proverbs 3:13–19 TNK

Reading: St. Quodvultdeus, bishop, Father of the Church † 450

On the Creed 1.6.4–5, 9–11

Let our Bridegroom ascend the wood of his bridal chamber; let our Bridegroom ascend the wood of his marriage bed. Let him sleep by dying; let his side by opened, and let the virgin Church emerge from within. Just as Eve was made from the side of Adam while he slept, so too the Church was formed from the side of Christ while he hung on the Cross. For his side was pierced, as the Gospel recounts, and immediately there flowed forth blood and water which are the twin sacraments of the Church: the water in which the Bride is cleansed; the blood which became her dowry. . . . Rejoice, rejoice, O Bridal Church, for if these things had not taken place in Christ, you would not have been formed from him. Sold, he bought you back! Killed, he loved you; and because he loved you so much, he willingly died for you. Oh the great sacrament of this marriage! Oh how great the mystery of this Bridegroom and Bride! Human words fail to explain it! From out of the Bridegroom the Bride is born and as she is being birthed, she all at once is united to him.

Evening Prayer

Antiphon: Let us glory in the Cross of our Lord Jesus Christ.

Psalm 133:1–3 ✠ Psalm 80:1–14 ✠ Psalm 42:1–5

Scripture: Galatians 6:14–16

Reading: St. Augustine, bishop, Father and Doctor of the Church † 430

Sermon 218.6

Because the placard [on the Cross] was written in three languages, namely Hebrew, Greek, and Latin, this amounts to a declaration that he would reign not only over the Jews, but over the Gentiles as well. Thus, in the same passage of the Psalm where it says, *But I have been appointed king on Zion his holy mountain,* where of course the Hebrew language ruled the day, it continues as though Greek and Latin were subordinate, *The Lord has declared to me, You are my Son, today I have given birth to you: ask of me, and I will give you the nations for your inheritance, and as your possessions even the ends of the earth.*

September 29—Feast of the Archangels

Morning Prayer

Antiphon: Blessed be God; blessed by all his holy angels. (Tobit 11:14)

Psalm 34:1–10 ✠ Psalm 102:1–22 ✠ Psalm 91:1–16

Scripture: Daniel 7:9–10; 12:1–3

Reading: St. Ephrem, deacon, Father and Doctor of the Church † 373

Hymns on the Faith 4.1–3

> A thousand thousands stood in place, ten thousand ten thousands rushed about.
> Thousands and ten thousands were not capable of investigating the One.
> All of them, therefore, stood in silence to serve him.
> He has no companion except the Offspring that is from him.
> Seeking him must be in silence. When watchers began to investigate
> they confronted silence and were restrained.
> The Firstborn entered a womb, but the pure one did not perceive it.
> He arose and emerged with birth pangs, and the fair one felt him.
> Glorious and hidden was his entry, but human at his exit.
> What wonder and consternation to hear: Fire entered the womb,
> clothed itself in a body and emerged. . . .
> Gabriel, that chief of the angels, hailed him as Lord.
> He called him Lord to teach that he is his Lord and not his equal.
> For Gabriel, Michael is his equal.
> The Son is the Lord of the servants. His nature is as awesome as his name.
> A servant is not capable of investigating him since,
> no matter how much the servant becomes greater,
> the One whose servant he is, is far greater than he.

Evening Prayer

Antiphon: God makes his angels winds, and his servants flames of fire.

Psalm 103:1–4 ✠ Psalm 137:1–8 ✠ Psalm 148:1–14

Scripture: Hebrews 1:1–9 NT

Reading: St. Ephrem, deacon, Father and Doctor of the Church † 373

Paschal Hymn 13.13–15

> He was spat upon, the Lord of the Universe,
> upon whom even the seraphim cannot fix their gaze.
> Cherubim and seraphim, at the moment he was offended,
> they hid their faces, fearing to even look.
> When they mocked him, Michael trembled.
> Gabriel likewise, was astonished, stupefied, and perplexed.

NOVEMBER 1—SOLEMNITY OF ALL SAINTS (WEST)

Morning Prayer

Antiphon: Wisdom has sent forth her servants.

Psalm 5:1–12 ✠ Psalm 80:1–14 ✠ Psalm 30:1–24

Scripture: Proverbs 9:1–6 TNK

Reading: St. Hippolytus, bishop and martyr, Father of the Church † 235

Commentary on Proverbs 9

Christ, meaning, the Wisdom and Power of God the Father, *has built a house for herself*, taking flesh from the Virgin, just as John previously said, *The Word became flesh and made his dwelling among us*. So too, the wise prophet bears witness: She who existed before the world was made, and who is the source of life, She who is the infinite, *The Wisdom of God, she has built a house for herself*, through a mother who knew no man, specifically when assuming the temple of the body. *And she has raised her seven pillars*; that is, the fragrant grace of the all-Holy Spirit, as Isaiah says: *And the Seven Spirits of God shall rest upon him*. Some others allege that the seven pillars are seven divine ranks that uphold the creation by the holy and divinely inspired doctrine; namely, the prophets, apostles, martyrs, hierarchs, hermits, saints, and the righteous ones. Regarding the phrase, *She has slaughtered her beasts*, this refers to the prophets and martyrs who in every city and country are slain like sheep day and night by the unfaithful. They are killed on behalf of the Truth, crying aloud: *For your sake we are killed all day long, we were reckoned as sheep for the slaughter*. And again, *She has mingled her wine* in the bowl, meaning that the Savior, uniting the divinity like pure wine with the humanity in the Virgin, was born of her both God and human without confusion of the one in the other.

The verse, *And she has furnished her table*, refers to the promised knowledge of the Holy Trinity. It also denotes the most precious and undefiled Body and Blood which are administered day after day and sacrificially offered at the mystical divine table, as a memorial of that first and most memorable table of the mystical and divine supper. And again the phrase, *She has sent forth her servants*, namely Wisdom has done so in Christ, summoning them together with raised proclamation. By the line, *Let whoever is simple come to me*, she proclaims, demonstrably alluding to the holy apostles who traveled the whole world, and summoned the nations to knowledge of her in truth with their sublime and divine preaching. And again, *And to those who desire understanding she said*, that is to say, to those who have not yet received the power of the Holy Spirit—*Come and eat my bread and drink the wine I have mingled for you*. By this Wisdom means, that she gave her divine flesh and most precious blood to us, to eat and drink of it for the remission of sins.

Evening Prayer

Antiphon: Behold the great cloud of witnesses on every side.

Psalm 133:1–3 ✠ Psalm 80:1–14 ✠ Psalm 131:1–18

Scripture: Hebrew 12:1–4

Reading: *Syrian Liturgy for Martyrs*

The martyrs were clothed with the armor of the Holy Spirit and like eager warriors they embraced the combat in order to receive the crown of martyrdom. And the Holy Spirit joined them, and like a mother with her children, she lovingly encouraged them saying: Behold the moment when the watchers above are content and the devil is angry and trembling, seeing your crowns and the garment of glory in which you are robed, O victors!

The Spirit, she says to the martyrs in combat: Do not fear my beloved ones. I enter into the fray with you. I strengthen you so that you can fight and win and take the crown. The pains and tortures that the servants of error prepare for you, I will render them mild and acceptable to you, that is why you need not fear them.

The blessed martyrs go up to the heavenly Jerusalem. The Spirit, she meets them and greets them saying: Welcome, my brothers and my children, babes of the heavenly paradise. Come in and inherit the kingdom of eternal life.

November 2 — Feast of All Souls (West)

Morning Prayer

Antiphon: Now let us honor the illustrious dead, our ancestors in their successive generations.

Psalm 5:1–12 ✠ Psalm 80:1–14 ✠ Psalm 21:1–23

Scripture: Sirach 44:1–15

Reading: St. Mechtild of Hackeborn, nun and mystic † 1299

Book of Special Grace 5.8

There was on the top of [the deceased Brother's] head an amazingly ornate crown in which one especially saw an ornament of the Lord's Passion, by which one knew what special devotion he had regarding the Lord's Passion. Admiring it, [Mechtild] said to the Lord, "O my sweetest God, why was this soul so quickly taken out of the world, which could have done so much good by way of word and example?" The Lord responded, "His ardent desire brought it about; he is to me as a weaned child resting upon its mother [breast], so that his soul cleaved to me, and for that reason he merited to find rest in me. His merit and glory had been accepted such as it was because to a considerable extent his expectation preceded it. And in that expectation I myself caused him to find rest on my breast."

℘ 📖 ☙

Evening Prayer

Antiphon: You have been placed with the spirits of the saints who have been made perfect.

Psalm 133:1–3 ✠ Psalm 80:1–14 ✠ Psalm 30:1–24

Scripture: Hebrew 12:18–24

Reading: St. Francis de Sales, bishop, Doctor of the Church † 1622

Consoling Thoughts 4.13

The most sweet St. Bernard, while still a youth residing at Chatillon-sur-Seine, on the night of Christmas, waited in the church until the divine office started, and as the poor child waited he fell into a light slumber during which he saw in the spirit, a vision being quite vivid and clear, how the Son of God, having espoused human nature and become a little infant in the bowels of his mother, was virginally born from her sacred womb with a humble gentleness mixed with celestial majesty. This vision so filled his heart with such great joy that throughout all his life he experienced intense recollections of it and the memory of this mystery concerning the birth of his Master always brought him spiritual joy and unparalleled consolation.

Alas! If a mental vision of the temporal birth of the Son of God so powerfully ravished and delighted the heart of a child, well then, what will it be like when our minds gloriously illumined by the blessed brilliance, shall behold that eternal birth by which the Son proceeds, God from God, divinely and eternally born from God? Then shall the soul be deified, filled with God and made like God, by an eternal and immutable participation in God who unites with the soul as fire inflames the iron which it permeates, communicating its light, splendor, warmth and other properties, to such an extent that one takes it for the same fire.

November 21—Presentation of Mary in the Temple

Morning Prayer

Antiphon: He has clothed her with the robe of salvation, like a bride adorned with her jewels.

Psalm 5:1–12 ✠ Psalm 26:4–9 ✠ Psalm 64:1–13

Scripture: Wisdom 7:7–14 LXX

Reading: St. Maximos the Confessor, monk, Father of the Church † 662

Ambigua 1.41

The Wisdom and Intelligence of God the Father is the Lord Jesus Christ who encompasses the universe of all created things by the power of his wisdom, and contains all their constitutive parts through his intelligence, being by nature the Creator and Supervisor of all creation. By bringing into unity through his person everything which is distanced from him, he resolved their conflict, and reunited into a peaceful friendship and indivisible concord everything which is in the heavens and on the earth, as the divine Apostle said.

The natures are made new once again. The Divine Nature accepts a physical birth like our own, something prodigious and voluntary by the goodness and immeasurable loving kindness that God has for humanity. Our own nature produces a paradoxical birth without seed, for a God who is outside the body but who becomes incarnate in flesh endowed with a rational soul, outside the laws of natural reproduction, yet indistinguishable from our nature except being without sin. What is most paradoxical is none of the norms of virginity were diminished except that this birth rendered her a mother. A most proper innovation, not only because God the Word who was born without any beginning in an indescribable fashion from God the Father is now born in time and in the flesh, but also because our nature produces flesh without any seed and a virgin gives birth without any loss of virginity.

Evening Prayer

Antiphon: She served God in the Temple, night and day, with fasting and prayer.

Psalm 137:1–8 ✠ Psalm 83:1–12 ✠ Psalm 27:1–9

Scripture: 1 Corinthians 3:16–17; 6:19–20

Reading: Syrian liturgy, *Syro-Malankara Rite, Sunday before the Nativity*

Praise to the Eternal Child who for our salvation came to a second birth in the flesh from the Virgin, full of grace. To him belongs glory, honor, and praise, at this time of the Evening Prayer. . . When we ponder the wondrous mystery of your saving grace, O Christ our Lord and God, and your first eternal birth from God and your second and saving birth from Mary, we give thanks for your power beyond reckoning and the abundance of your compassion and mercy. Although your eternal birth was hidden and concealed from the angelic watchers, by your will and that of your Father as well as your Holy Spirit, you descended to the second birth out of love so that you might rescue us from our servitude to our captor.

December 8—Solemnity of the Immaculate Conception of Mary (West)

Feast of the Conception by St. Anna of Mary (East)

First Evening Prayer

Antiphon: Wisdom will never stay in a body in debt to sin.

Psalm 39:5–10, 17 ✠ Psalm 80:1–14 ✠ Psalm 38:1–13

Scripture: Wisdom 1:4–7 LXX

Reading: St. John of Damascus, priest, Father and Doctor of the Church † 749

The Orthodox Faith 3.1

By the good pleasure of God the Father, the Only-Begotten and Word God, who has his being within the bosom of God the Father, one in essence with the Father and the Holy Spirit, he existed before the ages and without any beginning. The Only-Begotten, who existed in the beginning and was with God the Father and was God, being in the form of God, bent down the heavens and descended; that is to say, he humbled without humiliation his lofty standing and condescended to his servants with a condescension both ineffable and incomprehensible, for this is what the descent signifies. And God, being perfect, became a perfect human being, bringing to perfection the newest of all new things, the only new thing under the sun, through which the infinite power of God is manifested. For what is greater than for God to become human? Now without undergoing change, the Word became flesh by the Holy Spirit and of the Holy and Ever-virgin Mary, Mother of God, presiding as Mediator between God and Man. He, the only lover of humanity, was conceived in the immaculate womb of the Virgin not by the will, or desire, or co-operation of a male, nor by pleasurable generation, but by the Holy Spirit and the first offspring of Adam. And he became obedient to the Father by healing our disobedience through a nature like ours which he assumed, even by becoming for our sake a model of that obedience without which it is impossible to obtain salvation.

Morning Prayer

Antiphon: I have called you from your mother's womb.

Psalm 5:1–12 ✠ Psalm 39:5–10, 17 ✠ Psalm 80:1–14

Scripture: Wisdom 7:21–26 LXX

Reading: St. Hildegard of Bingen, abbess † 1179

Letter 47

    Indeed, Man whom you formed is deceived by the devil. Thus all human nature is contaminated because every human being is conceived in sin by carnal desire. Furthermore human nature has become perverted and crooked so that no human being can deliver another from the captivity of the devil. Wherefore in yourself, [O Holy Divinity], you ordained an earthly garment for your Son drawn from virgin soil, produced by the seed of no one, whose warm blood was heated by the warmth of the Holy Spirit. This garment is born from flesh as an egg which when a hen broods over it, keeping it warm, brings forth a chick. In this fashion the Virgin bore a Son by the warmth of the Holy Spirit brooding over her, and as a little chick would never hatch from the egg without the warmth of the hen, so too the Virgin never would bring forth a Son without the warmth of the Holy Spirit.

Second Evening Prayer

Antiphon: When he took her to himself she was holy and immaculate.

Psalm 133:1–3 ✠ Psalm 39:5–10, 17 ✠ Psalm 80:1–14

Scripture: Ephesians 5:25–32

Reading: St. Ephrem, deacon, Father and Doctor of the Church † 373

Hymns on the Nativity 16. 8–11

> You aren't simply a human being that in an ordinary fashion
> I would sing you a lullaby. For your conception is a novelty
> and your birth is a miracle. Without the Spirit
> who could sing to you? A new utterance
> of prophecy stirs within me.
> What shall I call you, you who are so different from us,
> yet become one of us? Shall I call you Son?
> Shall I call you Brother? Or shall I call you Bridegroom?
> Shall I call you Lord, you who gave birth to [me] your mother
> according to a new birth out of [your] waters?
> For I am [your] sister from the House of David,
> who is a second father [to you]. I am also mother
> because of your conception [in me], and bride
> because of your sanctifying chastity; handmaid and daughter
> by means of [your] blood and water, I whom you redeemed and baptized.
> Son of the Most High who came to dwell in me
> by means of a second birth. He bore me as well
> by a second birth. I put on the glory of him
> who put on the body, the garment of his mother.

DECEMBER 25 — SOLEMNITY OF THE BIRTH OF CHRIST

Morning Prayer

Antiphon: It was one and the same who from all eternity and always is the Son of God, born of the Father, who began to be the Son of Man at a point in time, born of the virgin (Augustine, *Sermon* 186.1).

Psalm 5:1–12 ✠ Psalm 109:1–7 ✠ Psalm 39:5–10, 17

Scripture: Isaiah 9:5–6

Reading: St. Augustine, bishop, Father and Doctor of the Church † 430

Sermon 184.3

> Born of his mother he sanctioned this day for the ages, while born of his Father, he created all ages. That birth could have no mother, while this one required no man as father. In short, Christ was born both of a Father and of a mother; both without a father and without a mother; of a Father as God, of a mother as a human being; without a mother as God, without a father as a human being. Therefore, *Who shall declare his begetting*, whether that one without time or this one without seed; that one without beginning or this one without precedent; that one which never ceased to be, or this

one which never was before or after; that one which has no end, or this one which has its beginning in its final purpose?

Rightly, therefore, did the prophets announce that he would be born, while the heavens and angels announced that he truly had been born. The one who sustains the world lay in a manger, inarticulate infant and yet Word. Him whom the heavens cannot contain, the womb of one woman bore.

Evening Prayer

Antiphon: Born of a Father without any time of day, he was born of a mother this day! (Augustine, *Sermon* 186.3).

Psalm 133:1–3 ✠ Psalm 109:1–7 VULG ✠ Psalm 39:5–10, 17

Scripture: Luke 2:1–20

Reading: St. Augustine, bishop, Father and Doctor of the Church † 430

Sermon 185.1

Today is called the birthday of the Lord on which the Wisdom of God manifested herself as an infant, and the Word of God without words uttered a human sound. Yet that hidden divinity was signified to the Magi by a celestial witness and was announced to the shepherds by angelic voices. And so we celebrate this day with great solemnity every year on which was fulfilled the prophecy: *Truth has sprung up from the earth, and Justice has looked down from the heavens.* Truth, which resides in the womb of the Father, has sprung up from the earth so that she might also dwell in the womb of a mother. Truth, by which the world is upheld, has sprung up from the earth so that she might be held in the hands of a mother. Truth, which incorruptibly nourishes the happiness of angels, has sprung up from the earth to be suckled at human breasts.

Christmas Week

Day 1

Morning Prayer

Antiphon: By Christ's birth from his mother he is subjected to human weakness, but by his birth from his Father he is resplendent with majesty. (Augustine *Sermon* 190.3)

Psalm 5:1–12 ✠ Psalm 39:5–10, 17 ✠ Psalm 21:3–5; 9–11, 22–23

Scripture: Isaiah 7:10–14

Reading: St. Augustine, bishop, Father and Doctor of the Church † 430

Sermon 186.3

If the one who is the Son of God did not himself become a son of man, how can the Apostle say to the Romans: *set apart for the Gospel of God, which he had previously promised by the prophets in the Holy Scriptures, concerning his Son who was made for him of the seed of David according to the flesh*? Here you have the Son of God, which of course he always was, made of the seed of David according to the flesh, which he always wasn't. Likewise, if the one who is the Son of God was not himself made a son of man, how is it that *God sent his Son, born of a woman*? . . . And who, after all, was sent by the Father, if not the only-begotten Son of God?

Born of a Father without any time of day, he was born of a mother this day! This day, which he created, he chose for his own creation, just as he was born of a mother whom he created. This very day, from which each subsequent day receives an increasing measure of light, symbolizes the activity of Christ by whom *our inner self is renewed day by day*. Certainly it is befitting that the Eternal Creator when created in time should have as his day of birth that day which marks temporal creation's cycle.

Evening Prayer

Antiphon: How much more could this Word, such a great Word as this, make fruitful a mother's womb by assuming a body, while still not departing from the Father's bosom! (Augustine, *Sermon* 187.2).

Psalm 133:1–3 ✠ Psalm 39:5–10, 17 ✠ Psalm 21:3–5; 9–11, 22–23

Scripture: Matthew 1:18–25

Reading: St. Augustine, bishop, Father and Doctor of the Church † 430

Sermon 187.1

My mouth shall speak forth the praise of the Lord, of that Lord *through whom all things were made*, and who was himself made [flesh] in the midst of all things; who is the Revealer of his Father, the Creator of his mother; the Son of God born of the Father without a mother, the Son of Man born of a mother without a father; . . . the Word, God before all time, the Word made flesh at the appropriate time. The Founder of the sun, found under the sun; ordering all the ages from the bosom of his Father, he consecrates this day from the womb of his mother; remaining in the former, coming forth from the latter; Producer of heaven and earth, brought forth under heaven on earth; unspeakably wise as God, wisely speechless as a babe.

Day 2

Morning Prayer

Antiphon: Who shall declare his generation?

Psalm 5:1–12 ✠ Psalm 39:5–10, 17 ✠ Psalm 21:3–5, 9–11, 22–23

Scripture: Micah 5:1–3

Reading: St. Leo the Great, pope, Father and Doctor of the Church † 461

Sermon 30.1

You are well aware, dearly beloved, that we have often carried our duty to provide you with an inspiring sermon regarding the excellence of today's feast. We do not doubt in the least that the power of divine solicitude has shown so brightly in your hearts that what is rooted in you by faith has likewise been grasped by your mind. The birth of our Lord and Savior, not only that of his divinity from the Father but that of his humanity from his mother as well, far exceeds the ability of human eloquence. Thus the text *Who shall recount his generation?* may rightly be referred to either birth. In this very matter which cannot be explained properly, a reason for not discussing the subject always springs to mind, not because there is liberty to think a multitude of thoughts, but rather because no tongue can sufficiently discourse on the dignity of the matter.

Evening Prayer

Antiphon: Wisdom has built for herself a house.

Psalm 133:1–3 ✠ Psalm 39:5–10, 17 ✠ Psalm 21:3–5, 9–11, 22–23

Scripture: Galatians 4:1–5

Reading: St. Leo the Great, pope, Father and Doctor of the Church † 461

Sermon 30.3

As blessed John said, *The Word became flesh and dwelt among us. Among us*, indeed, us whom the divinity of the Word conjoined to himself. We are his very flesh, the flesh that had been assumed from the Virgin's womb. If thus flesh had not been from our nature, had it not been truly human, then the Word made flesh would not have dwelt among us. But he did in fact dwell among us, for he made the nature of our body his very own, as it says, *Wisdom has built for herself a dwelling*, not just from any material, but from the substance which is properly ours.

Day 3

Morning Prayer

Antiphon: Who shall declare his generation?

Psalm 5:1–12 ✠ Psalm 39:5–10, 17 ✠ Psalm 21:3–5, 9–11, 22–23

Scripture: Wisdom 18:14–16

Reading: St. Augustine, bishop, Father and Doctor of the Church † 430

Sermon 188.2

Now then, for a few moments, let us direct our ears and minds to the following, and see if perhaps we can say something fitting and worthy, not about the matter *In the beginning was the Word, and the Word was with God, and the Word was God*, but about *the Word became flesh*; to see if perhaps we can say something appropriate because *he dwelt among us*; or if, perchance, he may be satisfactorily spoken about at the point when he willed to be made visible. That, after all, is the very reason why we celebrate this day on which he deigned to be born of a virgin, a means of generation which he himself caused to be told about by human beings. But as for that eternity in which as God he was born of God, *who shall declare his generation?* In eternity there is no such day to solemnly celebrate. There, day does not pass away to return with the revolving year; day remains without any sunset because it didn't begin with a sunrise.

Evening Prayer

Antiphon: The One who was born of the Father but not made by the Father, was made in the mother whom he had made so that he might be born from her (Augustine, *Sermon* 191.1).

Psalm 109:1–7 ✠ Psalm 39:5–10, 17 ✠ Psalm 21:3–5, 9–11, 22–23

Scripture: John 1:9–14

Reading: St. Augustine, bishop, Father and Doctor of the Church † 430

Sermon 190.2

So, Christians, let us celebrate this day, not as a feast of the divine birth, but of his human birth, by which he accommodated himself to us so that by the Invisible One being made visible, we might pass through visible reality to the invisible. For we of the Catholic faith must hold that there are two births of the Lord: one divine, the other human; the one timeless, the other in time. Both nativities, moreover, are awe-inspiring! The first without a mother, the second without a father. If we cannot comprehend the latter, when can we expound on the former? Who will grasp this new, unheard of novelty, unique in the history of the world, wherein the unbelievable became believable and in an unbelievable manner was believed throughout the whole world?

Day 4

Morning Prayer

Antiphon: Christ as God is born of the Father; Christ as Man is born of a mother (Augustine, *Sermon* 194.1).

PRAYING—WITH THE SAINTS—TO GOD OUR MOTHER

Psalm 109:1–7 VULG ✠ Psalm 39:5–10, 17 ✠ Psalm 21:3–5, 9–11, 22–23

Scripture: Isaiah 9:5–6

Reading: St. Augustine, bishop, Father and Doctor of the Church † 430

Sermon 194.1

Hear, O children of light who have been adopted into the Kingdom of God. Hear O dearest brothers and sisters. Hear and *exult, you just in the Lord, so that praise might befit the upright*. Hear what you already know; reflect upon what you hear; love what you believe; proclaim what you love. Just as we are celebrating the anniversary of this day, so you should expect a sermon befitting the feast.

Christ as God is born of the Father, Christ as Man is born of a mother. Born of the Father's immortality, and born of the mother's virginity; of his Father without a mother, of his mother without a father; of the Father without time temporal, of the mother without seed seminal; of the Father as the beginning of life, of the mother as the end of death; of the Father ordering all days, of the mother consecrating today.

Evening Prayer

Antiphon: God was born from God and yet the number of gods did not increase (Augustine, *Sermon* 195.1).

Psalm 133:1–3 ✠ Psalm 39:5–10, 17 ✠ Psalm 21:3–5, 9–11, 22–23

Scripture: Matthew 1:18–25

Reading: St. Augustine, bishop, Father and Doctor of the Church † 430

Sermon 195.1

Our Lord Jesus Christ, the Son of God, is likewise a son of man. Born of a Father without a mother, he created every day; born of a mother without a father, he consecrated this day; invisible in his divine nativity, visible in that of humanity; in both births awe-inspiring. Thus it is difficult to determine to which birth the Prophet referred when foretelling, *Who shall declare his generation?* Was it regarding that nativity in which it is never true that he was not yet born, having a co-eternal Father, or that nativity whereby he was born in time of a mother whom he had already created, or whether regarding that nativity whereby he was always being born since he always existed? For who shall recount how Light was born from Light and how both are but one Light; how God was born from God and yet the number of gods did not increase? How one can speak of his being born as if it were an accomplished event when in that birthing there is no passage of time resulting in a past, nor progression becoming a future, nor was the birth present as if it were transpiring up to that point and yet was incomplete? Consequently, who shall declare this generation when what it is to be declared remains superior to the confines of time, while the speech of the one who declares passes with time?

Day 5

Morning Prayer

Antiphon: The Word was born from God before the morning star.

Psalm 109:1–7 ✠ Psalm 39:5–10, 17 ✠ Psalm 21:3–5, 9–11, 22–23

Scripture: Micah 5:1–3

Reading: St. Gregory the Illuminator, Catholicos, Father of the Church † ca. 332

Armenian Catechism 388

Now see what the grace of the prophetic Spirit in Micah says to us: *And you, O Bethlehem, have attained no less a destiny; from you will arise for me a leader, a prince of the House of Israel, whose goings forth have been from the beginnings of the days of the world.* "From the beginning" indicates his divinity; "Bethlehem" signifies the flesh. The Archangel says, *She will give birth to a son, and they will name him Jesus.* And the Psalmist sang, *before the sun his name.* One refers to his birth in the flesh; the other indicates his divinity born from the Father before the morning star.

᪽ 📖 ᪺

Evening Prayer

Antiphon: The Word was born from the Almighty, not made.

Psalm 133:1–3 ✠ Psalm 39:5–10, 17 ✠ Psalm 21:3–5, 9–11, 22–23

Scripture: Luke 2:1–18

Reading: St. Bede the Venerable, priest, Father and Doctor of the Church † 735

Homily on the Gospels 1.7

And it came to pass when the angels had departed from them into heaven that the shepherds were speaking to one another, saying "Let us go over to Bethlehem and see this Word which has come to be, which the Lord has made and shown to us." And so they went with haste and found Mary and Joseph, and the infant lying in a manger. The shepherds made haste with happy joy to see what they had heard, and because they searched for it with ardent love they were worthy to find suddenly the Savior for whom they sought. . . . *And let us see,* they said, *this Word which has come to be.* What a proper and pure confession of holy faith this is! *In the beginning was the Word, and the Word was with God, and the Word was God.* The Word, born of the Father, was not made, because God is not a creature. In this divine birth he could not be seen by human beings, but in order that he might be seen *the Word was made flesh and dwelt among us.*

PRAYING—WITH THE SAINTS—TO GOD OUR MOTHER

Day 6

Morning Prayer

Antiphon: Born of his Father he created his mother (Augustine *Sermon* 195.2).

Psalm 109:1–7 ✠ Psalm 39:5–10, 17 ✠ Psalm 21:3–5, 9–11, 22–23

Scripture: Isaiah 7:10–14

Reading: St. Augustine, bishop, Father and Doctor of the Church † 430

Sermon 195.1–2

Our Lord Jesus Christ, the Son of God, is likewise a son of man. Born of a Father without a mother, he created every day; born of a mother without a father, he consecrated this day; invisible in his divine nativity, visible in that of humanity; in both births awe-inspiring. Thus it is difficult to determine to which birth the Prophet referred when foretelling, *Who shall declare his generation?* Was it regarding that nativity in which it is never true that he was not yet born, having a co-eternal Father? . . . And who will declare that other generation from the Virgin, in which conception in the flesh was accomplished without union in the flesh, and in which giving birth brought fullness to her breasts when she would nurse, while not depriving her of virginal integrity when she gave birth? *Who shall declare his generation* in either or both of the nativities?

This is the Lord our God; this Man is the Mediator between God and man, our Savior! Born of the Father he created his mother; created as a man in his mother he glorified the Father. Christ is the only Son of the Father without female parturition; the only son of his mother without male copulation.

Evening Prayer

Antiphon: Our Lord had two births: one divine, the other human (Augustine, *Sermon* 196.1).

Psalm 109:1–7 VULG ✠ Psalm 39:5–10, 17 ✠ Psalm 21:3–5, 9–11, 22–23

Scripture: John 1:1–18

Reading: St. Augustine, bishop, Father and Doctor of the Church † 430

Sermon 196.1

Today, a day of festivity has dawned for us: the birthday of our Lord Jesus Christ. It is his nativity, the day on which the Eternal Day was born. And this is today, because beginning with today, daylight increases.

Our Lord Jesus Christ had two births: one divine, the other human, both awe-inspiring. The first was without a woman for mother, the second without a man for father. What the holy Prophet Isaiah said, *Who shall declare his generation?* can be referred to both acts of generation. Who could worthily discourse on God's act of generation? Who could worthily discourse on the Virgin's act of parturition? The first is apart from any day, the second occurred on a given day, both beyond human imagination, both requiring great admiration.

Consider the first form of generation: *In the beginning was the Word, and the Word was with God, and the Word was God.* Whose Word? The Father's very own. Which Word? The Son himself. The Father could never exist without the Son. And yet the One who was never without a Son, engendered a Son. God engendered, but without commencement. There is no beginning for One engendered without beginning.

December 27 — The Feast of John, Apostle and Evangelist

Morning Prayer

Antiphon: I am my beloved's and he is mine.

Psalm 5:1–12 ✠ Psalm 80:1–14 ✠ Psalm 42:1–5

Scripture: Song of Songs 2:16–17

Reading: St. Gregory of Nyssa, bishop, Father and Doctor of the Church † ca. 395

Song of Songs 1

Now the discourse reveals a dispensation regarding the Church. For those who were first instructed by grace and became eyewitnesses of the Word did not overlook the good word in themselves, but passed on the same grace that were given to those who came after them. For this reason the maidens exclaim to the bride who, having come face to face with the Word, was the first to be filled with good things and be made worthy of the hidden mysteries: "*Let us rejoice and be glad in you*, for our common joy is your rejoicing. Because you yourself love the Word's breasts more than wine, we, ourselves, likewise shall imitate you and love your breasts more than human wine, for through them you give drink to those who are infants in Christ."

In order to make the meaning of the passage even clearer, ponder the following: John, who reclined on the Lord's chest, loved the breasts of the Word, and having placed his own heart like a sponge upon the fountain of life was filled with an ineffable draught of the mysteries residing in the heart of the Lord. Thus John presents to us the breast filled by the Word and fills us with the hidden good things he received from the wellspring of goodness, loudly proclaiming the Word who exists for all eternity. Therefore, we most fittingly say to the Word, *We will love your breasts more than wine.*

PRAYING—WITH THE SAINTS—TO GOD OUR MOTHER

Evening Prayer

Antiphon: Grace abundantly flows from the Bridegroom's spiritual breasts (Gregory of Nyssa, *Song of Songs* 2).

Psalm 133:1–3 ✠ Psalm 80:1–14 ✠ Psalm 18:1–14

Scripture: John 13:22–25

Reading: St. Ephrem, deacon, Father and Doctor of the Church † 373

Hymns on Virginity 25.2–3

> Blessed are you, O woman, whose Lord and Son
> entrusted you to one molded in His image.
> The Son of your womb did not injure your love,
> but to the son of His womb He entrusted you.
> Upon your bosom you caressed Him when He was little,
> and upon His bosom He caressed him likewise,
> so that when He was crucified He repaid all that you had given Him in advance,
> the debt owed for His upbringing.
> For the Crucified One repaid all debts;
> even your due was repaid by Him.
> He drank from your breast visible milk,
> but the other drank from His bosom invisible mysteries.
> With confidence He approached your breast;
> confidently the other approached and lay upon His bosom.

The Liturgical Calendar: Moveable Feast Days

The Baptism of the Lord—Sunday after January 6

First Evening Prayer

Antiphon: Christ entered the River Jordan to wash away our sin.

Psalm 133:1–3 ✠ Psalm 80:1–14 ✠ Psalm 113A:1–9

Scripture: Genesis 8:1–12

Reading: St. Peter Chrysologus, archbishop, Father and Doctor of the Church † 662

Sermon 160.3–4

Today Christ entered the waters of the River Jordan in order to wash away the sin of the world. John himself testifies that he came for this reason: Behold the Lamb of God, behold the one who takes away the sin of the world. Today the servant clasps his Lord, a human being his God, John embraces Christ. He embraces in order to receive pardon, not to grant it. Today, as the prophet said, *The voice of the Lord is over the waters.* . . .

Today the Holy Spirit hovers over the waters in the form of a dove, so that just as that dove announced to Noah that the flood waters covering the earth had receded, likewise by this dove it would be known that the perpetual shipwreck of the world had ceased. But she did not carry a twig from the old olive tree, as the former one did, rather, she pours out a new chrism all over the head of Christ our Parent, thus fulfilling what the prophet declared: *God, your God, has anointed you with the oil of gladness in the presence of your companions.*

Morning Prayer

Antiphon: The Dove fluttered above the Messiah and she sang over him.

Psalm 5:1–12 ✠ Psalm 80:1–14 ✠ Psalm 76:13–20

Scripture: Matthew 3:13–17

Reading: Syrian hymns, mid to late second century

Odes of Solomon 24:1–5

The Dove fluttered above the head of our Lord Messiah,
because the head was hers.
And she sang above him,
and her voice was heard.
Then the inhabitants were afraid,
and the foreigners were disturbed.
The flying creature abandoned its wings,

and every creeping thing died in its burrow.
And the deep chasms opened and closed;
they were seeking the Lord like those about to give birth.

Second Evening Prayer

Antiphon: Christ sanctified the waters for our sake.

Psalm 133:1–3 ✠ Psalm 80:1–14 ✠ Psalm 113A:1–9

Scripture: Luke 3:21–38

Reading: Syrian liturgy

Syro-Malankara Rite, First Sunday after Epiphany Vespers

> A great marvel it was in the house of the angelic watchers
> and among all peoples and tribes on earth
> that God experienced a baptism not needed for the Holy One.
> He came to sanctify the waters for the children of Adam
> enabling them to be born again by the Holy Spirit,
> so as to become children of the heavenly Father,
> that he might enter them into the Book of Life in heaven.

CHRISTIAN UNITY—SECOND SUNDAY OF ORDINARY TIME (WEST)

Morning Prayer

Antiphon: Let those *who were born not from blood, nor from the will of flesh, but from God* offer concord to God as peace-loving children (Leo I, *Sermon* 26.5).

Psalm 5:1–12 ✠ Psalm 121:1–9 ✠ Psalm 132:1–3

Scripture: Ephesians 4:1–16

Reading: St. Leo the Great, pope, Father and Doctor of the Church † 461

Sermon 26.3

If like minds and similar wills seek each other out for human friendship, and differences in lifestyles can never reach complete harmony, how can somebody become a sharer of peace with God if that person finds pleasure in what displeases God and desires to delight in the very things one knows are offensive to God? That is not the attitude of children of God. No, such a perspective does not resonate with your adopted noble status. Let the *chosen and royal race* respond to the dignity of its divine regeneration; let it love what its Father loves; and let it not experience discord in anything with its Maker, so that the Lord should not have to say again, *I have given birth to children and raised them, yet they have renounced me. Oxen recognize their owner, and the ass knows its master's stall, but Israel does not realize who I am, and my people have not acknowledged me.*

༄ 📖 ༺

Evening Prayer

Antiphon: May they be so completely one that the world will realize it was you who sent me.

Psalm 133:1–3 ✠ Psalm 121:1–9 ✠ Psalm 132:1–3

Scripture: John 17:1–23

Reading: St. Augustine, bishop, Father and Doctor of the Church † 430

Sermon 265.11

Charity is possessed only in the unity of the Church. Those who cause divisive wounds don't have it, as the Apostle Jude remarks, *These are the ones who set themselves apart, worldly people, not having the Spirit.* "Who set themselves apart." Why do they? Because they are "*worldly people, not possessing the Spirit.*" They seep away because they don't possess the coagulating property of charity. The hen, who becomes enfeebled for the sake of her chicks, is full of this charity, lowering her voice with her little ones, extending her wings over her brood. The Lord declared, *How often I would have gathered your children together!* He says, gather, not separate. Because, he noted elsewhere, I have other sheep which are not of this fold; I have to bring them along as well, so that there may be one flock and one shepherd.

Ash Wednesday (West)—First Day of the Great Fast (East)

Morning Prayer

Antiphon: A son of Adam is now the immortal Son of Man.

Psalm 62:1–11 ✠ Psalm 8:1–9 ✠ Psalm 29:1–12

Scripture: Sirach 17:25–32

Reading: Syrian hymns, mid to late second century

Odes of Solomon 36:1–8

>I rested upon the Spirit of the Lord,
>and she lifted me up to the heights,
>and made me stand on my own feet
>in the Lord's high place
>before his perfection and glory.
>While I continued giving glory by the composition of his odes
>she brought me forth before the presence of the Lord
>and because I was the Son of Man,
>I was called Light,
>the Son of God;
>because I was the most praised among the praised;
>and the greatest among the great ones.
>For according to the greatness of the Most High,
>so she made me;
>and according to his newness,
>he renewed me.
>And he anointed me from his fullness,
>and I was one of those who are near him.
>And my mouth was opened
>like a cloud of dew,
>and my heart spouted forth
>like a spout of righteousness.
>And my approach was in peace,
>and I was established in the Spirit of providence.

Evening Prayer

Antiphon: Christ was tempted so that we might learn by his example.

Psalm 133:1–3 ✠ Psalm 17:1–31 ✠ Psalm 25:1–12

Scripture: Matthew 4:1–11

Reading: St. Anthony of Padua, priest, Doctor of the Church † 1231

Sermon on the First Sunday in Quadragesima 1.4

> The Son of God came, therefore, at the favorable time, and by obeying God the Father, restored that which was lost, and healed those opposed by their opposite. Adam was placed in Paradise where, overflowing with pleasures, he succumbed. Jesus was placed in the desert where, giving himself to fasting, he overcame the devil. See how the two temptations in Genesis and Matthew parallel one another. *The serpent said, "The day on which you shall eat"*; and, *Approaching, the tempter said to him, "If you*

are the Son of God, say to these stones becomes loaves." Here you have the temptation regarding appetite. Next, *You shall become like gods;* followed by *Then the devil took him to the Holy City and set him on the parapet of the Temple.* Here you have vainglory. Finally, *Knowing good and evil* paralleled by *Once again the devil took him to a very high mountain and showed him all the kingdoms of the world and their glory. He said to him, "I will give you all of this if you bow down and worship me."* Inasmuch as he is distorted, he utters extortion; behold avarice.

Wisdom, on the contrary, precisely because she always acts wisely, trumped the triple temptation with a triple citation from Deuteronomy. When the devil tempted Jesus to give in to his appetite, Jesus responded, *Man does not live by bread alone*, as if to say, "As the exterior person lives by physical bread, the interior lives by heavenly bread, namely the word of God." The very Word of God, that is the Son, is Wisdom, *she who proceeds from the mouth of the Most High*. "The word 'wisdom [*sapientia*]' comes from 'to whet one's appetite, to savor [*sapore*].'" Thus the bread of the soul is the savor [*sapor*] of wisdom [*sapientia*]; through her one savors the good things of the Lord: *O taste and perceive that the Lord is good.*

✠

Sunday of Orthodoxy—First Sunday of Lent (East)

Morning Prayer

Antiphon: In the beginning was the Word, and the Word was with God, and the Word was God.

Psalm 5:1–12 ✠ Psalm 72:1–28 ✠ Psalm 25:1–12

Scripture: John 1:15–18 NT

Reading: St. John of Damascus, priest, Father and Doctor of the Church † 749

The Orthodox Faith 1.8

The everlasting God gives birth to God's own Word, a perfect being, without beginning and without end, in order that God, whose nature and existence are outside of time, should not give birth in the passage of time. Obviously, with a human being it is quite another matter, for humans are subject to birth and death, process and increase, being clothed within a body, possessing a nature which is male and female. For the male needs the female's assistance. But may the One who surpasses all things, and transcends all understanding and comprehension, be gracious to us!

Therefore, the holy catholic and apostolic church teaches that the Father simultaneously exists with his Only-begotten Son who is born from him without time, change, or being affected, in an incomprehensible manner, known only by the God of the universe. They exist simultaneously, just as fire does with its light, without the fire being first and the light following, but both simultaneously. And just as the light is

PRAYING—WITH THE SAINTS—TO GOD OUR MOTHER

continually being given birth to by the fire, being continually contained within it, and in no way separated from it, so too is the Son born of the Father without ever being in any way separated from him, but eternally existing within him.

Evening Prayer

Antiphon: Study the Scriptures believing that in them you have eternal life.

Psalm 133:1–3 ✠ Psalm 1:1–6 ✠ Psalm 88:1–28

Scripture: 2 Timothy 3:12–17

Reading: St. Leo the Great, pope, Father and Doctor of the Church † 461

Letter 28

Not knowing, therefore, what he should believe concerning the Incarnation of the Divine Word and neither being willing to labor so as to enlighten his mind from the breadth of the Sacred Scriptures, Eutyches ought to have at least attentively learned the common and standard profession of faith which the faithful confess the world over: namely, that they believe in One God, the Father Almighty, and in Jesus Christ, his only Son, our Lord, who was born of the Holy Spirit and the Virgin Mary. By these three statements the machinations of almost all heretics are destroyed. For when one believes in God the omnipotent Father, then the Son is demonstrated to be coeternal, in no fashion differing from the Father, because he was born God from God, omnipotent from the omnipotent, coeternal from the Eternal One, not later in time, not inferior in power, not unequal in glory, not separate in essence. This same eternal only-begotten Son of the eternal Father was born of the Holy Spirit and the Virgin Mary. This birth in time did not minimize in the least bit his divine and eternal birth, nor did it add to it.

Lenten Daily Readings

Day 1

Morning Prayer

Antiphon: How good is God to those who place their hope in the Lord.

Psalm 5:1–12 ✠ Psalm 7:1–17 ✠ Psalm 50:1–19

Scripture: Sirach 19:19–29

Reading: St. Francis de Sales, bishop, Doctor of the Church † 1622

Introduction to the Devout Life 4.13.4

Whenever we experience these spiritual delights and consolations, we must humble ourselves very much before God. Let us be on guard lest we say, "O, how good I am!" No, Philothea, these good things cannot make us better, for as I said earlier, true devotion does not consist in these things; rather, let us say, "O how good is God to those who hope in him, to the soul that searches for him!" The one who has sugar in his or her mouth cannot say that the mouth is sweet, but only that the sugar is sweet. Likewise, even though this spiritual sweetness is very good, and God who has given it is exceedingly good, it does not follow that the one who receives it is also good. Let us be mindful that we are still little children who depend on milk, and that the bits of sugar are given to us because we still possess tender and delicate spirits which need some bait and lure to entice us to the love of God.

That being said, speaking in general and under ordinary circumstances, let us humbly receive these graces and favors, and esteem them to be exceedingly great, not so much because they are so in themselves, but because it is the hand of God that places them in our hearts, as a mother would in order to soothe her child puts bits of candy one by one into its mouth. If the child has understanding, it would place a greater value on its mother's displays of affection and caresses than on the sweetness of the candy. Therefore, Philothea, it is a great matter to experience these delights, but it is the delight of delights to recognize that it is God's loving and maternal hand that places them in our mouth, heart, soul, and spirit.

Evening Prayer

Antiphon: Blessed are the pure of heart for they shall see God.

Psalm 133:1–3 ✠ Psalm 138:1–14 ✠ Psalm 26:1–14

Scripture: Matthew 5:1–12

Reading: St. Gregory of Nyssa, bishop, Father and Doctor of the Church † ca. 395

On Perfection

If anyone is truly *the temple of God*, not containing any idol or evil shrine within one's self, this person has received participation in the Divinity through the Mediator, having been made pure through the reception of his purity. For *Wisdom does not enter into a soul that plots evil*, as Scripture says, nor does *the pure in heart see anything else in himself besides God*, and clinging to God through incorruptibility, receives the entire good kingdom within. More properly speaking, what has been said becomes clearer to us if we couple it with what the Lord said to the Apostles through Mary, *I am going to My Father and your Father, to My God and your God.* Now it is the Mediator between the Father and the disinherited who says this, the One who reconciled the enemies of God to the true and only Divinity. For when, according to the prophetic message, human beings were alienated from the Life-giving Womb because of sin, and wandered away from the Womb in which they were molded, they spoke falsehood instead of truth. Thanks to this, the Mediator, assuming the first-fruit of our common nature, made it holy through his soul and body which was not mixed with or receptive of any evil, thus preserving the first-fruit of our nature within himself. He did this so that, having taken it up to the Father of incorruptibility through his own incorruptibility, the entire race might be drawn up along with him due to its related nature, and so that the disinherited might be granted adoption and the enemies of God be given a share in his divinity.

Day 2

Morning Prayer

Antiphon: When I say that God is the Source, I do not introduce process and duration, nor do I interpose any intermediary between the Progenitor and the Offspring (Gregory, Nazianzus *Theological Orations* 20.7).

Psalm 41:1–11 ✠ Psalm 89:1–17 ✠ Psalm 118:73–80

Scripture: Proverbs 8:22–31 TNK

Reading: St. Gregory of Nazianzus, Patriarch, Father and Doctor of the Church † 389

Theological Orations 30.2

The Lord created me as a beginning of his ways with regard to his works. How shall we address this? We will not accuse Solomon. We will not reject offhandedly what he has said because he later fell. Shall we say that this passage doesn't refer to Wisdom Herself, She who is like knowledge and artistic reason in whom all things subsist? For Scripture, in fact, often personifies many things, even inanimate objects such as *The Sea said* this or that, and *The Deep declared, She is not in me*, and *The heavens proclaim the glory of God*; or better yet a command is given to the Sword, and the Mountains and Hills are asked the reason for their leaping. We do not say that this case is anything like that, even though some of our predecessors used such forceful arguments. No, let us admit that this text refers to the very Savior, the True Wisdom.

Let us together examine the passage a bit. Among all existing things, what doesn't have a cause? Divinity. No one can indicate the origin of God, for if so that would be older than God. And what is the cause of the humanity which God took for our sakes? Our salvation obviously, What else could it be? Thus since we clearly find here *He created me*, and *He gives birth to me*, the line of reasoning is straightforward. That which we find linked with a cause, relate it to the humanity; that which we find absolute and without a cause, relate it to the Divinity. *He created me*, isn't that an expression with regard to a cause? In fact, *He created me*, she says, *as a beginning of his ways with regard to his works*. Now *the works of his hands are truth and judgment*, in view of which the unction of Divinity was received; now this anointing is of the humanity. But on the other hand, *He gives birth to me*, is not connected with a cause. Therefore what argument will disprove that Wisdom is said to be created with regard to her birth here below, and Offspring with regard to her first birth which is more incomprehensible?

Evening Prayer

Antiphon: Listen my child to your Mother's teachings.

Psalm 1:1–6 ✠ Psalm 102:1–22 ✠ Psalm 122:1–4

Scripture: 2 Timothy 1:3–5

Reading: St. Gregory of Nyssa, bishop, Father and Doctor of the Church † ca. 395

Song of Songs 1

Christ employed Solomon as an instrument and speaks to us through Solomon's voice first in Proverbs and then in Ecclesiastes, and after these in the Song of Songs he discourses about the path of philosophy and shows us the ascent to perfection stage by stage. Accordingly, not all stages of life in the flesh have every natural capacity, nor do our lives make progress is the same manner at different periods. For example, the infant does not participate in adult activities, and neither is an adult picked up in the arms of its nursing mother; rather, each stage of development has its own proper activity. Likewise, one can observe in the body's stages of growth an analogy to the soul wherein is found a certain order and sequence leading one to a life in accordance with virtue.

For this very reason, Proverbs instructs in one way and Ecclesiastes teaches in another, while the philosophy of the Song of Songs transcends both by its loftier doctrine. The teaching in Proverbs propounds sayings proper to the person who is still young, adapting its admonition to that stage of life. [Recall that Christ used Solomon as an instrument and speaks through his voice.] *Hear, my child, your father's instruction and do not reject your mother's injunctions.* Note that the soul is at a stage of life when it is tender and easily formed. Furthermore, it still needs maternal instruction and paternal admonition.

Day 3

Morning Prayer

Antiphon: Truly God is in this place and I did not know it.

Psalm 54:1–16 ✠ Psalm 100:1–9 ✠ Psalm 118:9–16

Scripture: Genesis 28:10–22

Reading: St. Francis de Sales, bishop, Doctor of the Church † 1622

Letter 1402

 My dearest child, you ask if our Lord thinks about you and if he looks upon you with love? Yes, my dearest daughter, he thinks of you, and not only about you, but about the least "hair of your head." This is an article of faith, and there's no need to doubt it whatsoever. But I know very well that you don't doubt it, but you're only giving expression to the aridity, dryness, and insensibility that the lower portion of your soul is now experiencing. *Truly God is in this place, and I didn't know it* remarked Jacob. That is to say, I didn't perceive God's presence; I had no feeling of it; it didn't seem so to me. I have addressed this in my book, *Treatise on the Love of God*, dealing with the death of the will and its resignations, but I don't remember in which section.

 That God looks upon you with love, you can't have any doubt; for God lovingly regards even the most terrible sinners of the world, looking for the smallest true desire they have for conversion. Tell me, my dearest daughter, Don't you have the intention of being God's? Don't you want to serve God faithfully? And who gives this desire and this intention, if not God himself in his loving regard? To examine whether your heart is pleasing to him, is not the right approach, but whether his heart pleases you. And if you gaze upon his heart, it will be impossible for it not to please you, for it is a heart so gentle, so sweet, so graciously humble, so amorous of poor creatures if only they recognize their misery, so gracious towards the miserable, so good towards the penitent. And who would not love this royal heart, paternally maternal towards us?

Evening Prayer

Antiphon: For me, to live is Christ.

Psalm 6:1–10 ✠ Psalm 113B:9–19 ✠ Psalm 30:1–24

Scripture: Romans 7:24—8:13

Reading: St. Francis de Sales, bishop, Doctor of the Church † 1622

In *The Consoling Thought of St. Frances de Sales*, ed. Rev. Pere Huguet, trans. Fr. Pustet (New York: Fr. Pustet & Co., 1857), 120–21; unplaced to the 18th French edition

 To travel well, we should apply ourselves to the present day's journey, and not concern ourselves about the final one before we have finished the first. Remember this: we sometimes amuse ourselves so much about being good angels, that we hardly labor to become good men.

 Our imperfection will accompany us to the grave. We cannot walk without touching the ground. It is not necessary to lie or wallow there; neither is it necessary to think of flying; for we are so small, that we have not yet got wings. We die little by little so we must also die to our imperfections day by day. O precious imperfections! which show us our misery, exercise us in humility and self-contempt, in patience and diligence, and in spite of which, God has regard to the preparation of our heart, that it may be perfect! . . .

Our imperfections need not please us; we must say with the great Apostle: *Miserable man that I am! who will deliver me from this body of death?* But they need not astonish us, or take away our courage; we should rather draw submission, humility, and diffidence in ourselves from them, but not discouragement, nor affliction of heart, much less doubtfulness of the love of God towards us. Thus God does not love our imperfections nor venial sins, but He loves us much notwithstanding them. As the weakness and infirmity of an infant displeases its mother, yet she does not cease to love it, but loves it tenderly and compassionately; so God, while he does not approve of our imperfections or venial sins, ceases not to love us tenderly.

Day 4

Morning Prayer

Antiphon: Whoever keeps watch for Wisdom will soon be free of cares.

Psalm 64:1–13 ✠ Psalm 118:17–24 ✠ Psalm 120:1–8

Scripture: Wisdom 6:12–20 LXX

Reading: St. Francis de Sales, bishop, Doctor of the Church † 1622

Consoling Thoughts 1.18

My eyes are always on the Lord, for he will set my feet free from the snares and traps. Have you fallen into the snares of adversity? Well, don't dwell on your misfortune or the traps into which you have fallen prey; dwell on God and let him take care of things. God will care for you. *Cast your preoccupations on him, and he will nourish you.* Why trouble yourself with second guessing the events and troubles of the world since you don't know what you ought to wish for, and God will always wish for you everything you could wish for that doesn't harm you? Wait, then, with a quite spirit for the outcomes of the Divine Good-Pleasure, and let God's will be enough, for it is always very good. Thus wise did Our Lord command his Well-beloved saint Catherine of Siena, "Think on me, and I will think for you."

A hundred times a day, then, let us dwell on this loving will of God, and grounding our will in the divine will, let us devoutly exclaim, "O infinitely sweet Goodness! How lovable is your will! How desirable are your favors! You have created us for eternal life and your maternal breast, enlarged with sacred nipples of incomparable love, abounds with the milk of mercy, whether to forgive the repentant sinner, or to bring the just to perfection. Why then should we not cause our wills to cling to yours, like little children fastened to their mother's breast in order to suck the milk of your eternal blessings?"

PRAYING—WITH THE SAINTS—TO GOD OUR MOTHER

Evening Prayer

Antiphon: We are made so as to desire relationship God.

Psalm 15:1–11 ☩ Psalm 121:1–9 ☩ Psalm 4:1–8

Scripture: Genesis 1:26–27 TNK

Reading: St. Francis de Sales, bishop, Doctor of the Church † 1622

Consoling Thoughts 1.1

The pleasure and confidence which the human heart naturally finds in God can only proceed from the affinity that exists between the Divine Goodness and our soul. There is a great, but secret affinity between the two, a resemblance that each one knows but too few understand, an affinity of which one cannot perceive the depths. We are created in the image of God; we have an extremely close affinity with the Divine Majesty.

But besides this resemblance and likeness, there exists an unrivalled correspondence between God and Man for their reciprocal perfection. Not that God could receive any perfection from a human being, but because a human being can only become perfected by the Divine Goodness, so too, the Divine Goodness cannot outside of itself be so well-disposed for goodness, except in regard to our humanity. The one has a great need and capacity to receive the Good, and the Other a great abundance and inclination to shower with goodness. Nothing is better suited to poverty than generous affluence, and for affluence, nothing better suited than destitute poverty. And the greater the influence it can exert, the stronger its inclination to give of itself freely. The needier the poverty is, the more eager it is to receive, like a void wishing to be filled. Thus the encounter between affluence and poverty is sweet and desirable; and one could hardly say which one has the most contentment, abundance to be showered and self-communicated, or deficiency and poverty to receive and retain, if our Lord had not said that it is more blessed to give than to receive. But where there is more happiness, there is more satisfaction; the Divine Goodness then has more pleasure in giving its graces than we do in receiving them.

Sometimes mothers have their breasts so productive and full that they cannot wait to give their breast to some infant, and while the baby takes the breast with great eagerness, the nursing mother gives it to the babe more willingly, the infant sucking, driven by hunger, and the mother nursing, driven by her fruitfulness. Similarly, our deficiency needs the divine abundance because of its dearth and necessity, whereas the divine affluence has no need of our poverty except through the excellence and perfection of its goodness.

Day 5

Morning Prayer

Antiphon: My soul pants for you, my God, like a deer panting for water.

Psalm 62:1–11 ✠ Psalm 41:1–11 ✠ Psalm 142:1–12

Scripture: Sirach 24:1–3, 18–22 LXX

Reading: St. Francis de Sales, bishop, Doctor of the Church † 1622

Treatise Concerning the Love of God 3.10

  Now Theotimus, imagine yourself with the Psalmist to be the stag, hard pressed by the hounds and no longer having any breath or legs left, as he eagerly plunges into the waters for which he panted, with what determination he presses and envelopes himself in that element. It's as if he would willingly drown and become all water in order to enjoy more fully this refreshment. Ah! What union there shall be of our heart with God above in heaven where after these infinite desires for the True Good, never assuaged in this world, we will find there the living and powerful wellspring. Then, truly, it shall be as when as one sees a hungry little baby tightly grasping the side of its mother and attached to her nipple, eagerly pressing this sweet fountain of delectable and most desired liquid, that one would think either it would plunge itself into its mother's breast, or else grasp and suck all of that breast into itself. Thus let our soul be panting with an extreme thirst for the True Good so that it might encounter the inexhaustible wellspring in the Divinity! O True God, what holy and sweet ardor to be united and joined to the bountiful breasts of all Goodness, either to be altogether drowned in it, or to have it entirely pour into us!

Evening Prayer

Antiphon: Let us approach the throne of grace with confidence.

Psalm 18:1–14 ✠ Psalm 50:1–19 ✠ Psalm 22:1–6

Scripture: Hebrews 4:1–16

Reading: St. Francis de Sales, bishop, Doctor of the Church † 1622

Consoling Thoughts 2.16

  Do as little children do. As long as they feel their mother holding them by the sleeves they walk about courageously, run around everywhere, and don't become alarmed at the slightest trip brought on by the weakness of their legs. Thus, while you perceive God holding you by the good will and resolution he has given you to serve him with, walk courageously, don't become the least bit alarmed by the little disturbances and jolts you experience. There is no need to grumble about them as long as from time to time you throw yourself into his arms and give him a loving kiss. Go joyfully, with an open heart, and if you can't always go as joyfully as you would wish, at least always approach with courage and confidence. Our Lord acts towards us just like a good mother who allows her child to walk all alone in a soft meadow where the grass is thick, or on a mossy bank, because she knows that if her child falls, it will not be hurt, whereas on the rough and dangerous path she carefully carries the child in her arms.

Day 6

Morning Prayer

Antiphon: In you the orphan finds maternal compassion (Hosea 14:4 TNK).

Psalm 72:1–28 ✠ Psalm 56:1–11 ✠ Psalm 78:8–12 TNK

Scripture: Hosea 11:1–4 TNK

Reading: St. Francis de Sales, bishop, Doctor of the Church † 1622

Consoling Thoughts 1.21

And we, like little children of our heavenly Father, can advance in two ways: first, by the steps of our own will conformed to his, always holding with the hand of our obedience that of his divine will and following it wherever it may lead. This is what God requires of us by manifesting his will, for when he wishes that I do what he commands, he wills that I have the ability to accomplish it. And secondly, we can also advance with Our Lord without having any self-will, simply allowing ourselves to be carried along, according to his Good Pleasure, like an infant in the arms of its mother, by an admirable contentment which one can call union, or more so the unity of our will with God's.

Evening Prayer

Antiphon: Your love is beyond all telling.

Psalm 21:1–11 ✠ Psalm 123:1–8 ✠ Psalm 118:25–32

Scripture: Romans 8:35–39

Reading: St. Francis de Sales, bishop, Doctor of the Church † 1622

Consoling Thoughts 1.22

Indeed, a hundred times a day we ought to contemplate the loving Providence of God which always has its heart turned towards us by foreknowledge, as we should always have our hearts turned towards his by confidence. Placing our hearts in his divine will we should cry out with devotion: "O infinite sweet goodness, how lovable is your will and how desirable are your favors! You have created us for eternal life, and your maternal breast, burning with incomparable love, abounds with the milk of mercy, whether to pardon the penitent, or to perfect the just." Why then do we not fasten our wills to yours like little infants who attach themselves to the breast of their mothers in order to suck the milk of your eternal blessings? Oh how true it is that God is a thousand thousand times more worthy of being loved than is loved, and that no power of love could ever love God enough.

Day 7

Morning Prayer

Antiphon: I am my Beloved's.

Psalm 91:1–15 ✠ Psalm 124:1–5 ✠ Psalm 112:1–9

Scripture: Sirach 15:1–8 LXX

Reading: St. Mechtild of Hackeborn, nun † 1299

Book of Special Grace 3.9

One time when Mechtild was greeting her Beloved most heartily, he responded, "When you greet me, I greet you in return; when you praise me, I myself am praising within you; and when you render thanks, I give thanks, I in you, and through you I give thanks to God the Father." She then asked, "My Beloved, what is that greeting which my soul makes when I don't feel anything?" The Lord replied, "My greeting is nothing other than my most sweet feeling in the soul. A mother fawns over her child in her bosom, teaching it and uttering words of greeting and consoling it. Being a child, it cannot yet act on its own, but the child will act according to what its mother has taught it, and all the while, she, with her maternal heart, supports her child, from time to time smothering it with kisses. In the same fashion I instruct the soul, by divine inspiration and a movement of love, to greet me."

Evening Prayer

Antiphon: I am like a weaned child, on its mother's breast.

Psalm 118:49–56 ✠ Psalm 130:1–3 ✠ Psalm 101:1–28

Scripture: 1 Corinthians 3:1–2 NT

Reading: St. Francis de Sales, bishop, Doctor of the Church † 1622

Consoling Thoughts 2.3

It is a common matter among those who begin to serve God, and who have not yet experienced the withdrawal of grace and other spiritual trials, that as soon as they begin to lose the feeling of sensible devotion and the sight of that delightful light which was drawing them to run in the paths of God, they of a sudden lose their breath and fall down into great sorrow and faintheartedness. People well versed in these things give the following explanation: They say that the rational nature cannot for long remain famished and without any delight, whether heavenly or earthly. Rather, as souls elevated above themselves by the experience of superior pleasures, they easily renounce all visible objects, so that when, by a divine disposition, this spiritual joy is withdrawn from them, finding themselves already deprived of physical consolations and not having yet been accustomed in the least to wait patiently for the return of daylight, it seems to them that they are neither in heaven nor on earth, and that they are going to remain buried alive in a perpetual night. In this way they have become like infants who have just been weaned, and who still seek their mother's breast; they only know how to languish and cry, becoming annoying to everyone, but particularly to themselves.

In order not to fall into discouragement, be mindful:

1. That God ordinarily gives some foretaste of the heavenly delights to those who enter into his service in order to draw them away from the pleasures of the world and to encourage them in the pursuit of divine love, like a mother who accustoms her baby to the breast by putting on it a bit of honey.

2. That, nevertheless, this Good God who, by a disposition of his Wisdom, sometimes takes away from us the milk and honey of consolation, so that weaned, we might learn to eat the hard and substantial bread of a rigorous devotion, trained by the testing of temptations and distasteful situations.

Day 8

Morning Prayer

Antiphon: God's tenderness is like that of a mother.

Psalm 107:1–6 ✠ Psalm 125:1–6 ✠ Psalm 51:1–5 TNK

Scripture: Sirach 14:20–27 LXX

Reading: St. Ephrem, deacon, Father and Doctor of the Church † 373

Paschal Hymn 2.12–18

> In the Will of the Son is found His treasure.
> Everywhere he willed it, he distributed his riches.
> For his Word is the Treasure of treasures.
> There where he opens it, are his creatures enriched.
> The gift which he gives is the source of every good.
> And if he dispenses any excess his creatures greatly rejoice.
> His Will, that is the great key,
> with which is opened the hidden bowels of his tender mercy.
> His Goodness is tender

bringing about health like a Nursing Mother.
His Justice is judicious,
bringing about threats like a Nanny.
The power of his Goodness displays kindness towards all.
She binds up all wounds like a skilled physician.

Evening Prayer

Antiphon: God heals us like a doctor, lovingly tending her patient.

Psalm 118:57–64 ✠ Psalm 118:33–40 ✠ Psalm 29:1–12

Scripture: Baruch 4:4–8, 30 LXX

Reading: St. Ephrem, deacon, Father and Doctor of the Church † 37

Nisibene Hymns 11.1–8

> Your chastising is like a mother of our infancy.
> Her rebuke is merciful because you have restrained
> your children from folly, and they have been made wise.
> Let us seek your justice, for who is capable
> of measuring its help? Since by it the undisciplined
> on numerous occasions are made chaste.
> Many times, your hand, my Lord, has made the sick whole,
> for it is the hidden healer of their diseases,
> and the wellspring of their life.
> Exceedingly gentle is the finger of your justice,
> in love and compassion she touches the wounds
> of the one who is to be healed.
> Exceedingly mild and merciful is her scalpel to the wise.
> Her sharp remedy in its powerful love
> excises the part that is corrupt.
> Exceedingly welcome is her wrath, to the one who is discerning,
> but her remedies are despised by the fool who takes delight
> in the troubles caused by his members.
> Exceedingly eager is she to mend the incision she has made.
> When she has smitten, she pities, that out of these two
> she may produce healing.
> Exceedingly welcome is her wrath and her anger pleasant,
> and sweet her bitterness, sweetening bitter things
> that they may be made pleasant.

PRAYING—WITH THE SAINTS—TO GOD OUR MOTHER

Day 9

Morning Prayer

Antiphon: Wisdom declares, "I proceed from the mouth of the Most High."

Psalm 118:145–52 ✠ Psalm 126:1–5 ✠ Psalm 118:65–72

Scripture: Sirach 24:1–9 LXX

Reading: St. Ephrem, deacon, Father and Doctor of the Church † 373

Homily on the Lord 1

The First-born, who was engendered according to his nature, experienced another birth outside his nature in order that we could understand as well that after our natural birth, we must experience another birth outside our nature. As a spiritual being he was incapable of becoming physical until the time of his physical birth. Likewise, physical beings, unless they experience another birth, cannot become spiritual. The Son, whose birth is beyond scrutiny, experienced another birth which can be investigated. Thus by the former we learn that his majesty is beyond limits, and by the latter we realize that his goodness is boundless. For his majesty excels without bounds, whose first birth is incapable of the mind's imagination; and his goodness overflows without limit, whose second birth is proclaimed by every tongue.

Evening Prayer

Antiphon: The Word experienced a second birth so that we might be born again.

Psalm 138:1–14 ✠ Psalm 127:1–6 ✠ Psalm 118:33–40

Scripture: John 1:9–14 NT

Reading: St. Ephrem, deacon, Father and Doctor of the Church † 373

Homily on the Lord 2

> It is He who was engendered of Divinity according to his nature,
> and of humanity which was not according to his nature,
> and of baptism which was not his habit;
> so that we might be engendered of humanity according to our nature,
> and of Divinity which is not according to our nature,
> and of the Spirit which is not our habit.

Thus the One who was engendered of Divinity experienced a second birth so as to bring us to rebirth. His birth from the Father is not to be scrutinized, but believed. And his birth from a woman is not repugnant; rather, it is noble.

Day 10

Morning Prayer

Antiphon: God's tender maternal mercy has carried us since our conception.

Psalm 129:1–8 ✠ Psalm 138:1–14 ✠ Psalm 50:1–19

Scripture: Isaiah 46:1–5 TNK

Reading: St. Faustina Kowalska, nun † 1938

Divine Mercy in My Soul 1726

Christ and Lord, you are leading me over such precipices that, when I look at them, I am filled with fright, yet at the same time I am at peace as I snuggle close to your Heart. Close to your Heart, I don't fear anything. In these trying times, I act as a little child supported in its mother's arms. When it sees anything menacing, it clutches its mother's neck more firmly and feels secure.

Evening Prayer

Antiphon: Do not be afraid, I am full of compassion and mercy, calling you to repentance.

Psalm 140:1–5 ✠ Psalm 131:1–18 ✠ Psalm 118:73–80

Scripture: Revelation 1:9–20

Reading: St. Faustina Kowalska, nun † 1938

Divine Mercy in My Soul 603

At evening, when I was in my cell, I unexpectedly saw a bright light and a gray cross hidden high up inside the light. Suddenly, I found myself caught up close to the cross. I fixed my gaze on it but could not understand anything, and so I prayed, asking what it might mean. At that moment I saw Jesus and the cross disappeared. The Lord Jesus was sitting in a great light; his feet up to the knees were immersed in the light, so that I could not see them. Jesus bent down toward me, looked at me lovingly and spoke to me about the will of the Heavenly Father. He told me that the most perfect and holy soul is the one that does the will of his Father, but there are not many such souls, thus he regards with special love the soul who lives according to his will. And Jesus told me that I was doing the will of God perfectly . . . *and for this reason I am uniting myself with you and communing with you in such a special and intimate way.*

God embraces with his incomprehensible love the soul who lives according to his will. I understood how much God loves us, how simple he is, although beyond comprehension, and how easy it is to commune with him, despite his great majesty. With no one do I feel as free and as much at ease as I do with him. Even a mother and her child who sincerely loves her do not understand each other as much as God and I do.

Day 11

Morning Prayer

Antiphon: Self-knowledge is the beginning of wisdom.

Psalm 142:1–12 ✠ Psalm 118:41–48 ✠ Psalm 138:1–14

Scripture: Wisdom 7:7–14 LXX

Reading: St. Faustina Kowalska, nun † 1938

Divine Mercy in My Soul 297–298, 505

O Jesus, Supreme Light, grant me the grace of knowing myself, and pierce my dark soul with your light, filling the abyss of my soul with your own self. . . .

O my Jesus, the Life, the Way, and the Truth, I implore you to keep me close to you as a mother clasps her baby to her bosom, for not only am I a helpless child, I am a conglomeration of misery and nothingness as well.

All my nothingness is drowned in the sea of your merciful love. With the confidence of a child, I throw myself into your arms, O Father of Mercy, to make up for the lack of faith of so many souls who are afraid to trust in you. Oh how very few souls really know you! Oh how I burn with desire that the Feast of Mercy be known by souls! Mercy is the crown of your works. You provide for all with the love of a most tender mother.

Evening Prayer

Antiphon: Like a loving mother, God never rejects her children.

Psalm 133:1–3 ✠ Psalm 127:1–6 ✠ Psalm 145:1–10 TNK

Scripture: Romans 11:1–32

Reading: St. Melito of Sardis, bishop, Post-Apostolic Father of the Church † ca. 180

On Pascha 82–83

You did not recognize the Lord, you did not know, O Israel, that it is he, the First-Born of God, he who *was born before the daystar*, who caused the light to spring forth, who made the day to shine, who separated the darkness, who established the first foundation, who hung the earth, who drained the abyss, who fixed the firmament, who set the universe in order, who arranged the stars in the heavens, who caused the luminaries to shine, who created the angels in the heavens, and established their thrones there, who fashioned for himself a human being upon the earth.

Palm Sunday

Morning Prayer

Antiphon: Blessings on the One who comes in the name of the Lord!

Psalm 5:1–12 ✠ Psalm 80:1–14 ✠ Psalm 117:8–26

Scripture: Matthew 21:1–11

Reading: St. Francis de Sales, bishop, Doctor of the Church † 1622

Consoling Thoughts 1.2

In its love and tender mercy the Divine Goodness prepared all the means, general and particular, of our salvation. Yes, without a doubt, like a mother who prepares the cradle, the linens, the baby clothes, and even the nourishment, for the infant she is about to give birth to, so too, our Lord, in the desire of birthing us into salvation and making us his children, prepared on the tree of the Cross everything necessary for us: our spiritual cradle, our linens, our swaddling clothes, our nourishment, and everything else required for our happiness. These are all the means, all the enticements, all the graces with which he leads our souls and draws them to perfection.

Evening Prayer

Antiphon: Follow the example of Christ, the shepherd and bishop of your soul.

Psalm 133:1–3 ✠ Psalm 80:1–14 ✠ Psalm 79:1–19

Scripture: 1 Peter 2:21–25

Reading: St. Francis de Sales, bishop, Doctor of the Church † 1622

Treatise Concerning the Love of God 12.12

Don't you know, Theotimus, that the high priest of the Law carried on his shoulders and over his chest the names of the children of Israel, that is, the precious stones upon which the names of the leaders of Israel were engraved? Well, look at Jesus our great Bishop and behold him from the moment of his conception; consider that he carries us upon his shoulders, receiving the commission to redeem us by his death, *death on the cross*. O Theotimus, Theotimus, the Savior's soul knows us all by given name as well as surname. Above all, on the day of his Passion, while he offered up his tears and his prayers, his blood and his life for everyone, he emitted in particular just for you these loving sentiments: "Alas, O my Eternal Father, I take upon myself and accept the charge of all of poor Theotimus' sins, to suffer torments and to die in order that he might remain safe and not perish at all, but live. O that I might die so that he might live! O that I might be crucified so that he might be glorified!" O sovereign love of the heart of Jesus that will bless you so devotedly for all eternity!

Thus, within his maternal breast, his divine heart foresees, disposes, merits, and obtained all the benefits that we possess, not only in general for everyone, but in particular for each person. And his sweet breasts prepare for us the milk of his influences, attractions, inspirations, and the sweetness by which he draws, leads, and nourish our hearts to life eternal.

☦

Holy Thursday

Morning Prayer

Antiphon: Come to the banquet, and feast to your heart's content.

Psalm 5:1–12 ✠ Psalm 80:1–14 ✠ Psalm 22:1–6

Scripture: Proverbs 9:1–6, 11 TNK

Reading: St. Peter Chrysologus, archbishop, Father and Doctor of the Church † 450

Sermon 99A.1

It says, *And it happened that when the Lord had entered the home of a certain leader of the Pharisees to dine on the Sabbath, they themselves were closely observing him. . . .* Nevertheless, the Lamb of God was eating there, not to be fed but to be slaughtered, as if he knew nothing about it. He was eating in plain view, brothers and sisters, not as if he knew nothing, but so that at the very least by his companionship, by their very camaraderie as well as the gracious manner in which he shared a meal with them, their inhumanity might be checked, their anger soothed, their envy extinguished. Thus by his very humanity these human beings might now be brought back to their humanity, they might entertain affection, experience graciousness, welcome their Parent, esteem God's benevolence, recognizing virtues, loving God's curative actions, and earnestly seek rather than assail God's healing wholeness.

Evening Prayer

Antiphon: Let us prepare for the Feast.

Psalm 133:1–3 ✠ Psalm 80:1–14 ✠ Psalm 22:1–6

Scripture: Matthew 26:17–30; Luke 22:39–44

Reading: Bl. Marguerite of Oingt, prioress † 1310

A Page of Meditations 31–33, 36, 39

Sweet Lord Jesus Christ, my heart will never be at perfect peace until I know how to love you with all my heart; there is nothing in all of this world that I desire as much as this. Sweet Lord, I left my father and my mother and my brothers and everything in this world for love of you, but this is worth far too little because the riches of this world are nothing but sharp thorns; whoever has more of them has more misfortune. And because of that, it seems to me that I have rejected nothing but misery and poverty; but you know, sweet Lord, that if I owned a thousand worlds and could use everything from them at my command, I would leave everything for love of you, and if you granted me whatever there is in heaven and on earth, I would not consider myself content unless I had you, for you are the life of my soul, and I have—nor do I want to have—any father or mother besides you.

Are you not my mother and more than mother? The mother who bore me labored at my birth for one day or one night, but you, my sweet and lovely Lord, were in pain for me not just one night or day, but you were in labor for more than thirty years! O Sweet and Lovely Lord, how bitterly you were in labor for me all through your life! But when the time drew near when you had to give birth, your labor was such that your holy sweat was like drops of blood which poured out of your body onto the ground....

Oh, Sweet Lord Jesus Christ, who ever saw any mother suffer such a birth! When the hour of birth came you were placed on the hard bed of the cross where you could not move or turn around or stretch your limbs as someone who suffers such great pain should be able to. Yet seeing this, they stretched you out and fixed you with nails. You were so stretched out that there was no bone left to become disjointed, and your nerves and all your veins were ruptured. Truly it was no wonder that your veins were ruptured when you gave birth to the whole world all in one day....

Oh, lovely Lord God, who ever saw at any other time that a mother wanted to suffer such a physically disgusting death for the love of her child? Surely, no one ever saw this, because your love was beyond all other loves.

Good Friday—Great and Holy Friday

Morning Prayer

Antiphon: With a loud cry, God gave birth to us on the Cross.

Psalm 5:1–12 ✠ Psalm 21:1–23 ✠ Psalm 117:8–26

Scripture: Isaiah 66:9 VULG

Reading: St. Anthony of Padua, priest, Doctor of the Church † 1231

PRAYING—WITH THE SAINTS—TO GOD OUR MOTHER

Prologue to Sunday Sermons

In Ecclesiasticus it says, *I shall irrigate the garden in my estate, and I shall abundantly water the fruit born to me.* Now the garden is the soul in which Christ as the gardener plants the sacraments by faith, he then waters the garden and makes it fruitful with the grace of compunction. With this in mind the text adds, *and I shall abundantly water the fruit born to me.* This means that our souls are like fruit born of the Lord, born of his pain. Like a woman in the labor of childbirth, he gave birth to our souls in the anguish of his Passion, as the Apostle remarks, *With a loud cry and abundant tears he made his offering.* And in Isaiah we read, *Shall not I myself, who cause others to give birth, give birth? declares the Lord.* God, therefore, abundantly waters the fruit born of him when he puts to death carnal pleasures by the myrrh and aloes of his Passion.

Evening Prayer

Antiphon: You died in giving birth to us and gave birth to us by dying.

Psalm 133:1–3 ✠ Psalm 21:1–23 ✠ Psalm 117:8–26

Scripture: John 16:17–21 NT

Reading: St. Anselm of Canterbury, archbishop, Doctor of the Church † 1109

Prayer to St. Paul 10.197–204

But you, Jesus, good Lord, are you not also a mother? Is it not a mother, who, like a hen, gathers together her chicks under her wings? Truly, Lord, you are a mother. For both those who are in labor and those who have given birth have received this capability from you. More than they, you have died in giving birth and you have given birth by dying, even though they have given birth. Because if you had not given birth, you would not have endured death, and if you had not died, you would not have given birth. Through your desire to engender children into life, you tasted death, and in dying, you begot them. You did this in your own self, they did this by your command and with your help; you as author, they as ministers. Therefore, you, Lord God, are the great Mother.

Another Morning Prayer

Antiphon: Jesus was offered as a silent ewe before her shearers.

Psalm 5:1–12 ✠ Psalm 136:1–6 ✠ Psalm 39:5–17

Scripture: Isaiah 53:1–7 TNK

Reading: St. Ephrem, deacon, Father and Doctor of the Church † 373

Paschal Hymn 13.12–21

> Why did he offend them?
> He was spat upon, the Lord of the Universe,
> upon whom even the seraphim cannot fix their gaze.
> Cherubim and seraphim, at the moment he was offended,
> they hid their faces, fearing to even look.
> When they mocked him, Michael trembled.
> Gabriel likewise, was astonished, stupefied and perplexed.
> Because the creation did not have a veil
> with which to hide his face, as with a garment
> she opened the gates of darkness—like Shem and Japheth
> not wanting to see the shame—of her Pure Lord.
> And when he let out a cry, the Spirit, echoing his voice,
> in the Holy Sanctuary, She, too, cried out.
> When she heard that he had bowed his head and cried out,
> she tore the Temple curtain, totally horrified.
> Creation clothed herself in a garment of mourning,
> girding herself in darkness, because of the Son of her Lord.
> The Shekinah of the Sanctuary tore the Temple curtain,
> like Her veil, because of Her dearly Beloved.

Another Evening Prayer

Antiphon: Christ our Passover has been sacrificed.

Psalm 133:1–3 ✠ Psalm 49:7–22 ✠ Psalm 112:1–9

Scripture: Luke 11:47–51 NT

Reading: St. Gregory of Narek, monk and priest † 1003

Prayers 44.1–2

> And you, even though you are capable of achieving
> the Incarnation without experiencing suffering,
> you deigned in my stead, a sinner, to drink the cup of death
> with the totality of your humanity and the entirety of your Divinity.
> Your Holy Spirit also took care to save me, Source of Life,
> being of the same essence as you and your Father,
> and sharing in essence the same honor with
> the One who begot you and you, the Only-begotten.
> Unity-Trinity, perfect in three distinct but inseparable Persons,
> without beginning and beyond time,
> totally beneficent,

entirely life-giving,
who grants peace to all,
who created beings and fashioned all things,
glorified for his indivisibility and unique nature.
The Father, compassionate, heavenly, powerful,
One of the Divine Essence,
because of my transgressions, for me who merits death,
offered you up, you the Only-begotten from the unfathomable Womb.

Great and Holy Saturday

Morning Prayer

Antiphon: Like a mother searching for her lost children, God came to us.

Psalm 5:1–12 ✠ Psalm 80:1–14 ✠ Psalm 51:1–5 TNK

Scripture: Isaiah 54:7–13 TNK

Reading: St. Gregory of Nyssa, bishop, Father and Doctor of the Church † ca. 395

Against Eunomius 3.2:50–51

By grace, [Christ] is the firstborn either *of the dead*, or *of creation*, or *among many brothers and sisters*. Now all of these passages have the same view in mind even though each indicates a particular idea. He becomes firstborn from the dead, who first by himself loosed the pangs of death so that he might likewise make the birth pangs of the resurrection a passage for all. Again, he becomes the firstborn among brothers and sisters, who is born before us through the new birth of regeneration in water, the birth pangs of which the hovering of the Dove served as midwife. Thereby he makes those who are correspondingly transformed in him by a similar birth, into his own brothers and sisters, and becomes the firstborn of those who after him are born of water and of the Spirit.

Evening Prayer

Antiphon: The Firstborn entered the bowels of the earth that we might enter the Womb of God.

Psalm 133:1–3 ✠ Psalm 80:1–14 ✠ Psalm 15:1–11

Scripture: 1 Peter 3:18—4:6

Reading: St. Hippolytus, bishop and martyr, Father of the Church † 235

Sermon on the Great Canticle

The One who rescued from the depths of Hades the first-formed Man of earth, being bound with the chains of death; the One who descended from on high, and lifted the earthly to heaven, who became the Proclaimer of Good News to the dead, and the Redeemer of souls, even the Resurrection of the buried, this One was the helper of vanquished humanity. The First-born Word was made like humanity so that he might experience the first-formed Adam by means of the Virgin. The One who is spiritual sought out the earthly in the mother's womb. The Ever-living One sought out the one who, through disobedience, is subjected to death. The One who is celestial called the one who is terrestrial to the things that are above. The One who is nobly born, by his own subjection, desired to set the slave free. He transformed into diamond the Man who had been dissolved into dust and made the serpent's food. The One who hung upon the Tree was manifested to be Lord over the conqueror, and thus through the Tree, He is discovered to be the Victor.

Therefore, those who do not now recognize the Son of God as incarnate, they shall know him as Judge when he comes in glory, he whom they now despise as humiliated in an inglorious body. For the apostles came to the tomb on the third day and did not find the body of Jesus, just as the children of Israel went up the mountain and looked for the tomb of Moses, but did not find it.

✠

Easter—Great and Holy Pascha

Morning Prayer

Antiphon: Risen from the tomb, Christ goes to God's womb.

Psalm 5:1–12 ✠ Psalm 80:1–14 ✠ Psalm 109:1–7

Scripture: Isaiah 49:13–16 TNK

Reading: St. Anthony of Padua, priest, Doctor of the Church † 1231

Sermon for the Sunday in the Octave of Easter 1.11

The Lord says in Isaiah, *I have written you in my hands*. Note that for writing three things are required: paper, ink, and pen. The hands of Christ were like paper, his blood like ink, and the nails like the pen. Christ, therefore, has inscribed us in his hands for three particular reasons: 1) to show the Father the scars of the wounds he bore for us so that God might have mercy upon us; 2) so that he would never forget us, wherefore it says in Isaiah, *Can a woman forget her infant, and not have pity of the child of her womb? And even if she should forget, yet I shall not forget you. Look, I have inscribed you in my hands*; 3) he has written in his hands what type of people we should be and in whom we should believe.

Evening Prayer

Antiphon: Behold my hands; behold my side that gave you birth.

Psalm 133:1–3 ✠ Psalm 80:1–14 ✠ Psalm 29:1–12

Scripture: John 20:24–29

Reading: St. Anthony of Padua, priest, Doctor of the Church † 1231

Sermon for the Sunday in the Octave of Easter 1.8

Jesus stood in the middle of his disciples and said to them: "Peace be with you." And when he had said this he showed them his hands and his side. Luke puts it this way, *See my hands and my feet, that it is truly I.* It appears to me that the Lord had four reasons for showing the Apostles his hands, his side, and his feet: 1) to show that he had truly risen and to take away all doubt from us; 2) so that the dove, which is the Church or the faithful soul, might build a nest in his wounds as if in the clefts of the Rock, and hide herself from the face of the hawk seeking to seize her; 3) to impress upon our hearts the most significant signs of his Passion; and 4) he shows the wounds to us begging us to be compassionate and not to crucify him again with the nails of our sins. Thus he shows us his hands and side, as if saying, "Here are the hands that formed you, behold them pierced with nails. Here is my side, out of which you faithful, my Church, have been born, just as Eve was given birth to out of Adam's side. My side has been opened by a lance so that it might open for you the gate of Paradise which had been shut by a cherub wielding a fiery sword." The power of the blood flowing from Christ's side, removed the angel and blunted the sword, and the water from his side extinguished the fire.

FEAST OF DIVINE MERCY—SECOND SUNDAY AFTER EASTER (WEST)

Morning Prayer

Antiphon: God abounds in maternal mercy and compassion.

Psalm 5:1–12 ✠ Psalm 80:1–14 ✠ Psalm 51:1–5 TNK

Scripture: Sirach 4:1–11 VULG

Reading: St. Faustina Kowalska, nun † 1938

Divine Mercy in My Soul 1541

    Today the Lord said to me, . . . *Write this for the benefit of afflicted souls: when a soul sees and realizes the gravity of its sins, when the whole abyss of the misery into which it has immersed itself is disclosed before its eyes, let it not despair; but with trust let it throw itself into the arms of my mercy, as a child into the arms of its beloved mother. These souls have right of priority to my compassionate heart; they have first access to my mercy. Tell them that no soul that has called upon my mercy has ever been disappointed or brought to shame. I especially delight in the soul that has placed its trust in my bounteous goodness.*

Evening Prayer

Antiphon: The greater the sin, the greater the maternal mercy.

Psalm 133:1–3 ✠ Psalm 80:1–14 ✠ Psalm 50:1–19

Scripture: 1 Peter 1:3–5 NT

Reading: St. Faustina Kowalska, nun † 1938

Divine Mercy in My Soul 423

    Praise the Lord, O my soul, for everything, and glorify his mercy, for his goodness is without limit. Everything will pass, but his loving mercy knows no limit or end. Even if evil will attain its measure, in mercy there is no measure.

    O my God, even in the punishments with which you chastise the earth I see the abyss of your mercy, for by punishing us here now on earth you free us from eternal punishment. Rejoice, all you creatures, for you are closer to God in his infinite mercy than a newborn babe is to its mother's heart. O God, you are compassion itself for the greatest sinners who sincerely repent. As great the sinner, greater still is his right to God's mercy.

SOLEMNITY OF THE ASCENSION OF OUR LORD

Morning Prayer

Antiphon: The Queen advances in pre-eminence to the right hand of God.

Psalm 109:1–7 ✠ Psalm 46:1–8 ✠ Psalm 44:1–17

Scripture: Proverbs 8:12–21 TNK

Reading: St. Methodius of Olympus, bishop and martyr, Father of the Church † 311

PRAYING—WITH THE SAINTS—TO GOD OUR MOTHER

Banquet of the Ten Virgins 7.8

There are sixty queens and eighty concubines and young maidens without number. Yet one is my dove, my perfect one. Perceiving this in another sense, one could say that the bride is the undefiled flesh of the Lord, for the sake of which he came down, leaving his heavenly Father, so that he may embrace it in a flash of splendor, thus becoming incarnate within it. Thus likewise by way of metaphor he calls it his Dove, because the dove is a tame and domestic creature which is readily adapted to live with human beings. Indeed, it alone, so to speak, was found to be pure and immaculate, surpassing everything else in adornment and beauty of justice to such an extent that not even those who formerly were most prestigious in divine favor could approach it in comparison of virtue. Therefore was this flesh judged worthy to share intimately in the Kingdom of the Only-Begotten, through espousal and union with him.

And so in Psalm 44, the queen who advances in preeminence to the right hand of God, robed in golden raiment of virtue, she whose beauty the King desired, she is, I repeat, this undefiled and blessed flesh which the Word brought to heaven and established at the right hand of the Father, ornately draped in a gown spun of gold, that is, with the discipline of incorruption, which is allegorically called, *golden borders*.

Evening Prayer

Antiphon: Divinity placed humanity at the right hand of God.

Psalm 133:1–3 ✠ Psalm 46:1–8 ✠ Psalm 109:1–7 VULG

Scripture: Hebrews 1:1–9 NT

Reading: St. Ephrem, deacon, Father and Doctor of the Church † 373

Hymns on the Nativity 21.4–5

> This is the night that blends heavenly watchers with [earthly] vigilants.
> The Watcher came [down] to make watchers in creation.
> Behold those who keep vigil have become partakers with watchers.
> Those who give praise have become companions with the seraphim.
> Blessed is the one who becomes a lyre for your praise,
> and who's recompense is your mercy!
> Now let us sing about the birth of the First-born
> how Divinity in the womb wove for herself a garment.
> She clothed herself and emerged in birth;
> in death she stripped it off.
> She stripped it off once, and put it on twice.
> When the sinister hand snatched it, she wrested it back,
> and she placed it at the Right Hand.

Another Morning Prayer

Antiphon: As a mother bird, Christ lifts us up on her wings.

Psalm 5:1–12 ✠ Psalm 46:1–8 ✠ Psalm 109:1–7

Scripture: Isaiah 31:4–5 TNK

Reading: St. Augustine, bishop, Father and Doctor of the Church † 430

Sermon 264.2

Christ actually looked upon the disciples, as he himself worthily said, just as a hen does upon her chicks. In fact, as a hen herself becomes enfeebled due to the feebleness of her chicks—for, as you recall, of all the many types of birds that bring forth their young within our view, we know of no other bird than the hen which shares weakness with her chicks—so, the Lord compared himself with her because, on account of our feebleness he was willing to become enfeebled by the assumption of flesh. Now, [at his Ascension], however, it was befitting for his disciples to be lifted up, for them to begin thinking of him in a spiritual manner as the Word of God, as God with God, as One through whom all creation was made.

Another Evening Prayer

Antiphon: I gazed into heaven and saw Jesus standing at God's right hand.

Psalm 133:1–3 ✠ Psalm 46:1–8 ✠ Psalm 109:1–7 VULG

Scripture: Ephesians 1:17–20

Reading: St. Augustine, bishop, Father and Doctor of the Church † 430

Sermon 244.3–4

What then is the meaning of the words: *Do not touch me, for I have not yet ascended to my Father?* [Christ says:] You see me as a man and so think of me as a man, then *I have not yet ascended to my Father.* I am indeed human, but don't let your faith stop there. *Do not touch me* in such a way as to believe I am only a human being, for then *I have not yet ascended to my Father.* I am ascending to my Father, and so truly touch me; that is, advance, understand that I am equal to the Father, and then touch me, and you will be saved.

You see that I have descended, yet you still do not see that I have ascended. . . . *I emptied myself taking the form of a slave, made in human likeness, and in condition found as a man.* This is what was crucified, what was buried, what was raised again. But you do not yet see and touch the other truth: *Being in the form of God he did not consider it robbery to be equal to God.* That I have ascended, you do not yet see. By touching the earth, don't lose heaven. By clinging to me as a man, don't fail to believe in me as God. . . .

[Augustine comments:] Do you want him to ascend to the Father in your eyes? Then believe that *Being in the form of God he did not consider it robbery to be equal to God*. It was not robbery, because it was his nature. What is gotten by robbery is unlawfully grasped, what is gotten by nature is simply recognized. *Being in the form of God he did not consider it robbery to be equal to God*. Accordingly he was born and was always born; both born and always born, and born without beginning. . . . There is no interval of time between the Father and the Son. The Father engendered and the Son was born. Without the limitations of time the One engendered; and without the limitations of time the One was born, through whom all time was created. Touch him in this way, and he has ascended for you to the Father.

Fathers of First Ecumenical Council—Sunday before Pentecost (East)

Morning Prayer

Antiphon: The Only-Begotten is born of the Father, from God's very being.

Psalm 5:1–12 ✠ Psalm 109:1–7 ✠ Psalm 72:1–28

Scripture: 1 Timothy 3:14–16

Reading: First Ecumenical Council (Nicea I) 325

Nicene Creed, Greek text

We believe in one God the Father Almighty, maker of all things both visible and invisible, and in one Lord Jesus Christ, the Son of God, the Only-Begotten, born of the Father, that is from the essence of the Father, God from God, Light from Light, True God from True God, begotten not made, one in being with the Father, through whom all things came to be, both those in heaven and those in the earth; for us human beings and for our salvation he came down and became incarnate, became human, suffered and arose on the third day, ascended into the heavens, is coming to judge the living and the dead; and in the Holy Spirit.

Evening Prayer

Antiphon: These remained faithful to the teaching of the Apostles.

Psalm 133:1–3 ✠ Psalm 1:1–6 ✠ Psalm 88:1–28

Scripture: Acts 15:6–7, 28; 16:4

Reading: First Ecumenical Council (Nicea I) 325

Nicene Creed, Latin text

We believe in one God the Father Almighty, maker of things visible and invisible, and in one Lord Jesus Christ, the Son of God, born of the Father, that is from the substance of the Father, God from God, Light from Light, True God from True God, born not made, one in substance with the Father, which the Greeks call *homoousion*, through whom all things were made, whether those in heaven or those in the earth; who for us human beings and for our salvation, came down, was incarnate, was made human, suffered and arose on the third day, ascended into heaven, is coming to judge the living and the dead; and in the Holy Spirit.

Solemnity of Pentecost

Morning Prayer

Antiphon: In the latter days I shall pour out my Spirit.

Psalm 5:1–12 ✠ Psalm 80:1–14 ✠ Psalm 143:7–12 TNK

Scripture: Numbers 24:2–9 TNK

Reading: Byzantine liturgy for Pentecost

Apolysis after Kneeling Prayers

May Christ, our True God, have mercy upon us, he who emptied himself by leaving the womb of the Father, assuming our human nature and making it divine, and ascended into heaven and was enthroned at the Father's right hand, and sent down the Holy, Divine, and Eternal Spirit, one in being with him and the Father, co-eternal and equal to them in honor and glory. He sent the Spirit upon the Apostles who were thus enlightened by him, and through them the whole universe. May this same Christ save us also through the intercession of his all-pure Mother, of his glorious apostles worthy of all praise, and of all his saints, for he is good and the lover of humanity.

PRAYING—WITH THE SAINTS—TO GOD OUR MOTHER

Evening Prayer

Antiphon: And we shall come and abide in you, I and my Father, and the Spirit.

Psalm 133:1–3 ✠ Psalm 80:1–14 ✠ Psalm 143:7–12 TNK

Scripture: John 14:19–26 PESH

Reading: Syro-Malankara Rite

First Sunday after Pentecost, Evening Prayer

> Turn your ears towards the throne of the Godhead
> and receive from it precious pearls, words of life.
> Study the Testaments of Light and put your faith in them.
> By these Two you shall obtain life that knows no end.
> Pay heed to the New, but listen to the Old as well. Keep them together
> for it is the same Truth that they speak to you.
> Glory to the Father who revealed mysteries through the Prophets.
> Adoration to the Son who made them known through the Apostles.
> Thanksgiving to the Spirit, Ocean of riches and wisdom, who distributes
> gifts among the children of Adam. O Holy Spirit, Mother of the poor,
> visit those who are in need, heal the sick, show compassion to sinners,
> and pardon the dead who rest in hope of you. To you be all praise.

✠

FEAST OF THE HOLY SPIRIT—MONDAY AFTER PENTECOST (EAST)

Morning Prayer

Antiphon: The Spirit of God sanctifies and re-animates us!

Psalm 50:1–19 ✠ Psalm 138:1–14 ✠ Psalm 142:1–12

Scripture: Nehemiah 9:18–21 TNK

Reading: St. Ephrem, deacon, Father and Doctor of the Church † 373

Hymns on the Nativity 5.7–10

> The Gracious One, seeing that humanity
> was poor and prostrate, made feast days
> as treasuries, and opened them wide
> for the faint of heart, so that the feast would rouse
> the faint of heart to arise and become rich.
> Behold, the First-born has opened his feast for us,
> like a vast treasure-house. This one day,

the most perfect of the year, alone opens
this treasury. Come, let us prosper
and become rich before it is closed.
Blessed are the vigilant who plunder from it
the spoils of life. Such great disgrace shall shame
the one who sees his neighbor carrying away treasures
yet rests and nods off in the treasury, emerging empty-handed.
On this feast day let everyone hang a garland
on the door of his heart. The Holy Spirit, may she
desire to enter through the door and dwell therein
sanctifying the interior. Behold, She moves about
to every door searching where She might dwell.

Evening Prayer

Antiphon: The Spirit of God has been given to us, let us glorify God!

Psalm 133:1–3 ✠ Psalm 80:1–14 ✠ Psalm 103:1–34

Scripture: John 14:12–17 PESH

Reading: St. Ephrem, deacon, Father and Doctor of the Church † 373

Commentary on the Diatessaron 19.15

Go into the entire world and baptize them in the name of the Father, and of the Son, and of the Spirit; he didn't say: "in the name of the Father and in the name of the Son and in the name of the Spirit" in order to show that they are one single nature, because he names three persons in one single name. . . . Therefore the Spirit is God because she is from God. The Name of God dwells among human beings because certain ones of them are called *gods*, and moreover we have by grace the name of the Father and of the Son. Thus Man is called "god," like Moses who was glorified more than Pharaoh. But a human being has never been called a *living Spirit*. It is not said of Eve that she was Adam's sister or his daughter, but rather that she came from him; likewise, it is not to be said that the Spirit is a daughter or sister, but rather that she is from God and consubstantial with God.

✠

Solemnity of the Holy Trinity—First Sunday after Pentecost (West)

Morning Prayer

Antiphon: The Trinity created humanity for whom the world was prepared.

Psalm 5:1–12 ✠ Psalm 80:1–14 ✠ Psalm 109:1–7

Scripture: Genesis 1:26–27 TNK

Reading: St. Theophilus, bishop, Post-Apostolic Father of the Church † 181

To Autolycus 2.9–10

    Certain people of God, possessing the Holy Spirit and thus becoming prophets, receiving from God inspiration and Wisdom, became God-taught, holy and righteous. Therefore, they were considered worthy of receiving this reward: that they should become instruments of God and embrace the Divine Wisdom. It was through this Wisdom that they spoke about the creation of the world and everything else. They predicted pestilences, famines, and wars. But there was not just one or two of these prophets, but many of them at various times and circumstances amongst the Hebrews. . . . They have all spoken consistently and harmoniously with each other, concerning previous events and what is going to take place, and what is even now unfolding before our very eyes. Therefore, we are persuaded that things will happen just as those things predicted have already taken place.

    First of all, with one accord they taught us that God made everything out of nothing. For nothing co-existed with God or developed with God who was and is his own domain, who experiences no need, existing before the ages. God willed to be known, and thus created humanity for whom the world was prepared. For that which is created has needs; that which is Uncreated doesn't need anything. Thus God possessing the Word internally, within the depths of the womb, engendered the Word, and brought it forth with Wisdom [the Spirit], before everything else.

Evening Prayer

Antiphon: We have faith in the Triune God of Love who unites with us out of love.

Psalm 133:1–3 ✠ Psalm 80:1–14 ✠ Psalm 109:1–7

Scripture: John 16:12–16 PESH

Reading: St. Isidore of Seville, Father and Doctor of the Church † 636

Letter 6.10

But when we speak and distinguish the Persons of the Holy Trinity, we should take great care that we do not seem to divide the indivisible and most simple essence of the one God. For if we do not understand the ineffable meaning of the Father "to beget"; and likewise, regarding the Son eternally "to be born," "to be begotten," or "to go forth" is beyond our estimation, then just as incomprehensible is it concerning the Holy Spirit "to be sent" or "to proceed," et cetera, "from the Father and the Son," for such things are said about the distinctions of the Persons. But if we do not perceive these matters with reason, let us receive them by faith, so that we may deserve to be eternally saved.

✠

Solemnity of Corpus Christi—Thursday after Holy Trinity (West)

Morning Prayer

Antiphon: Come, buy wine and milk.

Psalm 5:1–12 ✠ Psalm 131:1–18 ✠ Psalm 22:1–6

Scripture: Sirach 24:4, 22–31 VULG

Reading: St. Bonaventure, cardinal, Doctor of the Church † 1274

Mystical Treatise on the Death of the Lord 15.4

Let us listen and understand the true voice of the Wisdom of God, the Only-begotten of the Father, Sweet Jesus, saying: *Whoever eats of me will hunger still, whoever drinks of me will thirst for more*. . . . Yes surely, I will make haste and drink; *and without money and without price, I will buy the wine and milk* which the Wisdom of the Father Most High, the Most Blessed Jesus, *has mixed for us in the cup* of his Body, that is his Precious Blood, the price of our life! *Come* with me, all you who love the beloved Jesus, and *buy not with perishable things, with silver or gold*, but by an exchange of the way you live and act, purchase that *wine and milk*, the most pure blood that inebriates the perfect as wine and nourishes the little ones as milk. If you are perfect and full of strength, the blood of Jesus is to you strong wine straight from the grapes. If you are weak, and still a nursling, it is for you nourishing milk. Drink, therefore, of this blood most pure.

PRAYING—WITH THE SAINTS—TO GOD OUR MOTHER

Evening Prayer

Antiphon: I am the living bread that comes down from heaven.

Psalm 133:1–3 ✠ Psalm 80:1–14 ✠ Psalm 22:1–6

Scripture: John 6:48–58

Reading: St. Cyril of Alexandria, Patriarch, Father and Doctor of the Church † 444

Commentary on John 4.3

As the Living Father has sent me, and I live by the Father, so anyone who eats me, shall also live by me. When we speak of his Incarnation we mean that he was completely made human. "Just as the Father has made me human," he says, "and since I am God the Word, having been born Life out of that which is by nature Life Itself, and becoming human have filled my Temple, that is my Body, with my own nature; likewise whoever will eat of my flesh shall *live because of me.* For I took mortal flesh, but since I dwelt in it, being by nature Life—because I am from the living Father, I re-orientated and restructured all things into my own life. I have not been conquered by the dissolution of the flesh, but rather have conquered it, as God. Therefore just as, (for I will say it again not hesitating whatsoever for your benefit) even though I *was made flesh,*" he says, (for this is what *being sent* signifies) "I live again because of the Living Father, preserving within myself the natural excellence of God who gave me birth, thus whoever by partaking my flesh, receives me within, shall live, completely reconfigured and transformed entire into me, who possesses the power to give life, because I am, so to speak, from the root of the Life-giver, namely from God the Father." Now he says he was incarnate from the Father, and indeed Solomon says, *Wisdom has built for herself a house.*

✠

SOLEMNITY OF THE SACRED HEART OF JESUS—FRIDAY AFTER SECOND SUNDAY AFTER PENTECOST (WEST)

Morning Prayer

Antiphon: Answer me, O Yahweh, for your steadfast love is bounteous, in your abundant maternal compassion, turn to me. (Psalm 69:16 TNK)

Psalm 143:7–12 TNK ✠ Psalm 40:9–13 TNK ✠ Psalm 145:1–10 TNK

Scripture: Isaiah 63:7–9 TNK

Reading: St. Gertrude the Great of Helfta, nun † 1302

The Herald of God's Loving-Kindness 3.63.2

Placing Gertrude upon his bosom as one does an infant showering it with a thousand caresses, the Lord bent down and with his divine mouth to her ear attentively consoled her saying, "Just as a tender mother is in the habit of wiping away all the woes of her little child with her kisses, so too, by the most sweet whisperings of my loving words, I wish to assuage all your pains and difficulties." After she had savored these things resting upon the Lord's bosom, repeatedly receiving sweet and endless divine consolations, the Lord showed her his Heart, saying, "Intently study now, my beloved, all the interior depths of my Heart and attentively examine with what faithfulness you have invoked me for anything, and see how I have gathered it there and arranged it for good, for the most profitable and salutary benefit of your soul."

Evening Prayer

Antiphon: The Divine Heart is the treasury of all graces.

Psalm 40:9–13 TNK ✠ Psalm 51:1–5 TNK ✠ Psalm 145:1–10 TNK

Scripture: Galatians 5:22–25 VULG: "The fruit of the Spirit is love, joy, peace, patience, endurance, goodness, generosity, meekness, faith, modesty, continence, and chastity. Against such there is no law. Those who belong to Christ have crucified their flesh with its passions and desires. If we live by the Spirit, let us walk according to the Spirit."

Reading: St. Mechtild of Hackeborn † 1299

Book of Special Grace 2.2

On a certain Sunday, when they were singing *Asperges me* [Sprinkle me], [Mechtild] asked the Lord, "My Lord, in what shall you now wash and cleanse my heart?" And immediately the Lord with indescribable love bent towards her like a mother to her child, completely embracing her and said, "In the love of my Divine Heart I bathe you." And he opened the gateway of his sweet Heart, even the treasury of divinity, into which she entered as into a vineyard. And she saw there a river of living water flowing from the East to the West, and surrounding the river were twelve trees bearing twelve fruit, that is the virtues which blessed Paul enumerated in his epistle: love, joy, peace, et cetera. This water is called the river of love, and thus her soul entered into it and was washed of every stain.

Fathers of Fourth Ecumenical Council— Fourth Sunday after Pentecost (East)

Morning Prayer

Antiphon: God gave them up until she who was to give birth gave birth.

Psalm 5:1–12 ☧ Psalm 72:1–28 ☧ Psalm 25:1–12

Scripture: 1 Timothy 3:14–16

Reading: Fourth Ecumenical Council (Chalcedon) 451

Definition of Chalcedon

Therefore, following the holy fathers, we, [the fathers of this sacred council], all with one voice, teach the confession of one and the same Son, our Lord Jesus Christ: the same perfect in divinity and perfect in humanity, the same truly God and truly a human being possessing a rational soul and a body; consubstantial with the Father according to divinity and the same consubstantial with us regarding humanity, like us in all respects except for sin; before the ages born from the Father as regards divinity, and in the last days the same one for us and for our salvation born from Mary, the virgin *Theotokos* [Mother of God] as regards humanity; one and the same Christ, Son, Lord, Only-Begotten.

ಌ 📖 ಌ

Evening Prayer

Antiphon: The virgin womb gave birth to God made flesh: God-with-us!

Psalm 133:1–3 ☧ Psalm 1:1–6 ☧ Psalm 88:1–28

Scripture: Matthew 1:18–25

Reading: Fathers of the local Eleventh Council of Toledo, 675

Symbol of Faith

We proclaim and believe that the holy and ineffable Trinity—Father, Son, and Holy Spirit—is one God by nature, of one substance, of one nature as well as of one majesty and power.

And we profess that the Father is not begotten, not created, but unbegotten. For he himself, from whom the Son has received his birth and the Holy Spirit his procession, has his origin from no one. He is therefore the source and origin of the whole godhead. . . .

We also confess that the Son was born, but not made, from the substance of the Father, without beginning, before all ages, for at no time did the Father exist without the Son, nor the Son without the Father. . . . In everything the Son is equal to God the

Father, for he has never begun to exist nor ceased to be born.... We must believe that the Son is begotten or born not from nothing or from any other substance, but from the womb of the Father, that is from his substance. Therefore the Father is eternal, and the Son is likewise eternal. If he was always Father, he always had a Son, whose Father he was, and therefore we confess that the Son is born from the Father without beginning....

We also believe that the Holy Spirit, the third Person in the Trinity, is God, one and equal with God the Father and the Son, of one substance and of one nature, not, however, begotten or created, but proceeding from both, and that he is the Spirit of both....

The Holy Trinity itself has indeed deigned to reveal it clearly to us: in these names by which he wanted the single Persons to be known, it is impossible to understand one Person without the other; one cannot conceive of the Father without the Son, nor can the Son be found without the Father. In truth, the very relationship expressed in the personal names forbids us to separate the Persons, for, although it does not name them together, it implies them. No one can hear any one of these names without necessarily also understanding the Other. While then these Three are One and this One is Three, each of the Persons retains his own characteristic: The Father has eternity without birth; the Son has eternity with birth; and the Holy Spirit has procession without birth with eternity.

☩

FATHERS OF THE SIX ECUMENICAL COUNCILS— SEVENTH SUNDAY AFTER PENTECOST (EAST)

Morning Prayer

Antiphon: The Council of the holy ones was assembled.

Psalm 5:1–12 ☩ Psalm 1:1–6 ☩ Psalm 25:1–12

Scripture: 1 Timothy 3:14–16

Reading: Second Ecumenical Council (Constantinople I) 381

Nicene-Constantinopolitan Creed, Greek text

We believe in one God the Father Almighty, maker of heaven and earth, of all things both visible and invisible, and in one Lord Jesus Christ, the Son of God, the Only-Begotten, born of the Father before all ages, Light from Light, True God from True God, begotten not made, one in being with the Father, through whom all things came to be; for us human beings and for our salvation he came down from heaven and became incarnate from the Holy Spirit and the Virgin Mary, became human and was crucified on our behalf under Pontius Pilate and suffered and was buried, and arose on the third day according to the Scriptures, and he ascended into heaven and is seated at the right hand of the Father; he is coming again with glory to judge the living and the dead, whose kingdom will have no end; and in the Holy Spirit, the Lord and Giver of Life, who proceeds from the Father, who with the Father and the Son is worshipped and glorified, who spoke through the Prophets; in one, holy, catholic, and apostolic church; we confess one baptism for the remission of sins; we look forward to a resurrection of the dead and the life of the world to come. Amen.

Evening Prayer

Antiphon: It has been decided by the Holy Spirit and the Councils.

Psalm 133:1–3 ✠ Psalm 1:1–6 ✠ Psalm 88:1–28

Scripture: Acts 15:1–29

Reading: Third Ecumenical Council (Ephesus) 431

First Letter of Cyril, Greek text

 The Holy and Great Council, therefore, stated that the Only-begotten Son, born of the Father according to nature, True God of True God, Light from Light, the One through whom the Father made all things, came down, became incarnate, became human, suffered, arose on the third day and ascended into heaven. We likewise should follow these words and these teachings, considering what is meant by saying that the Word from God became enfleshed and became human. For we do not declare that the nature of the Word was changed and became flesh, nor that he was transformed into a whole human being composed of soul and body. Rather we claim that the Word in an ineffable and inconceivable manner united to himself according to subsistence, flesh enlivened by a rational soul, and so became a human being and was called son of man, but not by God's will or good pleasure alone, nor by the assuming of a person alone. Rather we profess that two different natures did come together to form a unity, and from both arose one Christ, one Son. It was not as if the distinctness of the natures was destroyed by the union, but rather divinity and humanity together made perfect for us one Lord and Christ, together marvelously and mysteriously combining to form a unity. Thus it is said that the one who existed and was born of the Father before all ages, was born according to the flesh of a woman, without his Divine Nature either beginning to exist in the holy Virgin, or needing of itself a second birth after that from his Father.

Solemnity of Christ the King—Last Sunday in Ordinary Time (West)

Morning Prayer

Antiphon: The Lord's Anointed is King of all creation.

Psalm 5:1–12 ✠ Psalm 80:1–14 ✠ Psalm 60:1–8

Scripture: Daniel 7:13–14

Reading: St. Hippolytus, bishop and martyr, Father of the Church † 235

Concerning the Antichrist 26.1–2

    As Daniel says, *I saw in a vision of the night, and behold on a cloud of heaven came one like a Son of Man, and he appeared before the Ancient of Days. And to him was given dominion, honor, and the kingdom, and all peoples, tribes, and tongues will serve him. His authority is an everlasting authority which will not pass away, and his kingdom will not be destroyed.* This indicates that all authority is given to the Son by the Father so that he is established king and judge of every creature *in heaven, on earth, and under the earth*; "in heaven," because the Word was born from out of the Father's heart before all creation; "on earth," because he became a human being among human beings, forming a new Adam out of himself; and "under the earth," because he was reckoned among the dead, having preached to the souls of the saints, conquering death by his death.

Evening Prayer

Antiphon: Christ, the Word of God, is King of kings, and Lord of lords.

Psalm 133:1–3 ✠ Psalm 80:1–14 ✠ Psalm 46:1–8

Scripture: Revelation 19:11–21

Reading: St. Ephrem, deacon, Father and Doctor of the Church † 373

Hymn on the Resurrection 1.4–7

    His knowledge chased away
    the error of lost humanity.
    Through Him, the Evil One was bewildered and confounded.
    Throughout the people He poured out all Wisdom.
    Blessed be his treasury!
    From on High, Power descended to us;
    from the womb, Hope shone out for us.
    From the tomb, Life rose up for us;

on the Right Hand, the King is enthroned for us.
Blessed be his magnificence!
From on High he flowed like a river.
From Mary he budded forth like a shoot.
From the Wood of the Cross he hung down like a fruit.
He rose up to Heaven as the first-fruit offering.
Blessed be his will!
The Word came forth from the Father's Womb,
and clothed himself in a body in another womb.
He proceeded from one Womb to another,
and chaste bosoms are filled with him.
Blessed be the One who dwells within us!

Advent Daily Readings / Nativity Fast (East)

Day 1

Morning Prayer

Antiphon: A star shall come out of Jacob, a scepter arise out of Israel.

Psalm 5:1–12 ✠ Psalm 118:65–72 ✠ Psalm 3:1–8

Scripture: Numbers 24:2–3, 15–17 TNK

Reading: St. Ephrem, deacon, Father and Doctor of the Church † 373

Hymns on the Nativity 27.19–20

> I give thanks for your first birth, hidden and concealed from every creature.
> I also give thanks for your second birth, revealed and younger than all creatures made by your hands.
> Unique to two births, one celestial and the other terrestrial,
> one the stranger, strange to all,
> and one the kinsman, completely allied to humanity.

Evening Prayer

Antiphon: There is only one Mediator who was sent at the appointed time.

Psalm 133:1–3 ✠ Psalm 118:73–80 ✠ Psalm 4:1–8

Scripture: 1 Timothy 2:1–7

The Liturgical Calendar: Moveable Feast Days

Reading: St. Quodvultdeus, bishop, Father of the Church † 450

On the Creed 3.4.1–4

Indeed, faith and truth preach that Christ was born of a virgin. Such you have accepted by faith; such you have declared you believe when you responded: "I believe." This birth of God and Man was brought about for the sake of humanity. Proceeding from the heart of the Father, this sublime Majesty poured itself into a mother's womb. God's benevolence made it necessary that humanity, found fallen, might be found restored to God the Father through a Mediator. This second birth, however, my beloved brothers and sisters, is just as marvelous. Can anyone describe the first birth by which the Son was born of the Father without any mother? If we cannot explain this first birth, then when are we ever going to be able to even begin to explain that second birth? If the first birth so taxes our understanding that it gives way to faith, when will we ever grasp the second, which even the hearts of the prophets were unable to comprehend?

Day 2

Morning Prayer

Antiphon: God displays tender maternal compassion.

Psalm 41:1–11 ✠ Psalm 118:81–88 ✠ Psalm 56:1–11

Scripture: Deuteronomy 30:1–5 TNK

Reading: St. Leo the Great, pope, Father and Doctor of the Church † 461

Sermon 24.1

Indeed, dearly beloved, the goodness of God has always cared for humanity, in various ways and with many measures. God has tenderly imparted numerous providential gifts to ages past, but *in these last days* has exceeded all the abundance of his usual generosity. At this time, Divine Mercy herself came down in Christ for us sinners, Truth herself for the wayward, and Life herself for the dead. As a result, the Word who is co-eternal and co-equal with the Father, took up our lowly nature into unity with divinity, and being God born of God, was likewise born a human being from a human being. This indeed had been promised from the foundation of the world.

Evening Prayer

Antiphon: We await the Appearing of our Great God and Savior.

Psalm 1:1–6 ✠ Psalm 118:89–96 ✠ Psalm 101:1–28

Scripture: John 1:9–14 NT

PRAYING—WITH THE SAINTS—TO GOD OUR MOTHER

Reading: St. Gregory the Illuminator, Catholicos, Father of the Church † ca. 332

Armenian Catechism 391

Now we have yet to tell you about the birth of the Son of God from the Virgin; the details of how it took place we shall recount in sequence. For indeed the beginning of the Uncreated Word did not start from after the birth from the Virgin, but before all ages he was born from the Father and then subsequently descended for our sake and was born in the flesh from the Virgin. But regarding the birth from the Father who gave birth to him, he alone knows. The second birth happened by God's grace for humanity in order that God might bestow life to humankind, and save the earth from the first curse, as well as renew it by coming with blessings upon his heels.

Day 3

Morning Prayer

Antiphon: The Word is eternally born of God and temporally born of the Virgin.

Psalm 54:1–16 ✠ Psalm 118:89–96 ✠ Psalm 112:1–9

Scripture: Isaiah 7:14; 9:5–6

Reading: St. Cyril of Jerusalem, bishop, Father and Doctor of the Church † 386

Catechetical Lectures 12.4

Now recall what was said yesterday regarding the Divinity. Believe that the very same Only-begotten Son of God was born yet again of a virgin. Be convinced by what John the Evangelist says, *And the Word became flesh so that it might dwell among us.* For the Word indeed is eternal, born of the Father before all ages, but recently assumed flesh for our sake. But many retort and ask, "What cause was so great that Divinity should descend into humanity? And is it God's nature at all to be associating intimately with human beings? Besides, is it even possible for a virgin to bear a child without intercourse with a man?" Since there is much controversy and the strife is many-sided, come, let us by the grace of Christ, and the prayers of those who present, proceed to resolve each objection.

Evening Prayer

Antiphon: At last we shall see God face to face.

Psalm 6:1–10 ✠ Psalm 118:97–104 ✠ Psalm 79:1–19

Scripture: 1 Corinthians 13:1–13

Reading: St. Francis de Sales, bishop, Doctor of the Church † 1622

Treatise Concerning the Love of God 3.12

O Holy and Divine Spirit, eternal Love of the Father and of the Son, be propitious to my immaturity. Then, Theotimus, our understanding shall behold God, yes I declare it, it shall see God *face to face*, contemplating by means a view of true and real presence, the Divine Essence herself, and in her infinite beauties: all power, all goodness, all wisdom, all justice, and the rest of the profundity of perfections.

This understanding shall see clearly then, the infinite knowledge which God the Father had from all eternity of his own beauty, and wishing its full expression in himself, he pronounced and eternally declared the Word, the Verbum, or the most unique and infinite speech and diction, which, comprising and representing all the perfection of the Father, can be only one true God self-same, without division or separation. Then we shall truly see that eternal and wondrous generation of the Word and Divine Son, by which he was eternally born to the image and likeness of the Father. . . . O Theotimus, what joy, what exultation to celebrate this eternal birthing which is manifested *in the splendor of the saints*, to celebrate it by beholding it, and to behold it by celebrating it!

Day 4

Morning Prayer

Antiphon: Wisdom delighted in the children of God.

Psalm 64:1–13 ✠ Psalm 118:97–104 ✠ Psalm 3:1–8

Scripture: Proverbs 8:22–31 TNK

Reading: St. Bede the Venerable, priest, Father and Doctor of the Church † 735

Homily on the Gospels 1.8

However, to as many as accepted him he gave them the power to become children of God, to those who believe in his name. Let us consider, dearly beloved brothers and sisters, how great is the grace of our Redeemer and how great is the abundance of his tender sweetness! He is the only one born of the Father, yet he did not choose to remain the only one; he descended to earth where he might acquire siblings for himself to whom he could grant the Kingdom of his Father. He was born God from God, yet he did not wish to remain the only Son of God; he deigned to become also son of man, without losing what he had been, but taking up what he had not been, so that by this he could transform human beings into children of God, and make them co-heirs of his glory, and so they might by grace begin to possess what he himself has always possessed by nature.

Evening Prayer

Antiphon: Our forbearers in the faith were guided by the Cloud.

Psalm 54:1–16 ✠ Psalm 76:13–20 ✠ Psalm 42:1–5

Scripture: 1 Corinthians 10:1–5, 11–13

Reading: St. Cyril of Alexandria, Patriarch, Father and Doctor of the Church † 444

Commentary on John 4.4

> Again, it is written as an example for us in the Book called Numbers, *And on the day that the tabernacle was taken up, the cloud covered the tabernacle, that is, over the Tent of Testimony, and at evening prayer there was upon the tabernacle the appearance of fire, until morning. Thus it always was, the cloud covered it by day and the appearance of fire by night. And when the cloud rose from the tabernacle, then afterwards the children of Israel set out on the journey; and in the place where the cloud came to rest, there the children of Israel pitched their tents. At the command of the Lord shall they set forth on their journey, and the children of Israel shall keep the charge of God and not depart. By the voice of the Lord shall they break camp and by the command of the Lord shall they journey forth.* Do you see how they are commanded to follow, and to journey with the journeying of the cloud, and to break camp with it and again to rest with it? For accompanying their guide was salvation for those of Israel, and even now for us is the never departing Christ. For he was with them in ancient times in the form of the tabernacle and cloud, as well as fire.
>
> But as far as we are able, the historical narrative shall be transposed to a spiritual interpretation. For when *Wisdom,* as it is written, *built for herself a house,* and pitched the more authentic tabernacle, that is, the temple of the Virgin, God the Word, who is in the womb of God the Father, descended into the temple in an incomprehensible and God-worthy fashion, and was made human, so that for those who are already enlightened, and *walk as in the day*, as Paul says, he might become a cloud overshadowing them, dissipating the heat of our passions arising from our infirmities; while to those who are still ignorant and wandering about, living as if in a night and darkness, he might become a fire illuminating them and transforming them into spiritual fervency.

Day 5

Morning Prayer

Antiphon: God the Word comes forth from the mouth of the Most High.

Psalm 72:1–28 ✠ Psalm 137:1–8 ✠ Psalm 118:105–12

Scripture: Sirach 24:1–11 VULG

Reading: St. Bede the Venerable, priest, Father and Doctor of the Church † 735

Homily on the Gospels 1.5

He was born into the world after us, but by the merit of his virtue and kingdom he is justly called the *first-born* of us all. Regarding his own divine birth he can properly be said to be *first-born* because, before generating any creature by making it, the Father brought forth a Son co-eternal with himself; and before generating any children of adoption for himself by redeeming them through the Word of Truth, the eternal Father gave birth to the Word, co-eternal with himself. Thus the Word himself, the very Son of God, his Virtue and Wisdom, declares, *I came forth from the mouth of the Most High, firstborn before every creature.* Now Mary gave birth to her first-born son, that is, the son of her substance; she gave birth to the One who was born God from God before every creature, and in that humanity in which he was created, he rightfully preceded every creature.

Evening Prayer

Antiphon: From generation to generation, our God is full of maternal compassion.

Psalm 84:1–13 ✠ Psalm 102:1–22 ✠ Psalm 88:1–28

Scripture: Matthew 1:1–17

Reading: St. Augustine, bishop, Father and Doctor of the Church † 430

Sermon 51.8

Matthew goes on to say: *All the generations, from Abraham to David, are fourteen generations; and from David to the transmigration into Babylon are fourteen generations; and from the transmigration into Babylon to Christ are fourteen generations.* Then, recounting how Christ was born of the Virgin Mary, he further related: *Now the generation of Christ was in this manner....* By enumerating the list of progenitors he spelled out why Christ is called the son of David and the son of Abraham. But now the tale has to be told regarding how he was born and appeared among human beings. And so there naturally follows the narrative concerning which we believe that not only was our Lord Jesus Christ born of the everlasting God, coeternal with the One who engendered him before all times, born before all creation, and through whom all things have been made; but was also born in time by the Holy Spirit of the Virgin Mary—and this we equally confess as the former. You, I am speaking of course to my fellow Catholics, you remember and you know that this is our faith; this we profess and confess. For this very faith myriads of martyrs have been slain all over the world.

PRAYING—WITH THE SAINTS—TO GOD OUR MOTHER

Day 6

Morning Prayer

Antiphon: I am your God, your savior from eternity.

Psalm 91:1–15 ✠ Psalm 141:1–7 ✠ Psalm 118:113–20

Scripture: Isaiah 43:10–14

Reading: St. Bede the Venerable, priest, Father and Doctor of the Church † 735

Homily on the Gospels 1.5

> *Behold a virgin,* he says, *will be with child and give birth to a son, and his name shall be called Immanuel, which means "God with us."* The Savior's name, by which he is called "God with us" by the prophet, signifies both natures of his one person. For the one who was born before time from the Father, is God himself in the fullness of time, became Immanuel (i.e., God with us) in his mother's womb, because he deigned to receive the weakness of our nature into the unity of his person when *the Word was made flesh and dwelt among us.* In a marvelous manner he began to be what we are while not ceasing to be what he has been, assuming our nature in such a fashion that he himself should not lose what he has always been.

Evening Prayer

Antiphon: Born from the Father without a mother, born from a mother without a father; both births are awe-inspiring.

Psalm 15:1–11 ✠ Psalm 112:1–9 ✠ Psalm 109:1–7

Scripture: Romans 11:33–36

Reading: St. Augustine, bishop, Father and Doctor of the Church † 430

Sermon 189.4

> The birth of Christ from the Father was without a mother; the birth of Christ from his mother was without a father; both births are awe-inspiring. The first nativity is eternal, the second temporal. When was he born of the Father? What do you mean, "when"? You're asking "when," when there, there is no passage of time. Don't ask about "when" there. Ask about it here; it's good to ask when he was born of his mother. But it's not a good idea to ask about when he was born of his Father. He was born and time doesn't pertain in that instance. He was born eternal from the Eternal One, and is co-eternal. Why be amazed, God is God. Consider his divinity and your basis for amazement disintegrates.

✠

The Liturgical Calendar: Moveable Feast Days

DEVOTION TO THE SACRED HEART OF JESUS

Day 1

Morning Prayer

Antiphon: We are taught that all things have one Mother, one Cause of their existence (Gregory of Nyssa, *Song of Songs* 2).

Psalm 5:1–12 ✠ Psalm 118:121–28 ✠ Psalm 145:1–10 TNK

Scripture: Song of Songs 2:16–17

Reading: St. Gregory of Nyssa, bishop, Father and Doctor of the Church † ca. 395

Song of Songs 1

Now when the soul has been cleansed and no longer is obscured by the leprosy of the veil of flesh, it sees the treasury of all good things. A name for this treasury is the heart from which flows to the breasts the abundance of divine milk by which the soul is nourished, drawing forth grace in proportion to its faith. Therefore the souls proclaims, *Your breasts are better than wine*, signifying the heart by the symbol of the breasts. No one would be guilty of deception when understanding the heart to represent the hidden and secret power of God. One would correctly consider the breasts to stand for the activities of God's power in our regard by which God nurses each one's life, graciously bestowing the nourishment according to each one's needs.

Evening Prayer

Antiphon: The Heart of God abounds in patience and long-suffering love.

Psalm 133:1–3 ✠ Psalm 4:1–8 ✠ Psalm 144:1–10

Scripture: 2 Peter 3:8–9

Reading: St. Bernard of Clairvaux, abbot, Doctor of the Church † 1153

Sermons on the Song of Songs 9.5

Now let us see what this esteem for the Bridegroom's breasts means. [*For your breasts are better than wine, sweetly smelling of the finest ointments.*] . . . The two breasts of the Bridegroom are two proofs of his innate mildness, namely, his patience in awaiting the sinner and his receptive clemency for the penitent. This twofold and intense sweetness overflows from the heart of the Lord Jesus in the form of tireless expectation and generous pardon.

PRAYING—WITH THE SAINTS—TO GOD OUR MOTHER

Day 2

Morning Prayer

Antiphon: God's maternal heart will never forget us!

Psalm 5:1–12 ✠ Psalm 118:121–28 ✠ Psalm 24:1–22

Scripture: Isaiah 49:13–16 TNK

Reading: St. Faustina Kowalska, nun † 1938

Divine Mercy in My Soul 1490

O Jesus, Wellspring of Life, sanctify me. O my Strength, fortify me. O my Supreme Commander, fight for me. Only Light of my soul, enlighten me. My Leader, guide me. I entrust myself to you as a newborn babe does to its mother's love. Even if everything were to rise up against me, and even if the ground were to fall out from under my feet, I still would be at peace close to your Heart. You are always a most tender mother to me, and you surpass all mothers.

ಐ 📖 ಐ

Evening Prayer

Antiphon: The counsel of the Lord endures forever; the thoughts of God's heart from generation to generation (Psalm 32:11 LXX).

Psalm 133:1–3 ✠ Psalm 118:17–24 ✠ Psalm 72:1–28

Scripture: Matthew 11:28–30

Reading: St. Mechtild of Hackeborn, nun † 1299

Book of Special Grace 2.16

At one time, Love surrounded [Mechtild] with a garment as radiant as the sun. Both the soul and Love were standing in the presence of Jesus Christ like beautiful virgins. The soul was consumed by a great desire to draw closer to Jesus; for although she was gazing upon his kingly countenance, it was not enough for her. While she was overwhelmed with desire the Lord waved his hand, and Love took her and led her to the Lord.

The soul bent over to the mellifluous heart of her unique Savior, savoring the drink of sweetness and delight flowing from his side. Then all her bitterness was transformed into sweetness; all her fear into security. She also sucked out of Christ's heart a lovely fruit which she then took and put into her mouth. This fruit was perpetual praise which comes from the heart of God. For all praise given to God flows out from him who is the beginning and the end of all that is good. After that she received another fruit, the fruit of thanksgiving, for the soul cannot do anything by itself unless it is anticipated by God.

The Lord said to [Mechtild of Hackeborn]: "Now I also require most of all, one fruit from you." She replied: "O my sweetest God, what is this fruit?" The Lord answered: "This one—that you place every joy of your heart in me alone." She responded: "O my only Beloved, how can I do this?" Jesus replied: "My Love will accomplish this within you." Then she exclaimed with joyous feelings of gratitude: "Ah! Ah! Love! Love! Mother!" The Lord said: "You have called Love—Mother. Yes, my Love will become your Mother, and like a child you will suck from her interior consolations and ineffable delights. She will feed you, give you drink and clothe you, providing for all your needs like a mother cares for her only daughter."

Afterword

Now you have read the excerpts and have had a chance to reflect upon them. Hopefully this devotional book has been beneficial to you for your own relationship with God and/or scholarly enrichment. I derived the vast majority of texts from sermons, meditations, and church hymns composed by saints for public edification. This is the primary reason why I chose the format of prayer and worship because this is the very context in which the feminine imagery of God arose and was originally embedded.

I was struck at how easy it was to find a feminine text applicable for every feast day in the liturgical calendar, whether fixed or movable. This testifies to how thoroughgoing in the life of the Church the usage of feminine imagery was (and can be). I found texts in the Law, Prophets, and Writings (Old Testament) as well as in the New Testament. I likewise culled passages from every century from writers in both Western and Eastern Christendom. Not only did inspired authors of Sacred Scripture as well as saints throughout Christian history employ feminine imagery to describe God's relationship with us, but both of them also utilized maternal metaphors to depict the eternal relationship between the First and Second Persons of the Trinity. Feminine imagery aptly affords us insight into the relationship between God Almighty and her Wisdom, eternally conceived within the depths of her being. The depiction of God through feminine analogies is an integral part of the Deposit of Faith as found in Sacred Scripture and the Apostolic Tradition passed down through the ages in every culture. As St. Vincent of Lérins declared, the authentic Apostolic Tradition is that "which was held by everyone, everywhere, always."[1] I have found passages from five Ecumenical Councils, all thirty-three Doctors of the (Catholic) Church, another thirty-six Fathers, and a total of seventy-one saints from every century. Consequently, it is incumbent upon the Body of Christ to appreciate and to re-appropriate this life-giving aspect of the Deposit of Faith.

The selections that have been provided in this book are the fruit of many years of reading and research. I am convinced that many, many more passages remain to be uncovered in the writings of the Fathers, Doctors, and saints of the Catholic and Orthodox Churches. The scope of my reading has been limited by time, and the duties and joys of being a husband and a father, of teaching at a university, of being a son, brother, friend, and member of society. If you happen to know of a text not included in this book, as listed in Appendix B, I would sincerely appreciate your informing me about it.

Dr. Daniel F. Stramara Jr.
Rockhurst University
Kansas City, Missouri

*Do not displace the ancient landmarks
established by your predecessors.
—Proverbs 22:28*

---

1. Vincent of Lérins, *Commonitorium*, 4.3.

Appendix A

Chronological List of Authors and Church Writings

2 Clement	2nd century
Diognetus	2nd century
St. Justin Martyr	165
Minucius Felix	2nd century
Odes of Solomon	2nd century
St. Melito of Sardis	180
St. Theophilus of Antioch	181
Acts of Peter	190
St. Irenaeus	202
St. Clement of Alexandria	215
Didascalia	early 3rd century
St. Hippolytus	235
Tertullian	240
Origen	254
St. Cyprian of Carthage	258
St. Dionysius of Rome	268
St. Methodius of Olympus	311
Nicaea I	325
St. Gregory the Illuminator	332
St. Aphraates	350
Liber Graduum	mid 4th century
St. Hilary of Poitiers	367
St. Athanasius	373
St. Ephrem	373

Note: Ecumenical Councils and Doctors of the Church are in italics.

APPENDIX A

St. Basil the Great	379
Constantinople I	381
St. Cyril of Jerusalem	386
St. Gregory Nazianzus	389
St. Macarius the Great	391
St. Gregory of Nyssa	395
St. Ambrose of Milan	397
St. Cheremon	400
St. John Chrysostom	407
Synesius of Cyrene	414
St. Jerome	420
St. Augustine of Hippo	430
Ephesus	431
St. Cyril of Alexandria	444
St. Peter Chrysologus	450
St. Quodvultdeus of Carthage	450
Chalcedon	451
Theodoret of Cyrhus	460
St. Leo the Great	461
Pseudo-Dionysius	5th century
Oecumenius	early 6th century
St. Romanos Melodius	556
Cassiodorus	580
St. Anastasius of Antioch	599
St. Gregory the Great	604
St. Sadhona	630
St. Isidore of Seville	636
St. Maximos the Confessor	662
Council of Toledo XI	675
St. Anastasius of Sinai	700
St. Bede the Venerable	735
St. John of Damascus	749
John of Dalyatha	780
St. Rabanus Maurus	856
St. Paschasius Radbertus	860
St. Gregory of Narek	1003
St. Peter Damian	1072
St. Anselm of Canterbury	1109
St. Bernard of Clairvaux	1153

Bl. Guerric of Igny	1157
St. Aelred of Rievaulx	1167
St. Nerses IV	1173
St. Hildegard of Bingen	1179
St. Hëlinand of Froidmont	1230
St. Anthony of Padua	1231
St. Bonaventure	1274
St. Thomas Aquinas	1274
St. Albert the Great	1280
St. Mechtild of Hackeborn	1299
St. Gertrude of Helfta	1302
Bl. Angela of Foligno	1309
Bl. Margaret of Oignt	1310
St. Gregory Palamas	1359
Bl. Henry Suso	1366
St. Birgitta of Sweden	1373
St. Catherine of Siena	1380
St. Nicholas Cabasilas	1391
Council of Florence	1439
St. Teresa of Avila	1582
St. John of the Cross	1591
St. Peter Canisius	1597
St. Laurence of Brindisi	1619
St. Robert Bellarmine	1621
St. Francis de Sales	1622
St. Alphonsus Liguori	1787
St. Thérèse of Lisieux	1897
St. Faustina Kowalska	1938
Bl. John Paul II	2005

Appendix B

Alphabetical List of Authors and their Critical Texts

Abbreviations

CCCM	Corpus Christianorum: Continuatio mediaevalis
CCSG	Corpus Christianorum: Series graeca
CCSL	Corpus Christianorum: Series latina
CSCO	Corpus scriptorum christianorum orientalium
CSEL	Corpus scriptorum ecclesiasticorum latinorum
GCS	Die griechischen christlichen Schriftsteller der ersten Jahrhunderte
GNO	Gregorii Nysseni Opera
PG	Patrologiae graeca
PL	Patrologiae latina
PO	Patrologia orientalis
PS	Patrologia syriaca
PTS	Patristische Texte und Studien
SC	Sources chrétiennes
SOCC	*Studia orientalia Christiana Collectanea*

2 Clement 14:1–3

> *The Apostolic Fathers*, ed. J. B. Lightfoot and J. R. Harmer (Grand Rapids: Baker, 1984), 49–50.

Acts of Peter 39

> *Les Actes de Pierre* (Paris: Letouzey et Ané, 1922), 452–56.

APPENDIX B

Aelred of Rievaulx

> Mirror of Charity (*De speculo caritatis*), 2.12.29–30 in CCCM 1:79; 2.19.59 in CCCM 1:94.
>
> Rule of Life for a Recluse (*De institutione inclusarum*), 25–26 in CCCM 1:657–58; 31 in CMMM 1:668, 671.
>
> Sermon (*Sermones*), 36.4–6 in CCCM IIA:295.

Albert the Great

> Commentary on Isaiah (*Super Isaiam*), 49:15 in *Opera omnia ad fidem codicum manuscriptorum edenda* (Münster, Germany: Aschendorff, 1951–) 19:491; 66.13 in 19:627.
>
> Commentary on the Psalms (*Commentarii in Psalmum*), 26:10 in *Opera omnia* 15:387.

Alphonsus Liguori

> How to Converse Continually and Familiarly with God (*Modo di conversare continuamente ed alla familiare con Dio*), 1–2 in S. Alfonso M. De Liguori, *Opere Ascetiche* (Roma: Redentoristi, 1933) 313–14; 6–9 in 316–17.

Ambrose of Milan

> Concerning Virgins (*De virginibus*), 1.5.21–22 in *Corpus scriptorum latinorum paravianum*, ed. Egnatius Cazzaniga (Rome, 1948), 10–12.
>
> The Mystery of the Incarnation of Our Lord (*De Incarnationis Dominicae Sacramento*), 1.2.11, 13 in CSEL 79:229–30.
>
> The Patriarchs (*De Patriarchis*), 11.50–51 in CSEL 32.2:152–53.

Anastasius of Antioch

> Oration on the Holy Trinity (*Oratio de SS. Trinitate*), 1.12 in PG 89:1317A–B.

Anastasius of Sinai

> Sermon on the Making of Man (*Sermones in constitutionem hominis secundum imaginem Dei*), 1.1 in CCSG 12:9–11.

Angela of Foligno

> Memorial (*Memoriale*), 7 in *Il libro della beata Angela da Foligno: editizione critica*, Spicilegium Bonaventurianum XXV (Grottaferrata: Collegii S. Bonaventurae, 1985), 318.

Anselm of Canterbury

> Meditations (*Meditatio*), 4 in PL 158:732A–B.

Alphabetical List of Authors and their Critical Texts

Monologion (*Monologion*) 42; in Michel Corbin, *L'oeuvre d'Anselme de Cantorbery*, (Paris: Editions du Cerf, 1986), 1:146, 148.

Prayer to St. Paul (*Oratio*), 10.197–238 in Michel Corbin, *L'oeuvre d'Anselme de Cantorbery*, (Paris: Editions du Cerf, 1986), 5:40–41.

Anthony of Padua

Prologue to Sunday Sermons (*Sermones Domincales et Festivi*), in *Sermones Domincales et Festivi* (Patavii, Italy: Edizioni Messagero, 1979), 1:2.

Sermons on the First Sunday in Quadragesima (*Sermone in Dominica I in Quadragesima*), 1.4 in ibid., 60–61.

Sermons on the Sunday in the Octave of Easter (*Sermone in Dominica in Octava Paschae*), 1.8 in ibid., 237–38; 1.11–12 in ibid., 243–45.

Sermons on the Second Sunday after Easter (*Sermone in Dominica II Post Pascha*), 2.3 in ibid., 250.

Sermons on the Fourth Sunday after Easter (*Sermone in Dominica IV Post Pascha*), 4.4 in ibid., 312.

Aphraates the Persian Sage

Demonstrations (*Demonstrationes*), 1.8–9 in PS 1:20–21; 6.6 in PS 1:268–69; 6:13 in PS 1:288–89; 6.14 in PS 1:292–96; 17.7–8 in PS 1:796–800; 18.10 in PS 1:840.

Athanasius of Alexandria

Defense of the Nicene Creed (*De decretis Nicaenae synodi*), 3.13 in PG 25:445D–447A; 5.21 in PG 25:453A–C.

Discourse against the Arians (*Oratio Contra Arianos*), 4.24 in PG 26:504B–505A; 4.27 in PG 26:509B–C.

Augustine of Hippo

Commentary on the Psalms (*Enarrationes in Psalmos*), Second Discourse on Psalm 26 2.17–18 in CCSL 38:164; Second Discourse on Psalm 30 2.1.4 in CCSL 38:193; Second Discourse on Psalm 30 2.1.9 in CCSL 38:197; First Discourse on Psalm 58 1.10 in CCSL 39:736; Psalm 67 22 in CCSL 39:885; First Discourse on Psalm 90 1.5 in CCSL 39:1258; Second Discourse on Psalm 90 2.2 in CCSL 39:1267; First Discourse on Psalm 101 1.8 in CCSL 40:1431–32; Psalm 130 9 in CCSL 40:1905–6; Psalm 143 in CCSL 40:2073–74.

Confessions (*Confessione*), 4.1.1 in PL 32:693C; 7.18.24 in PL 32:745C–D.

On the Literal Meaning of Genesis (*De Genesi ad litteram*), 1.18.36 in PL 34:260A–B.

On the Trinity (*De Trinitate*), 4.20.27–28 in CCSL 50:196–98.

APPENDIX B

Questions on the Gospels (*Quaestionum Evangeliorum*), 1.36 in CCSL 44B:28.

Sermons (*Sermone*) 51.8 in PL 38:337D-338A; 51.11 in PL 38:339B; 105.11-12 in PL 38:623C-624A; 135.4 in PL 38:747C-748A; 140.2 in PL 38:773B; 140.5 in PL 38:775B; 184.3 in PL 38:997A; 185.1 in PL 38:997C; 186.1 in PL 38:999C; 186.3 in PL 38:1000C-D; 187.1-2 in PL 38:1001A-D; 188.2 in PL 38:1003D-1004A; 190.2-3; PL 38:1007D-1008D; 191.1 in PL 38:1010B; 194.1 in PL 38:1015B; 195.1-2 in PL 38:1017D-1018B; 196.1 in PL 38:1019:A-B; 199.3 in PL 38:1028B-C; 214.6 in PL 38:1068D; 218.6 in PL 38:1085C; 225.1-2 in PL 38:1096A-1097A; 244.3-4 in PL 38:1150B-1151A; 264.2-3; PL 38:1213A-C; 264.5 in PL 38:1217B; 265.11 in; PL 38:1223D-1234A; 189.4 in *Miscellanea Agostiniana* (Roma: Vatican, 1930-31), 1:211.

Tractate on the Gospel of John (*Tractatus in Iohannis Evangelium*), 15.6-7 in CCSL 36:152-53; 21.1 in CCSL 36:212.

Basil the Great of Caesarea

Long Rules (*Regulae fusius tractatae*), 2.2 in PG 31:912B-C.

On the Six Days of Creation (*Hexaemeron*), 2:6 in SC 26:168/70.

Bede the Venerable

Allegorical Exposition on the Sayings of Solomon (*Super Parabolas Salomonis Allegorica Expositio*), 3.31 in PL 91:1028A.

Exposition on the Gospel of Matthew (*In Mathaei Evangelium Expositio*), 4.23 in PL 92:101B-C.

Homilies on the Gospels (*Homelia Evangelii*) 1.5 in CCSL 122:34-36; 1.6 in CCSL 122:40-41; 1.7 in CCSL 122:47-49; 1.8 in CCSL 122:53-54, 57-58.

Bernard of Clairvaux

Letters (*Epistolae*) 322; *S. Bernardi Opera Omnia* (Romae: Editiones Cistercienses, 1977), vol. 8.2:256-57.

Sermons on the Song of Songs (*Sermones super Cantica Canticorum*) 9.4-6 in SC 414:202-08.

Birgitta of Sweden

Fifth Book of Revelations (*Revelaciones Libri V*), Sixth Interrogation, 12-15 in Birger Bergh, *Sancta Birgitta: Revelaciones Book V* (Uppsala, NJ: Almquist & Wiksell, 1971), 108; Thirteenth Interrogation, 62-65 in 149-50; Fifteenth Interrogation, 25-29 in 159-60.

Bonaventure

Mystical Treatise on the Death of the Lord (*Vitis mystica seu tractatus de Passione Domini*), 15.4 in *S. Bonaventurae Opera Omnia* (Quaracchi: Ad Claras Aquas, 1882-86), 8:181, 182.

Alphabetical List of Authors and their Critical Texts

Cassiodorus

Exposition on the Psalms (*Expositio Psalmorum*), 26.10 in CCSL 97:240; 56.2 in CCSL 97:508; 90.4 in CCSL 98:831; 130.2 in CCSL 98:1193.

Catherine of Siena

Dialogue (*Il Dialogo*), 14 in *Il Dialogo della divina provvidenza* (Rome: Edizioni Cateriniane, 1968), 40–41; 70 in 156–57; 72 in 159–60; 96 in 225–28; 141 392–93; 151 in 439–40.

Chalcedon

Concilium Chacedonense Definitio Fidei, in *Decrees of the Ecumenical Councils*, ed. Norman P. Tanner (Washington, DC: Georgetown University Press, 1990), 1:86.

Cheremon (as found in)

John Cassian, *Consolations* (*Consolatio abbatis Chaeremonis tertia*), 13.14 in SC 54:173–74; 13.16 in SC 54:175; 13.17 in SC 54:178–79.

Clement of Alexandria

Christ the Educator (*Paedagogus*), 1.5.12.1–2 in SC 70:132; 1.5.14.2–4 in SC 70:136; 1.6.34.3–36.5 in SC 70:172–76; 1.6.37.2–3 in SC 70:178–80; 1.6.39.1—42.3 in SC 70:180–88; 43.2–44.1 in SC 70:188–90; 1.6.45.1–2 in SC 70:190–92; 1.6.45.4—46.1, 47.2–3 in SC 70:192–96; 1.6.49.2–3, 50.3–4 in SC 70:198–202; 1.7.53.3, 55.2—56.1 in SC 70:206, 210.

Exhortation to the Greeks (*Protrepticus*), 10 in *Clement of Alexandria*, trans. G. W. Butterworth Loeb Classical Library (Cambridge, MA: Harvard University Press, 1939), 196–200.

Hymn to Christ the Educator, in SC 158:194, 198–202.

Who Is the Rich Man That Shall Be Saved? (*Quis dives salvetur*), 23.2–4 in GCS 17.2:175; 36.1–37.2 in GCS 17.2:183–84.

Constantinople I

Concilium Constantinopolitanum I, in *Decrees of the Ecumenical Councils*, ed. Norman P. Tanner (Washington, DC: Georgetown University Press, 1990), 1:24.

Cyprian of Carthage

Testimonies against the Jews (*Testimoniorum libri tres Adversus Judaeos*), Prologue in PL 4:675D–677B; 2.1 in 696B–C.

Cyril of Alexandria

Commentary on John (*Commentarium in Iohannem*), 1.9 in *Sancti Patris Nostri Cyrilli in D. Joannis Evangelium* (Oxford: Clarendon, 1872), 1:134–35; 1.10 in 1:157; 2.1 in 1:217–19; 4.3 in 1:537–38; 4.4 in 1:563–64.

APPENDIX B

Commentary on Luke (*Commentarium in Lucam*), 11 in PG 72:686D–688A; 15 in PG 72:800B–D; 18.29 in PG 72:860B–861A.

Commentary on Matthew (*Commentarium in Matthaeum*), 23:37 in PG 72:440D.

Dialogues on the Trinity (*De Trinitate dialogi*), 2 in SC 231:300, 302.

Cyril of Jerusalem

Catechetical Lectures (*Catechesis*), 6.6–8 in PG 33:548A–552A; 7.1–3 in PG 33:605A–608B; 9.2 in PG 33:640A–B; 9.9 in PG 33:648A–B; 9.15 in PG 33:653B–656A; 11.1–2 in PG 33:692A–B; 11.4–5 in PG 33:693C–697A; 11.7 in PG 33:697B–700B; 11.19–20 in PG 33:716A–717A; 12.4 in PG 33:729A–B.

Didascalia Apostolorum (Syriac version)

Didascalia 9 in CSCO 401:102–4.

Diognetus (anonymous)

Letter to Diognetus, 9.2–6 in *The Apostolic Fathers*, ed. J. B. Lightfoot and J. R. Harmer (Grand Rapids: Baker, 1984), 497.

Dionysius of Rome (as found in)

Letter (*Epistula*), in Athanasius, Defense of the Nicene Creed (*De decretis nicaenae synodi*), 26 in PG 25:461D–465A.

Ephesus

Concilium Ephesinum, First Letter of Cyril (Greek text), in *Decrees of the Ecumenical Councils*, ed. Norman P. Tanner (Washington, DC: Georgetown University Press, 1990), 1:41–42; Formula of Union (Greek text) in 1:69–70.

Ephrem

Commentary on the Diatessaron, 1.2 in *Saint Ephrem: Commentaire de l'Evangile concordant texte syriaque*, ed. Louis LeLoir, Chester Beatty Monographs 8 (Dublin: Hodges Figgis, 1963), 2; 19.15 in CSCO 137:276–77.

Homily on the Lord (*Sermo de Domino nostro*), 1–2 in CSCO 270:1–2.

Hymns on the Crucifixion (*De crucifixione*), 3:16–17 in CSCO 248:54.

Hymns on the Faith (*De fide*), 4:1–3 in CSCO 154:9–10.

Hymns on the Nativity (*Sermones de nativitate domini*), 1:41–51 in CSCO 186:6–7; 3:2–3 in CSCO 186:20; 3:9 in CSCO 186:21; 4:146–54 in CSCO 186:38–39; 5:7–10 in CSCO 186:46–47; 13:7–9 in CSCO 186:74–75; 16:8–11 in CSCO 186:84–85; 21:1–8 in CSCO 186:104–6; 27:14–20 in CSCO 186:139–40.

Hymns on the Resurrection (*De resurrectione*), 1:4–7 in CSCO 248:79; 3:7–9 in CSCO 248:86–87.

Hymns on Virginity (*Sermones de virginitate*), 5.8 in CSCO 223:19l; 25.2–9 in CSCO 223:89–91; 31.1 in CSCO 223:113; 52.6–7 in CSCO 223:167–68.

Nisibene Hymns (*Carmina Nisibena*), 11:1–8 in CSCO 218:31–32.

Paschal Hymns (*De azymis*), 1:11–15 in CSCO 248:2–3; 13:12–21 in CSCO 248:20–21; 20:12–18 in CSCO 248:38–39.

Faustina Kowalska

Dzienniczek: Miłosierdzie Boże w duszy mojej (Warsaw: Wyd. Księży Marianów, 2004) [translations in Italian, Spanish, and English were consulted]; Divine Mercy in My Soul #230, in *Diary of Saint Maria Faustina Kowalska: Divine Mercy in My Soul* (Stockbridge, MA: Marian, 2006), 115–16; #239 in 118–19; #249 in 123; #264 in 128; #297–98 in 138–39; #505 in 217; #423 in 188; #603 in 253; #1490 534, #1541 in 547–48; #1726 in 610.

Florence

Concilium Florentinum decretum pro Armenis, in *Decrees of the Ecumenical Councils*, ed. Norman P. Tanner (Washington, DC: Georgetown University Press, 1990), 1:534–38.

Francis de Sales

Consoling Thoughts (*Pensées consolantes*), 1.1 in *Pensées consolantes de saint François de Sales recueillies dans ses écrits*, ed. Pere Huguet, 18th ed. (Paris: Casterman), 37–39; 1.2 in 42; 1.15 in 91–92; 1.18 in 103–4; 1.21 in 107–8; 1.22 in 111; 2.3 in 132–33; 2.16 in 191–92; 2.21 in 215; 3.3 in 263–64; 3.11 in 298; 4.4 in 347–50; 4.13 in 376; 4.14 in 382–84; unplaced to the 18th French ed.: *The Consoling Thought of St. Frances de Sales*, ed. Pere Huguet, trans. Fr. Pustet (New York: Pustet, 1857), 120–21, 137–38.

Introduction to the Devout Life (*Introduction à la vie devote*), 4.13.2–4 in *Oeuvres de Saint François de Sales* (Annecy, France: Niérat, 1892), 3:321–25.

Letter 1402 to the Mistress of Novices, Sister de Blonay at the Visitation of Lyons, in *Oeuvres de Saint François de Sales*, 18:170–71.

Treatise Concerning the Love of God (*Traité de l'Amour de Dieu*), 3.10–12 in *Oeuvres de Saint François de Sales*, 4:198–205; 12.12 in 4:343–45.

Gertrude the Great of Helfta

The Herald of God's Loving Kindness (*Legatus memorialis pietatis*), 3.30.38 in SC 143:160, 62; 3.42.2 in SC 143:194, 96; 3.63.1–2 in SC 143:250, 52; 3.72.1–2 in SC 143:288, 90.

Spiritual Exercises (*Exercitium pro recuperanda innocentia baptismali*), 7 in SC 127:260, 278–80, 288–90.

APPENDIX B

Gregory the Great of Rome

Forty Gospel Homilies (*Homiliae Evangelium*), 34 in PL 76:1249.

Gregory the Illuminator

Armenian Catechism (*Vardapetowt'iwn Srboyn Grigori*), 259 in Agat`angelos, *Patmut`iwn Hayoc`*, critical ed. by G. Tēr Mkrtč`ean (Tiflis, Armenia: 1909), 134, in consultation with Robert W. Thomson, *The Teaching of Saint Gregory: An Early Armenian Catechism* (Cambridge: Harvard University Press, 1970), 41; 382, 388, 391 in Mkrtč`ean 191–95 and Thomson 80–83.

Gregory of Narek

Commentary on the Song of Songs (*In canticum canticorum*), 1, trans. Vincenzo Mistrih, in SOCC 12:496; 7.13 in SOCC 13:243; 8.5 in SOCC 13:247.

Prayers (*Oratione*), 5.1 in SC 78:76–77; 33.4 in SC 78:207–9; 44.1–2 in SC 78:246.

Gregory of Nazianzus

Theological Orations (*Orationes*), 20.7 in SC 270:72; 29.2 in *Gregor von Nazianz: Orationes Theologicae Theologische Reden* (Freiburg: Herder, 1996), 170–72; 30.2 in 223–26.

Gregory of Nyssa

Against Eunomius (*Contra Eunomium*), 2:104 in GNO 1:257; 2:144–46, 148–49 in GNO 1:267–68; 2:154 in GNO 1:270; 2:298–300, 304 in GNO 1:314–15; 2:417–20 in GNO 1:348–49; 3.1:28–30 in GNO 2:13–14; 3.1:43–49 in GNO 2: 18–20; 3.2:50–51 in GNO 2:68–69; 3.8:9–10 in GNO 2:241–42.

Against Those Who Defer Baptism (*Adversus eus qui different baptismum oratio*), in PG 46:421B.

Commentary on the Song of Songs (*Commentarius in Canticum Canticorum*), 1 in GNO 6:17–18, 33–35, 40–41; 2 in GNO 6:46, 56; 6 in GNO 6:181–83; 7 in GNO 6:212–14; 15 in GNO 6:468–69.

Inscriptions of the Psalms (*In inscriptiones Psalmorum*), 2.11 in GNO 5:119; 2.15 in GNO 5:161–62.

On the Christian Mode of Life (*De instituto christiano*), in GNO 8.1:44–45.

On Infants' Early Deaths (*De infantibus praemature abreptis*), in GNO 3.2:83–84.

On the Life of Moses (*De vita Moysis*), 2.137, 140 in GNO 7.1:76–78.

On the Lord's Prayer (*De oratione dominica*), 1 in GNO 7.2:17–18.

On the Making of Man (*De hominis opificio*), 25.6–7 in PG 44:217A–B.

On Perfection (*De perfectione*), in GNO 8.1:205–6.

On the Three-Day Period of the Resurrection (*De tridui spatio resurrectione*), in GNO 9:291–92.

Gregory Palamas

Homily (*Homilia*) 56, as translated from the French by John Meyendorff in *L'Introduction à l'étude de Grégoire Palamas* (Paris: Editions du Seuil, 1959), 247–48, from *Palamas*, ed. Sophoklēs Oikonomos (Athens, 1861), 206–8.

Guerric of Igny

First Sermon for Epiphany (*De Epiphania Sermo Primus*), 6 in SC 166:250.

Second Sermon for the Feast of Sts. Peter and Paul (*Sermo secundus in sollemnitate apostolorum Petri et Pauli*), 2–3 in SC 202:384, 386.

Second Sermon on the Nativity of Mary (*In nativitate beatae Mariae sermo secundus*), 1 in SC 202:486.

Hëlinand of Froidmont

Sermons (*Sermone*), 14 in PL 212:591–94.

Henry Suso

The Life of Henry Suso (*Das Leben des seligen Heinrich Seuse*), 3 in Karl Bihlmeyer, *Heinrich Seuse* (Frankfurt: Minerva, 1961), 14–15.

Hilary of Poitiers

Commentary on Matthew (*Commentarium in Matthaeum*), 24.11 in SC 258:176–78.

Homilies on the Psalms (*Tractatus in psalmum*), 56.3 in CSEL 22:169; 130.5 in CSEL 22:659.

On the Trinity (*De Trinitate*), 4.21 in SC 448:52, 54 (also CCSL 62:123–24); 6.16 in SC 448:200 (also CCSL 62:214).

Hildegard of Bingen

Book of Divine Works (*Liber divinorum operum simplicis hominis*), 2.19 in PL 197:764C–765A; 4.105 in PL 197:898A–C.

Know the Way (*Scivias*), 2.1.7 in CCCM 43:115–16; 2.2.4 in CCCM 43:126–27; 2.3.25 in CCCM 43:149–50; 2.6.35 in CCCM 43:263; 3.2.20 in CCCM 43A:366.

Letters (*Epistula*), 47 in PL 197:238A–B.

Hippolytus of Rome

Against Noetus (*Contra Noetum*), 10 in *Hippolytus of Rome: Contra Noetum*, ed. and trans. Robert Butterworth, Heythrop Monographs 2 (London: Heythrop College, 1977), 69, 81, 83.

Commentary on Luke 2 in PG 10:700D–701A.

APPENDIX B

Commentary on Proverbs (*Commentarium in Proverbia*), 9 in PG 10:625C–628C.

Concerning the Antichrist (*Peri antichristou*), 26.1–2 in *L'anticristo: De Antichristo/Ippolito*, ed. Enrico Norelli (Firenze, Italy: 1987), 96.

Refutation of All Heresies (*Refutatio omnium haeresium*), 10.33.1–2, 11 in PTS 25:410, 412.

Sermon on Elchana and Anna (*Sermone in Elcanam et Annam*), in PG 10:864B.

Sermon on the Great Canticle (*Sermone in magnum Canticum*), in PG 10:865A–C.

(as found in) Jerome, Letters (*Epistolae*), 36.16 to Pope Damasus in CSEL 54:283.

Irenaeus of Lyons

Against Heresies (*Adversus haereses*), 3.24.1 in SC 211:471–75; 4.38.1 in SC 100:942–48; 4.20.1 in SC 100:627; 4.20.3–4 in SC 100:633–35.

Proof of the Apostolic Preaching, 8 in PO 12.5:15.

Isidore of Seville

Letters (*Epistulae*), 6.10 in PL 83:904D.

Jerome

Commentary on Isaiah (*Commentarium in Esaiam*), XI 40:9–11 in CCSL 73.1:459.

Commentary on Matthew (*Commentarium in Matheum*), 4.37 in SC 259:184.

Homilies on Matthew (*Homilia in Matthaeum*), 18:7–9 in CCSL 78:505.

Homilies on the Psalms (*Tractatus de Psalmo*), #20 in CCSL 78:128; #36 in CCSL 78:224–25; #68 in CCSL 78:421.

Letters (*Epistulae*), 18B in CSEL 54:97–98.

John of the Cross

Ascent of Mount Carmel (*Subida del Monte Carmelo*), 1.2.1–4 in *S. Juan de la Cruz* (Burgos, Spain: Editorial Monte Carmelo, 1997), 163–64.

John Chrysostom

Baptismal Instructions (*Sermones ad neophytes*), 3:17–19 in SC 50:161–62.

Homilies on John (*Homiliae 26 in Joannem*), on 3:6 in PG 59:153 column 1B–C.

Homilies on Matthew (*Homiliarum in Matthaeum*), 76.5 in PG 58:700B–C; 82.5 in PG 58:743D–744B.

How to Choose a Wife (*Et quales ducendae sint uxores*), 3 in PG 51:229A–C.

On Luke 15:11 (*In Evangelium secundum Lucam 15.11*), in PG 61:781A–B.

Alphabetical List of Authors and their Critical Texts

John of Dalyatha

Homilies (*Homiliae*), 19 in Manuscript Vatican Syriac 124f.348a.

Letter (*Epistula*), 51.10–11 in PO 39:478.

John Paul II

Catechism of the Catholic Church (*Catechismus catholicae ecclesiae*), 40–43, 239 (Rome: Libreria Editrice Vaticana, 1997).

Orientale Lumen (May 2, 1995; online: http://www.vatican.va/holy_father/john_paul_ii/apost_letters/documents/hf_jp-ii_apl_02051995_orientale-lumen_en.html), 9.

Justin Martyr

Dialogue with Trypho (*Dialogus cum Tryphone Judaeo*), 135 in PTS 47:303–4.

First Apology (*Apologia Maior*), 21–23 in PTS 38:63–66.

Lawrence of Brindisi

Commentary on Genesis (*Explanatio in Genesim*), 1 in *S. Laurentii a Brundusio Opera Omnia* (Patavii, Italy: Ex Officina Typographica Seminarii, 1928) 3:133–35.

Leo the Great

Letters (*Epistolae*), 28 in PL 54:757B–759A.

Sermons (*Tractatus*), 24.1 in CCSL 138:109; 26.3 in CCSL 138:128; 30.1 in CCSL 138:152; 30.3 in CCSL 138:154.

Liber Graduum

Book of Steps (*Liber Graduum*), 12.1 in PS 3:285–88.

Macarius the Great

Collection of Homilies III (*Homiliae collectiones III*), 6.3 in SC 275:110; 8.1–2 in SC 275:140–48; 16.2 in SC 275:182–84; 22.2–3 in SC 275:258–60; 27.1 in SC 275:314; 27.3–4 in SC 275:320–24.

Spiritual Homilies (*Homiliae spirituales*), 7.1 in PTS 4:71; 31.4 in PTS 4:249; 46.3 in PTS 4:302.

Marguerite of Oingt

A Page of Meditations (*Pagina meditationum*), 31–33, 36, 39, 47–53 in Antonin Duraffour, *Les oeuvres de Marguerite D'Oingt* (Paris: Les Belles Lettres, 1965), 77–80.

APPENDIX B

Maximos the Confessor

Ambigua (*Ambigua*), 1.41 in PG 91:1313B–C; 1.71 in PG 91:1413B–C.

Centuries on Knowledge (*Capita theologiae et oeconomiae*), 1:100 in PG 90:1124C–D.

Centuries on Love (*Capita de charitate*), 2:30 in *Massimo Confessore: Capitoli sulla carità* (Rome: Editrice, 1963), 106.

Letters (*Epistolae*), 8 in PG 91:444C; 13 in PG 91:521B–525B; 14 in PG 91:537A–B.

Scholia on Letter 9 of Dionysius (*S. Maximi scholia in epistolas S. Dionysii Areopagitae*), 9 in PG 4:560A–B.

Mechtild of Hackeborn

Book of Special Grace (*Liber specialis gratiae*), 2.2 in *Revelationes Gertrudianae ac Mechtildianae* (Paris: Monks of Solesmes, 1877), 2:137; 2.16 in 2:149–50; 3.9 in 2: 207–8; 4.7 in 2:263–64; 4.50 in 2:304; 4.59 in 2:310–11; 5.8 in 2:332.

Melito of Sardis

Fragment 15 in SC 123:240.

Hymn in SC 123:128.

On Pascha (*Peri Pascha*), 82–83 in SC 123:106, 108.

Methodius of Olympus

The Banquet of the Ten Virgins (*Convivium decem virginum*), 7.8 in SC 95:194–96.

Minucius Felix

Octavius (*Octavius*), 18.7–8 in Jean Beaujeu, *Octavius: Texte* établi *et traduit* (Paris: Les Belles Lettres, 1964), 26–27; 19.14–15 in 31; 35.4–5 in 61.

Nerses IV of Armenia

Jesus, Son, Only-Begotten of the Father (*Hisus, Ordi*), 205–6 in SC 203:78–79; 328–31 in SC 203:104; 334–36 in SC 203:105–6; 748–54 in SC 203:185–86.

Nicaea I

Nicene Creed (*Concilium Nicaenum I*), Greek and Latin texts, in*Decrees of the Ecumenical Councils*, ed. Norman P. Tanner (Washington, DC: Georgetown University Press, 1990), 1:5.

Nicholas Cabasilas

Life in Christ (*De vita in Christo*), 1.4 in PG 150:500C–D; 1.6 in PG 150:504A–B; 2.9 in PG 150:541–B; 4.10 in PG 150:601D–604B.

Odes of Solomon

Ode 8:8–16 in Majella Franzmann, *The Odes of Solomon: An Analysis of the Poetical Structure and Form*, Novum Testamentum et Orbis Antiquus 20 (Göttingen: Universitätsverlag Freiburg, 1991), 63–64; 19:1–5 in 146; 24:1–5 in 183; 28:1–7 in 207; 35:1–7 in 244; 36:1–8 in 248; 40:1–6 in 270.

Oecumenius

Commentary on the Book of Revelation (*Oecumenii Commentarius in Apocalypsin*), 12.7.4–5 in *Traditio Exegetica Graeca* (Louvain: Peeters, 1999), 8:281.

Origen

Against Celsus (*Contra Celsum*), 4.18 in SC 136:226.

Paschasius Radbertus

Commentary on Matthew (*Commentarium in Matthaeum*), 10 in CCCM 56b:1142–44.

Peter Canisius

Autobiography (*Confessionum Canisii*), 1.2 in *Beati Petri Canisii: Epistulae et Acta* (Freiburg: Herder, 1896), 1:12.

A Sum of Christian Doctrine (*Christianae Doctrinae*), 1.9 in *S. Petri Canisii* (Rome: Pontificia Universitas Gregoriana, 1933), 1:85.

Peter Chrysologus

Sermons (*Sermone*), 29.5 in CCSL 24:172; 31.1 in CCSL 24:78; 32.4 in CCSL 24:84; 33.1–2 in CCSL 24:86–87; 45.1–2 in CCSL 24:251; 49.1–2 in CCSL 24:269; 50.2–3 in CCSL 24:277–78; 55.6 in CCSL 24:310; 69.2 in CCSL 24a:415–16; 80.6 in CCSL 24a:494; 89.5–6 in CCSL 24a:550–51; 99A.1 in CCSL 24a:613–14; 160.3–4 in CCSL 24b:991; 164.5 in CCSL 24b:1012.

Peter Damian

Concerning Divine Omnipotence (*De divina omnipotentia*), 8.1–20 in SC 191:418, 20; 17.21–36 in SC 191:472, 74.

Concerning True Happiness and Wisdom 3 (*De vera felicitate et sapientia*), in PL 145:833B–C.

Letters (*Epistulae*), 81 in *Die Briefe des Petrus Damiani* (Munich: Monumenta Germanae Historica, 1988), 2:418, 429; 86 in 2:478–79.

On the Perfection of Monks (*De perfectione monachorum*), 1 in PL 145:293A.

Pseudo-Dionysius

Letters (*Epistulae*), 9.1 in PTS 36:194–96.

APPENDIX B

Quodvultdeus of Carthage

> On the Creed (*De Symbolo*), 1.3.15–18, 20 in CCSL 60:311–12; 1.6.4–5, 9–11 in CCSL 60:320–21; 3.4.1–4 in CCSL 60:354.

Rabanus Maurus

> Commentary on Sirach (*Commentarium in Ecclesiasticum*), 1.1 in PL 109:765A.
>
> Scriptural Allegories (*Allegoriae in Universam Sacram Scripturam*) in PL 112:939D–940A.

Robert Bellarmine

> Commentary on the Psalms (*Explanatio in Psalmos*), 45.1 in *Roberto Bellarmino, Explantio in Psalmos* (Rome: Pontificiae Universitatis Gregorianae, 1931), 239–40; 90.1 in 522; 90.4 in 525; 109.4 in 647–48; 130.2 in 750–51.

Romanos Melodius

> Hymn of the Resurrection (*Canticum in Resurrectione*), 6.1–2 in SC 128:578–80.

Sahdona

> Book of Perfection (*Liber de perfectione*), 3.13 in CSCO 201:32–33; 4.50–51 in CSCO 201:103.

Synesius of Cyrene

> Hymn (*Canticum*) II.1–10, 85–116 in critical text by Christian Lacombrade, *Synésios de Cyrène: Hymnes* (Paris: Les Belles Lettres, 1978), 61, 63; V.59–74, 89–91 in 82–83.

Teresa of Avila

> Conceptions of the Love of God (*Conceptos del amor de Dios*), 4.4–5 in *Santa Teresa: Obras Completas* (Burgos: Editorial Monte Carmelo, 1997), 1219–21; 7.9 in 1237.
>
> Interior Castle (*Castillo Interior*), 4.3.10 in 692; 7.2.6 in 807.
>
> The Way of Perfection (*El Camino de Perfección*), 31.9–10 in ibid., 556–57.

Tertullian

> Treatise against Praxeas (*Adversus Praxean*), 6.1–2 in *Corona Patrum Q. Septimii Florentis Tertulliani: Adversus Praxean* (Torino: Società editrice internazionale, 1985), 154; 7.1–32 in 156; 11.1–3 in 166, 68.

Theodoret of Cyrhus

> Commentary on the Psalms (*Interpretatio in Psalmos*), 109 in PG 80:1769 D–1772A.

Commentary on the Song of Songs (*In canticum canticorum*), 2 in PG 81:105B–C; 3 in PG 81:116C–D; 7–8 in PG 81:200A–201B, 204B–C.

Theophilus of Antioch

To Autolycus (*Apologium ad Autolycus*), 2.9–10 in SC 20:120–22.

Thérèse of Lisieux

Conseils et souvenirs 1, in *Sainte Thérèse de l'Enfant-Jésus: Histoire d'une âme écrite par elle-même* (Lisieux, France: 1958), 261.

Thomas Aquinas

Against the Gentiles (*Summa contra Gentiles*), 4.11–12 in *Sancti Thomae de Aquino Opera Omnia* (Rome: Ed. di san Tommaso, 1970–76), 15:35–36.

Commentary on the Psalms (*Commentarium super Psalmorum*), 44:2 in ibid., 14:319.

Exposition on the Song of Songs (*In Canticum Canticorum expositio*), 1 in ibid., 14:354.

Golden Chain on the Gospel of Matthew (*Catena Aurea in Matthaei Evangelium*), 23 in ibid., 11:268.

Lectures on the Gospel of John (*Super Evangelium Ioanem*) in ibid., 11:215, 218.

Summa Theologiae, IIaIIae.45.6 in ibid., 3:175–76.

Toledo XI

Council of Toledo XI (*Concilium Toletanensis XI*), in *Concilios Visigóticos e Hispano-Romanos*, ed. José Vives (Barcelona: Instituto Enrique Flórez, 1963), 344–50.

Appendix C

Liturgical Hours

Compline—Night Prayers

May God Almighty grant us a quiet night and a bright new dawn. Amen.

Scripture Reading

You, O Lord, show your mercy. Thanks be to God.

Examination of Conscience: I confess to Almighty God, to blessed Mary Ever-Virgin, to blessed Michael the archangel and all the angels, to blessed John the Baptist, to the holy Apostles Peter and Paul, to blessed Father Benedict [*or patron saint*], to all the saints (and to you my brothers and sisters), that I have sinned exceedingly in thought, word, and deed: through my fault, through my fault, through my most grievous fault. Therefore, I call on blessed Mary Ever-Virgin, blessed Michael the archangel and the heavenly hosts, blessed John the Baptist, all the holy Apostles, our blessed Father Benedict [*or patron saint*], all the saints, (and you my brothers and sisters) to pray for me to the Lord our God.

May Almighty God have mercy upon us, forgive us our sins, and bring us to life everlasting. Amen.

> O God, Defender of my cause, answer me as I call out to you.
> From distress set me free; have mercy, and hear my prayer.
> O people how long will you be dull of heart,
> loving what is empty and running after deception?
> See how the Lord glorifies his devoted servant.
> The Lord always hears me when I call upon him.
> Though disturbed and distraught, sin not.
> Ponder well in your hearts, in stillness throughout the night.
> Offer sacrifices of righteousness,

APPENDIX C

and put all your trust in the Lord.
Many keep saying: "Who shall show us what is truly good?"
O Lord, let the light of your countenance shine upon us.
With your joy and your gladness fill my heart, O Lord,
and may wheat and wine now abound for your people.
At peace in your Presence I shall fall gently asleep,
for you alone, O Lord, make my dwelling secure.
Doxology

You who abide in the secret place of the Most High,
who find rest in the shadow of Shaddai,
say to the Lord: "My Refuge and my Fortress,
my God in whom I trust!"
For he shall set you free from the fowler's snare,
and from deadly poisons protect you.
With his pinions he shall overshadow you,
and under his wings you shall find refuge.
You need not fear the terrors of the night,
nor the arrows that fly by day,
nor the plague that prowls in the darkness,
nor the disease that devastates at noon.
A thousand may fall at your side,
ten thousand fall at your right,
you it shall never come near.
His arm is a mighty shield to encircle you.
You shall witness the destruction round about,
and shall see how the wicked are repaid.
Because you have taken the Lord for your refuge,
and have made the Most High your helper,
no evil shall befall you,
no affliction strike your dwelling.
For to you has he appointed his angels,
to protect you in all your paths.
In their arms they shall lift you up,
lest you trip and stumble over a stone.
On the wild beast and serpent you shall tread,
trample the roaring lion and the dragon.
"All who cling to Me I shall rescue,
lift them on high since they know my Name.
Whenever they call I shall answer and be close at hand,
from distress I shall rescue them, and endow them with glory.
With everlasting life I shall satisfy them,
and bid them drink deeply of my salvation."
Doxology

Now, O Master, you have fulfilled your promise.
At your bidding your servant may rest in peace,
for my own eyes have beheld the Savior,
prepared for all peoples to see.
He is your Radiance to enlighten the nations,
the very Glory of your people Israel.
Doxology

Guard us O Lord, like the pupil of your eye. Hide us in the shadow of your wings.

(Let us conclude our prayers.)

O Lord, we ask you to visit this house and drive far away from it all the snares of the enemy; send your holy angels and saints to dwell herein, who may keep us in peace, and let your blessings always be upon us. We ask you this through our Lord Jesus Christ, your Son, who lives and reigns with you and the Holy Spirit, one God, forever and ever. Amen.

May the almighty God bless you, Father, Son, and Holy Spirit.

[OR: May the almighty and merciful Lord: Father, Son, and Holy Spirit, bless us and keep us.]

Amen. Let us bless the Lord. Thanks be to God.

Morning Prayers—Abbreviated Format

O Lord, open my lips and my mouth shall declare your praise. Doxology

Antiphon — Psalm — Doxology

Old Testament Canticle (song)

Antiphon — Psalm — Doxology

Antiphon — Psalm — Doxology

Scriptural Reading — Church Reading

Benedictus: Blessed be the Lord, the God of Israel for he has visited and redeemed his people. God has raised up for us a horn of salvation in the house of his servant David, just as he promised through the mouth of his holy prophets from of old; that we should be saved from our enemies and from the hand of all who hate us; to show mercy to our ancestors and to be mindful of his holy Covenant and of the oath he swore to our father Abraham, to grant us that we, being delivered from the hand of our enemies, might serve God without fear, in holiness and righteousness all the days of our lives.

APPENDIX C

And you, child, shall be called the prophet of the Most High; for you will go before the Lord to prepare his ways, to give his people knowledge of salvation through the forgiveness of their sins, because of the maternal mercy of our God through which the Dawn from on High shall visit us to give light to those who sit in darkness and in the shadow of death, to guide our feet into the path of peace.

Intercessory Prayers — Lord's Prayer — Doxology

Evening Prayers—Abbreviated Format

O God, come to my assistance. O Lord, make haste to help me. Doxology

Antiphon — Psalm — Doxology

Antiphon — Psalm — Doxology

New Testament Canticle (song)

Antiphon — Psalm — Doxology

Scriptural Reading — Church Reading

Magnificat: My soul proclaims the greatness of the Lord; my spirit rejoices in God my Savior, because he has looked upon the lowliness of his handmaid. Behold, from now on, all generations shall call me blessed. The Mighty One has done great things for me, and holy is his name. His maternal mercy is from generation to generation upon all those who revere him. He has shown great might with his arm, he has scattered the proud in the imagination of their hearts. He has cast down the mighty from their thrones, and raised up the lowly. He has filled the hungry with good things, and the rich he has sent away empty-handed. He has helped Israel his servant, remembering his tender mercies, according to the promise to our forbearers, to Abraham and his descendants forever.

Intercessory Prayers — Lord's Prayer — Doxology

Bibliography

Albright, William F. "The Names Shaddai and Abram." *Journal of Biblical Literature* 54 (1935) 173–204.

Cross, Frank Moore. "Yahweh and the God of the Patriarchs." *Harvard Theological Review* 55 (1962) 244–50.

Isaac, E. "1 (Ethiopic Apocalypse of) Enoch." In *The Old Testament Pseudepigrapha*, edited by James H. Charlesworth, 1:5–89. Garden City, NY: Doubleday, 1983.

Metzger, Bruce M. "The Fourth Book of Ezra." In *The Old Testament Pseudepigrapha*, edited by James H. Charlesworth, 1:517–59. Garden City, NY: Doubleday, 1983.

Myers, Jacob M. *I and II Esdras*. Anchor Bible 42. Garden City, NY: Doubleday, 1974.

Stuhlmueller, Carol. "Apocrypha." In *New Catholic Encyclopedia* 1:549–58. 2nd ed. Detroit: Thomson/Gale; Washington, DC: Catholic University of America, 2003.

Taft, Robert. *The Liturgy of the Hours in East and West: The Origins of the Divine Office and Its Meaning for Today*. Collegeville, MN: Liturgical, 1986.

Uspensky, N. D. *Evening Worship in the Orthodox Church*. Translated by Paul Lazor. Crestwood, NY: St. Vladimir's Seminary Press, 1985.

Vatican II. "Decree on Ecumenism" (*Unitatis Redintegratio*). In *Vatican Council II: The Conciliar and Post Conciliar Documents*, edited by Austin Flannery. New rev. ed. Northport, NY: Costello, 1984.

Walker, Norman. "New Interpretation of the Divine Name Shaddai." *Zeitschrift für die Alttestamentliche Wissenschaft* 72 (1960) 64–66.

www.ingramcontent.com/pod-product-compliance
Lightning Source LLC
Chambersburg PA
CBHW060302010526
44108CB00042B/2608